CW01513210

MANUA
– FOR THE –
AWAKENING
WARRIOR

"The Trojan Warrior [aka Jedi Warrior] project described in this superb book changed my life. This training protected me from moral injury in Iraq and Afghanistan and prevented PTSD while enhancing my performance in high-risk operations. These transformational enhancements will bolster decision-making, resilience, warrior ethos, and organizational readiness throughout the national defense enterprise."

FRED KRAWCHUK, U.S. ARMY SPECIAL FORCES COLONEL (RET.),
DEPUTY DIRECTOR FOR OPERATIONS AT
SOUTHEASTERN EUROPEAN TASK FORCE, AFRICA

"I was mesmerized by the page-turner narrative of this 'Mission Impossible'— how Joel and Michelle brought these inner practices to the Special Forces. A story of dedication, discipline, experimentation, bravery, and love. This is crucial training for us now, as we too are engaged in a battle for the human spirit and the Spirit of Life."

MARGARET J. WHEATLEY, ED.D., TEACHER AND AUTHOR OF
WHO DO WE CHOSE TO BE? AND LEADERSHIP AND THE NEW SCIENCE

"*Manual for the Awakening Warrior* by Michelle and Joel Levey is one of those rare books that offers down to earth pragmatic skills for living a fulfilled life as well as the depth of wisdom that is necessary for a genuine transformation of self, institutions, and, may I say, nations. I unequivocally recommend this book for anyone who wishes to walk the warrior's path of skillful action, grounded compassion, and pragmatic wisdom."

RICHARD STROZZI-HECKLER, AUTHOR OF
EMBODYING THE MYSTERY AND IN SEARCH OF THE WARRIOR SPIRIT

MANUAL
– FOR THE –
AWAKENING WARRIOR

THE SPECIAL FORCES
SECRET MIND-BODY-SPIRIT
TRAINING PROGRAM

A Sacred Planet Book

JOEL & MICHELLE LEVEY

Destiny Books

Rochester, Vermont

Destiny Books
One Park Street
Rochester, Vermont 05767
www.DestinyBooks.com

Destiny Books is a division of Inner Traditions International

Sacred Planet Books are curated by Richard Grossinger, Inner Traditions editorial board member and cofounder and former publisher of North Atlantic Books. The Sacred Planet collection, published under the umbrella of the Inner Traditions family of imprints, includes works on the themes of consciousness, cosmology, alternative medicine, dreams, climate, permaculture, alchemy, shamanic studies, oracles, astrology, crystals, hyperobjects, locutions, and subtle bodies.

Cataloging-in-Publication Data for this title is available from the Library of Congress

ISBN 978-1-64411-606-7 (print)
ISBN 978-1-64411-607-4 (ebook)

Printed and bound in India at Replika Press Pvt. Ltd.

10 9 8 7 6 5 4 3 2 1

Text design and layout by Priscilla Harris Baker
This book was typeset in Garamond, with Brother 1816 and Gill Sans used as display typefaces

Artwork from *Evolutionary Tactics: A Manual for the First Earth Battalion* by Lieutenant Colonel Jim Channon

To send correspondence to the author of this book, mail a first-class letter to the author c/o Inner Traditions • Bear & Company, One Park Street, Rochester, VT 05767, and we will forward the communication, or contact the authors directly at **wisdomatwork.com**.

Scan the QR code and save 25% at InnerTraditions.com.
Browse over 2,000 titles on spirituality, the occult, ancient mysteries, new science, holistic health, and natural medicine.

A person with outer courage dares to die.
A person with inner courage dares to live.
ATTRIBUTED TO LAO TZU

*This book is dedicated to the evolutionary warrior
spirit and courageous presence brilliantly embodied in
Colonel Kenneth W. Getty, the twenty-five brave souls from
the Tenth Special Forces who participated in this pioneering
program, Lieutenant Colonel Jim Channon, Patricia and
Daniel Ellsberg, Tenzin Gyatso the Dalai Lama,
Joanna Macy, Greta Thunberg, and all awakening
wisdom warriors working for the greater
good throughout the four times—
past, present, future, and
within timeless awareness.*

Contents

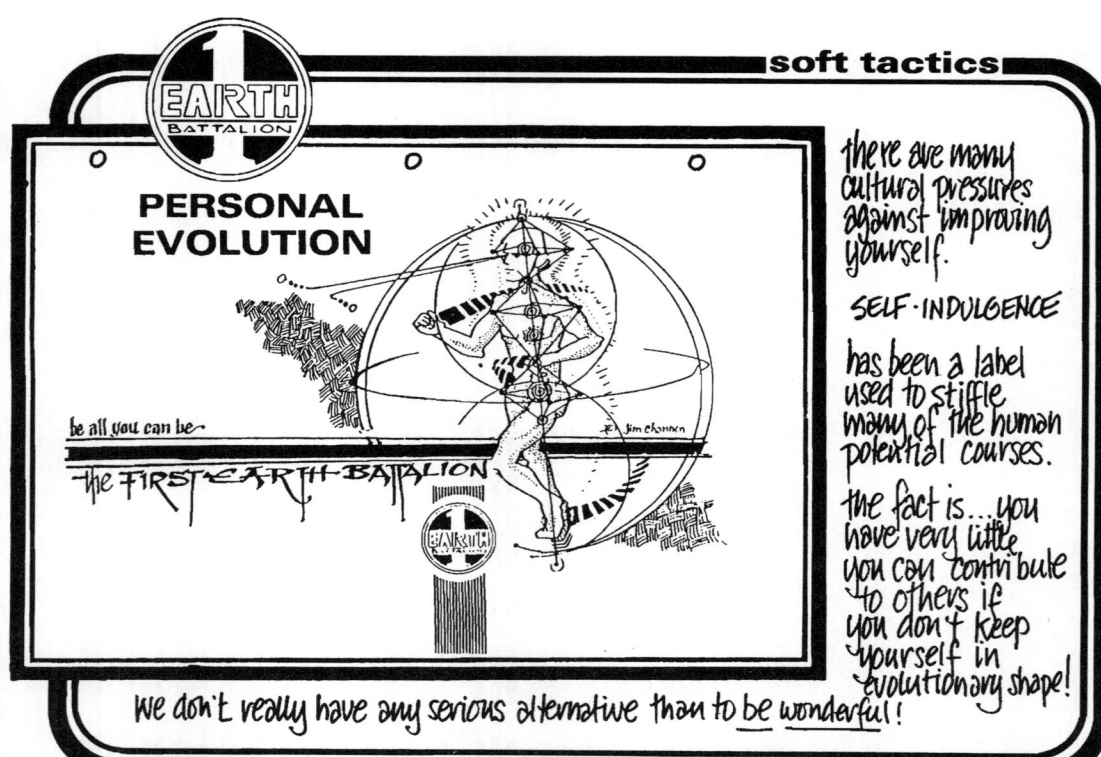

1 EARTH BATTALION

PERSONAL EVOLUTION

be all you can be

the FIRST EARTH BATTALION

— Jim channon

EARTH

there are many cultural pressures against improving yourself.

SELF·INDULGENCE

has been a label used to stifle many of the human potential courses.

the fact is...you have very little you can contribute to others if you don't keep yourself in evolutionary shape!

we don't really have any serious alternative than to be <u>wonderful</u>!

THE FIRST EARTH BATTALION

INTRODUCTION

A Special Kind of Courage

Without a global revolution in the sphere of human consciousness, nothing will change for the better in the sphere of our being as humans, and the catastrophe towards which this world is headed, be it ecological, social, demographic or a general breakdown of civilization, will be unavoidable. . . . The salvation of this human world lies nowhere else than in the human heart, in the human power to reflect, in human meekness, and in human responsibility.

VACLAV HAVEL, FORMER PRESIDENT OF THE
CZECH REPUBLIC, "SPEECH TO THE U.S. CONGRESS,"
FEBRUARY 22, 1990

As you read these words, you are crossing a threshold into a remarkable story illuminating the special kind of courage needed in our world today to be fully present and wisely responsive to whatever life may bring. This book reveals the story of the historic, once-secret Jedi Warrior program for the U.S. Army Special Forces and its origins in Lieutenant Colonel James B. Channon's visionary manual *Evolutionary Tactics: A Manual for the First Earth Battalion*.[1] In the early- to mid-1980s we, along with several inspired colleagues, developed and implemented an immersive six-month pioneering program to train twenty-five Green Berets* in advanced mind-body-spirit

---

*To respect their anonymity, we have changed the names of soldiers we weren't able to reach to get permission for using their names in this book.

1

training. Using this remarkable story of the Jedi Warrior program as a springboard, we weave together a wealth of wisdom that offers a glimpse of how each of us, not just elite warriors, can awaken to our own innate extraordinary potentials to thrive amid great challenges and opportunities and in doing so develop our communities and inspire generations to come.

Our intention in revealing this mind-blowing story is to illuminate the potent relevance of this program for all who are seeking to live wisely, meaningfully, and courageously in these profound times. We'll offer insights, guidelines, principles, and personal practices to help you follow this path and realize these potentials for yourself and for the benefit of those within the sphere of your influence.

The metacrisis we face in our world today makes it clear that old norms of business as usual are woefully inadequate, unsustainable, and unwise and are killing us in many ways. Things are heating up. The oceans are rising. Fragile unsustainable systems are collapsing. It's time now to equip ourselves for this Earthwalk in wiser ways together. Never before in human history have the stakes been so high, the existential dangers so vast, the timeline for wise and effective response so urgent, or the need for wise, compassionate, courageous, and capable leadership and engagement so great. The challenges and opportunities of these pivotal times call for a massive upgrade of our personal and collective consciousness and capabilities.

This book is your invitation and guide to join the global r/evolution in the sphere of human consciousness, to learn new skills that open and activate your mind, heart, and will, and to realize extraordinary capacities that can expand your potential to serve the greater good. The methods and insights described in these pages have been tested and refined over decades of research, study, practice, world travel, and teaching. Many of these methods have been empirically tested and validated over millennia of applied research in ancient warrior-monk and contemplative disciplines. Understanding these transformational disciplines will help you to realize your extraordinary human potentials and live as a force for good.

These times call each of us to awaken the special kind of courage it takes to keep our eyes, minds, and hearts wide open in our rapidly changing and increasingly complex world and to be ever more deeply attuned and wisely responsive to the needs within and around us. Our hope and prayer is that you will take this story to heart and experience a deep yearning rising within you to discover the precious "special forces" within yourself. Through this awakening may you open your eyes and mind to a deeper view of our collective, extraordinary human potentials and the treasures of our deep humanity that are seldom dreamed of, pursued, or realized. Many are hearing the call and enlisting in this noble endeavor. May you find and gather a circle of wise and trusted allies and mentors to make this journey with, and together awaken to this special kind of courage to live your lives wisely and compassionately and help others to do the same.

A Deep Bow to the Warrior Spirit within Us All

The archetypal warrior spirit runs deep in our bones as a vital element of our ancestral evolutionary journey. Without this vital spark of confident, courageous, and empowering presence, we would accomplish little that is worthwhile in our lives or world. Though only some of us are called to assume the role of soldiers fighting in battles with lethal weapons, the warrior spirit awakens in each of our lives, regardless of age, gender, title, worldview, political inclinations, or station in life each time we step up to meet a challenge, take a stand for something we care about, or step into the role of leadership.

The role of warriors in our modern world is broader than most people may think. In today's world, warriors assume not only the role of members of the military, law enforcement, and first responders who serve their communities in high-stress contexts but also of courageous leaders and activists in many communities and organizations around the globe. These leaders embody the courage, dedication, discipline, and willingness to step up and risk their own safety and well-being to care for others and protect the greater good.

Our appreciation for the role of modern-day warriors in our world is also inspired by Elizabeth A. Stanley, who is director of the Center for Security Studies at Walsh School of Foreign Service at Georgetown University and a former U.S. Army intelligence officer.

> I know the profession of arms from the inside out: from its integrity, nobility, heroism, and selfless service on the one hand, to its horrors, traumas, shadow behaviors and deep suffering on the other. . . . Warriors—at their most impeccable and most effective—must embody what one Marine lance corporal once described to me as "both the monk and the killer." This truth makes many civilians, especially those at the liberal end of the political spectrum, very uncomfortable. A true warrior must be able to still her body and mind to call forth strength; exhibit endurance during harsh environmental conditions; have awareness of herself, others, and the wider environment so she can make discerning choices; access compassion for herself, her compatriots, her adversary, and the locals where she is deployed; and show self-control during provocation so that she doesn't overreact. And yet, if the moment demands, she must also have the capacity to kill, cleanly, without hesitation and without remorse.
>
> This is the paradox of warriors: they don't seek aggression out, but if they encounter aggression that cannot be resolved nonviolently, they must meet it decisively. In other words, the warrior must be able to access vulnerability and strength simultaneously. It is only by accessing both qualities fully at all times that the warrior can engage in right action.[2]

When the power of the archetypical warrior spirit is immature and undisciplined, it can easily go astray, assuming the dominating stance of *power over* others, causing inconceivable damage, harm, and suffering, as we so widely witness in our world. Yet, when the warrior spirit is matured and properly honed, disciplined, honored, and deployed by those who know how to wisely wield its potential as *power with*, it can be an inspiring and enduring force for protection, leadership, and service.

The power of this warrior spirit may be simply expressed through a kind word, action, thought, or prayer. It may be conveyed by compassionately and courageously responding to reckless, threatening, or harmful behavior with a disarming skillfulness that dissipates, resolves, or deescalates the tensions or aggressive latencies present in the field, while protecting those who are vulnerable. This compassionate courage may also manifest as fierce decisiveness striking at the heart of a situation to disarm or neutralize dangerous people intent on harming others, destroying habitats, or pillaging natural resources vital to the lives and well-being of communities and future generations—even at the risk of their own lives. Without this special kind of courageous, caring, and protective warrior spirit, we would not have survived the many dangers we have faced individually and collectively. As William James, the father of modern psychology, once mused, "ancestral evolution has made us all warriors!"

Ultimate Warrior and Beyond

The identifier for this historic advanced human potential training program for the Special Forces has morphed over time. In its initial conception it was envisioned as the ultimate warrior training program, as inspired by Channon's vision, described in *Evolutionary Tactics*. Later, in its contractual phase, the program was christened with the code name Trojan Warrior, a reference that evokes an intriguing image of a Special Forces group secreted away deep within the belly of the U.S. Army, gestating to later emerge as a victorious transformational force to penetrate more deeply into previously inaccessible territory, analogous to the ancient Greek warriors hidden in the wooden Trojan horse. This was how the soldiers we trained generally referred to the program.

Over time as word spread and the mythical overtones of the program ignited people's imaginations, the program gravitated toward the identity of the Jedi warrior and came to be known by that name. This was further inspired by our graphic designer, Paul Ackerman, who came up with a brilliant logo for the program, drawing inspiration from the traditional crossed arrows insignia for the Green Berets and switching out the arrows for two glowing light sabers with the Special Forces motto *De Oppresso Liber*, Latin for "Liberators of the Oppressed," emblazoned below the image, and *Vi Cit Tecum*, Latin for "May the Force Be with You" inscribed below that.*

However you choose to identify this program, it was an epic endeavor. The deep changes within the hearts and minds of the military leaders who had conceived of an ultimate warrior training program opened the portal for this pioneering program to be conceived and realized within the Special Forces command structure. To honor the creative spirit and mythic power of its possibilities, we refer to this as the Jedi Warrior program throughout the book.

The Noble Intention behind Jedi Warrior

Extraordinary missions call for extraordinary levels of skills and training. For perspective, consider that at the time of writing this book, the estimated cost of training and equipping an ordinary soldier is around $20,000 to $25,000, while the investment in training and equipping a Navy SEAL or

---

*It was on the night train to *Surat Thani* in Thailand that the potency of the Jedi Warrior meme came vividly alive for us. As we rattled and swayed along through the Thai countryside, we marveled at the elegant beauty of many tall spires of Buddhist temples reaching to the vastness of space. Expressing our delight at seeing such beauty, our colleague Chaiwat said with a wise smile, "Ah, these are called *chedis* (pronounced Jedis). They are symbols for the awakened mind of enlightenment." Hearing this, we realized that given George Lucas's early travels in Asia, the term chedi may have been the source of his inspiration for the word *Jedi* to describe the quality of awakened warriors with the wisdom presence of great monks. Lucas has clearly stated in various interviews that Jedi were designed to be Buddhist monks who happened to be very good at fighting.

Army Green Beret is between $1,500,000 and $2,000,000. If we had been training ordinary soldiers with ordinary assignments, as our programs for other military units had done, we would have had less time and a modest budget and would have stuck to providing very basic introductory training in mindful awareness, self-regulation, and peak-performance training. We wouldn't have had a charter to explore the more profound implications and applications of personal mastery disciplines and wisdom traditions.

In the extraordinary case of the Jedi Warrior program, we had the inconceivably rare opportunity to design and deliver a robust, generously funded, six-month-long, immersive, multidisciplinary program for twenty-five fortunate members of two elite Green Beret Special Forces teams. In the mission scenarios these soldiers trained for, they could literally have found themselves in the position of igniting or preventing the next world war. The stakes for their success were inconceivably high. This program was described by military analysts at West Point Military Academy as "the most exquisite orchestration of human technology we've ever seen" and by founders of the human potential movement as "the most advanced and technically sophisticated leadership and human performance training program ever to be delivered in modern times."

The potent "secret sauce" for this historic program was formulated from the inspired synergy of compelling mythos and methodologies from varied sources. Among these were: Jim Channon's *Evolutionary Tactics*, George Lucas's vision of Jedi warriors in his Star Wars series, and the profound embodied warrior wisdom of Morihei Ueshiba's martial art of aikido, along with other warrior-monk traditions. We also drew from the psychophysical sciences of advanced biofeedback and neurofeedback training for self-regulation and self-mastery, the wisdom of advanced peak performance and contemplative sciences. These various traditions, practices, and sciences were woven together and focused on developing the extraordinary capacities of already elite and powerful Special Forces warriors who were preparing to deploy on what might have become the most dangerous and existentially impactful covert missions our world had ever seen. This supercharged blend of ancient, modern, mythical, and technoshamanistic traditions created an incomparable learning laboratory for our awakening wisdom warriors and for ourselves, and we were deeply grateful for the privilege to play such a pioneering role in creating and delivering this program from its inception.

At the time we were invited to develop Jedi Warrior, initial reports were beginning to emerge estimating that as many as two to five times more soldiers were dying from suicide after they returned home from combat than had died in combat. Estimates would eventually reach as high as twenty times more suicides among veterans than combat deaths, with as many as forty-four U.S. military veterans dying each day by their own hand. The courageous and visionary military leaders we were working with carried a heavy burden of regret and shame for the tremendous suffering that so many veterans had witnessed and participated in the gut wrenching, soul shattering horrors of the war. These caring leaders were acutely aware that this scourge of suffering flowed on in the continuum of veterans' lives long after they left the service. Highly motivated to search for a deeper wisdom to guide military training for future generations of warriors, they were clear that it was vital to provide education in life- and mission-related skills necessary for soldiers to recognize and befriend their inner enemies so they could stop the wars raging or smoldering within them, realize new degrees of self-awareness, self-regulation, self-mastery, and ethical discernment, and muster the special kind of courage and dedication required to accomplish this. It was this noble intention that gave rise to the invitation for us to develop this first of its kind program.

The research on people returning from military deployment makes it clear that they are likely to experience some degree of PTSD, anxiety, and depression. Data collected by the U.S. Military Mental Health Advisory Team revealed that troops who screened positive for mental health problems after deployments in Afghanistan and Iraq were three times more likely to report that they engaged in unethical behaviors while they were deployed, which resulted in a debilitating moral injury that continued to haunt them. It became clear in these cases that their distress was not so much about the nature of the conflict itself or whether they should have engaged in it, but rather was about whether they crossed a line and did something they didn't feel was right. The mental health implications for people in other walks of life who also suffer moral injury and resulting devastation are of similar concern.

As combat veteran Stanley observes:

> The profession of arms is unlike any other. It is the only profession that requires leaders to nurture, mentor and train their subordinates—in fact, love them—but then be willing to send these same subordinates into harm's way, to kill and perhaps be killed. And it is the only profession that requires subordinates to respect and trust their leaders enough to willingly follow orders that may lead to their own wounding, dismemberment or even death. Given the difficulties inherent in waging war, we have an obligation to train our warriors to embody as much capacity for self-regulation and nonharming as is possible. With training and deliberate practice, warriors can learn to see clearly exactly how things are, tolerate what's happening without getting jerked around by impulses or reactivity, and then choose the most effective course of action in the service of others—without sacrificing their own humanity in the process.[3]

Another factor motivating the development of the Jedi Warrior program was that it emerged while the Cold War was raging. At this time there was also a tense but little-known psi-ops mind race emerging with increasing research on the nature and potential weaponization of extraordinary psychic powers.*

---

*"Psi-ops" focus on developing and deploying extraordinary powers of mind for military purposes. This is radically different from the more commonly referenced "psyops" that focus on altering attitudes and beliefs of individuals or groups to change their behavior.

This research was generously funded by the U.S. military and their counterparts in the Soviet Union and China. Our own early research in this area was through colleagues working on studies at Stanford and Princeton and with colleagues involved with the "psychic discoveries behind the Iron Curtain."[4]

This research focused primarily on the domains of remote viewing and the nonlocal psychokinetic mental influencing of electronic, biological, and material targets. At a more mundane and immediate level of threat, there was also a growing concern among U.S. military leaders that the Soviets were quietly applying advanced psychophysical training protocols with their elite military units, called the *Spetsnaz,* whose mission was to equip the Soviet Special Forces with the same high-level capacities that led to their supremacy in the world of international sports. The Jedi Warrior program was regarded by some as a counter measure to match or surpass the Soviets in advanced psychophysical training for elite warriors with the goal of giving our Special Forces troops a significant advantage over their ruthless Soviet counterparts.

We'd like to acknowledge upfront that some of our readers may have ethical concerns regarding offering sophisticated psychophysical training to increase the capacities of elite military operatives. As you will see, we have certainly wrestled deeply with such concerns ourselves. We appreciate the wisdom of our dear colleague Professor Amishi Jha, director of contemplative neuroscience and professor of psychology at the University of Miami, who has worked extensively in military training and research related to mindfulness, mental health, attention, resilience, and force readiness. When asked about how advanced mind training might be applied to creating more adept killers, Amishi astutely responded: "I've had people challenge me, 'You're just trying to create super soldiers.' My response is that if a soldier has a machine gun that can destroy an entire village, I want to make sure that person has the capacity to really know what they're doing and have full control over their faculties, to be able to withhold as appropriate, not be reactive. So, a super soldier in many ways is one that can control when to *not* pull the trigger, not to just pull the trigger."[5]

Speaking to the importance of such clear-minded discernment in an astute article titled, "Leading with Attention: Mindfulness Takes Hold as Army Embraces the Now," Lieutenant General Walter Piatt, Colonel Deydre Teyen, and Amy Adler, a senior scientist at the Center for Military Psychiatry and Neuroscience, noted that "Paying attention—being present in the moment and fully focused on the now—is a capability that can make the difference between good decisions and great decisions. . . . improving attention can literally mean the difference between life and death. Without this focus, soldiers are limited to reacting, their minds always somewhere else and never on the task at hand. . . . Through most of our technology, everything can look like a target, but leaders must be able to discern if it is or is not. To be able to pay attention in that moment, to see the complexity and be able to discern what is and is not a threat, remains a basic skill that soldiers must acquire. It is one thing to be good with a weapon; it is another thing to know when not to use it. Both skills are vital for soldiers who have a split second to decide."[6]

Evolutionary Tactics

The portal to the possibility of the Jedi Warrior program was initially opened by our colleague Bud Pōmaika'i Cook who introduced us to Channon, the inspired imagineer, social architect, and author of *Evolutionary Tactics.* His weaving of words and artwork had the power to induct his readers into totally new psychospheres of perspective. Channon not only created a vast vision for the future highest purpose of the military on planet Earth, but he also later worked with dozens of leading global organizations to illuminate and illustrate their corporate visions for a future worth celebrating on a global scale. Channon was the commander of the U.S. Army's First Earth Battalion, an actual yet mythical force. The vision put forth in his book, and the groundswell of mind-set shifts that rippled from it, seeded the mind field within the military and beyond for our Jedi Warrior program to sprout and grow into a robust, well-funded program for the Special Forces. We are deeply grateful for Channon's blessings, encouragement, and permission to weave images from his inspired work into this book.

Channon was considered one of the brightest, most futuristic visionaries of the U.S. Army in the 1970s and early 1980s. He was trained as a military intelligence officer and served ten years in the infantry. As a platoon leader on three tours of Vietnam, Channon said that he lost only one soldier in combat and never killed an innocent civilian.

Channon was also a visionary artist whose skills were widely coveted by senior military officers who would rely upon him to illustrate their briefings with his dynamic, illuminated, wall-sized colorful "monstergrams" that summarized the information conveyed in a briefing in blazing images. Channon was so renowned for his work that General Thurman, before he briefed the U.S. Army senior leadership, would ask, "Where's Jimmy?"—and fly him in from the West Coast as needed. As such, Channon helped to define and pioneer the field of dynamic "graphic facilitation."

Channon landed a job in public affairs and was soon assigned as the army's interface with Hollywood. During this time he initiated a revolutionary scouting mission to explore the various emerging human potential movements that were burgeoning in California with the goal to gather insights, inspirations, and methods that might inform and inspire a vision for the role the U.S. Army could play in the year 2000. Channon traveled far and wide in his quest to discover the best and the brightest that the human potential scene had to offer during the colorful, paisley-patterned times of the late 1970s and early 1980s. Channon's research was encouraged and supported by the Task Force Delta think tank based at the U.S. Army War College at Carlisle Barracks, Pennsylvania.

Our first encounter with Channon was at his home on the Salish Sea, near Joint Base Lewis-McCord, south of Seattle. Beaming a huge and mischievous smile, he arrived in uniform with a rich display of chest candy—colorful service ribbons and medals. Channon was a formidable presence, with a disarming wit and a vocabulary replete with a creative barrage of potent visions that were mind and paradigm expanding. A master storyteller, Channon would use his words and gestures to riff in all ways cosmic, using the airbrush of illuminating, psychoactive memes, masks, and sweeping mural-size paintings to animate his visions of extraordinary human potential.

Little did we know at that first meeting that we would become lifelong friends, cowizards, and creative collaborators working together on dozens of visionary projects, or that we would become neighbors developing a thriving ecocommunity on the island of Hawaii where we cohosted many gatherings over twenty years. We, along with several others, would later create SportsMind, a training and consulting firm that would be a delivery vehicle for Channon's vision of the First Earth Battalion to leaders and teams in hundreds of organizations around the globe.

Channon described the Earth Battalion as "protomythological—looking at the future while rooted in a historic framework." The motto of the First Earth Battalion was "Dare to Think the Unthinkable," in the most creative, far-reaching, and beneficial sense of the word. The Earth Battalion dedication reads as follows:

The Earth Battalion declares its primary allegiance to **people** and **planet**. You can become a part of that allegiance right where you are simply by allowing the exquisite human being inside to come out. When it's out . . . then help others to come out and work together to stay out—building the paradise that is possible when we cooperate with each other and our mother earth.[7]

Channon's vision for the First Earth Battalion was affirmed and emboldened by President Jimmy Carter's embrace of environmental stewardship, renewable energy, and protection of natural resources and wildlands as being essential for sustained national security. Carter himself was a graduate of the Naval Academy at Annapolis and served as a naval officer for seven years. He later served as the thirty-ninth president of the United States from 1977 to 1981. In 2002 he was awarded the Nobel Peace Prize for his work to find peaceful solutions to international conflicts, advance democracy and human rights, and promote economic and social development. Carter had aspired to the daunting goal of making the U.S. government "competent and compassionate," responsive to the American people and their needs. In the Middle East, through the Camp David agreement of 1978, he helped bring amity between Egypt and Israel. He succeeded in obtaining ratification of the Panama Canal treaties. Building upon the work of his predecessors, he established full diplomatic relations with the People's Republic of China and completed negotiation of the SALT II nuclear limitation treaty with the Soviet Union.

Channon was inspired to invite leaders in the military and beyond to seriously consider shifting their attention and priorities toward new missions for solving the problems of today's and tomorrow's world. The missions proposed for the First Earth Battalion included: human disaster rescue group, ecodisaster rescue group, natural disaster rescue group, as well as force of heart, force of will, force of arms, force of spirit, ecopioneers, urban pioneers, and space pioneers.

Evolutionary Tactics states that "soldiers are in the business of life and death. As a leader during war, I must know that if my soldiers are to die . . . that it's for the right reasons. When at peace they deserve nothing less than a chance of personal evolution. Soldiers can be a real part of the evolution of this Earth. Anything less . . . is just something less."[8]

To accomplish these aims, Channon called for the army to develop the First Earth Battalion, an elite cadre of warrior-monks trained in the best of modern and ancient martial, scientific, ecowise, and mystical traditions. Channon envisioned their roles as meditation leaders, spirit and martial arts wizards, nutritionists, herbalists, vexillographers (flags and banners), cinematographers, futurists, general systems theorists, minstrels, holographers, and more. All this shifted the military minds of his time, and they began to envision what it might look like to actually manifest this vision, which opened the way for the Jedi Warrior program.

In his inspiring foreword to the Task Force Delta concept paper called "The First Earth Battalion: Ideas and Ideals for Soldiers Everywhere," Colonel D. Mike Malone wrote:

> The track of time comes hurtling up out of the past from somewhere billions of years ago back in history. It flicks by us as we stand here now in the present and then thrusts on for billions of years out ahead of us into the future, bound for some place called infinity.
>
> Two things we know about time: its march is inexorable . . . and it always gives rise to change. Change, then, is like time, inexorable, inevitable, and pervasive—and so powerful and complex a thing that in just five billion years, change has produced, from inorganic matter and countless millions of experiments, complex living things such as social insects and humankind.
>
> Any concept of change is a concept of time. Thus, any concept of change must involve past, present, and future. Task Force Delta's effort, as a concept of change, needs the track of time . . . the lessons of history, the realities of the present, and the dreams and visions of the future.
>
> Our "First Earth Battalion" is a place to dream. A place to think the unthinkable. It's the prime place to put our thoughts of the future just as we must maintain our perspective of the past and contact with the complexities of the present. It's an "Earth" battalion because of what we know about a shrinking world, and about interdependencies among people, nations, and natural resources . . . interdependencies which everyday are becoming more evident to us all. It's a battalion because our

effort is directed to our Army, and the battalion is an entity which all of us soldiers from top to bottom, can comprehend.[9]

In Channon's foreword to the manual, he further outlined his vision of the Earth Battalion.

Making this planet whole . . . requires the ethical use of force. But even subcultures of force must evolve. . . . The Army is no exception. Soldiers can be the principal moral ethical basis on which things political can harmonize in the name of the Earth. . . . Earthkind has grown from pack to village . . . from village to tribe, from tribe to territory . . . and from territory to nation. It is time to go from nation to planet. First Earth Battalion hereby declares its primary allegiance to the planet . . .

The Earth Battalion is potential oriented, not mission oriented, so any definition of what it is or does tends to limit what it can become. . . . At the moment it is a spirit among other things . . . it may be a pilot community of warrior monks who completely recycle all resources, live amid new nuclear reactors, awaiting deployment to tension spots . . . or a think tank methodology for the U.S. Army—a banner for the closet great-hearts wherever they are—a bonding agent for the idealist activists in the service and out—a home for the ethical evolution of force—an alternate form of service to the planet.[10]

Deep Resilience

The stakes in our world today are so high that we need to radically accelerate our evolution. While some say that resilience will be our "new sustainability," the evolutionary momentum we need to thrive and survive in these complex times will certainly require more than merely maintaining or bouncing back to a meager status quo. As Krishnamurti so wisely reminds us, "It is no measure of health to be well adjusted to a profoundly sick society."

Through our work with Jedi Warrior and beyond, we have come to appreciate what we call deep resilience as an agile regenerative skill that increases our capacity for developing our strength, confidence, wisdom, and effectiveness through finding the courage to fully show up for, learn from, embrace, and be strengthened by each new wave of challenge that life may bring.

Having pioneered the integration of such methods into mainstream medicine, higher education, business, sports, and the military for nearly five decades, we have worked with people around the globe from diverse cultures and walks of life and witnessed the meaningful, often-radical transformation of thousands of people. In our work developing and delivering the Jedi Warrior program, we drew deeply from both modern and ancient wisdom traditions and generously adapted and translated these potent transformational technologies to inspire and empower the soldiers we trained. We knew that properly framed and skillfully articulated and presented, these methods of mastery are readily assimilable, hyperrelevant, and of universal value to people from every profession, walk of life, culture, or tradition.

The Great Unraveling and Great Turning

The Jedi Warrior training emerged like a wise immune response within these pivotal times that many regard as the time of the Great Unraveling—a time of existential global-scale metacrisis, replete with the implosion, disintegration, and collapse of many of the unsustainable systems, structures, identities, assumptions, antiquated paradigms, and ways of living that humanity has come to rely upon in the treadmill of unrelenting "progress."[11] In these critical times, many global leaders are struggling to keep their heads above the rising waters of complexity and not succumb to overwhelm, bewilderment, burnout, or short-sighted reactive responses that only create more unanticipated problems. Some appreciate the need to radically upgrade their psychophysical capacity to wisely lead, while others bluster about with misguided actions that distract people from focusing on their incompetence and growing irrelevance as leaders.

Many wise people say we also live in the time of the Great Turning—away from the global domination of the myth of continual growth that is consuming and destroying the life-support systems of the planet and pivoting toward a more life-sustaining civilization.[12] Humanity has drifted so far away from being guided by a wisdom deeply rooted in discerning science and deep ecology that we are beginning to reorient ourselves individually and collectively toward ways of living together on this rare and precious tiny blue marble of a planet that are more sensible, resilient, regenerative, and congruent with the many dimensional systems of nature and reality. In this Great Turning there is a growing recognition of the wisdom traditions of indigenous people, who have nurtured and cared for their people and Earth for millennia, as a valued source of inspiration. Will we pivot deep and fast enough to save our world from devastation? Time will tell, and it's up to us all.

VUCAA Times

In the international spheres of our work in the world, many global leaders are increasingly referring to these as "VUCA times," that is times of *volatility, uncertainty, complexity,* and *ambiguity.* We are experiencing unprecedented change, upheaval, collapse, surprise, and transformation in every dimension of our lives—personal, organizational, social, and environmental. Inspired by one of our colleagues, we added an additional A to VUCA to acknowledge the utter *absurdity* of so many powerful forces at play that seem to be moving away from a wisdom-informed responsiveness to the radical needs and nature of these times.[13] These VUCAA times bring chaos and uncertainty in our lives and world, as well as a myriad of emergent opportunities and new expressions of creativity. These include innovative, life-affirming, altruistic community, entrepreneurial, and global initiatives that encourage more wise and sustainable ways of living in our world. Depending upon the capacities developed by individuals, organizations, and communities, VUCAA times are likely to bring out both the best and the worst in people.

The VUCA acronym was first coined in 1985 by economists and university professors Warren Bennis and Burt Nanus in their book *Leaders: The Strategies for Taking Charge.* The VUCA meme quickly found its way into the curriculum and lexicon of the U.S. Army War College as a fitting description of the swift and unexpected fall of the Iron Curtain and the demise of the Soviet Union and the Eastern Bloc and later as an apt description of the modern battlefield.

The challenge is to learn and implement new ways of seeing and wisely responding amid conditions of volatility, uncertainty, complexity, and ambiguity. VUCA has come to be a succinct description for the conditions of both the modern battlefield and the theater of colliding, collapsing, and emerging polycrises within which all of human affairs are currently unfolding. Here we find both great danger and opportunity, as reflected in the Chinese symbol for crisis. In these VUCAA times, many hearts quiver with a tender sense of solastalgia, the kind of tender, soul deep grief that arises as we experience the decimation of natural habitats, forests, wetlands, coral reefs, rivers, climate patterns, and homelands that were precious, meaningful, or sacred to us but are no longer here.[14]

What Color Is Your Apple?

Each person who reads this book will experience their own unique rich mix of insights, interpretations, and reactions. To illustrate this, count to three, and then reach out into the space before you and imagine picking up an apple. Ready? One . . . two . . . three . . .

Holding this apple in your hand, now look at it. Notice, do you have a yellow apple? A green apple? A red or multicolored apple? Does your apple still have the stem on it? Are there any leaves attached to the stem? Is the apple you picked up a crunchy piece of delicious fruit—or an electronic device? Notice if you can clearly see the apple or not? Can you feel its weight and mass—or not? Can you smell its subtle fragrance—or not?

When we invite people in audiences to engage in this simulation, there are inevitably many different images that appear to people's minds when we simply say the word *apple*. If children are in the audience, the images multiply as they tend to be more creative and conjure up apples with sparkles, jewels, candy stripes, or rainbow colors.

Keep in mind that we simply wrote "pick up an apple" without referencing any details. You then proceeded to mentally generate whatever colors, stems, leaves, fragrances, and so on that you experienced. In the same way, as you read this book, we encourage you to be curious about and mindful of how you will inevitably conjure up your own interpretations, associations, and mental fabrications of embellishing this story. In this way we encourage you to appreciate that regardless of what we write here, you are partnering with us as an active coproducer of this already amazing story.

In this spirit, please keep in mind that each of us involved in the design and delivery of this program, and each of the twenty-five soldiers who participated, plus their senior officers, would certainly have his/her own version of this story. The narrative we offer in these pages represents our unique set of views, memories, experiences, and perspectives, having been with the project from its inception to its completion.

Legacy

This story comes to you as we honor the heartfelt request of Colonel Kenneth W. Getty, who asked the two of us to write this book and offer the world our views and version of this historic training program. As the inspiring and visionary leader who initially conceived of and oversaw this pioneering program, we owe him a deep debt of gratitude.

Shortly before Colonel Getty's death, we reached out to him to discuss a proposal we had been asked to submit to the Surgeon General's Office for a simplified version of the Trojan Warrior program, targeting a wider audience in the military community. In our conversations with him, Colonel Getty thanked us for all the insights he had gained and the life skills he had learned through our work together. He reflected on how he carried the lessons he learned with him when he went on to teach at the Army War College and then to lead the Special Operations Command for Europe.

Colonel Getty mused on how fortunate we all had been to participate in this extraordinary training and lamented that so few modern-day warriors have had the opportunity to learn the skills and develop the capabilities of our Jedi Warriors prior to being deployed into harm's way. His heart ached with sadness, regret, and compassion for the great suffering that arises due to the absence of such embodied wisdom, and the severe, debilitating stress and lingering trauma that so many soldiers face being deployed into modern arenas of warfare.

Colonel Getty had witnessed firsthand the great price that so many warriors pay for not receiving adequate training in even the most basic self-awareness, self-regulation, and self-mastery skills necessary to wisely cope and resiliently adapt to the extremely stressful, often traumatic, and enduring consequences of this profession and was saddened knowing that so much of this great suffering could be prevented if warriors were properly trained in the skills this book presents.

Colonel Getty was insightful and pragmatic. In one media interview he noted:

While generally enthusiastic about the challenge and the refreshing change of pace, we had to dilute the idea that it was meditation. We just offered them the option of developing other faculties that would make them better soldiers and better human beings. For some, the idea of talking about spirituality was very difficult. Macho men just don't talk about such things. . . . We are looking to turn out better human beings overall. These men won't always be in the Army, and we want to turn a better man back into the civilian world.[15]

When we were interviewing Colonel Getty shortly after he retired, Michelle asked him what he was most proud of from all his decades of service to his country and his exemplary leadership for his community of warriors. He leaned back, smiled, and said, "Honestly, Michelle, what I'm most proud of is the number of covert humanitarian operations that our teams were able to run over the years that helped thousands of people, that no one ever heard about because these operations were so stealthily and skillfully carried out." Hearing this, we both looked at each other with a sense of deep respect and appreciation for the profound legacy of rippling beneficial influence that this inspiring warrior had created through his work as a senior military leader.

As a cherished friend and wise mentor, Colonel Getty encouraged us to pursue every avenue available to us to publish and widely share these vital teachings and reminded us of his longstanding request that we document our experience and unique perspectives on this historic program in a book someday. That day has now arrived, and this book that you are reading would not have come about without his courageous and compassionate dedication to this transformational work to change the lives of those within his sphere of influence and elevate the wisdom and compassion guiding the human systems he was embedded within. May we all strive to have such ennobling impacts on the individuals, communities, and living systems that weave the fabric of our lives, work, and world.

Revolutionary Spirit

We now begin our story with a call to a special kind of r/evolutionary courage from Jim Channon:

> We live in a universe that has evolutionary potential. Unfortunately, there are folks who would freeze the potential in order maintain personal or corporate control. Therefore, warriors are required to protect the POSSIBILITIES and nurture THE POTENTIAL.
>
> It requires courage to come out, reach out, and effect positive change in ourselves and in the larger systems we serve. It requires courage to LOVE. It requires courage to accept that we ourselves can push the universe into higher states of order![16]

PART ONE

THE ROOTS OF JEDI WARRIOR TRAINING

One of the grandest moments
in personal development
trainings is to watch people
"pop out of the jelly" caught
all of their lives in a set of
belief systems that have
blocked them from realizing
we are all one family......
often a zeroing experience
like warfare ... or a truly
loving group of friends that
causes people to realize
they are <u>CONNECTED</u> to all of
those around them in
a <u>deep</u> & <u>profound</u> way.

this is the planets newest
spectator sport ...
<u>CONSCIOUSNESS WORK</u>

THE FIRST EARTH BATTALION

ONE

The Genesis of Jedi Warrior

Another name for God is surprise.
BROTHER DAVID STEINDL-RAST

The golden light of an early August day in 1982 filtered through the plants in the office window, and I (Joel) was in the rhythm and flow of patient care at Group Health Cooperative Medical Center in Seattle. As the director of the Stress Management, Biofeedback, and Pain Control Center, my days were dedicated to guiding individuals in exploring the inner terrain of their mind-body, helping them to nurture the special forces of awareness, awaken self-compassion, and gain greater confidence, resilience, and self-mastery.

I was returning from a break when my receptionist Donna halted me midstride in the hallway. "Joel, Bud Cook is on the line," she said. "He says it's urgent to talk with you right away."

I chuckled to myself, wondering what Bud had in mind. Bud was a dear friend and a former student of mine from a graduate program in the psychology of consciousness that I had designed and taught at Antioch University. He was also an adept sports psychologist and inspiring martial arts instructor, with a generous spirit, a hearty laugh, and a formidable presence. The last time Bud had called it had been about an idea for working with the Seattle Mariners. The time before that it was about training ski instructors in mind fitness aboard a sailboat cruising the Caribbean. Neither of those ambitious ideas had come to pass. *Now what's Bud cooking up this time?* I wondered. Little did I know that fateful call would open a portal to a transformational journey that would radically change the course of our lives, challenge and unravel many deeply held views, and potentially help to stop the next world war. Getting straight to the point, Bud asked, "Hey, Wiz, how would you like to design the ultimate warrior training program for the Green Berets?"

There was a long, deep silence on my end. He continued, "This is for real. Listen. I just came back from a meeting with Task Force Delta, and some officers well placed in the chain of command asked for a proposal. They are seriously interested, and you're the first person who came to mind to design this. Are you game?"

Bud had my attention. He went on to explain that he had developed a connection with Lieutenant Colonel Jim Channon from the U.S. Army War College at Carlisle Barracks in Pennsylvania. For the past three years, Jim's assignment had been to explore the human-potential movement in search of inspirations and ideas that could inform the army's vision for the new warrior in the twenty-first century.

So why was the army interested in extraordinary human potential? It turned out that in the 1960s and 1970s there were widespread reports of psychic discoveries behind the Iron Curtain. I was well aware of these studies and had engaged in some parallel research and collaboration during my time in the labs at the University of Washington. Understanding that the security, intelligence, and military implications of psychic powers were enormous, many U.S. intelligence agencies had launched into a flurry of activity, funding research to understand and develop America's own extraordinary powers. Over the years, research at Stanford Research Institute, Princeton School of Engineering, Menninger Foundation, and many other respected laboratories explored the phenomena of mental telepathy, remote viewing, psychokinesis—the power of mind to influence or move material objects at a distance from the body and other extraordinary human capabilities. This research consistently produced mind-boggling results that demonstrated not only that such special psychic powers were real but also, more importantly, that "ordinary" people could be trained to develop these extraordinary capabilities.

In thousands of rigorous, well-controlled, and replicated studies, researchers showed that our mind-bodies are capable of reaching out into the fabric of space and time in ways that produce measurable results that are often statistically significant at billions to sometimes trillions of times beyond what would be expected by chance. And though these results were inexplicable by any existing theories relied upon by mainstream science, the lack of coherent explanation didn't refute the overwhelming amount of evidence for mind creating measurable change and sourcing accurate information at a distance.

In the late 1970s, the People's Republic of China publicly reported that several thousand of its children aged eight to fourteen were capable of telepathy, clairvoyance, x-ray vision, or psychokinesis. At the same time, the Central Intelligence Agency, National Security Agency, Defense Intelligence Agency, Lawrence Livermore Laboratories, and the U.S. Army had already begun to pour millions of dollars into their own similar research. The U.S. Army's program was headquartered at Fort Meade, Maryland, and was part of the Intelligence and Security Command (INSCOM). Leaders there included Generals Edmund Thompson and Albert Stubblebine, Colonel John Alexander, and Lieutenant Colonel Jim Channon, all of whom were assigned to the U.S. Army War College at Carlisle Barracks.

Drawing insights from his colleagues at the War College and from his own far-reaching and "far-out" explorations, Jim distilled his findings and synthesized his inspirations into a mind-expanding masterpiece titled: *Evolutionary Tactics: A Manual for the First Earth Battalion*. The manual offered a compelling higher-order vision for the evolving archetype of the U.S. Army's most advanced soldiers for the twenty-first century—ones with techno-wizardly skills tempered by deep-spirited principles and the intuitive wisdom and spiritual power of a mystic, sage, and warrior-monk. As a prescient vision for the Jedi Warrior program, Channon wrote in *Evolutionary Tactics*:

> I envision an international ideal of service awakening in an emerging class of people who are best called *evolutionaries*. I see them as soldiers, as youth, and as those who have soldier spirit within them. I see them come together in the name of people and planet to create a new environment of support and protection and nurturing of the mother earth. Their mission is to protect the possible and to nurture the potential. They are the evolutionary guardians who focus their loving protection and affirm their allegiance to the people and planet for their own good and for the good of those they serve. I call them evolutionaries, not revolutionaries, for they are potentialists, not pragmatists. They are pioneers, not palace guards.
>
> As their contribution to a hopeful future, the warrior monks bring evolutionary tactics. They recognize that the world community of peoples demands hope from those who would operate as servants of the people. Services rendered by the warriors of the First Earth Battalion are specifically designed to generate workable solutions to defuse the nuclear time bomb, promote international relations, spread wise energy use, enforce the ecological balance, assist wise technological expansion, and above all, stress human development.
>
> Armies are both the potential instruments of our destruction and the organized service that can drive humanity's potential development. They are the "turn key" organizations that could either shift the energy of our world into a positive synergistic convergence or bring us to the brink of the void. We have no choice but to encourage world armies to accept and express the nobility they already strive to attain . . .

This will not be the first time that warrior monks have been active in our world. In Vedic traditions, the warrior monk was a philosopher and teacher, and therefore a powerful transformational player. In the Chinese culture, the warrior was both a healer and teacher of martial arts. History affirms our own belief that there is no contradiction in the warrior and the service-oriented monk prototypes living a completely harmonious, blended, and parallel path when the basic ethic and service is "loving protection" of evolution and humankind. There is no contradiction in having armies of the world experience the same ethic as they evolve in peaceful cooperation toward the greater good of all . . .

It is sometimes difficult to determine how we have set ourselves against each other as nations, and even the more frustrating when we realize that the people of these nations are not really very different inside, and in fact have the same desires for growth and environmental balance and for prosperity that we have. But this is reality. And soldiers who have grown up in an "arms race" world are obviously doing their job of protection when they come up with a new and more effective weapons package. But it is time for another approach, to use all of this military power for another end. It is time to give as much reward for the evolutionary contribution made by a soldier or an army as we have given in the past for the destructive contributions made on behalf of national defense. I know that this process will begin with the transformation of soldiers and evolutionaries everywhere on the face of our planet home. There are young men and women who already aspire to this level of service and who are ready to make a permanent commitment. They will begin to meet in small groups to provide a support system for the personal transformation of group members. And on a small scale, these groups will begin selecting evolutionary programs in their units and their communities. This manual serves as a handbook for the development of these evolutionary players and the development of their operating teams.[1]

Evolutionary Tactics was essentially the unclassified briefing slides from the army's research, and it was soon destined to become a widely distributed underground cult classic among visionary leaders within the intelligence and military community—and beyond. Although decidedly "new edge" at the time, this War College project was not entirely visionary or theoretical. Inspired by the research they had conducted, and by the vision of the First Earth Battalion, Colonel Alexander would go on to become a leader in the Los Alamos National Lab's nonlethal weapons program. General Stubblebine would take up a career doing research and training in extraordinary human powers and potentials. Looking back now at humanitarian and peacekeeping missions of the army since that time, it is possible to recognize many elements true to the original spirit of the First Earth Battalion vision. As far as our intelligence goes, no other program in military history has gone as far to advance this vision as the work in the story we are about to tell.

Bud continued to share that Jim had invited him to appear as the guest aikido master at a recent Task Force Delta conference near Washington, D.C. This meeting was to also serve as Jim's retirement party and was slated to be one of the most outrageously wild, creative, and cosmic events in military history. As part of the inspiring multimedia fantasia and three-day ritual that Jim had created, all of the Delta Force attendees were invited to step into the possibility of awakening the virtues and strengths of their own inner "warrior-monk archetype." This aesthetically elaborate, compelling, and emotionally potent event laid the stage for our friend Bud, as the resident aikido sensei, to make a profound impression on the crowd. Embodying the spirit of the warrior-monk that Jim was portraying, Bud inspired many of the leaders who were present. As a result, he was approached by a couple of the senior officers and requested to pull together a team to develop a robust proposal for bringing Jim Channon's vision alive as an actual "boots on the ground" military training program.

Bud related how these officers were deeply inspired by the extraordinary human potentials that Jim had invited them to consider and embody. It was clear that developing a military in which the next generations of Special Forces warriors had deeper psychophysical wisdom and more expansive wholistic training was the direction they knew that the army needed to go. The problem was that even the most advanced, existing military-training programs at that time paid little serious attention to developing the inner qualities, strengths of character, self-mastery skills, or extraordinary potentials that Jim and Bud had been presenting to them.

These leaders realized that these potentials for radical improvement were enormous; yet, they didn't have the knowledge or experience necessary to design a sophisticated, integrative training program that could bring the vision alive. They sensed that Bud might. The officers also expressed their haunting concerns prompted by the disturbing findings of some studies just released at the time that more than twice as many veterans had died of suicide than had died in combat, and they lived with the lingering grief, shame, and heartbreak of this on a daily basis. They were wise enough to understand that there were devastating wars going on inside many of their men and women caused by the unresolved trauma from military missions they had been deployed on, and that when these internal conflicts got out of control, they could cause tremendous and needless further suffering.

They also knew that under pressure, some people had developed a set of skills that helped them stay present, centered, clear minded, and open-hearted and thereby connected to the action and better able to think clearly, see what's really going on, and respond with skillful wisdom. Such extraordinary skills made it more likely that these soldiers would recognize and choose the wisest options that would result in the least pain and the most likelihood of resolving the conflict. They wanted to encourage their troops to develop these extraordinary skills, but they just weren't sure how to accomplish this.

Bud related that these Special Forces officers were most sincere and had said to him, "Look, we're excited by the possibilities, and we owe it to our people and to our country to explore this new frontier in developing our warriors. But we just don't have the expertise that we'd need to design a training program like this. We sense that you do and that you could put together a team with the kind of mental-fitness technology and people technology we need to build and equip the next generation of Special Forces operatives. We're not really sure what this training would look like or what the elements of it would be, but we invite you to give this some thought, pull together your team, and put a proposal together for us. We'll take the ball from there and see if we can make this happen."

Standing there in my office I listened to Bud's description of the cascade of events that had led to his call, and a kaleidoscope of images and thoughts exploded in my mind. I was astonished by the sheer audacity of Bud's invitation and told him that I'd need to give some more thought to his proposal and do some serious soul searching with Michelle and that I would get back to him soon.

As I hung up the phone and turned to pick up my charts and greet my next patient, I felt like a massive explosion had just taken place in the depths of my own psyche. At some level, perhaps many levels, I was in a state of shock, yet it seemed cushioned by an unexpected quality of peace and exhilaration mixed with dread, confusion, creativity, and possibility. My psyche reeled as a stream of images, dangers, opportunities, and potential scenarios flooded through, tugging on the worldview and identity I had constructed over the years and had come to know so well.

As synchronicity would have it, the timing of Bud's call was significant. A number of my patients were military veterans who were struggling with trauma that ran deep in their psyches, their bodies, and their relationships. Also, when Bud called, the first nuclear-warhead-armed Trident submarine was scheduled to arrive within a few days at the new Bangor Trident base on the Kitsap Peninsula just west of Seattle. Many of our closest friends and colleagues were gearing up to block roads, climb fences, or paddle out in their kayaks in protest. Most of them would be arrested.

As the reverberations of Bud's invitation continued to move deeper into my psyche, the question that kept coming to mind was, How could we teach the Green Berets to recognize and befriend their inner enemies and stop the war inside? I wondered what could, and would, happen if we accepted this invitation. I began to envision what "success" in a case like this would look like. What might it mean for the men, for us, and for our world?

These reflections kept rumbling through the day like aftershocks from the collision of two tectonic plates in my psyche. Driving home that evening, I found myself both excited and apprehensive about sharing this news with Michelle. I sensed that in her heart of hearts she had the wisdom, courage, and inner strength it would take to embrace an opportunity and challenge of this magnitude.

From Conscientious Objector to Military Adviser

As you may have gathered, the idea of accepting an assignment training elite teams of U.S. Army Special Forces troops was at least a few magnitudes out of order in my psyche. I grew up in a family with a rich blend of suffering and faith. Some of my fondest early memories are of being a very young child playing around the kitchen while my grandfather Abe was *davening* with his skullcap, prayer shawl, and prayer books as the sun rose over the peaks of the Cascade mountains east of our home. He'd repeat the same ritual in the evening, taking time to pray and read the Psalms of David before he went to bed. Growing up, Gramps was my father figure and role model, and from him I was strongly impressed that there was a larger mystery underlying all of life that was worthy of reverence and deep communion.

From my mother I learned lessons of courage and fierce determination. One morning when I was six years old, I awoke to find Gramps in tears, carrying my mother in his arms from the hallway where she had collapsed, half paralyzed, to her bed. He and my grandmother rushed her to the hospital where she lapsed into an encephalitic coma. For weeks she lay comatose, with hundreds of people in our community praying for her, though with scant hope in their hearts and minds. After three painfully long weeks, Mom woke up. As she explained it, she was lost in a dream-world and knew that if she didn't find her way back, something terrible would happen to me. Compelled by her sheer strength of will and an ocean of grace, she found her way back into her body and willed herself to wake up. The problem was that when she did come back, she was fully paralyzed. A well-meaning surgeon offered to perform an operation that would cut her spinal cord to allow her to sit more comfortably in a wheelchair for the rest of her life. She was terrified and took the counsel of her uncle Bill, chief of staff at Providence Hospital, who had suggested that we give her some time and try a less radical approach. For months the nurse-nuns and physical therapist at Providence worked with her, trying everything they could think of to help her. Months later, Mom walked up to that same surgeon at a community event and asked him to dance.

My grandmother Hilda was a passionate and caring woman who held an incredible amount of tension in her body and lived with a lot of pain. She used to get migraine headaches and needed cortisone shots every month or two to get her back muscles to relax. Her brother Bill, the Providence chief of staff, suggested that she try working with a "kooky doctor" down the hall from him, named George Watmore, who was one of the grandfathers of biofeedback training. As a young boy I'd go with her sometimes as she'd hook up with his big machines that measured her muscle tension levels. With Dr. Watmore's wise coaching, Grandma learned to internalize the feedback she was receiving from his instruments and monitor her own tension levels so that she could relax and release tension when she noticed it was accumulating.

I barely escaped the fate of going to the same dingy old high school that my grandmother had attended. Fortunately for me, my mother and I moved from the sleepy little pre-Boeing mill town of Everett to Bellevue, a more affluent "Boeing suburb" of Seattle, where I attended a new, progressive, high-tech high school not far from where Microsoft's headquarters are today. It was a magical-mystery-tour time to be in high school: the late 1960s, in the heat of the war in Vietnam, the dawning of the Age of Aquarius and acid rock, and a time of considerable soul searching regarding social justice and issues of race, gender, war and peace, authority, and beyond. Much to my delight, the school was populated in large part by a cadre of very hip, turned-on, socially engaged faculty who were eager and well equipped to expand the minds of their lucky students.

I passionately embraced the formal and informal curriculum of these times and delighted as the creative assignments of my teachers helped give form and concepts to the principles, values, and sense of wonder I had grown up with. My studies focused largely on contemplating the nature and meaning of life, the origins of consciousness and the universe, the nature of mystery and spirit. I thrived on the assignments, reading about the life of Siddhartha the Buddha, the works of Hermann Hesse and Carl Jung, the Zen teachings of Alan Watts, and the writings of many great philosophers of the ages. My former Jesuit priest science teacher, Tom Fackenthal, inspired in me the faith that science could also be a spiritual path and stretched my heart and mind farther toward their true cosmic proportions. My formal studies were generously supplemented by the fellowship of a remarkable community of kindred souls who spent many evenings and weekends exploring peacemaking, alternatives to war, Quaker philosophy and nonviolent protest and social action, methods of meditation, and rock concerts. We plumbed the profound mysteries of our lives through every means available in those magical and mind-blowing times. As I watched friends from school go off to war, I intensified my studies of spirit, deep ecology, nonviolence, and social justice, sought refuge in the wise counsel of inspiring elders, American Friends Service Committee draft protest counselors, and marched in propeace rallies. The notion of participating in a dirty war in Southeast Asia based on deceptions and corrupt ambitions was simply not an acceptable option for me. I resolved not only not to participate in the killing but to take a stand. In this spirit, my high school studies culminated in the formal presentation of my CO or conscientious objector thesis as my senior English project. This paper gave voice to a sequence of epiphanies and visions that had ripened in my soul a profound reverence for the unity and sanctity of all life and the wisdom of the survival of the kindest.

My formal and informal pursuits of these early years laid the foundation, set the direction, and forged the intention that would guide the travels, studies, protests, meditation retreats, consciousness research, and clinical training that filled the next decade of my life until that fateful morning when Bud called out of the blue asking if I would help design the ultimate warrior training program for the U.S. Army Green Berets. Can you imagine what rumbled through my mind upon hearing his words? As fate and good karma would have it, my beloved Michelle was (and is) a kindred soul in such pursuits. She had been even more fiercely involved as an activist in the anti–Vietnam War movement. Taking an especially strong stand against the war in support of the war resisters, she became an expat in 1969 and was granted political asylum in Sweden. Years later she immigrated to Canada where she continued to reside happily until we met in 1982, and she realized it was time to return home to the States. In our coming together, the long years of her self-imposed exile gently and unexpectedly came to an end. I watched Michelle's face closely as I told her of Bud's call. It lit up at the sheer irony of this invitation coming to two peaceniks like us, but she was quiet and reflective and let it soak in for a few moments before she responded.

With Your Blessing

Together we explored the implications of our involvement in the project and its coincidence with the arrival of the Trident. As we pondered the possibilities, we came to a rather profound realization. What if Bud had invited us to spend six months training the crew of a Trident submarine, with nuclear weapons on board, in mind-body disciplines? Wouldn't we feel that by the time we had immersed them in this type of training, they would be more likely to have the wisdom and skills necessary to be more centered, self-reflective, and intuitive and be able to think more deeply and clearly under extreme pressure? As a result, wouldn't the world actually become a safer place?

Though perhaps a bit too idealistic or even flippant at the time, the profundity of this insight continued to ring true in the daze that followed. A comprehensive, wholistic program that would inspire the strengths and capacities of true warriorship could develop a deeper awareness within the soldiers that could then give rise to a deeper insight regarding the interdependent forces at play in the complex situations they would encounter. Properly trained, these men or women would be equipped to recognize more subtle cues and more critical options and potentials. Under extreme and unreasonable stress, they ultimately would be more capable of self-regulating their bodies and calming their nervous systems, making wiser decisions based in the clarity, reasoning, and intuition necessary to take into consideration a greater sense of the whole. Seeing their missions and the circumstances they would encounter in a deeper light could enable them to bring a deeper attunement, wisdom, awareness, and, ultimately, compassion to doing what they needed to do in ways that would minimize the collateral damage in all its many harmonics.

As we talked into the night, we began to sense that accepting this invitation would be a wise and life-altering decision, one that would potentially result in the most impactful peace work that we'd ever have a chance to do in our lives.

While the potential for incredible benefit was enormous, it occurred to us that the potential also existed for our good intentions and efforts to unravel into a myriad of nightmare scenarios. What if the men we trained took what we taught them and just became more fearless killers? What would happen if they really developed greater powers of mind and bodies and used those powers in terribly harmful ways? We seriously wondered what kind of karma we'd be creating by participating in the training of the army's most elite and capable Special Forces troops.

The more we contemplated these haunting possibilities—both for better and for worse—the clearer it became that embarking on this path could be devastating or immensely beneficial in its direct and longer-term humanitarian and karmic implications. We realized that we would be wise to seek the counsel of mentors whom we respected. Bemoaning the fact that one of our closest teachers, Kalu Rinpoche, had just left Seattle, we decided to call him in Portland.

Kalu Rinpoche was a truly extraordinary man. An esteemed master of the profound inner science traditions, Kalu was the classic example of an authentic Himalayan Tibetan yogi who was trained in the same ancient disciplines as the great Milarepa and other revered saints whose awakening spirits emblazoned the caves and monasteries of medieval Tibet and inspired countless generations to follow in their path. With the tragic invasion of Tibet by the Chinese in 1949 and 1959, and the ensuing holocaust of the Tibetan people and culture that continues to this day, over a million Tibetans had perished, while nearly all of Tibet's ten thousand monastic universities, libraries, research institutes, and medical schools were totally destroyed. At peril of his life, Rinpoche himself had fled over the Himalayas to India and had miraculously and arduously walked from that ancient and distant world into our modern one, carrying with him a treasury of wisdom teachings with profound meaning for people in modern times.

Rinpoche (a title meaning "precious one") was recognized as a reincarnation of his predecessor, who was also acknowledged as a remarkable and accomplished yogi, or inner scientist, in the highly advanced and altruistically founded traditions of Tibetan inner science traditions. Kalu was a kind and remarkable teacher, and he selflessly filled his role as mentor in a most inspiring and genuine manner. Well into his eighties, Kalu was ancient going on timeless in his appearance. Sitting with him, he was vividly present yet seemed to have the ephemeral nature of a fragile luminous soap bubble that might just pop and vanish at any moment. The moments with him were precious. It was commonly said that Kalu's striking and unusual appearance had inspired Steven Spielberg in his modeling of ET. Rinpoche knew us well, and over the years we had been fortunate to spend many months in retreats, traveling and studying with him. In fact, it was during our travels with Rinpoche that we had originally met and realized our path together as a couple.

By grace and good fortune, Rinpoche's translator, Chokyi, answered the phone. Chokyi, whose English name is Richard Barron, was a close friend and one of the world's finest Tibetan translators. We explained to Chokyi what we had been invited to do and asked if he could possibly ask Rinpoche for his advice. Should we even consider working on a project like this? Was it wise, "karmically" advised, or not?

Chokyi received our request in stride and with a friendly reassurance said, "What an amazing opportunity. Hold on and I'll go ask Rinpoche for his thoughts on this right now."

Michelle and I hovered on the phone for about ten minutes for Chokyi to return. His warm voice was comforting when he finally returned, and he was clearly excited. "Oh," he said, "Rinpoche thinks this is a wonderful opportunity for you and gives you his blessings and full support." His next words touched us in the most profound way. "He says that if you have the opportunity to work with people who have enormous power but may lack the wisdom and compassion to use that power wisely, and if you can give them the skills and knowledge to help them bring a deeper wisdom to what they do—see more options and make wiser choices—then, by all means, accept the invitation."

Thanking Chokyi for his help, we said good-bye. Hanging up the phone, we looked at each other with an "oh my gosh, what have we gotten ourselves into?" fusion of excitement and bewilderment. We were both surprised by the intensity of endorsement and support that Rinpoche expressed for our involvement in the project, and a bit dumbstruck at the looming possibility that we would actually go ahead with it!

A Synergy of Transformational Technologies

On the basis of our own deep soul searching, our conversations with other trusted friends, and the wholehearted encouragement of Kalu Rinpoche and other mentors, we called Bud and arranged a time to get together. Two days later, we met at our home to envision and map out a robust proposal for an intensive training program for the Special Forces. Collecting our thoughts and considering various training scenarios, we approached this with no holds barred. Our goal was to take a wholistic approach to developing a radically multidisciplinary program that would deliver a highly relevant and deeply transformational impact on the soldiers we would be working with.

Four and a half hours later, we had generated the first draft of our preliminary proposal for a six-month-long full-time program that would address the army's specs on producing integrated enhancements in physical, mental, team, and mission performance. It was elegant in its comprehensiveness and whole human systems approach, integral in its design, and well-grounded in the complex realities of the men's lives, work, and missions. In many ways, our design fleshed out the spirit and structure that Jim Channon had laid the conceptual foundation for when he bedazzled the army with his vision in *Evolutionary Tactics: A Manual for the First Earth Battalion.*

The protocol we came up with involved an elegant blend of advanced high-performance human technology drawn from many modern disciplines and traditions. Key components included high-performance physical training and nutrition; intensive training in aikido, a Japanese martial art that teaches one to sense and transform the energy of conflict; and a high-tech cyberphysiology lab with an arsenal of the latest biofeedback equipment to teach these Green Berets how to understand and optimize their mental, emotional, and physiological responses to extreme stress by learning to widen the window of their psychophysical capacity to respond to mission situations with greater skill, flow, wisdom, and agility.

The program design included a monthlong intensive meditation and martial arts immersion called the encampment. This focused training time would be held mostly in silence, providing a context in which the men could learn to master their attention, to deepen courage and patience, and to face, embrace, and transform their fears. Such a period of extensive mind-body training would offer an opportunity for the soldiers to recognize and befriend their inner enemies. By bringing a calmer, quieter, and more focused mind to meeting their real enemies they'd be better equipped to find and follow the wisest course of action in the field of operations.

We agreed that for our work to be successful, we'd need to test it during mission training to make sure the lessons learned would carry over into deployment, so we built in numerous mission simulations and field trainings in a variety of settings from the high seas to the most rugged mountains we could find. And lastly, we realized that for our program to have a lasting and transformational impact on the soldiers' lives, we would be wise to provide meaningful opportunities that would engage and include their families, so they could be informed, sensitive to, and hopefully supportive of what the men were learning.

Building upon the philosophical and to some degree the metaphysical foundations that Jim had articulated in *Evolutionary Tactics*, we set about weaving the best of all these worlds and disciplines together. The essence

43

of our design was simple, yet profound: meeting the men where they were at and leading them into an immersive course of physical, mental, emotional, and spiritual training that would begin at very tangible levels, and then guide them on a learning expedition into progressively subtler and more refined dimensions and territories of awareness, self-discovery, self-transformation, self-mastery, and self-transcendence. We'd start by developing skills at levels of awareness and experience that would be easily accessible and familiar to our trainees. We'd then build upon the confidence and responsive awareness of that level of learning to introduce the next most subtle level.

As we reviewed our curriculum design, we were confident of the potential for catalyzing a radical transformation of our trainees. We knew from experience that six months of intensive, disciplined mind-body-spirit training would gradually rewire the nervous systems of our men and that they would leave this program with a dramatically expanded neurological, psychological, emotional, and spiritual capacity. This immersive training would also radically impact and transform their identity and worldview. The big question was, What would these soldiers do with what they learned? We were inspired and excited to work with the men who would be drawn to volunteer for this program. (Little did we know what the army had in store for us!)

With this strategy in mind, we designed a refined curriculum that offered a dynamic synergy of inner and outer technologies with modern and ancient disciplines of training. To develop the embodied, somatic intelligence of the men, we would rely heavily on the martial art of aikido, which has a profound tradition of energetic, powerful moves for blending with and harnessing the power of an opponent. The aikido dojo would provide an outer laboratory to test the capabilities that would be emerging through the inner mind-body training in our biopsybernautics laboratory.

Our "Mind Lab" would offer advanced biofeedback built around a sophisticated, state-of-the-art computer-based system that monitored and measured the ever-changing levels of various physiological functions, such as muscle tension, blood pressure, skin temperature, and the electrical conductance of the skin, and then communicated that information to the individual. The Mind Lab training would culminate in a phase of intensive neurofeedback training to enhance the soldiers' mastery of attention and awareness and control of the very subtle workings of their minds and brains.

In synergy with the instrumented technology of the cyberphysiological disciplines, we would introduce a wide array of complementary "inner technologies" of mind fitness and meditation skills for developing alertness, mindfulness and mastery of attention, power and flexibility of focus, suppleness in running mental simulations, and visualizations helpful for self-healing and for establishing a clear, open, responsive presence. We were confident from our research and experience that learning and integrating these powerful skills and powers could increase the capacity of our soldiers in fulfilling their missions and, depending on the depth of their realizations, might allow for the emergence of extraordinary capacities that lay on the psychic frontiers of military operations.

The dynamic synergy and integration of aikido, biofeedback, and advanced mind training would offer a dynamic interfusion of inner and outer self-mastery skills. The outer, visible, and physical moves of aikido would establish a powerful and profound center of internal *ki*—energy and presence. Simultaneously, the internally focused biopsybernautic training in the Mind Lab would offer deeper and subtler grounding, which would inform and inspire observable and measurable performance enhancements on the aikido mat, in the laboratory, and in mission simulations and field exercises.

As we envisioned the optimal and ideal ultimate warrior training program, we would need to also develop the contextual, philosophical, and theoretical foundation for this work in order to ground the experiential, embodied, and intuitive learning within a meaningful frame of reference.

This was to be particularly important on this mission as we were to be training trainers who would be required to not only embody what they had learned, but to also inspire others through their presence and example, and to have a good theoretical grasp of the philosophy, history, science, and principles of the disciplines they would be teaching to others. To this end, our program design would invite the soldiers to explore the writings and teachings of great warriors of the past and inquire into the meaning of these teachings and principles for them as modern-day Special Forces troops.

Since the men would be assigned full-time to working with us, we realized that we needed to also build in time for them to stay current on their Mission Operations Skills (MOS training), keeping in mind that at any moment our troops could be pulled out of the training program and deployed on a critical, secret mission to a location of which even their spouses would be unaware.

Once we had finalized our proposal, we took our notes to our recently established SportsMind office, a one-room three-desk office in Seattle's Pioneer Square. To reach the door to our office you had to walk through a toy store called Magic Mouse Toys and climb the stairs at the far end of the store. Sounds of yapping toy dogs, children at play, and cash registers muffled the traffic noises on First Avenue below.

We were greeted by our new office manager, Jacque Nugent, a kind woman in her sixties and the mother of Bud's girlfriend. Jacque, who quickly came to be affectionately called Mom by all of us youngsters in the office, set to work making sense of our notes and turning them into an impressive-looking document. We wrote up the cover letter on our new SportsMind stationery and prepared the Fed Ex label, sending the package off to our contacts at the Pentagon. Before sending our proposal out the door, we all gathered around to say a little prayer over our package and sow the seeds of good things to come from our vision and statement of intention. Little did we know what would blossom as the result.

The FedEx delivery man made his way through the toy store and off our proposal went, carrying with it the visions, the wisdom, and the blessings of many of our teachers and their teachers. We had crossed another threshold in setting things into motion.

The anticipation for all of us was intense, and a couple of weeks passed with no word. Finally, Bud called again. "Hey, we just received a reply from the army about our proposal. Let's meet up at the office and take a look at this together."

An hour later we were back at the tiny one-room office in Pioneer Square with a sweeping view of Magic Mouse Toys. Amid the sounds of children playing, we looked over the special delivery letter that had arrived from the Pentagon. Our proposal had been sent to a group of logisticians at West Point Military Academy who responded, "This proposal represents the most exquisite orchestration of human technology we've ever seen." Bud was clearly delighted and, grinning ear to ear, exclaimed, "Well, I guess we'd better start packing our bags. This looks like thumbs-up to me." Chris, the voice of reason and business in the office reminded us, "Looks promising, but military contracts can take quite some time to finalize and approve. There's likely more design and paperwork than we can imagine yet to come. Let's get mobilized and stay optimistic, and time will tell."

And so, this odyssey began.

THE FIRST EARTH BATTALION

What are the limits to human potential? In the final analysis they seem to be a bad joke. The culture imposes a language of the possible. Most humans accept those limits and fail to increase their potential.. But where those limits are ignored.. people bend metal with their minds, walk on fire, calculate faster than a computer, travel to new places in their minds eye, stop their hearts with no ill effects, and see into the future. There are no limits in the EARTH BATTALION.

TWO

The First Earth Battalion, Birthplace of Jedi Warrior

We are often asked, "How did the army come to invite and fund a program of this nature and scope for the Special Forces?" Here's a glimpse of the story.

In March of 1969, Ron Ridenhour, an ex-GI, courageously stepped forward as a whistleblower writing a letter to then army chief of staff General William Westmorland. In his letter he disclosed a secondhand account of a horrific incident in which 410 Vietnamese civilians had been brutally abused and murdered by U.S. Army troops. The aftermath of what came to be known as the My Lai massacre severely compromised the integrity of the army and its leadership, giving rise to an inquiry that resulted in charges being filed against fourteen soldiers, extending up to the ranks of brigadier general.

As a result of the initial inquiry, Westmorland commissioned a much broader study based out of the U.S. Army War College to assess the "moral and ethical climate of the army and its leadership."

The findings of this 1970 Study on Military Professionalism were devastating and concluded that the climate of the Army was "conducive to self-deception because it fosters the production of inaccurate information; it impacts on the long-term ability of the Army to fight and win because it frustrates young, idealistic, energetic officers who leave the service and are replaced by those who will tolerate, if not condone, ethical imperfection. . . . It stifles initiative, innovation, and humility because it demands perfection or the pose of perfection at every turn."[1]

These findings were so shaming and intimidating to army leadership that the report was buried and sat on a shelf gathering dust for nearly nine years. When General Edward C. "Shy" Meyer was appointed chief of staff, this War College study was resurrected. As Meyer recalls, "I saw a focus on the part of the officer corps toward personal gain as opposed to a selflessness that I thought was essential. That focus was brought about through policies and procedures that encouraged ticket-punching and quick success, to the exclusion of values and principles."[2]

By 1981, Meyer established and deployed new goals targeting the restoration of emphasis on classical leadership values of ethics, professionalism, mission accomplishment, and concern for people within the army command. These rolled out to bases around the country and around the world with new programs to advance and develop these higher standards of leadership throughout all the leadership ranks of the army.

The genesis of Jedi Warrior began during this same transformational time in military culture and leadership. Jedi's roots trace back to the inspiration of General Don Starry, then commander of the U.S. Army Training Doctrine Command (TRADOC). TRADOC was researching the combat effectiveness of American battalions as compared with Soviet battalions, and their research had concluded that by 1985 both forces would be equipped with weapons and vehicles of roughly the same capacity. General Starry surmised that a key way to assure that American troops had the advantage would be to shift the focus to developing the capacity of the people in the armed forces. Given that radical improvements in weapons and technology were unlikely to occur in that time, Starry was convinced that developing and empowering people was the only way to make a clear and decisive difference in the combat readiness and effectiveness of military units.

General Starry was fascinated by how James Grier Miller's living systems theory could be beneficial for envisioning the army's leadership and organizational evolution to develop the extraordinary capacities it would need to respond wisely and effectively to future challenges. His interests led to the inception of the army's special Task Force Delta, an innovative think tank dedicated to mapping the vast territory of extraordinary personal and organizational performance and potentials. Task Force Delta was widely regarded as the most visionary, cost-effective, and transformational military unit ever conceived.

Task Force Delta and the First Earth Battalion

In military science, the "delta" was regarded as the difference between the current state of soldier potential and their ultimate unrealized potential. In that spirit, the purpose and mission of the task force was to bridge the gap between current ordinary capacity and the innate extraordinary potential of soldiers, working through individuals to inspire and improve the performance of teams and larger units throughout the army, extending into society.

General Starry recruited Colonel Mike Malone to take the lead of this new task force with an explicit mission to empower and develop people.

Malone was a legend within the U.S. Army, known by some as the army's Mark Twain. His down-home, lucid, and deeply personal writings reflected a profound intimacy with the guts and glory of military life, and his capacity to communicate and to uplift, open, and move people's hearts and minds was unsurpassed. Malone was regarded as one of the most inspiring leaders and communicators in the army. Malone made it his business to know who the innovators, influencers, and social architects were who were defining the training and lifestyle of soldiers. With his charisma and enthusiasm for his new mission, Malone was able to easily recruit a small eclectic cadre of army cultural creatives to join forces to explore and map the new frontiers of the evolutionary potentials and human dimensions of soldiers.

Task Force Delta's mission was to scan the horizons of the human potential world—delving into systems theory, peak performance, and flow states and ways to master stress and improve self-regulation—to inspire a new vision for the modern warrior. Given the historic times of this endeavor, their field of operations included the budding turned-on, esoteric, New Age, yogic, and contemplative science scene that was rocking America in those days. This research endeavor inspired a deep bond within the growing community of researchers and participants involved who were drawn to not only conceptually learn *about* these disciplines but to personally embody and emulate the noble qualities of extraordinary human potential and performance they were researching.

Lieutenant Colonel James Channon was the primary scout for the human potential movement in the magical realm of California. He pondered how to convey to colleagues within the army and beyond the visions, values, and powerful methods that he and his team were discovering. During a flight to a Task Force Delta meetup at Fort Knox in spring 1979, Jim sourced the visionary download to create a mythical army unit called the First Earth Battalion, which would serve as the delivery vehicle for the ideas and techniques that he and his task force team were developing.

On the evening of the third day of the session at Fort Knox, Channon invited his eighty colleagues to gather at the officers' club on base to be initiated into the First Earth Battalion. Present were a diverse collection of fellow explorers, from army captains to generals, plus a wide array of civilian allies, scientists, and consultants involved with Task Force Delta. Jim instructed the initiates to remove their shoes and enter the large meeting room in silence. The room was lit at the center with a single candle, sitting next to the iconic symbol of a dollar bill. The chairs were arranged in a circle with abundant plants gathered from the officers' club. Given Channon's unorthodox creative spirit, there was a rich mix of nervous anticipation and excited curiosity for how this evening would unfold. Jim stepped into the circle, wearing a ceremonial dress uniform, to begin the formal induction, saying, "For the next forty-five minutes, suspend your rational thinking. Then, after this ceremony concludes, apply your rational mind to help us decide if we have anything worthy of further exploration or not."[3]

Jim in his wizardly way then guided everyone in some mindful breathing and the intonation of the mantra *eeeee* to bring everyone into resonance with the Earth, whose presence, care, and well-being are essential for every warrior and living being on this planet. Awkward as it was for some, this audience was accustomed to following orders, and the ceremony flowed on.

After several waves of inductive exercises to harmonize and synchronize the group, Jim proceeded to guide everyone through envisioning a day in the life of a First Earth Battalion soldier. Weaving a rich montage of potent images, Jim guided participants through envisioning themselves engaging in over a hundred different ways of sensing, knowing, being, and doing that were integral to the lives of the warrior-monks of the Earth Battalion. This was followed by a lively karate *kata* from Colonel Malone, who embodied the nobility, grace, focus, and on-purposeness of this unconventional, yet embodied approach to warrior training.

As the initiatory ceremony concluded, Channon invited the newly initiated First Earth Battalion members to reflect together on what value these visionary exercises, ideas, and ways of being might have for the army and the planet. Channon was heartened that by far the largest number of responses resoundingly affirmed this radical revisioning for modernizing the army with an expansively meaningful mission that included extraordinary personal development in service of a larger altruistic and Earth-centric field of military and humanitarian operations. As Channon noted in his *Evolutionary Tactics*: "These Task Force Delta officers were concerned with tending the soldier's human spirit during unrewarding and difficult times. They reckoned that the First Earth Battalion was a great experimental vehicle to test new forms of bonding, new forms of mythology, and new ways to positively affect the quality of life and human spirit of the American soldier. That evening, at Fort Knox, the First Earth Battalion was born."[4]

Over time, the community of individuals within the ranks of the army command and beyond expanded to include hundreds of r/evolutionary members of the First Earth Battalion. Their conferences carefully examined the best scientific and applied studies on enhanced human performance exploring themes regarding leadership, integrity, combat readiness, creativity and innovation, team and culture development, meaning, purpose, inclusiveness, and inspiring ritual. The vision for the army's high-tech light division of agile, specially built Humvees emerged from the group. The excitement of being involved with such a thriving, altruistic endeavor to create a better, safer, wiser, and more wonderful world was fuel for this r/evolution. Unlike most think-tank conferences, the First Earth Battalion felt more like large, loving family gatherings. Men, aware and confident of their masculinity, would embrace one another warmly. Women were deeply involved and comprised nearly 30 percent of the Earth Battalion members. There was a genuine honoring, inclusion, and balancing of both masculine creative energies and feminine intuitional strengths. Their gatherings served as dynamic learning laboratories to understand, affirm, and embody the noble spirit of the First Earth Battalion vision.

Over the years, as the influence of Task Force Delta drew more attention and generated more excitement, General Marsh, the secretary of the army under President Reagan, suggested that the First Earth Battalion be established as an actual experimental unit within the army. After some deeper consideration it was decided that establishing an actual boots-on-the-ground battalion would impede the wider spread of new innovative ideas, as compared to creating the unbound access and engagement possible with a more virtual, mythological unit. The thinking was that the First Earth Battalion could function like a commissary of potent ideas and performance-enhancing practices that could be applied in a myriad of unique circumstances by individual soldiers, officers, and military units around the globe. Accessible by all, everyone who tapped into this inspiring resource base could feel a sense of belonging and identification with the First Earth Battalion, whereas if the battalion was constrained to an actual location, it would drastically limit such access and sense of belonging. Thus, maintaining its mythical status, engagement, and membership expanded widely over the years through the global distribution of countless photocopies, and later digital copies, of *Evolutionary Tactics: A Manual for the First Earth Battalion* to visionary leaders, peacekeepers, consultants, and awakening wisdom warriors around the globe, spawning and inspiring initiatives and alliances for decades to come.

In his inspired introduction to Channon's First Earth Battalion concept paper, Colonel Malone mused:

> Every discipline or field of knowledge represented in our Task Force has a future, somewhere out at the frontiers of knowledge. . . . Each of you reads or learns of new research and new developments in your field . . . dreams and visions changing from concept to achievement.
>
> Information science is beginning to replace cathode ray tube numbers and words with pulsating, multi-colored holograms. . . . Neurophysiologists are unlocking the secrets of controlling the hitherto fore autonomic nervous system, and biochemists are beginning to beget themselves.
>
> The First Earth Battalion is a place to bring these new developments, to contemplate their implications for our Army, to then paint these implications green, and describe what things look like, how things work,

and how things are done in an Army battalion somewhere out ahead of us on the track of time.

You're invited to envision the future, in whatever form your discipline dictates, then bring that to our Army. Jim Channon is hereby appointed C.O., First Earth Battalion, responsible for assimilating, integrating, and communicating what the future may hold for our Army. Hopefully, from this effort will grow some dialogues, some writing, some teaching, about "battlefield futures," cast in a context meaningful to soldiers—the battalion.

At the present time, to our knowledge, none of our schools teach courses or electives in battlefield futures. Futures itself is becoming a respected discipline. We're tapping this at agency and think-tank levels, but soldiers need to know. How can soldiers, without an appreciation of the future, ever begin to appreciate and anticipate the inevitability of change?

The First Earth Battalion is a place for all of us to look to the future, freed up perhaps from the notion that "we've never done it that way before," and driven instead by the idea that what the human mind can conceive, the human will can achieve. A place to ponder and assess and hope about the future, through a basic Army perspective, and to thereby perhaps, assimilate fully the knowledge and the mindset, that change is more than just Inevitable. It is essential and even desirable. If we look backward down that track of time, back as far as there were living things, one truth stands out across those 5 billion years: any living thing (individual or aggregate) that's not adapting, adjusting, learning, changing . . . is either dying or it's dead.[5]

By the time that Frank Burns stepped into the role of director of Task Force Delta some years later, it had become a thriving global incubator for the emerging fields of organizational development and transformation movement. Many of the brightest evolutionary spirits in the world were drawn to join the ranks of Task Force Delta, inspired to do radical work to transform the world by creating organizations in which people could thrive while expanding their missions to help create the best possible conditions for life to flourish on planet Earth. The only prerequisite for nonmilitary members to join the task force was that they were personally committed to the four values of confidence, candor, commitment, and courage. Weaving a dynamic synergy between brilliant minds researching extraordinary human performance within the military with wise colleagues from the organizational and academic worlds, the ripples of activity radiating from the Task Force incubator spread far and wide, inspiring radical innovations in the fields of leadership development and organizational transformation for decades to come.

As these empowered and influential members of Task Force Delta deployed into army briefing rooms and combat units and out to the boardrooms of many of the world's most influential and successful organizations, they went forth well-armed with powerful new tools and advanced social technologies to serve as r/evolutionary agents and ambassadors of the spirit of the Earth Battalion's evolutionary tactics, vision, and values. The mission of these leaders was to inspire, encourage, and guide those within their sphere of influence through the ennobling process of discerning and defining the highest, altruistic purpose and systems-based visions for their organizations as actual forces for good in our world, while simultaneously developing organizational cultures where people could thrive.

This movement was also fueled and inspired by Abraham Maslow's expansive vision for a continuum of human development, which spawned the budding human potential movement in the 1960s and 1970s. Inspired by Maslow's vision and Miller's living systems wisdom, Task Force Delta members sought to encourage and embody the highest human potentials, using the army and other global organizations as their learning laboratories and launchpads. The U.S. Army took Maslow's work to heart when

Task Force Delta morphed Maslow's "What man can be, he must be" into the phrase "Be all you can be," which became the advertising slogan in its recruiting campaign.

After retiring from the military, Frank Burns and Jim Channon both stepped into more expansive roles as inspiring leaders carrying on and widely spreading this r/evolutionary work in the public sphere through the work in organization development and transformation. SportsMind, the company that we formed with Channon and other allies in 1982, was initially conceived of as a delivery vehicle for the work and mission of the First Earth Battalion and Evolutionary Tactics into organizations around the globe. While the initial invitation to develop the Jedi Warrior program came to us through Bud while Jim was still in the army and active with Task Force Delta, it would ultimately be delivered through our work with SportsMind some years after Jim retired.

Evolutionary Force

It is fitting to conclude this chapter with the following endnote from Channon's concept paper where he first introduced the First Earth Battalion to the world:

> The First Earth Battalion is a growing network of warriors with the planet in mind. Their business is the ethical evolution of force. They seek mastery as they move consistently up the ethical hierarchy of force: from Force of Arms; to Force of Will; to Force of Spirit; and finally, to Force of Heart. Recent world events clearly show that alternative forms of force are needed and that the good in people needs more expression in the arenas of power and conflict . . .
>
> The battalion has warriors in the U.S. Army that are presently quietly teaching the concepts of soft tactics. The great hearts are coming out of the closet! Additionally, some of the world's most evolved warriors are

now being committed to train larger groups of warriors when assembled. We find that New Age Samurai are sprinkled throughout the world just waiting for a common banner under which they can serve. The First Earth Battalion is just such a banner. Rooted in service to people, planet, and the many paths to God. The First Earth Battalion opens its heart to the warrior in you. Join us now in spirit and later in action.[6]

REASONS TO BE

Soldiers are in the business of life and death. As a leader during war, I must know that if my soldiers are to die... that its for the right reasons. when at peace they deserve nothing less than a chance at personal evolution.

Soldiers can be a real part of the evolution of this EARTH. Anything less..is just something less.

THREE

Tenuous Times

Our scientific power has outrun our spiritual power. We have guided missiles and misguided men. Our hope for creative living lies in our ability to reestablish the spiritual needs of our lives in personal character and social justice. Without this spiritual and moral reawakening, we shall destroy ourselves in the misuse of our own instruments.

REVEREND MARTIN LUTHER KING JR.,
STRENGTH TO LOVE

In the summer of 1982, the modest Soviet trawler the *Gavril Sarychevtra* dawdled in the Strait of Juan de Fuca near our home in Seattle, ostensibly fishing but reportedly listening for sonar patterns that would help its military track the elusive new *Ohio* class of U.S. Trident nuclear submarines that were designed to be virtually undetectable. All the while U.S. Navy destroyers kept watch over the Soviet watchers. At that time Cold War tensions were at an all-time high, and the *Bulletin of the Atomic Scientists'* famed Doomsday Clock, created by Albert Einstein and University of Chicago scientists who helped develop the first atomic weapons in the Manhattan Project, was set at 23:57:00—just three minutes to midnight, midnight being the collapse of society and the destruction of our world.[1]

About 5:00 a.m. on Thursday, August 12, 1982, just two days after we received Bud's fateful "Hey, Wiz" call, the U.S. Coast Guard declared Hood Canal a security zone and instituted a thousand-foot restricted area for the nation's first Trident nuclear submarine, the *Ohio*, when it would arrive. Cries of "full alert" filled the protesters' camps along the shoreline as they readied their boats to block the approaching sub. The media rushed to local sailboats and fishing boats they had rented to get a closer look at the action. At 6 a.m., the Coast Guard announced it had closed Hood Canal under a previously unmentioned 1946 maritime law, and the protesters would not be let out of Oak Bay. This first generation of Salish Sea "kayaktivists" paddled, rowed, and motored their small crafts into a different part of Puget Sound, intent on stopping the *Ohio* on its way to its new home at Bangor Naval Station.

The *Ohio* was the newest—and arguably deadliest—weapon in the nation's nuclear arsenal. This dark behemoth the length of nearly two football fields was virtually undetectable when it was submerged. When loaded with its crew and deadly payload, the *Ohio*, and later generations of Tridents, would set forth from the pristinely beautiful, mountain-wrapped orca whale sanctuary of Puget Sound to patrol and menace the seas. This massive sub was designed to cruise deep in the ocean for three months at a time, and then quietly slip back into its home port to change out crews, restock food and supplies, and then redeploy, through endless cycles of deployment.

The United States had commissioned eighteen of these uber war machines, and the *Ohio*, the first of many that would follow, was coming to its new home at Naval Submarine Base Bangor in Washington state, the third-largest navy base in the United States, one of only two strategic nuclear weapons facilities, and the navy's largest fuel depot. The *Ohio* was arriving to load up an arsenal of weapons that had arrived on the ominous "white trains" that delivered the missiles to the Bangor facility. Fully locked and loaded, the *Ohio* could carry up to twenty-four intercontinental ballistic missiles out to sea with it. Each of those missiles packed as many as eight independently targeted warheads each with an explosive force ranging between 100 to 450 kilotons of TNT, the destructive power of seven to thirty times the power of the bomb that incinerated Hiroshima.

We stretched our minds to envision the fleet of fourteen *Ohio* class nuclear-armed submarines cruising silent and undetectable beneath the oceans of the world, plus another four *Ohio* subs specially loaded with Tomahawk missiles and other nonnuclear arms. Each of the fourteen nuclear-armed subs packed the firepower equivalent to between 1,267 and 5,760 Hiroshima bombs, depending on how their warheads are configured. The Trident fleet when fully locked and loaded would carry the equivalent of 17,738 to 80,640 Hiroshima bombs (i.e., fourteen subs times twenty-four missiles times eight warheads, each 6.6 to 30 times the explosive power of the Hiroshima bomb), lurking below the surface of the oceans of the world, as a deterrent, and a threat, to the world. With a range of up to 7,000 miles, traveling at Mach 24 (twenty-four times the speed of sound or 18,400 miles per hour), each of these 2,688 missiles could reach their distant targets in less than twenty-five minutes. To fire even one missile by mistake, or on purpose, would likely trigger a massive nuclear exchange that could devastate our world.

After Bud's call, and amid the teach-ins surrounding the Trident's arrival, we often thought of the gravity and impact of decisions that could be made by the commander and crew of a Trident war machine and, similarly, by the teams of Special Forces operatives we might train. This vision of critical decisions and their impacts inspired our work.

During the 1962 Cuban missile crisis, the Doomsday Clock was set at 11:58, two minutes to midnight, and the world narrowly escaped plunging into a devastating nuclear war due to the courage of a single man, Vasili Alexandrovich Arkhipov, a Soviet naval officer. As the flotilla commodore, as well as the executive officer on the diesel-powered submarine B-59, Arkhipov refused to authorize the captain and the political officer's use of nuclear torpedoes against the U.S. Navy, a decision that required the agreement of all three officers. Such an attack likely would have led to a global thermonuclear response, destroying large portions of the Northern Hemisphere and throwing the world into a nuclear winter, killing and starving billions of people. Thomas S. Blanton, then director of the U.S. National Security Archive, credited Arkhipov as "the man who saved the world."[2] He is an icon of a special kind of courage.

In the aftermath of this missile crisis, President John F. Kennedy offered a chilling address at American University, where he said, "A single nuclear weapon contains almost ten times the explosive force delivered by all the allied air forces in the Second World War." He noted, "The deadly poisons produced by a nuclear exchange would be carried by wind and water and soil and seed to the far corners of the globe and to generations yet unborn." In his concluding remarks he reminded the audience that "all we have built, all we have worked for, would be destroyed in the first 24 hours."[3] Kennedy was certainly no dove, and he had affirmed his willingness to use nuclear weapons. But his speech offered some raw, sobering honesty about nuclear war and the need to seriously negotiate with the Kremlin in the interests of averting planetary incineration—an approach that seems sorely lacking within the U.S. government and other nuclear powers today.

The Most Dangerous Man in America

Some years ago, we were fortunate to host our friends Patricia and Dan Ellsberg for a visit, vacation, and working session with us at our home and farm in Hawaii. Dan was working on his book *The Doomsday Machine: Confessions of a Nuclear War Planner,* which would reveal a chilling glimpse of the once-secret government scenarios for nuclear warfare that few people were aware of. Together, we were trying to sort out the best way to make this information as widely available as possible in hopes that this would mobilize necessary action to neutralize the threat. The gut-wrenching, soul-searching dialogue we had vividly illuminated and clarified many of our thoughts regarding our work with Jedi Warrior.

Dan had served as an officer in the Marine Corps, later joining the RAND Corporation as a strategic analyst working on national security. He later joined the Department of Defense where he was tasked with analyzing the escalating military engagement in Vietnam. The more he learned, the more he was convinced that the war was unwinnable and based on many lies. When he returned from Vietnam, Dan returned to RAND where he worked on *U.S. Decision-Making in Vietnam 1945–68*, a top-secret report commissioned by Secretary of Defense Robert McNamara. This report further inspired Dan's opposition to the war and led him to quietly, over eighteen months, photocopy the report and smuggle it out of the secure facility in order to bring it to public awareness, even at peril of his life. Afraid that Dan Ellsberg might expose his lies, Nixon ordered his aides to "destroy and silence the son-of-a-bitch" by "any means necessary. Is that clear?" Secretary of State Kissinger famously ranted that Ellsberg "is the most dangerous man in America."[4]

Though Dan had offered the document to numerous members of Congress, none of them chose to act on it. Inspired by the escalation and expansion of the war into Cambodia and Laos in 1970, Dan began to leak portions of the report to the *New York Times* and to other newspapers to bring the deceptions and lies of the war to public attention. For this courageous act, Daniel Ellsberg is regarded as the most famous whistleblower in the world for his release of the Pentagon Papers, which exposed government lies and led to the end of the ill-fated war in Vietnam. A special kind of courage.

As we sat on our lanai looking out across the ocean toward Maui, Dan painted a gut-wrenchingly vivid picture for us of the perils of a nuclear war scenario that he had helped to develop and document while working with the military. He shared his insight and angst, explaining in painful detail how the impact of even a limited nuclear exchange, on the order of a conflict between India and Pakistan, would eject nearly fifty million tons of soot into the upper atmosphere, causing a nuclear winter and decimating food crops, livestock, and fish around the globe, which within the first two years would result in the deaths of more than two billion people. If a full-scale nuclear war were waged between the United States and the USSR an estimated 150 million tons of soot from the blasts and resulting fires would be ejected into the atmosphere, blocking sunlight and leading to the starvation of most humans and other living beings on this planet. Keep in mind that these horrific scenarios don't even account for the deaths and suffering that would arise from radioactive fallout circulating the globe or the impact of the sun searing Earth if the ozone layer were to be destroyed by an atomic blast.

Such chilling images of global carnage made a deep impression on us and affirmed our engagement with Jedi Warrior. Horrific as these scenarios sound, keep in mind that people have devoted their lives to creating such war plans and the means to wage them. For example, in 1954, General Curtis LeMay, as the head of the Strategic Air Command, drew up plans for using 750 nuclear warheads preemptively against the Soviet Union. Tacticians working under "Bombs Away LeMay" estimated this firepower would kill up to one hundred million people. A 2019 military briefing by the Joint Chiefs of Staff was similarly bullish on winning a nuclear war. "Using nuclear weapons could create conditions for decisive results and the restoration of strategic stability," the document enthused.[5] Talk about psychic numbing! The only real conditions created by nuclear war would be death and the restoration of precivilization.

Our home in Seattle is seventeen miles, as the eagle flies, from Naval Base Kitsap, which has the largest cache of nuclear weapons on the planet. This base would certainly be ground zero for any nation seeking to take out the U.S. arsenal in a preemptive attack. Yet most people in Seattle and the Puget Sound region simply carry on with their daily lives, oblivious to this ominous presence. Of those who are aware, few venture forth to question, challenge, or impede it. Having come of age in the 1960s, immersed in the complex circumstances of those turbulent times, the opportunity for us to partner with Bud and Jim and recruit a remarkable team to design and deliver the ultimate warrior training program and be part of a deep-reaching movement to nudge the system toward the wisdom and vision of the First Earth Battalion was certainly compelling. The recognition that the ultimate warrior training program could help make the world a safer and saner place and potentially provide opportunities for critical military teams, such as Special Forces troops and crews of Trident subs, to participate in a version of the training we were creating was a humbling and motivating thought for us.

SportsMind

Realizing the potential impact that deep transformational training might have on warriors deployed on important missions who needed to make critical decisions was a profound inspiration for us in accepting Bud's invitation. This opportunity coincided with Bud and his colleague Chris Majer's plan to form a new boutique training and consulting firm that would provide the best of peak performance training, flow psychology, high-level human performance sciences, and organization transformation methodologies for teams and organizations. To accomplish this, Bud and Chris called us together with Jim Channon, Larry Burback, and Horst Abraham to envision this new organization called SportsMind, which would ultimately deliver the Jedi Warrior program.

Chris served as our CEO and business affairs guy. He nurtured our contacts, worked out the contracts, and was willing to take on business affairs that no one else on the team had the skills or mind for. He loved to be the center of attention and thrived in this role. We often called him El Jefe (the boss). Besides being an avid, aggressive rugby player, he also trained in aikido. As a student leader of the University of Washington's anti–Vietnam War movement, Chris had the notable honor of having once led thousands of peace marchers down Interstate 5, shutting down traffic to call attention to the lies and carnage of the war.

Larry was affectionately and honorifically referred to as "the Coach." He was one lean, good-hearted, humorous, well-honed hunk of masculine power, speed, and endurance informed by a deeply embodied wisdom of what the synergy in mind-body training looks like. Larry had a wide range of modes of engagement and could be charming, eloquent, and professionally appropriate. Given the opportunity and the appropriate crowd, he was also a master of the fine art of totally grossing out his drinking buddies, coworkers, or anyone in earshot. Larry had been a dedicated, hard-core, competitive athlete his whole life, and he loved to coach, inspire, and cajole people into realizing their highest potentials in every arena of their lives. He had played college football and international rugby, and the last we heard, he had completed sixty-five triathlons, including sixteen Iron Man triathlons. His wisdom regarding the science of applied physical fitness, wise nutrition, strength building, endurance, flexibility, and peak performance was mammoth, and he had achieved enough success and suffered enough to develop a huge heart and dedication to helping others. Larry was a guy you'd always want to have on your team, always willing to lend a helping hand and lift everyone's spirits with his ribald humor and huge compassion. On base with the soldiers, Larry would hands down win the award for the one person on our team who could go toe-to-toe with the worst and most off-color humor and would often leave our soldiers in tears of laughter.

Horst was the embodiment of the European gentleman and invincible athlete. He was an eloquent, finely honed, well-conditioned athlete, with professional training as an exercise physiologist, a world-class marathoner, and a member of both the Austrian Olympic skiing and sailing teams. Born in Austria in 1941, he first learned to ski on handcrafted wooden skis. After moving to the United States, he gained national recognition through his method of ski instruction, and in the 1960s, he assembled a group of experts in the field to develop the American Teaching Method (ATM), which became the new standard for American ski instruction and for ski training around the world. Horst was later inducted into the U.S. Ski Hall of Fame and his book *Skiing Right* became the handbook for the Professional Ski Instructors of America (PSIA). His inspiring presence in the field often elicited respect and admiration.

We all had our light and our shadows, and SportsMind would provide a learning laboratory for us all to be the best and worst of ourselves and to continuously learn and improve. When we first came together to launch SportsMind as a consulting business, we were a small, ragtag team of dedicated, visionary, highly talented, well-intended, yet naive corporate ninjas doing occasional programs while we all worked other jobs to support the emerging potential of our business. To the best of our knowledge, at that time no other organizations in the world were offering programs of this kind of deeply integrative, transformational work for leaders, teams, and organizations. The closest we had to a competitor in those days was Wilson Learning Systems, which offered an array of innovative, yet rather conventional, mainstreamed leadership and team-building programs. In contrast, our corporate and organizational programs were definitely on the extraordinary end of the spectrum and far more multidisciplinary in scope. As a result, SportsMind quickly became a magnet for the brightest and best consultants and trainers in the world who were seeking to open the new frontier of transformational learning in mainstream organizations. We expanded the ranks of our team to more than sixty diverse, talented people who were stoked to have the opportunity to work with other remarkable people to help transform the world by raising the awareness and consciousness of corporate leaders and teams whose decisions and actions had an international impact.

In time, we drew more high-profile clients and lucrative contracts and grew exponentially to become one of the most innovative, creative, and successful boutique training and consulting firms on the planet. Our clients included various divisions of the armed services and some government agencies, along with contracts and programs for thousands of employees and leaders in dozens of organizations around the world. On any given week, we would have as many as four teams in the field deployed around the globe. In the course of this work, Joel was once introduced to the vice president for Innovation at Nike as the director of soul development for SportsMind, which led to quite a chuckle for us all.

The ethos guiding our work at SportsMind carried a deep sense of the spirit and profoundly embodied presence and practicality of Morihei Ueshiba's aikido teachings. We also incorporated as well as a rich blend of the most high-tech biopsybernautic methods of biofeedback, mind fitness, and peak-performance training, along with wisdom drawn from ancient and modern contemplative sciences. Our goal was to model and inspire extraordinary human potential with leaders and teams around the globe to deepen their sense of awareness, care, and universal responsibility for how their decisions and actions impacted the world, now and for generations to come. Landing the contract for Jedi Warrior radically expanded our horizons of research, innovation, and development, allowing us to explore a much vaster range of disciplines, traditions, and teachings that few people had ever even dreamed of exploring.

In the early days of SportsMind, I (Michelle) played more of a supportive role and was less actively engaged in program design and delivery. However, as a codesigner of the original Jedi proposal, I felt called to join forces in a more directly involved way with the rest of the team, especially in working together with Joel to direct and develop the richness of the mind fitness, biofeedback, and personal mastery training components of the program. I brought my own rich mix of skills and talents and a wealth of insight from years of study, practice, and research in contemplative science and anthropology, along with a depth of experience from my work as a biofeedback and psychophysiological therapy clinician and firsthand cross-cultural encounters from having lived, studied, and traveled in diverse cultures around the world. I had come of age during the Vietnam War and had been actively involved in supporting the peace movement, participating in many antiwar demonstrations over the course of my college years and beyond. Having made the commitment to be totally honest and authentic with the warriors I would be working with in the Jedi Warrior program, this led to some powerful moments of shared vulnerability and truth-telling that opened into deeper levels of trust and a willingness to be real with one another.

I also had the unique role of being the only woman on the entire delivery team as well as the actual program itself. Though challenging in many ways, this aspect further activated my own special kind of courage and turned out to afford me a privileged position in that I was able to develop a quality of authenticity, empathic relationship, and emotional connection with the soldiers in ways and on levels that none of my other colleagues on the team were able to access.

About a year and a half into our program development for Jedi Warrior, we had a team meeting that concluded with the decision to launch a search for a team leader for the program who had a military background. We all decided to reach out to George Leonard, who was a trusted and respected mentor and adviser, to ask if he had any recommendations for a likely candidate. As George later wrote:

> I hesitated for maybe a half-second before answering. Jack Cirie was unquestionably the man for the job. A year earlier he had completed a rigorous two-moth training program in a discipline I had developed blending aikido and Western psychology. He had come to the program directly upon retiring as a lieutenant colonel for the Marines, with two combat tours in Vietnam and a chest full of medals. Those military credentials alone would command the respect of the Special Forces troops. But Cirie wasn't just a war hero. His proven leadership ability was tempered by playfulness and

poetry and a large measure of soul, which I defined as being the faculty of having ready access to deep authentic feelings.[6]

Based on George's enthusiastic endorsement, we invited Jack to fly out from D.C. to Seattle to meet us for an interview. Jack had an impressive résumé and a bright, passionate, inspiring spirit. He had served twenty years in the Marine Corps as an infantry officer, as a platoon commander from 1965 to 1966, and as an adviser to the Vietnamese army from 1969 to 1970. Jack had received the Bronze Star, the Silver Star, and the Legion of Merit. Between his two tours he attended Yale where he took intensive language courses in Vietnamese. During his last assignment, Jack had the title of special assistant to assistant secretary of the U.S. Navy and director of advertising for the Marine Corps. In this capacity, Jack worked with an advertising firm to produce one of the most famous and successful Marine recruiting ads ever made, entitled "A Few Good Men." For his creative effort, Jack was awarded the Legion of Merit, the highest peacetime medal the Marines grant. After he left the Marines, Jack embarked on a journey of self-healing and self-discovery, exploring the human potential movement, and it was here that he had come to know George. At the end of a long interview and a more casual social evening, Jack was invited to join our team.

Bridging the Gap

While Jack brought a tremendous amount of passion, insight, and expertise to developing the program, there was also noticeable tension between his style of leadership and the more collaborative synergistic mode of leadership that was the norm at SportsMind.

We worked hard to accommodate this style clash until, about two months before we were due to arrive on base to begin the program, Jack and Bud had a huge blowup over how the program would be delivered, resulting in the heartbreaking decision that Bud would not be directing aikido for the program.

Although it was clear that the two of them had their differences and there was some tension between them, the abruptness and finality of this meltdown left all of us in shock and deeply disappointed. This program had come together through the spark of Bud's vision, leadership, and tenacity, and it was his inspiring example that had drawn the attention of the military leaders at the First Earth Battalion session with Jim. Bud opened the door to this remarkable opportunity, and we had codesigned the program together for nearly three years. Jack was a latecomer to the program, and we were all still really getting to know him and learning how to work with his strong, often bullheaded, command-and-control leadership style.

A whirlwind of tumult and confusion ensued. The resulting outcome, much to the heartbreak of many of us on the team, was that not only would Bud be stepping out of our team for this program, but also leaving SportsMind for good. We were in shock. Though we tried to work out a way to keep Bud on the team, it seemed that the trust among Jack, Bud, and Chris had been irreconcilably shattered. Though Chris had been a longtime friend and colleague of Bud, he sided with Jack.

While Bud's departure and absence left a huge gap to fill on our team, it also left a large wound in our hearts because he had originally invited the two of us to codevelop and deliver this program with him. We found ourselves in a terribly awkward situation and were left with the heartache and challenge of wondering whether we should also depart from the team in solidarity with Bud, walking away from nearly three years of intensive work developing this program and other SportsMind programs, or if we would stay on and work through this somehow. This gut-wrenching time was exacerbated by the pressures to finalize our preparations, gather and pack our gear, and prepare to move all the way across the country to Massachusetts for nearly seven months to deliver the Jedi Warrior program. After considerable soul-searching and dialogue, we decided to stay

73

on and stick with the plan to deliver the program. We have, nonetheless, often wondered if there might have been some better or wiser way that we could have navigated that time of upheaval and disruption with Bud and with the rest of the team.

In the aftermath of this painful dissolution, with a mere six weeks until we were due to arrive on base, Jack put forth his proposal to invite Richard Strozzi-Heckler to join our team and step into the role of aikido instructor. Jack had trained with Richard at the Aikido of Tamalpais dojo, an internationally acclaimed school, and admired Richard's rich blend of aikido wisdom, plus his deep grounding in somatic science and psychology. Richard had cofounded the Aikido of Tamalpais with George Leonard. Though we had trained a bit at the dojo when we visited George in Marin, we never got to know Richard, so he was a completely unknown player to us.

The prospects of having only six weeks to bring a new core team member on board and fully up to speed on the program was a real stretch. In addition, developing a relationship, establishing trust, getting to know one another's skills and styles, and figuring out how we would work synergistically and aligned with a complex program design was daunting, to say the least. This challenging new development was stacked on top of the stress of completing our own final preparations for the program, pushing hard to wrap up our lives and work in Seattle, and making a massive move to our new home for the program due west of Boston. Squeezed by the vise of time, this whole bundle of circumstances certainly put our own self-mastery and self-regulation skills to the test!

As we scrambled to get to know Richard and bring him up to speed on the program history, design, and synergy plan, we quickly developed a strong connection. Fortunately, there was good synergy between our energy and styles, and the blend of the two of us with Jack and Richard had a lot of flow and strength to it as the core team. There seemed a mutual sense that we had the potential to weave our various gifts and talents together in powerful and synergistic ways and that we could also learn a great deal from one another in bringing the Jedi Warrior to life.

Shortly before the launch of Jedi Warrior, Michelle had the good fortune to participate in a conference at Harvard with the Dalai Lama where he reminded us that "physics has provided the basis for the design of the fission and fusion bombs, biology—germ warfare; chemistry—nerve gas. And all of them have helped bring us to the brink of doom. But they still do not provide keys to ultimate power. If we do destroy ourselves, it will be the minds of human beings, the unhealthy emotions of individuals, the fear, the hate, the jealousy, and the greed of individuals that will trigger these horrors."[7] We had reached out to His Holiness for guidance on our work and were touched and inspired by how swiftly he responded to offer his blessings, encouragement, and support. He too affirmed that if we had the opportunity to work with people with tremendous power and to help them train and discipline their minds to awaken a deeper wisdom to guide their power, this would be a very good opportunity.

As we complete this chapter, so many years later, the world is looking on aghast at the impacts of the Russian invasion of Ukraine, the expanding turmoil in the Middle East, increasing tensions between China and Taiwan, accelerating disruption and displacement due to the climate crisis, the uncertainties of AI, and renewed and realistic fears of intentional and accidental nuclear involvement, either through weapons or a meltdown at one of the huge nuclear plants. The Doomsday Clock just ticked forward to 23:58:31, just eighty-nine seconds to midnight, the closest humanity has ever been to midnight and the destruction of humanity on planet Earth. The stakes are still inconceivably high, and a special kind of courage, commitment, and skills are certainly necessary if humanity is to step back from the edge and learn to thrive together on this precious planet.

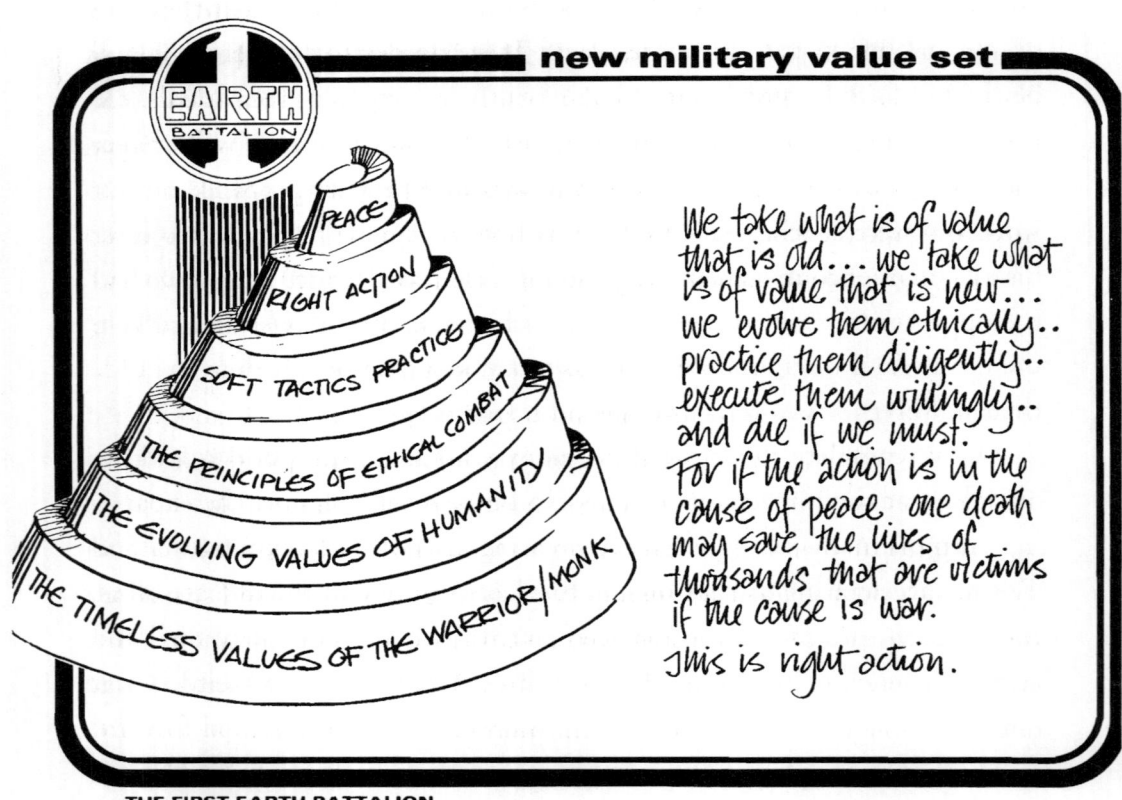

We take what is of value
that is old... we take what
is of value that is new...
we evolve them ethically..
practice them diligently..
execute them willingly..
and die if we must.
For if the action is in the
cause of peace, one death
may save the lives of
thousands that are victims
if the cause is war.

This is right action.

THE FIRST EARTH BATTALION

FOUR

Emergent Human Technologies for the Special Forces

The glee in the SportsMind office at Magic Mouse Toys was effusive when we received the go-ahead for our initial program proposal. Little did we realize, however, how massive in scope designing the ultimate warrior training program for the Special Forces would be. Nor did we imagine that we had a nearly three-year ride of red tape, contracting, and preparations ahead of us before launching the program.

During this time there would be countless back-and-forth communications, negotiations, and meetings to work out the final program design, which included determining equipment needed and costs, timing, and location; selecting the team; and designing the training spaces we would need. The investment of time, energy, and taxpayer dollars to fund this program was enormous. The upside of this prolonged planning was that we had a very wide window of time to seek out and connect with hundreds of colleagues, respected elders, and allies from many disciplines to discuss and explore potential elements of our program design.

Imagine having a virtually unlimited budget and access to all the resources that you need to design the most advanced, inspiring, holistic, and immersive six-month-long training program possible for twenty-five of the world's most elite professional warriors who might someday be in a position to start, or stop, the next world war. Our minds spun with a myriad of questions such as:

- What are our true motivations in accepting this opportunity? Are we in this for the money, the learning, the challenge, the prestige, to save lives, create a safer world, or—what?
- Where, or how, do we begin to design a program of this vast scope?
- Who do we turn to for inspiration, advice, and expertise?
- Who do we invite to work with us on our design and delivery team?
- How do we work together on your team, and how do we make decisions together?
- What program elements would be most essential and high priority?
- What strengths, skills, and qualities of being would be most essential to encourage the soldiers to develop?
- What criteria do we rely upon to select participants for this historic training program?
- How do we prepare ourselves physically, mentally, emotionally, and spiritually to deliver such a wide-reaching program to such an elite group of soldiers?
- What values, visions, and principles will guide us individually and as team?
- What measures will we gather, and how would we evaluate our success?
- Which elements or principles will be negotiable or bendable, and which will be nonnegotiable?
- What inner or outer resistance or challenges might we anticipate facing, and how will we most wisely and skillfully honor and respond to those resistances and challenges?
- What other questions should we be asking ourselves and others?

In preparing our proposal, our colleagues at SOCOM (Special Operations Command) provided us with the following description of the military environment to inform our design:

- The modern battlefield has become exceedingly complex and extremely demanding of the individual soldier's ability to adapt, respond, and recover.
- Training methodologies that focus only on limited aspects of human potential will create a limited soldier who must face a battlefield of unlimited dangers.
- The concepts, methods, and material technology needed to train for optimal human performance are available and have now been clearly validated as effective and applicable to the military.
- Our military forces will stay on the leading edge of modern warriorship by continuing to develop soldiers who can think clearly and act decisively and have the capacity to optimize their physical efforts and manage their personal energy by drawing upon substantial reserves of psychophysical and emotional energies.
- All the material presented must, therefore, be presented with the intention of creating a soldier who is totally prepared for current as well as future missions. The material must be so interwoven as to reinforce itself and not over- or underdevelop any aspect of the soldier's abilities.
- The focus on each of the program elements that forms a common thread in this approach is that increased awareness of mind-body-emotion relationship leads to greater control over every area of human performance and that greater control leads to more appropriate, powerful, and skillful actions, all of which promotes winning and surviving on the battlefield.

Informed by this input we came to an agreement that we would design and deliver a six-month full-time training program for two twelve-soldier

A-Teams of Green Berets from the Tenth Special Forces Group, plus their company commander. These soldiers were preparing to deploy as deep recon troops whose mission was to penetrate far behind enemy lines, dig in to gather and send out reconnaissance, perform whatever operations were necessary, and identify, recruit, and work with local collaborators. Once deployed, they would need to be operational for as long as they could, as they were unlikely to have a viable exit plan in many of their mission scenarios, and the likelihood of them returning home was highly improbable. Their area of operations would be cold, likely high elevations, deep behind the Iron Curtain and far from any resupply lines, so their capacity to be resilient, creative, self-regulated, and able to wisely manage their energy, as well as the quality of their relationships as a team, would be of paramount importance.

To succeed in their mission, these soldiers needed to embody a fluency and intimacy not only with stealth, power, and endurance, but also with skills that would strengthen and not deplete their cognitive resources, such as self-awareness, self-regulation, self-mastery skills, silence, stillness, lucid alertness, patience, discernment, and nonreactivity. They also needed to have the relational skills necessary to be empathic with those living in the regions they would be operating in and to build trust and recruit allies behind enemy lines to support them. In addition, we were training them to be trainers, capable of embodying and understanding what they had learned so deeply that they could teach others.

For perspective, some of the soldiers we trained in the early 1980s were similar to those who were later secretly dropped into the mountains and deserts of Afghanistan and Iraq, after 9/11 and before the two Gulf Wars. In fact, some of the soldiers we trained later engaged in covert activities in the first Gulf War in the early 1990s. These troops dug in days or weeks before any formal presence of U.S. troops was announced.

It is interesting to note that the year the Jedi Warrior program began, there were only 388 satellites in orbit, of which some were certainly spy satellites, and drone technology was in its infancy. In contrast, as of the writing of this book, there are more than 10,000 active satellites in orbit, plus countless stealth aircraft and unmanned drones that could be deployed. The number of satellites is projected to increase to between 58,000 and 100,000 by 2030. Since there were far fewer "eyes in the sky" in the years that Jedi was conceived and delivered, this meant that in those remote regions with restricted airspace, the intel necessary to inform operations and critical decision-making came from clandestine boots on the ground and watchful, alert, discerning human eyes such as those of the men we were training.

Training Domains

As we worked with our colleagues in the army to clarify the program specs, we agreed to the following program goals. First, that "Trojan Warrior [aka Jedi Warrior] was initiated as an experimental training program designed to enhance individual soldier and team abilities." The objectives of the program were "to increase the TOTAL fitness of these soldiers by using a 'holistic' training approach" and was mandated by SOCOM. The contract stated that this historic program was "to make full use of Emergent Human Technologies to enhance physiological and psychological awareness and control in Special Forces Detachment members." From the army's view the basic premise was that "the successful completion of the Trojan Warrior program will place the army in the forefront of human performance technology development. By validating, in a controlled, measured manner, the holistic approach of mind, body, and team training, the army will demonstrate its commitment to providing soldiers with the very best training that is available."

To realize these potentials for mission enhancement, we agreed that this training would focus on seven domains:

1. Advanced physical fitness training
2. Biopsybernautic training (mindfulness, meditation, mind fitness, biofeedback, and neurofeedback)

3. Aikido
4. Psychological orientation
5. Mission-related skills and field operations
6. Family engagement and special programs
7. Training the trainers

The Trojan Warrior project was designed to enhance soldier and team abilities—especially in areas of known or speculated "mission deficiencies." The army specs for the program entailed:

Physical Enhancements Training

- To understand new concepts for fitness
- To understand and optimize the effects of diet on performance
- To be able to fine-tune physical performance
- To be able to control pain and promote healing

Psychological Orientation and Enhancements Training

- To better manage the impacts of stress, shock, and trauma
- To enhance mind-fitness skills (such as mastering stress, concentration, mindfulness, discernment, cognitive capacity)
- To promote psychophysical integration for greater mental, physical, and emotional resilience
- To clarify key values (such as accountability, commitment, integrity, dedication, spirituality)
- To clarify beliefs and affirm the characteristics of the warrior

Team Cohesion

- To strengthen team qualities and bonding
- To strengthen leadership skills
- To reduce emphasis on individual effort

Mission Specific Training

- Increased ability to remain alert and motionless for extended periods of time on-site
- Intensive rest during short periods (such as infiltration, escape, and evasion)
- Circulatory and temperature control in extremities during operations (especially in cold weather environments)
- Control of psychological state during extended periods of stress exposure
- Premission acceptance of death potential to promote rational operations decisions in the field
- Values examination to increase understanding of and commitment to mission
- Self-pacing energy expenditures to provide for nondepleting energy reserves
- Ego diminishment to enhance authenticity and intellectual honesty
- Extended sensory awareness to enhance team security and mission capabilities.
- Super learning to reduce training time and increase efficiency and effectiveness.
- Biokinetic and physiological aspects to allow extended movement capabilities
- Psychological preparation to increase acceptance and appreciation of mission environment
- Increase confidence in their own leadership abilities
- Broaden the theological and hence spiritual base of the soldiers

Train Cadre of Trainers

- To prepare soldiers to be trainers for future holistic programs for Special Forces

The program methods were based on "the holistic model of human performance, which holds that optimal performance is the result of the synergy of all human factors—mind, body, and spirit." The instructional methodology "would also mirror this holism. In other words, each topic covered in the program would be related to other topics and to the overall goals for the program." All of us working on this project, both military and civilian, realized that we were being invited to go where no other military or Special Forces training program had ever gone before. The stakes were high, and our mandate was daunting—vast, multidisciplinary, and exciting for us all.

The most profound and vital elements of our Jedi Warrior program design lay in the dynamic synergy and interfusion of five essential domains of training:

1. **Embodied somatic disciplines** (aikido, physical fitness training, capoeira, energy healing, etc.) to develop extraordinary endurance, flexibility, coordination, strength, mind-body integration, balance, suppleness, agility, and the efficient use of force.
2. **Awareness-based disciplines** based in modern neuroscience and ancient contemplative sciences of mind-fitness training, meditation, and mindfulness to cultivate mindful presence, alertness, mastery of attention, discernment, deep resilience, empathy, and compassion.
3. **Advanced biopsybernautic disciplines** blending state-of-the-art biofeedback and neurofeedback training and technology with advanced mind-fitness and contemplative training to measure and amplify physical signals too subtle to easily sense and bring them up to a level that could be consciously monitored and interacted with in order to learn how to sense, self-regulate, and optimize those inner physiological states through the power of the mind. This approach to self-mastery training offered a profound and empowering example of mind-body integration and mind over matter.

4. **Psychological orientation** that focused on clarification of values and beliefs and identity, strengthening the characteristics of the warrior of personal accountability, commitment, spirituality, ethical discipline, moral intelligence, and integrity.
5. **Real-life mission-oriented skills and mission simulations** to test, measure, and affirm all the elements noted above.

This radically unique blend of advanced human performance disciplines and soldiering skills was virtually unheard of in modern Western Special Forces training. Jedi was also unique in its weaving in of energy work for healing, renewal, resilience, and recuperation; unflinchingly addressing the realities of death and dying; and the warm welcoming and inclusion of the soldiers' families and significant others. These five domains were mutually affirming and provided a rich testing ground to mirror the levels of awareness, skills, and self-mastery that each individual and team brought to enhancing their operational effectiveness in fulfilling their mission. The dynamic synergy among these five domains was the key to our potent program design.

Reading List

Our team put together a wide and varied reading list for Jedi Warrior that was intended to stretch and inspire the men's minds regarding how they viewed themselves as modern-day warriors. This had been based on our understanding (soon to be disproved!) that we were training trainers and that all the soldiers would be volunteers eager and excited to learn as much as they could about the various themes and disciplines related to the program. The readings included: Sun Tzu's classic *The Art of War*; Elmer and Alyce Green's epic book *Beyond Biofeedback*; *The Miracle of Mindfulness*, one of the very first popular books on mindfulness in the West written by the Vietnamese monk Thich Nhat Hanh, who had worked tirelessly to make peace between the warring factions in Vietnam and who was nominated by Dr. Martin Luther King Jr. for the Nobel Peace prize; various writings of Morihei Ueshiba; Michael Murphy's classic book *The Psychic Side of Sports,* cowritten with Rhea White and later published under the title *In the Zone: Transcendent Experience in Sports*; *The Superhuman Life of Gesar of Ling,* an epic tale of an iconic Tibetan warrior; and two articles: "Why Men Love War" by William Broyles Jr. and "Mars, Arms, Rams, Wars: On the Love of War" by James Hillman.

At Jack's insistence we also included an insightful article by cultural historian Charlene Spretnak, titled "Naming the Cultural Forces That Push Us toward War." The abstract reads:

Anthropology and archaeology have demonstrated that human societies can pass hundreds and even thousands of years in peace. Patriarchal cultures, however, go to war rather regularly. Militarism and warfare are continual features of a patriarchal society because they reflect and instill patriarchal values and fulfill essential needs of such a system. Men under patriarchy must prove dominance and control, must distance their character from that of "lowly" women, must survive the toughest violent initiation to enter full manhood, must shed the sacred blood of the hero, and must collaborate with death in order to hold it at bay. Such patriarchal pressures on men have traditionally reached resolution in ritual fashion on the battlefield. Unless peace efforts address the cultural pressures as well as the economic and political factors pushing us toward war, we will be unable to build a lasting peace.[1]

While this syllabus of readings offered a broad view of the field, if we were to assemble a reading list now, many years later, we would have a vastly expanded range of inspiring options to choose from.

Training the A-Teams

At the time of the Jedi Warrior program, there were four Special Forces groups, each prepared to deploy on missions in different regions of the world. We were assigned the Tenth Special Forces Group, which ran missions based in Europe and in what was then the Soviet Union. Each group was composed of three battalions, each with approximately three companies, which were in turn composed of four to six A-Teams or ODAs (Operational Detachment Alpha). An A-Team generally consisted of twelve soldiers, each of whom had a specific function (MOS or Military Occupational Specialty) on the team; however, all members of an ODA were engaged in extensive cross-training. Each A-Team was led by a detachment commander, who was the captain, and an assistant detachment commander, who was second-in-command, usually a warrant officer one or chief warrant officer two. The team also included the following enlisted soldiers: an operations sergeant known as the team sergeant, usually a master sergeant; an assistant operations and intelligence sergeant, usually a sergeant first class; and two each of weapons sergeants, engineer sergeants, medical sergeants, and communications sergeants, who are usually ranks of sergeants first class, staff sergeants, or sergeants. This structure allowed for six-man "split team" operations, redundancy, and mentoring between a senior NCO (noncommissioned officer) and his junior assistant.

The Jedi Warrior program would be offered to two A-Team detachments who were part of the Tenth Special Forces Group, each composed of twelve men, plus their company commander, Captain Dobson. Alpha Team had recently formed, with some men on the team for less than a month. They were still in a formative mode, slowly developing a sense of team cohesion. Their team company commander, Captain Thorne, was a bright, up-and-coming West Point graduate, with little experience as a team leader. In contrast, Bravo Team was a seasoned long-standing team, with a strong team identity as one of the best Special Ops teams around.

They knew it and were proud of it. Hua!* Their SCUBA-trained soldiers were generally older, more experienced, and more confident, both individually and collectively. Though it wasn't explained to us up front, the army leadership was interested in assessing how this kind of deep transformational training would be received by such different teams. As the program progressed, the strengths, weaknesses, and challenges of each of these teams would become apparent.

In a chance encounter with a Special Forces officer many years after the completion of the Jedi Warrior program, we came to learn that there had also been a third A-Team in play. Upon hearing of our role in this historic program, this officer said, "Oh yes, I know your program very well. I was on the Charlie Team that was the backup alternative team standing in the wings to step into the program if the Alpha or Bravo Teams were called up and sent out on a mission. We were continually briefed on the program. Oh, the stories I could tell you!" Hearing this, Michelle and I looked at each other with some disbelief. We had no idea that this had been in play during the whole program.

One of the senior officers overseeing the program described the situation.

As we entered the training process, I expected the training to accomplish exactly what was stated in the statement of work. To me the results would be apparent if I ended up with two detachments which had managed to subordinate individual egos for the common good; their internal communications process would allow for fast, accurate exchange of critical information during mission performance without the encumbrance of ego preserving the smoke screens, their leaders would implicitly know who to assign to critical tasks by being able to rapidly assess individual strengths, and each individual would know how to pace themselves and

---

*Hua (pronounced "hooah") is military slang signaling the speaker's acknowledgment and stands for "heard, understood, acknowledged."

other members of the detachment to deliver consistent performance throughout a mission whether it lasted five days or five weeks. Thus, the key enhancements which I expected to see were:

- a thorough knowledge of the limits and how and when to push the edges,
- simple, truthful, and effective interpersonal communications among all members of the detachment, and
- greatly increased physical, mental, and psychological endurance.[2]

The original program proposal stated that "the premise of the instructional method is that soldiers who will be participating will be highly self-motivated, mature, and comfortable with working and learning independently. The normal course of activities includes neither handholding nor threats." It also stated that the soldiers would be "intentionally exposed to both an abundance and variety of ways of doing and viewing things, and they would be left to decide for themselves the appropriate choices. This methodology is potentially the most powerful of teaching modes, but it is also very different from the normal military training experience."

The Wise Power of Courageous Compassion

Ultimately, our mission with Jedi Warrior was to encourage our soldiers to develop the special kind of courage it takes to be fully present, open, and connected to themselves, their field of operations, and the world. This quality of courageous presence will inevitably reveal all the places within us where we turn away or feel vulnerable or afraid. By turning toward these fears and vulnerabilities, we open the way to courage. This special kind of courage is a profound interfusion of both wisdom and compassion. Wisdom is the courageous capacity to look the world straight in the eye with clear discernment and behold the nature of circumstances just as they are. It inspires responsive, courageous compassion for ourselves, and for all living beings, who are vulnerable to the myriad shades of suffering that life and death may bring.

Lieutenant General Piatt et al. affirmed the wisdom and profound value of compassion for military operatives saying, "Compassion matters, because if we are to achieve the mission or succeed with a team, we must understand the environment, the people, and their struggle. The underlying ingredient across these practices, however, is learning to be present, and this lesson can be significant on both a personal and professional level."[3]

This union of wisdom and compassion reminds us that the root of "courage" is *cor,* from the Latin word for heart. In this sense, courage means "to stand by one's heart." Courage is about being willing to show up wholeheartedly, be present, and investigate what we fear, defusing tension and opening new degrees of insight, freedom, strength, and confidence through embracing the challenges that life may bring. Our courage reflects our willingness to be vulnerable, to step up and step out beyond our comfort zones into realms of challenge by going beyond our familiar frames of reference into uncharted territory. Dr. Gabor Maté illuminates the universality of this potential, saying, "The myth of normal is a cloak that disguises the immense diversity and complexity of the human experience, obscuring the truth that we are all vulnerable and flawed, yet capable of extraordinary resilience and growth."[4]

Having developed and taught numerous university graduate programs with enthusiastic and excited students, we were curious to meet the highly self-motivated individuals who would be inspired by the vision of this program and step up to volunteer to participate. Little did we know what awaited us and how the training journey would all unfold.

FIVE

The Embodied Wisdom of the Awakening Warrior

Since wars begin in the minds of men, it is in the minds of men that we have to erect the ramparts of peace.

UNESCO CHARTER

In designing a training program we are wise to ask, "What are we optimizing for?" In military training the stakes and stress are very high. Such training is designed to harden people and push them out of their comfort zones, to find new orders of strength that can enable them to override their pain and power through at all costs. Though such training develops certain strengths, it often results in degrading the physical, mental, and emotional reserves of soldiers, compromising their health, well-being, and operational effectiveness. The resulting exhaustion and, at times, enduring trauma of this kind of training can leave soldiers more vulnerable, anxious, and less capable once they are deployed to the battlefield.

When military exercises involve fierce competition for prized assignments, such as making the cut for slots in Special Ops, SEAL teams, Delta Force, or other elite units, the protocols employed can be brutal, debilitating, and even lethal. Such methods reflect systemic policies and mindsets that often ignore the wisdom of human performance science and don't give much value or time to developing the vital personal mastery skills necessary

THE FIRST EARTH BATTALION

for the consistently high-performance rest, renewal, healing, and restoration of vital energies necessary for optimal levels of health, well-being, and performance.

Over time, these policies and mindsets have created a painful legacy of untold suffering at the expense of many lives, both on the battlefield and due to suicides of veterans returning home debilitated from their military service. These factors all played a role in inspiring the design of the Jedi program to optimize for qualities that would develop the deep resilience, self-mastery, thrivability, and survivability of our soldiers.

Widening the Window

Key axioms of our Jedi Warrior training were that "stress is not a problem IF you don't let it accumulate!" and "you can only manage what you monitor." We understood that disciplined practice over time would retool the soldier's primary instrument, their mind-body, to restructure itself muscularly, energetically, biochemically, and neurologically to function at higher levels of well-being and performance. With the wholistic approach mandated by the Jedi Warrior contract, we had a charter to teach our soldiers skills to expand the scope of their performance to not only surpass previous records for physical and mission performance in the Special Forces but to also equip them with advanced self-mastery skills necessary to confidently rest, recover, and restore their inner strength after stressful or dangerous experiences.

In today's terms, Jedi Warrior had an explicit mission to help our Special Forces teams learn to mindfully monitor, wisely manage, and skillfully expand their window of tolerance (WOT) in order to increase their capacity for self-awareness, self-regulation, and self-mastery to assure their optimal performance and well-being. Daniel Siegel, UCLA psychiatrist and founder of the discipline of interpersonal neurobiology who first coined this term writes,

> When we are functioning within our Window, we have access to the power of "Response flexibility" which enables us to put a temporal and mental space between stimulus and response and between impulse and action. From a neurobiological perspective, this spaciousness of the mind enables us to pause and simply be with our experience with nonreactivity, to wisely consider the range of potential impacts and implications of our choices and actions before we engage the "doing" circuitry of mental, verbal, or physical action. Response flexibility offers us a way of choosing to be our "wisest self" possible in any given moment.[1]

Here's how this works:

When we are functioning within our window of tolerance, we have the capacity to be fully present and aware, to focus and attend to our inner and outer conditions, martial our full intelligence in order to perceive, think, learn, and reason clearly, be curious and inquire more deeply, have a coherent and realistic view of the reality of our circumstances, apply logic to making decisions, and consider the consequences of our actions.

Our physical state of well-being is also enhanced and we can rest, renew, regenerate, tap our vitality, and maintain our immune integrity and resiliency. Calm, clear minded, and cognitively capable, we are agile, adaptive, and responsive to whatever circumstances are present for us.

Within our window of tolerance, the social engagement and connection networks of our brain are fully online. We feel safe, at ease, and in harmony with our environment. We are high-functioning, engaged, and can relate meaningfully with people as we are empathically tuned-in, enabling us to accurately sense and interpret the states and needs of others, be supportive members of a team, maintain a sense of connection and relatedness to the humanity, needs, and drives of our adversaries, or even feel a sense of kinship, empathy and care for the well-being of whatever life-forms we may encounter.

For our Jedi warriors, learning to widen their WOT would provide greater access to their somatic, emotional, intuitive, and moral intelligences, including a visceral, gut-level knowing of what feels right in response to any situation. Stationed in their WOT, they would be connected to their wholeness, more astutely tuned into the inner and outer realities at play, and more likely to make wiser decisions that have better outcomes and create fewer unanticipated problems for themselves and others downstream.

Developing our capacity to skillfully respond to complex, stressful, and dangerous situations gives us greater confidence, power, and determination to show up wholeheartedly and stand strong while being adaptively agile and responsive to whatever challenges we may encounter.

At the heart of our window of tolerance is the treasured zone of peak performance. This is the "sweet spot" of our human potential for extraordinary human performance that can become ever more accessible to us through training and personal practice.

To understand how our nervous system is wired, it's helpful to appreciate that the descent out of our WOT into dysregulation happens in two stages.

At the first stage, our survival brain and instincts are activated, and our nervous system gears up to prepare us for fight or flight. At this stage, we maintain a sense of agency and choice that we can either fight our way out of this situation or run like hell to escape. Although there is a sense of possibility and engagement, the discerning, self-regulating parts of our brain are impaired and hijacked by the over-amped arousal of our sympathetic nervous system and the cortisol coursing through our bloodstream. This throws us off into chaotic, reactive states where we can feel out of control, anxious, agitated, panicked, frustrated, or angry. This moves us into mindsets and behaviors of othering, blaming, yelling, defensiveness, and harming. In this state our attention narrows and our capacity to think clearly and make discerning and accurate assessments and decisions is severely compromised.

In the clutches of the runaway sympathetic nervous system mobilized for survival and guided by whatever reactive, mindless habits drive us at an unconscious level, we can't rightly conceive of consequences for our choices and actions or care about the impacts of our actions on others. In this chaotic, dysregulated state we are not only in danger, but we are dangerous to others.

Yet if we have the good fortune to learn Jedi warrior skills, become adept in mindful self-awareness and self-mastery and learn to widen our window of tolerance, once we respond to the challenges that require us to fight or flee we will have the capacity to swiftly return to our WOT to rest and renew ourselves in preparation for whatever new challenges or waves of assault our life or mission may bring.

If, however, we move deeper into distress, or the dangers present in our lives escalate, we may then cross a second threshold into the danger zone of overwhelm where our evolutionary survival brain instincts compel us to freeze, faint, or dissociate. Departing from a "can do" attitude that feels powerful enough to fight or flee and then recover, at this stage we sink into helplessness, hopelessness, and depression. With this sense of loss of personal power and agency, the extreme dysregulation of our nervous system is dominated by the dorsal vagal branch of our autonomic nervous system leading us to turn away, numb down, or faint in an attempt to shield ourselves from danger. Our emotional availability and responsiveness flatten, and we languish in exhaustion.

Faced with such overpowering circumstances, the deep intelligence of our human psyche and nervous system kicks in. Turning away from the suffering to protect ourselves from the immense pain we are experiencing, we absence ourselves. Not surprisingly, the suffering we endure is often inflicted upon us as the abusive behavior of other tragically wounded, dysregulated, and traumatized souls who, in a sense, have lost their "right minds" and are deeply disconnected from their own deepest humanity.

Speaking to the ancient evolutionary wisdom of trauma and the price we pay for shutting down, Hübl and Avritt remind us,

The energy of intense suffering is pushed out of consciousness simply so that life can be allowed to go on. Denial permits us to survive the unsurvivable—for a while. Left too long, any unconscious defense mechanism becomes detrimental to life. . . . Suppression, resistance, and denial serve a crucial function in human survival . . . until they don't. When trauma remains too long denied, it begins to exact a steep price, a burden of debt that must eventually be paid, often by subsequent generations.[2]

While the survival wisdom of dissociative trauma response may be adaptive or even life-saving in the short term, if this trauma remains unresolved over time it can become toxic and leave us more vulnerable. When trauma is continually restimulated or triggered it can become a dangerously maladaptive habitual response to stressful encounters. The more we default to mindless absencing, rather than mindful presencing, the more we are in danger of unconsciously slipping into mental habits of denial, self-deception, desensing, projecting our delusions upon others, demonizing them, and then manipulating, blaming, abusing, or destroying them. All too often this culminates in self-destructive behaviors.

Given the heartbreaking number of suicides of veterans due to unresolved trauma endured in military service, Jedi warrior training was designed as a wise and potent antidote to such suffering. Our goal was to teach these soldiers the vital life skills necessary to widen their window of tolerance, expand the scope of their awareness, and awaken the courageous presence capable of clearly seeing and wisely responding to whatever challenges or dangers may arise within the perimeters of their awareness.

Lightening the Load

Our program was designed to focus on the disciplines of self-mastery required to wisely monitor and manage energy in order to optimize performance over lengthy deployments. The ability to rouse the optimal level of energy necessary to skillfully gear up, meet, and then recover from an encounter with a stressful challenge or threat is called allostasis. When conditions are conducive for us to feel safe and supported and our awareness and self-regulation skills are high, we will be able to more easily recover from whatever stress arousal we have experienced and carry a "low allostatic load." This means that we can easily rest, digest, regenerate, tend, and befriend after periods of being stressed or challenged. Low allostatic load is associated with higher levels of well-being and high vagal tone in our nervous system. This gives us greater capacity to feel well and at ease, have access to working memory, focus attention, regulate our blood sugar levels, maintain emotional balance, and engage effectively and harmoniously with other people. Well-regulated people are more likely to be part of solutions rather than cause more unintended problems for themselves or for others.

Over time, the accumulated strain of unrelenting stress without recovery erodes the vitality of our psychobiological systems, which are essential to maintaining our well-being, self-confidence, and ability to self-regulate. When we feel endangered, vulnerable, unable to rest or renew ourselves, and physical resources drain, our attention narrows and our cognitive capacities necessary for clear thinking and self-determination are compromised. We become more fragile. Understanding these profound mind-body dynamics, the Jedi Warrior curriculum was specifically designed to equip our soldiers with the self-mastery skills necessary to combat the threat of high-allostatic load that unaddressed could lead to chronic exhaustion, burnout, depression, insomnia, hypervigilance, racing and chaotic thoughts, mood swings, a wide range of draining chronic illnesses, harmful self-sabotaging coping strategies, addictive behaviors, and the crushing despair that often culminates in suicide.*

---

*Our ability to deeply rest and downregulate is related to our allostatic load, so much so that those who are fortunate to consistently have five healthy sleep habits—falling asleep easily, staying asleep, getting seven to eight hours of restful sleep, waking up rested, and foregoing sleep meds—are "30% less likely to die for any medical reason, 21% less likely to die from cardiovascular disease, 19% less likely to die from cancer, and 40% less likely to die of causes other than heart disease or cancer." Men with the robust self-regulation skills to realize these five sleep habits had a life expectancy that was 4.7 years greater than people who had none or only one of them. For women the impact is significant but only a gain of 2.4 years as compared with those who had none or only one of these sleep habits.[3]

At the societal level we see that wounded, dysregulated, and traumatized people are more likely to wound and traumatize others. As the integrity of vital social and environmental systems degrade, people are more likely to feel increasingly unsafe, uncertain, distrusting, defensive, victimized, out of control, and to become more dysregulated and at risk. Looking at the perpetrators of many of the acts of senseless violence in our communities and world, we see that extreme and harmful behavior is most often linked to individuals who are extremely dysregulated. Unsurprisingly, many of these wounded souls are victims of systemic or family abuse and trauma that has cascaded through ancestral lineages over generations of previously highly traumatized and dysregulated people.

Understanding this, we are wise to recognize and address the structural violence and systemic causes of trauma prevalent in our institutions and society that leave people feeling lonely, unsafe, powerless, uncared for, undervalued, lacking in choices for meaningful self-determination, and filled with rage. Such harsh social circumstances are breeding grounds for self-destructive and other harmful lifestyles, exploitation, and radicalization as we are witnessing playing out on a global scale in our world today. Recognizing these heartbreaking realities can mobilize us to truly "liberate from oppression" and to live and act with greater wisdom, kindness, and compassion, and invest in initiatives such as the Jedi Warrior program that offer wise alternatives.

Crossing the Line

Military leaders have witnessed the enormous losses and enduring suffering in their ranks due to an ignorance of the principles and life-skills that the Jedi warrior training was based upon. One Pentagon report indicated that psychological issues such as post-traumatic stress disorder exact a devastating toll in lost person-power, noting that mental health care accounted for almost 40 percent of all days spent in hospitals by service members that year. Four mental health issues—depression, substance abuse, anxiety, and adjustment problems such as PTSD—cost the Pentagon 488 years of lost duty in that year alone. Research indicated that 28 percent of soldiers suffer from severe levels of anxiety that diminish their mission readiness. When such levels of mental distress are allowed to fester unresolved, they can result in severe and debilitating mental disease, which causes further suffering to the soldiers, their families, and those in the perimeter of their influence. Swift or slow paths to suicide may then appear to be the only viable way out.[4]

Amishi Jha, who has worked extensively with military personnel, pre- and postdeployment, wisely observes, the more attention and working memory capacity people have, the more they are

> able to hold their own ethical compass and have their behavior be in line with their ethical code. So there is a really strong interrelationship between decision making, ethics, and these core cognitive capacities. If you degrade the capacity, you may not be able to live in line with what you know to be the right way to behave. So if we are able to bolster these capacities, increase attention and increase emotion regulation so that people are better able to align their behavior with what they know to be the right way to behave, we may have a chance of reducing errors and mistakes, and also the lifelong psychological disease related to that.[5]

The strong link between the impacts of stress and moral injury-related dysregulation and the degrading of cognitive capacity to monitor and manage emotions and control impulsive harmful behaviors is painfully clear. These factors combine to undermine mission performance and operational effectiveness and cause harm to soldiers and to others through their actions.

When we are able to support warriors and other professionals operating in harm's way to learn the basic self-awareness, self-regulation, and self-mastery skills necessary to widen their Windows of Tolerance, reduce allostatic load, and maintain access to their ethical compass, they will be more capable of staying true to their highest values without betraying them. They will be less likely to make choices and take actions that wound and traumatize themselves and others that they will later regret.

As Elizabeth Stanley, author of *Widening the Window: Training Your Brain and Body to Thrive During Stress and Recover from Trauma*, informed by her own recovery from traumatic military experience, writes,

> As an academic who teaches and writes about international security, I believed that mindfulness and body-based self-regulation skills could help with the cognitive degradation (well-documented in empirical research) associated with military stress-inoculation training. I believed it might help troops regulate their ANS [autonomic nervous system] and thus function more effectively while deployed. In military circles, this is called the "strategic corporal" concept, where an individual's choices or actions while deployed have tremendous effects on the nation's ability to accomplish its strategic goals. I also believed it might shield troops—and their families—against health disorders and behavioral symptoms of the stress spectrum after returning home.[6]

Embodied Wisdom and Alexithymia

Through our clinical stress management practice we became painfully aware of a dangerous life-compromising condition that is very common, yet very few people are aware that they suffer from it. This condition is called *alexithymia,* a term first used by Harvard psychiatrist Dr. Peter Sifneos to describe a problem shared by a large proportion of patients suffering from various stress-linked medical disorders. Looking at the Greek roots for the word we discover that *alexi* means "no words," and *thymia* means "for feelings."

One study found that 41 percent of U.S. veterans of the Vietnam War with post-traumatic stress disorder (PTSD) were alexithymic.[7] Another study found higher levels of alexithymia among Holocaust survivors with PTSD compared to those without.[8] Difficulty with recognizing, naming, and talking about their emotions is more common in men who conform to particular cultural notions of masculinity. Moreover, people suffering from alexithymia, impaired in their emotional intelligence and their embodied interoceptive awareness, may even take pride in their lack of empathy or inappropriate responses to the emotions of others. If this lack of empathy and self-awareness persists, their success in establishing enduring mutually supportive relationships will be severely compromised.

When we are unable to notice and accurately interpret our inner feeling states, the link between our embodied awareness and our sensemaking cognition is broken. When we live with alexithymia we unwisely and unknowingly put ourselves in harm's way. If we are not in touch with our internal state and have no words for our feelings, we will likely be unaware of the rising tide of subtle whispers of distress until they escalate into painful screams within or around us. An essential aspect of the Jedi warrior training was to develop our soldiers' skill and confidence to frequently return to a home base of embodied presence able to sense, name, and optimize their inner state of being.

We would explain to the soldiers that the more alexythymic we are, the farther out of balance we become before we have any conscious clue that something within or around us is not right. For this reason, alexithymia is regarded as a dangerous precursor to virtually every stress-related illness. If we have the inner awareness and self-regulation skill to avert this, we'll be more likely to recognize when something inwardly is "off" and inquire into it to set things right through natural responses of self-regulation that serve to restore our well-being. When we lack such self-awareness and self-management skills and are out of touch with our embodied experience, we are less effective and far more vulnerable as we become stressed about being stressed, and anxious about being anxious, as small imbalances escalate and spiral out of control into major crises.

Vast Horizons of Freedom

The suffering and suicides that gave rise to the creation of the Jedi Warrior program remind us that both personal and collective trauma lead us to disconnect and fragment our sense of wholeness. As the integrity of so many natural systems and social structures in our world are becoming increasingly fragile, the strain on these vital life support systems is manifesting as three major divides, each of which plays a role in personal, societal, and global unrest, violence, and war. These are the ecological divide, the social divide, and the spiritual divide.[9]

> **The ecological divide** arises through worldviews and actions that disconnect us from our living natural world.
> **The social divide** reflects the disconnect between self and others.
> **The spiritual divide** reflects our disconnection from the deeper dimensions of our true nature.

The pervasive theme bridging these divides is the sense of disconnection that is rooted in absencing or turning away from life as it is, often due to trauma. When we feel disconnected and out of touch with nature, with people, and with ourselves, we are more likely to relate to those around us and to the world itself as "other," something separate from ourselves to be ignored, exploited, or destroyed. This is heartbreaking since we can never actually be separated from nature, other living beings, or the deeper dimensions of ourselves, even though we may feel or believe that we are.

The Jedi Warrior program sought to encompass a broad view of the causes and resolution of violence and war. It affirmed that empowering skills can enhance survivability both on and off the battlefield, that healing can happen, and the experience of wholeness, connectivity, and aliveness once broken can be restored. To the degree that we develop appreciation for developing, maintaining, and restoring our vital life-affirming connections, we are more likely to survive and thrive, while to the degree that we experience ourselves as disconnected, our vitality, wisdom, resilience, survivability, and longevity are diminished.

As the Jedi program progressed, we would often remind our soldiers of the enormous courage required to be fully present, to honestly face, embrace, and bring wisdom and compassion to the vulnerability, woundedness, and suffering present in our lives and world and then to use the

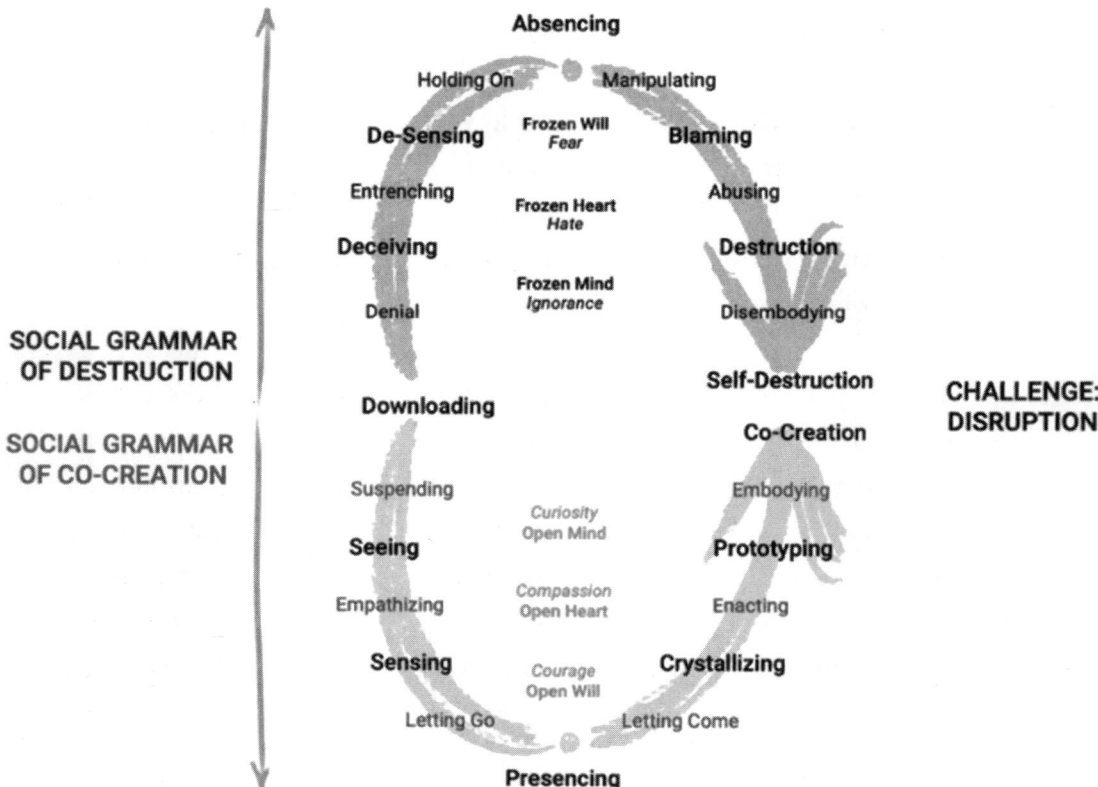

Fig. 5.1. Presencing and Absencing Model courtesy of Otto Scharmer

power of their insight and skills to bring healing to the wounds of warriors, their families, and communities. We would introduce our soldiers to the path of mindful presencing as a wise, powerful, and courageous alternative to the suffering caused by absencing. Presencing begins with showing up wholeheartedly, individually and collectively, curious, open, connected, and receptive to whatever the moment may bring. This courageous stance allows us to keep an open mind and suspend expectations and preconceptions that might otherwise be imposed on current reality to have it conform with past experience. This special kind of courageous presence opens our mind, heart, and will to the present moment, expands our access to intuitive intelligence, and brings us into an ever-deepening empathic resonance and intimacy with the nature of reality and those around us, opening vast horizons of freedom and responsive potential to help ourselves and others.

Wetiko

We've found an intriguing parallel between the detrimental mindsets and behaviors that arise due to absencing and disconnection and the concept of *wetiko* from Native American wisdom. Wetiko describes a "mind virus" at the core of humanity's gravest challenges. This "sickness of the spirit" operates through our unconscious, driving us toward actions that contradict our personal and collective well-being. It's an affliction of the soul, subtly infiltrating our collective consciousness.[10]

Wetiko denotes a psychospiritual state characterized by extreme self-centeredness, greed, and the voracious consumption of others' lives or resources. It embodies a mentality whereby individuals or societies become consumed by an insatiable quest for power, accumulation, and control, often disregarding the well-being of others and the greater good. This shriveling state of "malignant egophrenia" neglects empathy, cooperation, and the interrelatedness of all beings.[11]

By learning to recognize, understand, and liberate these harmful tendencies within our own lives, we are better equipped to empathically recognize and skillfully defuse these tendencies playing out in our world. The Jedi warrior training encouraged our soldiers to take their motto "Liberators of the Oppressed" to heart in a very personal way, and to develop the power, insight, and skills necessary to decolonize their minds from the culturally conditioned narrow-mindedness that occludes so much brilliant human potential and creates so much suffering in our lives and world.

SIX

Wise Counsel

Imagine how potent it would be to have a three-year charter to reach out to wise people around the globe, whose work and teachings had inspired you, with the question: "If you had the opportunity to create an immersive six-month-long training program for twenty-five people who may someday be in a position to start, or stop, the next world war, what would you teach them?" Jedi opened the way for us to do this.

The sheer novelty and profound implications of this program served as a remarkable key to open doors, especially in the many cases where when we boldly reached out to luminaries whom we had never met. Of all the people we reached out to, not even one turned us away. While we could write volumes on the wise counsel we received, we'll offer a glimpse here of some of those close encounters with mentors that inspired how we approached this program design.

Noetic Pioneers

One year before the Jedi Warrior program launched, we were invited to attend a conference on human consciousness, held at the White Memorial Campground, a United Methodist church camp in Council Grove, Kansas. Since 1969, the Interdisciplinary Conference on Voluntary Control of Internal States had held these yearly, weeklong conferences, to which they invited around one hundred distinguished and respected

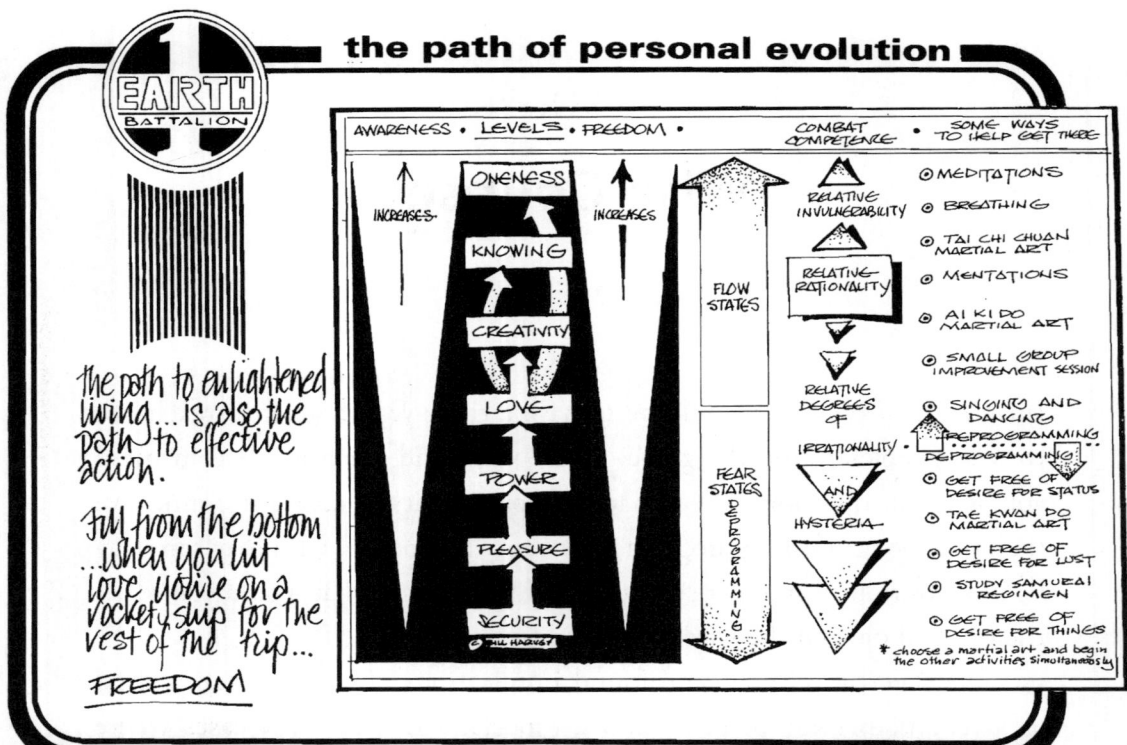

THE FIRST EARTH BATTALION

scientists, researchers, and teachers from a broad spectrum of disciplines and from dozens of nations, all working in the field of human potential. As a young research associate doing consciousness research at the University of Washington, Joel was grateful to attend this gathering of esteemed consciousness researchers exploring the further reaches of human consciousness.

To assure that everyone could speak openly and honestly about often controversial subjects, the conference had a strict policy of no recording and no posting of proceedings. This was established to ensure that researchers working with psychedelics (which had been targeted in Nixon's misguided war on drugs) or engaged in research on psychic and psychotronic phenomena (largely government funded), or exploring extra-ordinary states of consciousness and human capabilities, could candidly speak with fellow researchers and explorers about their often remarkable, paradigm-busting personal insights and academic research, without concern for professional repercussions.

The Council Grove Conference was the brainchild of two of our mentors, Drs. Elmer and Alyce Green. The Greens had established the world-renowned Voluntary Control of Internal States research laboratory at the Menninger Foundation, which was one of the world's most respected psychiatric institutes of its time. The stated purpose of the conference was "to develop an experimental and theoretical basis for a possible science of consciousness in which existential development and academic attainment are interrelated. This basic purpose underlies the inclusion of ancient systems for the development of voluntary control of internal states."[1]

Over the years, the scope of the conference had expanded to encompass a vast array of domains of inquiry related to research on extraordinary human potential and capabilities such as: flow states and peak performance; expanded sensory phenomena (such as ESP, psychokinesis, remote viewing, nondual unitive states, flow); energy medicine and healing; biofeedback and neurofeedback; meditation research and the contemplative sciences; indigenous wisdom and medicine traditions; and the primacy of consciousness. The streams of wisdom, insight, and experience flowing in this gathering offered a treasure trove of diverse perspectives and insight to inform our design for Jedi Warrior.

On the first morning of the conference, we spoke to the group and outlined the program we were developing. We asked our colleagues to seek us out afterward if they had any feedback on our program design. As we were finishing lunch that day, we were approached by Gary Zukav, the bright-eyed, soft-spoken author of *The Dancing Wu Li Masters*, a classic in the newly emerging exploration of the profound interphase of quantum theory and the noetic contemplative sciences. We had read and admired Gary's inspired book, but this was our first actual meeting with him. Gary suggested that we take a walk and talk about the program.

We walked through the tall prairie grass and came to sit on a bluff by the lake under a piercing blue sky. Gary, who presented as a very refined, quiet, gentle soul, revealed to us that prior to his research and writings on consciousness he had served as a Special Forces officer engaged in special operations during the war in Southeast Asia. We were surprised to hear this as he certainly didn't seem to fit our preconceived image of a a super-tough Special Ops kind of guy!

It was heartening to hear Gary express his confidence that the advanced wholistic training we were developing for the Special Forces would provide a valuable and enlightening advancement in the soldiers' training and mission preparedness. Gary explained that for us to be effective in delivering this program we would need to understand the nature of the work and missions that Special Forces troops did. He proceeded to describe in lucid, excruciating detail some of the missions he had been on, serving in the Special Forces during his deployment in Southeast Asia—the depths of moral injury and trauma he had witnessed and the confounding ethical dilemmas he had experienced.

After an hour of harrowing and at times gut-wrenching tales, Gary looked at us with his bright, clear eyes and said with great strength, "It is vitally important that you are both as authentic and for real as you can be with these men. They are trained like hunting dogs to search out any incongruities or inconsistencies, and if you show even a hint of any pretense or inauthenticity with these men, they will likely eat you for lunch!"

As the golden light of the setting sun reflected off the lake and danced through the wind-tossed prairie grasses, we meandered back to the conference center for dinner. It felt like we had just come back from a long and epic journey and were now returning to consensus reality after a timeless interlude in a mythical realm. Gary's wise and prescient advice would prove invaluable to us once we were on base with our Jedi Warriors.

Teach Them Courage

A couple of years before the program began, we had the rare opportunity to host one of our closest mentors, Zong Rinpoche, the eminent former abbot of Ganden, the largest monastic university in Tibet. Zong Rinpoche was from the Zong region in Eastern Tibet, so his name literally meant "precious one from Zong." Rinpoche had visited us in Seattle to offer some special lectures and workshops at Antioch University where Joel was on faculty, having designed and taught a couple of graduate psychology programs focused on consciousness and holistic health. During Rinpoche's visit to the Northwest, teaching in both Seattle and in Vancouver, British Columbia, we had many hours to talk about the contemplative sciences and their profound value for people living amid the complexities and stresses of our modern times.

We described the scope of the program we were designing and asked for his advice, saying, "Rinpoche, if you had the opportunity to devote six months to working closely with twenty five men who may someday be in a position to start, or stop, the next world war, what would be the most important wisdom to offer to them?" The venerable elder took our question into the vastness of his being and quietly sat with it for a few minutes, as though he were looking deeply into the fabric of time and potentialities, viewing various scenarios or simulations for our program. After a long silence, with kind bright eyes and a gentle smile, he simply replied through his translator, without further commentary, "Teach them courage."

Joel and I looked at each other, stretching our minds and trying to imagine what he meant by this somewhat cryptic response. How are *we* going to teach courage to these highly trained Special Forces troops? What would this mean for us and for the men we would be working with?

His pithy yet profound advice to us became a blend of a mandate and a koan, a deep spiritual question that transcends reasoning. As we said our goodbyes and thanked him for his kindness, he softly added, "I rely upon you for the success of this program." His words would continue to reverberate within us as a reference point to keep truing to throughout the grueling years of preparation and training to come.

We have since recounted Rinpoche's advice to numerous friends who are fluent in Tibetan and have gradually come to learn that Rinpoche had most likely used the Tibetan word *nyingthob*, which was translated for us then as "courage" but could also have been translated as: "patience," "forgiveness," "compassion," or "heart power."

Heart power is a literal translation and is interpreted as describing the capacity of someone to courageously and compassionately face their fears without turning away from their suffering. Such a courageous person embodies the strength necessary to look deeply into the nature of one's own reaction to fear with a strong, clear, stable heart and an open, curious, and compassionate mind. Interestingly, in the psychophysical sciences, such courage naturally emerges as one of the neural executive powers, reflecting a state of mental development and neural integration that emerges through intensive practice of mind-fitness disciplines such as mindfulness.

Extraordinary Human Potential

In the autumn before the program began, Joel had the opportunity, along with some of the other members of the SportsMind team, to visit and stay with Joan and Jim Channon at their home in Marin, California, and do some deep planning and design work together for the program. At that time Michelle was immersed in a three-month silent meditation retreat at the Insight Meditation Society, in Barre, Massachusetts, which was then a ground-zero training center for mindfulness education in the Western world outside of Asia.

One of the highlights of this working session was the opportunity for an illuminating dialogue with two of the most respected elders and founders of the emerging human potential movement—Michael Murphy, the visionary founder of the Esalen Institute at Big Sur, California, and George Leonard, an aikido sensei and pioneer in opening new frontiers of advanced human performance training as an integral part of expanding educational paradigms in the Western world.

The opportunity to meet with Jim, George, and Michael together was unparalleled. We couldn't think of three elder colleagues and mentors better suited to help us envision the design for Jedi Warrior. And so, we were blessed with a timeless afternoon and evening of deep conversation exploring the deeper dimensions of advanced transformational human technologies and the specific training protocols that we would weave into our design and delivery of Jedi Warrior.

The Esalen Institute, nestled in the wild beauty of the rugged California coast south of Monterey, opened its doors, and portals of possibilities, to the further reaches of the mind in 1962. Esalen was essentially the first modern global higher education and training center for all things credibly useful in raising consciousness and enhancing human health and performance. Its unique and inspiring presence and success in the world inspired a revolution of transformational learning and education, spawning countless similar centers of higher education to develop around the globe.

In Murphy's own words, the guiding philosophy of Esalen was to illuminate how "the cosmos, the universe itself, the whole evolutionary unfoldment, is what a lot of philosophers call slumbering spirit. The divine is incarnate in the world and is present in us and is trying to manifest." Esalen had provided fertile ground in the early stages of Jim's military assignment to research the wisdom and skillful means available within the human potential movement. Jim had immersed himself wholeheartedly in the multidisciplinary curriculum offered there, as well as in the soothing natural hot springs that were part of Esalen's allure. Jim's experiences there opened his eyes, heart, and mind to an expanded vision of what the highest, most ennobling, and planet-serving purpose for the military powers of our world could be and inspired his personal mission of devoting his life to helping people in the armed services—and beyond—to awaken more fully to their true nature and highest potentials.

The Esalen Institute also played a vital key role in inspiring generations of emerging leaders and entrepreneurs who created and transformed Silicon Valley (and thus the world) over the past fifty years. The institute was located just far enough away to be distant from the maddening crowds of Silicon Valley and the Bay Area, and yet was close enough to be easily accessible to seekers from there and beyond, serving as a nurturing oasis and meeting place for visionaries, mystics, entrepreneurs, and wisdom teachers. The Esalen Institute provided a vibrant crossroads on the modern-day Silk Road of the global human potential movement, hosting interdisciplinary dialogues, collaborations, and explorations and many East-West dialogues, bringing together teachers, researchers, philosophers, and scientists from modern and ancient wisdom traditions.

Esalen also played a relevant role regarding the secret mission of the soon-to-be Jedi warriors who were being prepared for deployment on a moment's notice on missions related to the escalating Cold War tensions between the United States and the Soviet Union. Through the inspiration of Michael and his wife, Dulce, the Esalen Institute served as ground zero for the Soviet-American Exchange Program (later renamed Track Two, an institute for citizen diplomacy). This initiative emerged at a time when Cold War tensions between the Soviet Union and the United States were at their peak, and threats of nuclear war were a real and present danger, lingering in the background of most people's minds in these countries. This courageous nongovernmental program was credited with substantial success in fostering peaceful, meaningful, and productive dialogue and exchanges between private citizens of these two clashing superpowers.[2]

In 1982, the Murphys pioneered the first U.S.-Soviet Space Bridge, allowing Soviet and American citizens to speak directly with one another via satellite communication. Their efforts helped to bring Soviet leaders to the United States for the first time to promote dialogue and mutual understanding with President H. W. Bush and influential leaders in business and government. After Gorbachev stepped down and effectively dissolved the Soviet Union, Jim Garrison helped establish the State of the World Forum with Gorbachev as its convening chairman. These successes inspired citizen diplomacy programs with China and an initiative to further understanding among Jews, Christians, and Muslims, as well as further work on Russian American relations, and these in turn have inspired the generations of citizen-to-citizen peacemaking initiatives that blossomed around the globe in the decades that followed.

Having grown up in the segregated South, George Leonard had a passion for social justice and healing social divisions. As senior editor for *Look* Magazine for seventeen years, George focused on the civil rights movement, politics, foreign affairs, and social change. He had received many national awards for his lucid writing on expanding the modern educational paradigm to encourage more wholistic and integral paradigms that would encourage and liberate our best selves in order to create societies and a world in which people could truly thrive.

Seeking ways to wisely embody what he was learning, George took up the martial arts practice of aikido in 1970, at forty-seven years of age, a time when most athletes bow out and retire, and went on to earn a fifth-degree black belt. In the course of his training, George not only studied aikido as a martial art but also delved deeply into the subtler energy awareness dimensions of this art as taught by Morihei Ueshiba (1883–1969), the founder of aikido, whose brilliant integrative style of teaching drew inspiration from diverse martial arts disciplines and wisdom traditions.

The potency, potentials, and dangers of these times informed and inspired our dialogue as we envisioned the elegant synergy of ancient and modern methods of mastery, transformation, and extraordinary human potential. It was a day of timeless flow, leaving us all with a sense of exhilaration from the synergy of sharing that came forth. We all felt a sense of being honored and privileged to participate in this historic endeavor of envisioning what George and Michael described as "the most advanced and technically sophisticated leadership and human performance training program ever to be delivered in modern times."

Mental Toughness

One of the most unique, challenging, and vital elements of Jedi Warrior training for the men was to be the encampment, a monthlong, intensive, highly disciplined immersion in deep, silent stillness coupled with close observation of the ever-changing, flowing, tangible, and subtle workings of the mind-body in responsive interphase with the world around them. The value of the encampment would be brutally tested in its impact as the men deployed from the encampment straight into an arduous mission simulation called "the Gut Check," which no other teams of Special Ops troops had ever successfully completed.

It was clear to us that the design of the encampment would be of the utmost importance. The disciplines and technologies of mental discipline and training are vast in scope and extremely scientific and rigorous. These inner technologies for refining awareness and developing insight into the nature of reality have been rigorously developed and empirically tested with inspiring results over thousands of years in monasteries, ashrams, and secret wisdom societies throughout the world and more recently in mind-fitness centers and universities. Properly understood, these mental disciplines, which enable the practitioner to understand and guide the powerful and subtle energies and functions of the mind-body-energy system, are on par with the high level of knowledge and mastery needed to develop the powerful outer technologies we rely upon in our material world, such as the internet or spacecraft guidance systems.

Though we consulted with many of our mentors on the design and protocols for the encampment phase of training, the primary structure and flow of instructions for the encampment emerged and coalesced during a memorable afternoon of deep dialogue with two wise and experienced Burmese meditation teachers, Rina Sircar, Ph.D., and her teacher, Taungpulu Kaba-Aye Sayadaw. Rina was a very dear mentor of ours and was one of the first faculty members of the California Institute of Integral Studies (CIIS) in San Francisco, teaching contemplative science long before it became more widely available in the West.

Rina had been a nun in the Burmese Theravadin tradition since she was four years old. She was not only a beloved teacher of many of the first wave of mindfulness teachers in the West, but also a friend and source of inspiration for many respected elder contemplative teachers from around the globe who would invite her to visit them when they came to teach in the Bay Area. Her clear, loving presence and inspirational teachings were a profound source of guidance for us and for many others in the beginning days of the Western mindfulness movement back in the early 1970s.

A powerful embodiment of peace, joy, selfless loving-kindness, and compassion, Rina was as unpretentious as can be. At gatherings and conferences with other contemplative teachers, she would usually be found sitting quietly on the sidelines, either content to be alone, radiating loving-kindness to all beings, or in deep quiet conversation with students who were eager to tap her wisdom or just be in the field of her *metta* (a Pali word meaning "loving-kindness"). In daily life, Rina tirelessly devoted herself to teaching and practice. She also worked deeply with health care professionals and people facing death, teaching them healing meditation practices mostly focused on loving-kindness and compassion.

Taungpulu Sayadaw was regarded as a national treasure of the Burmese contemplative traditions, and we were delighted to discover that he was visiting her and agreed to join our conversation. They generously devoted one long afternoon to sharing their insights and learnings distilled from their combined one-hundred-plus years of practice and study in the contemplative sciences and from their own deep experience in teaching meditation to military personnel in Asia. As we talked, they helped us map out a well-engineered path of practice that progressed gradually step-by-step to deeper and longer meditation sessions exploring subtler and subtler levels of the mind-body processes. While rigorous training was common for practitioners in the East, few Westerners had ever dreamed of engaging in such intensive psychophysical training in an immersive environment of silence for many weeks, if not months, at a time.

The instructions and design guidance that Rina and Sayadaw gave us for the encampment offered minute details regarding what to teach at each stage along this path of practice, what signs of progress to watch for, and when and how to proceed to the next level of training. We were touched by the humanity, love, care, wisdom, and practicality that they both brought to our conversation. Though Sayadaw presented as an austere and somewhat aloof elder, he was wholeheartedly engaged in our dialogue and would from time to time break into a big grin or chuckle, which, in a cultural act of humility, he would shyly hide with a large bodhi-leaf-shaped bamboo hand fan that he carried tucked in his robes.

This dialogue reflected Rina's profound and understated wisdom distilled from many decades of intensive mental training and many years of skillfully adapting ancient contemplative science teachings for people who had lived their whole lives in modern Western cultures. As our time together came to a close, Rina leaned back in her seat, smiled tenderly at us, and wisely advised, "But by all means, don't call this meditation. That might sound too soft or foreign to them. Call it mental toughness training!" We looked at each other with an appreciation for her insight in anticipating the potential challenges and opportunities that lay ahead.

Neurotechies

Over the years leading up to the launch of Jedi Warrior, we also had deep conversations on the pros and cons of various biofeedback and neurofeed-back systems and training protocols with many of the most respected pioneers in the field including Elmer Green, Pat Norris, and Peter and Sarah Parks from the Menninger Foundation, Edgar Wilson, Adam Crane, Hal Meyers, Carol J. Schneider, and Les Fehmi—all of whom were close friends and allies in this design phase.

During the annual meetup of this wise tribe of neurohackers and psychophysical researchers at the Biofeedback Society conference in Monterey, California, we were scouting out the latest biofeedback and neurofeedback technology, talking with manufacturers and with colleagues to gather intel to inform the design of our Mind Lab training center for Jedi and our selection of tech partners and suppliers and to inspire our training protocols.

It was exhilarating to have the opportunity and funding to design a state-of-the-art biopsybernautic training center where we would be training up to twelve-person teams of Special Forces troops. We honestly had never heard of anyone ever running a training like we were designing, or of anyone who had created a training center with the kind of collective training capabilities that we were building out, so the challenges and possibilities we faced were both at a very high level. Scouting for technology and allies to inspire and inform the design for our biofeedback and neurofeedback lab for this Special Forces program opened the portal to many neurogeek-out sessions with esteemed and far-thinking colleagues that would last far into many nights of this conference. Word quickly spread through this community that we were researching for this and shopping for gear, so we were clearly a strange attractor for many colleagues curious about the program or seeking to sell us on the merits of their systems.

At this conference we began a series of conversation with James Hardt, Ph.D., founder of the Biocybernaut Institute, a brilliant neurogeek who had trained closely with Joe Kamiya, one of the early pioneers of neurofeedback training. Jim himself was a uniquely talented adept and alpha brainwave virtuoso who through his own deep training and personal explorations in consciousness had created some very interesting and effective protocols for promoting states of deep, clear presence.

The spark of our conversation ignited into a blaze when Joel inquired into the possibility of doing shared neurofeedback and teaching our men to synchronize their brainwaves with each other. Jim totally lit up at this idea and described to us how his neurofeedback system could be expanded to enable us to not only run teams of twelve people simultaneously in training sessions but to also program a system wherein pairs of soldiers would learn to synchronize their brainwaves by receiving moment-to-moment feedback, indicating when they were or were not in neurosynch with each other.

We talked late into the night and left this conversation electrified with the potentials for this kind of advanced collective consciousness training. We agreed to continue this conversation with Jim's business partner, Foster Gamble, with whom he was developing a business plan to establish a line of high-end neurofeedback salons beginning with the first Mind Center in Silicon Valley.

Over the months to come, as our conversations evolved, we developed an initial design for the technical specifications and training protocols we would rely upon in building out the neurofeedback system and running the training for the Special Forces. The next step was for us to actually experience the training ourselves and to learn how to operate the system as guides and technicians for training the soldiers.

That springtime we set up base camp at our friends' home near the beach in Santa Cruz and prepared for nearly three weeks of immersive training with Jim at his Biocybernaut Institute that was housed on the campus of Agnew State Hospital in Santa Clara, California.

The first morning we made the very windy drive through the coast range of mountains to drop down into San Jose and then head north to the institute. After an orientation meeting with Jim and his team of neurote-chies we were guided to the preparation room where we were each outfitted with four neurosensors to record our EEG brainwaves. With sensors glued firmly to our scalps, which was no small feat for Michelle's impressive thick mane of long, wavy hair, we were each escorted off to take our seats for a five-hour immersion in our training chambers—two Faraday cages that were lightproof, soundproof, and electromagnetically shielded to provide an optimized environment for gathering EEG data free from the intrusion of the myriad of electromagnetic waves streaming to us and through us from local antennas, networks, light fixtures, and so on, that generate the dense electromagnetic environment that encases and penetrates our bod-ies at every moment of our lives. The opportunity to immerse ourselves for five to seven hours a day in such an energetically quiescent environ-ment was in itself a rare and precious opportunity, a kind of personalized neurohacking meditation retreat. Joel was quite at home being back in a Faraday cage again, as he had slept in the one in his lab at the University of Washington when he had moved into the lab during an intensive time of research and exploration.

Our shakeout cruise of this neurofeedback experience was comprised of a series of highly structured segments, each of which collected copious amounts of data to be analyzed by the institute. An average day at the lab involved a thirty-minute prep to clean the scalp and apply the neurosensors, five-plus hours training, and thirty to sixty minutes to wash up, debrief, and reflect with Jim and his crew. The unique and privileged opportunity to peer this deeply into the microfluctuations of our mind-brain-body pro-cess was exhilarating—and the days passed quickly. As we'd step out of the lab into the sunshine after being cloistered in our cybercave all day, we'd often play Frisbee together for twenty to thirty minutes, barefoot on the campus lawn, to ground ourselves and connect with each other, before we made the long, slow rush-hour drive with Silicon Valley commuters cross-ing over the Santa Cruz mountains on Highway 17.

One significant insight for the two of us in doing this training together was the moving recognition that our EEG baselines were quite different from each other. Michelle, being very detail oriented and precise in her noticing, thinking, and speaking, had a strong center of neural gravity in the high alpha, slower beta frequency bands (10–14 cycles per second/hz), which are often associated with clear, lucid, alert, wakeful presence. "On the other brain," Joel had an EEG baseline in the slower theta-alpha threshold (4–8 cycles per second) and was more likely to be attuned to more spatial, contextual, global modes of noticing, with less focus on details. Joel's EEG looked more like big rolling waves across the ocean, whereas Michelle's brainwaves were much closer together with higher curtains of alpha amplitude.

These complementary tendencies are constantly at play in the daily dance of our life-work relationship, and the neural calibrations that were native to each of us offered both the potential for great synergy and at times for some creative tension. For instance, in coauthoring this book, Joel's work was often in articulating general broad-brush descriptions, scenarios, and stories, which Michelle would then refine and polish up with far greater attention to subtle and specific nuances. Michelle's work was also to write up well-polished stories and segments for this book, for which Joel might offer insights or suggestions for weaving into other themes or segments of the book.

One of the most meaningful experiences we shared during this intensive training period happened spontaneously one day after we'd had a quarrel on our way to the lab and didn't have time to work it out before going into our sessions. We both carried the dissonance of this unresolved tiff into our neurofeedback sessions, which offered some interesting insight into how our emotions and states of mind do, indeed, profoundly impact our neural functioning and capacity.

Toward the end of his training day, Joel experienced a wondrous vision of Michelle entering his Faraday cage in a body of light from the upper-right corner, doing a somersault, and coming down to merge with him so that her heart interpenetrated with his heart and she was looking out through his eyes. Moved to savor this tender and profound sense of merging, intimacy, and interfusion, Joel let go of his brain training and simply rested in experiencing this precious gift of heartfelt unity. After a seemingly eternal moment, the image of Michelle's presence simply integrated into the afterglow of this deeply moving experience. At the same time Michelle had reported exactly the same experience but from her own subjective point of view and location.

As we gathered with our lab techs for a collective debrief at the end of the session, Jim excitedly showed us the EEG recordings from our sessions, where you could see the nanosecond that our EEGs had synchronized with each other and the exact onset where the intimate interfusion of our fields of consciousness and merging began. This was further confirmed by the time stamp of the white-noise beeps where the onset of this shared magical moment was indeed between the fifth and sixth beep in the vigilance phase of the training protocol, just as Joel had described. We were all amazed and grateful to have such clear empirical verification of this rare and precious experience. We spent some time unpacking this extraordinary experience and its profound implications for understanding the nature of personal and shared consciousness. Michelle remarked that it also had great potential applications for couples' therapy as the morning's tension had completely melted away!

That evening, watching the pelicans skimming across the crests of the breaking waves, serenaded by a flock of gulls and accompanied by curious harbor seals, we witnessed a most glorious sunset from the beach near our lodging in Santa Cruz and talked late into the night about the vast implications of our experience for the phase of our Jedi neurofeedback training, where we would actually provide explicit neurofeedback to guide the members of each team toward synchronizing their brainwaves with one another. Our unbidden but most welcome experience had opened a portal of insight into vast new frontiers of human potential and possible realms of research regarding shared intuitive and intimate mind spaces. We felt both honored and inspired by the opportunities that were being offered to us. To the best of our knowledge, this kind of EEG synchrony training had never been explored up to that time. The gift of our experience in the lab that day had opened our minds and hearts to envision a vast array of potentials yet to be fully realized.

General Kuno: Tibetan Freedom Fighter

Another mentor who influenced our view of what a modern-day warrior-monk spirit could be was Professor Narkyid, known to most people simply as Kuno. Kuno had served as a general in the Tibetan army. He was a Tibetan Buddhist monk, academic scholar, and biographer for the Dalai Lama.

Born in the tiny Himalayan village of Tsetang in central Tibet, Kuno went to study at Drepung Monastery when he was six years old. Drepung was a thriving monastic educational center of tens of thousands of monks. For many centuries Drepung had been the monastic seat of the Dalai Lamas, and while studying together as young monks, Kuno had become a close friend and confidant of the Fourteenth Dalai Lama, who was seven years younger.

The wheel of time turned, and the Chinese invaded and occupied Tibet, beginning in 1949, seeking a strategic advantage by dominating the Himalayan reaches of the Tibetan Plateau in Central Asia, which is rich in natural resources. The headwaters of rivers there provide water to billions of people throughout Asia. The Russian novelist, historian, and Nobel laureate Alexander Solzhenitsyn described this invasion and occupation—which led to the destruction of over ten thousand centers of higher education, libraries, medical centers, and culturally significant sites and the death of one out of five Tibetans—as "more brutal and inhumane than any other communist regime in the world."[3]

Many thousands of traumatized survivors languished for decades in gulag-style labor camps and prisons, where they were frequently tortured and often isolated in solitary confinement. They were severely punished for openly practicing their religious and cultural traditions and were "reeducated" in a highly indoctrinating and punitive manner in the invader's language. The nations of the world watched on without any effective intervention or sanctions. This brutal repression continues to this day, more than seventy years later. Their experiences remind us all of the importance of developing and maintaining a strong, capable military defense.

In response to this devastating invasion, Kuno and many of his fellow monastics disrobed from their monastic life to take up arms and raise a resistance force to defend Lhasa and the Dalai Lama.* In 1959, Kuno organized the escape of the Dalai Lama. In the dead of night dressed as a soldier carrying a gun, the Dalai Lama departed from the Norbulinka summer palace to begin the treacherous six-week trek over the snow-covered Himalayan mountains to seek safe refuge and asylum in India Kuno fled to India some months later, facing a much more dangerous crossing of the Himalayan wilderness due to the increased presence of Chinese patrols following the successful escape of the Dalai Lama. Once in India, Kuno played a vital role in establishing and serving in the Tibetan government in exile, writing the Tibetan constitution and creating the first Tibetan typewriter.

Twenty-two years after leaving Tibet, Kuno finally learned the fate of his mother from a nun who had been held with her in the same Chinese prison. The nun described how his mother had died in 1962 after both of her hips were broken in brutal beatings. True to her spirit, his mother, a devout Buddhist practitioner, meditated till the very end of her life. Upon

---

*Few people are aware of the clandestine role that the U.S. military played in supporting the Tibetan resistance movement. From 1959 to 1964, the United States brought hundreds of Tibetan freedom fighters to train in guerrilla-style resistance tactics at Camp Hale, a secret Colorado base. After months of training, these warriors were equipped with weapons and secretly air-dropped back into Tibet to bolster the Tibetan resistance. Heartbreakingly, due to political pressures, the United States ultimately abandoned these resistance fighters, and they were overtaken by the Chinese troops.

hearing this news Kuno was so heartbroken and enraged that for many years he could not endure being in the presence of Chinese people, eating Chinese food, or seeing anything red.

When his old friend the Dalai Lama first requested Kuno to be his personal biographer, Kuno hesitated. Weighing this request from the Dalai Lama, Kuno remembered the words spoken to him by a dying freedom fighter in Tibet: "Fulfill the wishes of Yeshin Norbu, the Dalai Lama." One day the Dalai Lama asked Kuno, "What do you get from all this hating? You are just suffering with a burden." The Dalai Lama chided him with his wry humor saying, "Plus, you are missing delicious food."

Kuno was fond of saying that "the Chinese had tried to brainwash him, but the Dalai Lama washed and cleansed his brain." It took him years of meditation and deep spiritual practice to strengthen and expand his compassion and melt away the hatred from his heart. Kuno found inspiration and strength through his faith in the presence and example of the Tibetan bodhisattva Chenrezig, who is regarded as the embodiment of universal compassion (similar to the spirit of Christ in Christian faith). Finally in 1989, while meditating at Sarnath, the sacred site in India where the Buddha gave his first teaching on the Four Noble Truths, the burden of Kuno's hatred of the Chinese dissolved completely from his heart, and he was at last free of this heavy weight. From that time on, not only did he feel comfortable wearing red clothes again and find genuine joy in the presence of Chinese people, but he was also once again able to eat and enjoy Chinese food!

Drawing inspiration from the Dalai Lama, Kuno lived the later years of his life as an inspiring teacher and example of our innate potential for radical transformation by finding the courage to face and conquer our inner enemies and stop the wars raging within us.[4]

Kuno's transformation echoes the profound teaching of the thirteenth Dalai Lama, the predecessor of the current Dalai Lama, who was very much involved in warrior-monk interventions related to mitigating the impending Chinese invasion of Tibet. He taught that,

The Bodhisattva is like the mightiest of warriors; but his enemies are not common foes of flesh and bone. His fight is with the inner delusions, the afflictions of self-cherishing and ego grasping, those most terrible of demons that catch living beings in the snares of confusion and cause them forever to wander in pain, frustration, and sorrow. His mission is to harm ignorance and delusion, never living beings. These he looks upon with kindness, patience, and empathy, cherishing them like a mother cherishes her only child. He is the real hero, calmly facing any hardship in order to bring peace, happiness and liberation to the world.[5]

Kuno's radical transformation from monk to warrior and from trauma to ennoblement offered great inspiration to us as we envisioned the Jedi Warrior program. You can imagine our delight when we had the good fortune to introduce Kuno to Jim Channon. They swiftly formed a deep bond as brother warrior-monk-artists with a global vision of peace and wise use of power.

One at a Time

Another treasured mentor to whom we reached out for advice with the program was Ram Dass, the iconic author and widely respected wisdom teacher who earlier in his life was also known as Professor Richard Alpert of Harvard. Ram Dass had lived a profound and colorful life from his time as a traditional psychology professor at Harvard to the magical mystery tour that he shared with Timothy Leary pioneering psychedelic research there in the late 1960s when it was still legal.

Through years of intensive research and experimentation with LSD, Richard had learned the tough lesson that what goes up, ultimately, comes down. Disillusioned by the lack of sustainable realization offered in the entheosphere, Richard journeyed to India in search of deeper wisdom teachings that would deliver more enduring transformational results. Through an unlikely sequence of synchronistic events and encounters, he came to meet and study closely with Neem Karoli Baba, a truly remarkable teacher. After taking to heart the wisdom of his teacher, Richard returned to the States with the name Ram Dass and published a treasure trove of inspiring books, including his classic *Be Here Now*, which turned millions of people on to the possibilities of integrating contemplative wisdom into their lives and living with deeper wisdom, love, and dedication to service to others.

We first met Ram Dass shortly after he returned to the States in 1972 and came to work, study, and eventually teach closely with him over many years, especially in the emerging field of conscious living and dying and wisdom-informed compassionate care work. He was one of the pioneers of this work, along with Stephen and Ondrea Levine, Dale Borglam, Joan Halifax, and Wavy Gravy, during the early years of the hospice movement in the mid-to-late 1970s, when it began to take root in health care communities. When we moved to the Boston area to work on the Jedi program, we knew that Ram Dass was caring for his ailing and dying father in Cohasset, Massachusetts, not far from the base. We called him about two weeks into the program to connect and to see how this tender time of caring for his father was unfolding. We talked for a while about the gifts and challenges he was facing in this labor of love, and then Ram Dass asked us how our work with the Special Forces teams was going.

We sighed a bit, describing how the men had a wide range of attitudes and levels of engagement with the program and lamenting that even though we had been promised all enthusiastic volunteers, it hadn't turned out that way. Ram Dass astutely asked, "So, how many of you are on your core delivery team?" We replied that there were four of us with varying roles and responsibilities. To this he beamed a hearty response, "Well, that's great. There's four of you and only twenty-five of them. Just pick them off one at a time!" He added: "Michelle, you'll clearly make a connection with some of the guys, and Joel, you'll resonate with others, and the other members of your team will also build relationships and find their allies and draw them in. If each of you just opens the door to bring even a

128

handful of the men on board, you'll melt through the resistance and have a bunch of allies ready to take this learning journey with you."

We chuckled at Ram Dass's insightful strategy and really took it to heart. Later that evening at dinner, we shared his advice with Jack, Richard, and Anne, and all agreed that this was a wise approach for us to keep in mind and a bit less maddening than feeling like each of us had to make a deep connection with all of the men at this early stage of the program. We would refer to Ram Dass's advice often as the program progressed.

Jedi Warrior provided us with an unparalleled opportunity to open doors to meaningful close encounters with hundreds of remarkable individuals who offered valuable insight and inspiration, which informed the training. In speaking with this diverse array of mentors and colleagues, we had the recurring vision that these wise friends were tapped into streams of energy and inspiration, flowing to them from their mentors—who in turn were inspired by their mentors and so on, back through millennia. We envisioned these streams of wisdom energy reaching back across countless generations in lineages with roots in the distant past spanning the globe. The wisdom flowing from the past through these many teachers to us inspired us to transform our own lives and to pass along this wisdom to those whom we were to teach, who would then pass it on to those they knew—a force rippling out for generations to come.

new soft tactics

typical battle scenario FIRST EARTH

they parachuted in that morning and stood in two lines facing each opposing army. the EARTH BATTALION satellite above...beamed this image to the globe. the EARTH watched as this potential catastrophy awaited the conscience of one or both of the commanders to act. For they would have to bloody the EARTH BATTALION people in their path before they could attack
...and the world would know who started it!

THE FIRST EARTH BATTALION

SEVEN

High Stakes, Huge Cost

While we had received the green light to proceed with the program, we still needed to visit the base to meet with the battalion commander and one of the Special Ops teams to have them check us out and give their thumbs-up to proceed with the program. Our team welcomed the opportunity to meet these soldiers, visit their world, and test some of our assumptions, and ourselves, in their company.

Our team flew to Boston to meet up with Colonel Getty, Major Hendrix, and a Special Ops team assigned to test us out at Fort Devens. The team of soldiers we were assigned to meet with had two field exercises scheduled for us. The first one was a rucking and rock-climbing challenge in the mountains near the base. En route to the trailhead of a popular climbing spot near the base, we had the opportunity to talk casually with the men. From our conversations in the various vehicles, it was clear that the men had not been briefed in any detail on the nature of our program, though they had some sense that it was focused on advanced training in mind-fitness and physical training. Beyond that they had no idea what our program was about.

We hiked through the multicolor splendor of autumn foliage for about fifteen minutes to the base of a rock face that we were going to scale. The climb itself was challenging, yet technically not too difficult, likely a grade of 5.3 to 5.6. The soldiers negotiated the face with relative ease and watched to see how our team would manage the climb. Joel managed to impress the men with his agility in finding a clean and novel line and navigating some of the more challenging elements of the pitch. When he reached the top, a few of the guys commented on his agility and observed that he must be doing yoga. "You bet! I've been studying yoga and t'ai chi since I was in high school," Joel replied with a beaming smile. Jack, Bud, and Chris struggled a bit more with the climb but made it without mishap.

We rested at the top of the climb to enjoy the view and talked casually with the men, welcoming the opportunity to hear about their lives and enjoy a stunning view of the mountain and brilliant autumn foliage. The conversations were warm and personal but reinforced the feeling that these soldiers had only the vaguest idea about what our program was about.

We hiked down the trail to the parking lot and loaded up to drive north to Portland, Maine, for the next leg of our twofold test. Our team was curious about what lay in store. We caravanned up the interstate highway to Portland, following Captain Dobson, who was in the lead. He had settled into a steady speed of fifty-five miles per hour on a wide-open highway, a gesture that seemed a vivid declaration that this man operated strictly by the book and likely obeyed orders. With most of the traffic streaking by, our team was a bit maddened by his strict adherence to not exceeding the speed limit, yet as we grew to know him in the ensuing months, we came to deeply admire and respect him for his unwavering dedication to being a role model and source of inspiration for those who reported to him.

Dodging Freighters

As we drove into Portland late in the afternoon, we made our way to a Coast Guard station in South Portland. We were briefed that our next test was to join the men for a swim across the harbor, launching from Bug Light Point and swimming to Fort Allen Park, a distance of about a mile. They were prepared for our arrival and had a Boston Whaler boat ready to accompany us. We pulled on wet suits and clipped into a rope line to swim tethered together and made our way to the boat launch just as the last light was fading from the sky. The water was cold, but the suits offered sufficient insulation to make it tolerable. We pushed out into the darkening, choppy bay.

As we began the swim, the men were in buoyant spirits, and there was a lot of banter as we headed out, with a few sea shanties sung. Once we were out a way from shore swimming in the dark, we began to realize that we had to find a safe path across the opening to a busy harbor with ferry lanes and dodge several freighters entering and departing the harbor. Our accompanying boat was in radio contact with the ships, but the stakes were still high and the dangers real. As the swim and night rolled on, the chill of the waters combined with fatigue began to set in, and we all needed to pace ourselves to accommodate the changing tides, the incoming and outgoing ships, and the occasional cramp that grabbed a leg like a searing shark bite.

Gradually the banter and singing subsided, and we all settled into synchronizing our strokes and managing our energy to have enough juice to make it all the way without needing to get pulled into the boat. At some point along the way, one of the guys on our team commented about the strain of needing to pee. One of the soldiers laughed and said, "I don't know about you, sir, but I don't have a date waiting for me on the other side, so just let it flow." There was a welcome sigh of relief and a wave of laughter to buoy us on.

As we approached the other shore, waves of encouragement carried us on. Reaching the beach, we all joined in a cheer for a safe crossing with everyone having made it across, and we were welcomed by warm drinks, dry towels, and snacks. Several men congratulated Jack as the most senior swimmer in the chain on having made the swim, and a few comments were offered that maybe we would make the cut on being able to keep up with them. Some commented that they wondered what new moves they might learn from us. We all slept well that night, a bit exhausted and exhilarated from the intensity and the success of our day of adventures and trials together.

Mandate: Get Them Home Alive!

Back at the base the next day, we were invited to a briefing with Colonel Getty, Major Hendrix, and Captain Dobson. We met in the lobby of the headquarters and were escorted up an elegant set of stairs to a well-appointed meeting room on the second floor with no windows but with long drapes on the walls and a very high ceiling. Colonel Getty opened the meeting with a warm welcome to us and announced that he was pleased that we had successfully passed muster with his teams and officially welcomed us warmly into the program. He then proceeded to remind us of the terms of our contract and to essentially swear us to secrecy, informing us that we were about to be briefed on the actual mission that the soldiers we would be training were assigned to.

There was a profound sense of gravity in his framing of this coming revelation, and we all felt a deep responsibility of being entrusted with a dangerous secret. At the time of our visit to the base, tensions between the United States and the Soviet Union were at an all-time high, and the Soviets had been on hair-trigger alert for nuclear attack for months. This was prompted by the threat posed by NATO deploying 108 Pershing II nuclear missiles in Europe with the ability to take out targets in the USSR in ten minutes. The tensions were exacerbated by the taunting tactics of U.S. military flights, which would head straight toward Moscow and then turn at the last minute before entering Soviet airspace. Just months before, a malfunction of Soviet satellite warning systems due to solar activity had triggered an incident that was regarded as the closest the United States and the USSR had ever come to launching an all-out nuclear war.

With a wave of his hand, the colonel signaled for the drapes on the wall to our right to be pulled open, revealing a large detailed topographical map of the field of operations, which lay deep within the interior regions of what was then the Soviet Union. The colonel proceeded to explain how the field of operations for the Tenth Special Forces Group was in Central and Eastern Europe, running clandestine operations behind the boundary lines for the Warsaw Pact countries in Eastern Europe. Our teams would be the eyes and ears of U.S. intelligence on the ground, doing deep reconnaissance far behind enemy lines.

The colonel and his staff proceeded to explain that if our soldiers were to be deployed, they would be dropped deep inside hostile territory in the depth of night, make their way to their target zones to dig in, gather, and send out reconnaissance regarding the movement of troops and supplies, and discover and develop allies and assets within the local communities that they were embedded within. Knowing all the while that their radio transmissions would be closely watched for and that their positions could be identified by triangulating the signals, they would need to move quickly and cover their tracks, and if pursued, they would be carrying minimal ammunition to fight back with, and so their best chances would be to travel light, remain agile, evade capture, and run rather than dig in for a fight. Knowing how to conserve and focus energy and optimize their minds and bodies would be key to their survival. Our program was considered of the utmost importance.

One other surprising part of this briefing was a firm word of caution for our team to keep in mind that, as we arrived in the local community and settled into our lodgings near the base, we should be cautious in casual encounters with local people because any one of them could be a KGB spy. This was framed as: "If you find yourself standing in line at the supermarket, and someone starts to talk with you, be careful what you say. They may well be KGB operatives." This certainly caught our attention. We were also strongly cautioned that we should just assume that our phones were bugged and be careful not to speak of any details on the phone about our work at the base. Given that at this time we were still in the midst of the Cold War, this was unsettling to say the least.

At the culmination of this presentation, Colonel Getty soberly declared, "The bottom line is that if things light up in some hot spot in the world and our teams are deployed, this will likely be a one-way ticket. These teams will be dropped in so deep behind enemy lines into hostile territory that there would be very little chance of extraction or exfiltration. We don't realistically expect more than one in ten of our guys to make it home alive."

Hearing the colonel's words hit deep and hard. All of us on the SportsMind team seemed to draw one deep breath together and let out a long sigh. Glances flashed between us. This was the first time this point had been mentioned in all our briefings to date. As the gravity of this sunk in, Chris asked, "So, Colonel Getty, are you saying that we're training these men for a suicide mission?" Colonel Getty replied with great poise and intensity, "No. What I'm asking is that your team give these guys everything you have to maximize their chances of getting home alive!"

After this briefing we shared lunch at the officer's club and then accompanied Colonel Getty and Major Hendrix to the Armistice Day Parade. For Jack, Larry, and Bud, this military-on-parade was more of a familiar sight and not a big deal. But for me (Joel), this was eye opening and the very first time I had encountered such a display of military presence, solemnity, and sentimentality. My only contact with veterans had been growing up with a grandfather who had fought in the artillery in World War I and a great uncle and cousin who had served as physician and nurse in frontline field hospitals in France during World War II.

The streets of the base parade path were lined with families of the soldiers and kids waving flags. A sense of somber celebration and quiet honoring was all-pervasive, honoring not only the lives lost in previous wars, but also the fact that everyone there in uniform might well be a casualty in wars and conflicts yet to come. The families of the men we'd be training wouldn't even know where their loved ones had been sent as their missions would be highly classified. If they were deployed, it was unlikely that they would return. There were many moist eyes and some tears being shed by wives, some older kids, and an occasional soldier.

Watching the parade and listening to the honoring of various individuals and groups who had died, there was a palpable feeling present in the collective field that many of those who had joined the service were motivated by a sincere wish to serve and protect noble ideals and defend vulnerable people. It was a testimony to the qualities of courage, valor, and compassion worthy of honor that prevail despite deceptions and undisclosed agendas that often precede a declaration of war.

Having come of age in the midst of the Vietnam era, we had witnessed a myriad of government lies exposed, ideals and familiar norms questioned, and people standing up to say no to war, the bombing of innocent civilians as collateral damage, and the desecration and destruction of ecosystems. Yet here was Joel, witnessing this spectacle of a military parade with all its pomp and circumstance, sitting with the base commander and his staff, and feeling truly moved with an admiration and sincere honoring of the dedication and sacrifice that so many men and women had made to defend their countries from aggressive invading foes.

At the end of this memorable initiatory day, our team circled up to reflect and unpack the revelations it had offered. It was crystal clear that we had all taken Colonel Getty's mandate to heart regarding "give these guys everything you have to maximize their chances of getting home alive!" This led us to reach out with a request to meet up with the teams the next day to hear from them in their own words how they felt about having a mission with such poor odds of survival.

Meeting with the teams the next morning, we mentioned the colonel's briefing of the previous day and asked them what their thoughts and feelings were about being assigned such a dire, high-stakes mission. After a brief silence, one of the team sergeants stepped up to explain, in a matter-of-fact, lighthearted way, "Look at it this way, we are in the U.S. Army, but we're Special Forces, the very best in the army, so we don't have to put up with all the ordinary army BS. We get the best training there is. We get the best gear and equipment you can ask for. We get to swim and scuba dive, ski, climb mountains, parachute, travel to exotic places, learn foreign languages, get advanced training that certifies us as paramedics. We handle and master the use of powerful exotic weapons, and we get to blow things up. What more could an all-American guy ask for? And if or when the balloon goes up, then we are going to be America's first line of defense. That's what we signed up for."

A wave of affirming nods, gestures, and HUAs rippled among the men. The sergeant continued, "So . . . I'm sorry, sir, but does that answer your question?" His declaration conveyed the essence of what we gleaned from our meeting and would inform our planning and preparations.

Up Against the Wall

Following this visit to the base, our team flew to Washington, D.C., to spend a few days with Jack and his wife, Anne, at their home and to do some planning work for the program informed by our time on base and the recent revelations of the missions for our teams. We had a sense of excitement as well as a sobering, overarching sense of the gravity and high stakes of this assignment. We were humbled yet excited by this opportunity to expand the horizons and dimensions of military training.

Nestled in Jack and Anne's living room at their brownstone in the nation's capital not far from the Pentagon and accompanied by their faithful dog, Shaba, who would be our comfort and companion throughout the program, we mapped out more of the fine mesh of details for our six months of training, confirmed the schedule, and made some final decisions on who our guest speakers would be and when their visits would be best timed. The work flowed with a sense of ease, and we were all in alignment with how the program would be structured and roll out and on the unique and special roles that each of us would play. Our time and work together were exhilarating, and we shared a collective sense that the significance and potential impacts of this program was vaster than any of us could fully fathom.

After a long day working out details of our program design, Jack stood up and with a clap of his hands said, "OK team, let's bundle up and go out for a walk." Stepping out onto the brisk, clear autumn air, onto the busy streets of D.C., we followed Jack to a location yet to be disclosed. Rounding a corner in the golden, late-afternoon sunlight, we crossed a street and found ourselves at the Vietnam Memorial. As we silently approached and touched the wall, it felt like a silent benediction for our work together. Jack walked the wall with a sense of grace, dignity, and solemnity, pausing here and there to point out names of fallen comrades from his two tours of duty in Vietnam. Standing there before the memorial wall, he shared stories of courage and valor of the men he served with on the battlefields of Vietnam, his eyes moistened by his reflections.

While the Vietnam Memorial commemorated the 58,300 fallen U.S. warriors, we also honored the many other lives lost in this war, holding in our thoughts the estimated 2,000,000 Vietnamese civilians, 1,100,000 North Vietnamese and Viet Cong fighters, 50,000 to 150,000 Cambodians, 50,000 Laotians, and tens of thousands more killed since the war ended by land mines and unexploded ordinances, most of whom were children.[1]

In time, our conversation turned to touch the heartbreak conveyed in the reports that had given rise to the Jedi Warrior program and the estimates that between two and twenty times more veterans had died from suicide than had died in actual combat. Taking to heart the sobering vision of an additional 174,900 to 1,166,000 men and women who had perished from various forms of swift or slow-burn suicide after their tours of duty, we felt a deeper appreciation for the depths of heartbreak, guilt, trauma, courage, and compassion of the senior officers who had enlisted us to design this ultimate warrior training program for the next generations of Special Forces warriors. We admired their humility in admitting that they

139

were searching for wiser disciplines for nurturing the strength and development of modern-day warriors that would create less enduring trauma and pain for them and others and were turning to us for this wisdom.

As the sun dropped lower in the sky, our minds stretched to envision the memorial wall expanding from its actual 493 feet and 6 inches, or 1.65 football fields in length, to encompass the total number of lives lost in this war, including the suicides. This expanded vision of the memorial wall reached the length of between 77 and 127 football fields in length—up to 7.25 miles long. This would be more than the entire reach of Pennsylvania Avenue in Washington, D.C., a sobering image reminding us of the millions of lives extinguished by this devastating war.

Bathed in the golden rays of the setting sun we tried to wrap our hearts and minds around this vast and sobering image of the men, women, and children who had been killed in combat or who had died due to the ongoing trauma, horrors, and impacts following this war. This potent image burned into our hearts the realization that our mission with Jedi Warrior was to offer our soldiers the most robust, meaningful, and wholistic arsenal of advanced wholistic personal mastery skills available to increase their capacity to recognize and befriend their inner enemies and to stop the war inside.

PART TWO

BOOTS ON THE GROUND: A GUIDE TO JEDI WARRIOR TRAINING

warriorwork

realization

BODYWORK — The moments when serenity guides your physical conflicts with another or your movement through life.

BIOWORK — The moment when the care of your body instrument is more important than the taste of the food in front of you.

HEADWORK — The moment you begin to see when you are just reacting from a mind program within a culturally induced trance.

HEARTWORK — The moment when you recognize that deep inside we are all one.

SPIRITWORK — The moment that you appreciate the perfect order in the universe, the biosphere and your mind. Then you will sense the power of a masterplan.

PSI WORK — The moment you feel the universe send its own kind of energy tingling through your body and your mind takes off.

ECOWORK — The moment that you know that the plants around you are conscious as well as the air and earth mother below.

PEACEWORK — The moment you dedicate your life to actions on behalf of PEOPLE AND PLANET . . . *then* you have become a player.

FRAMEWORK — The moment you see you can step out of an organizational pattern and reprogram the system.

How will you know when you get there?

answer these states of being honestly.

and you will be there . . .

THE FIRST EARTH BATTALION

EIGHT

Vi Cit Tecum

On August 3, we landed at Logan Airport in Boston and picked up our leased car to drive east through Boston and Cambridge and cut to West Acton where we would be spending the weekend moving into the modest two-story, four-bedroom Victorian house that would be our home and base camp for the next six months. This new home, just off the main street of West Acton, was about a twenty-minute drive out to Fort Devens and equidistant to Thoreau's fabled cabin retreat at Walden Pond. While we'd soon host a cavalcade of luminary guest speakers visiting for the program, our house would be home for the two of us, Jack and his wife, Anne, Richard (and at times his friend Catherine), and Shaba, Jack and Anne's beloved pup. This promised to be an odd but workable living arrangement for us as a team, having been uprooted from our homes, families, and communities, to dedicate the next six months to working on this program six to seven days a week, fourteen to sixteen hours a day. As we settled in, it was clear that we were all bone tired, having made this big move after months and years of preparation. Richard, having just come on board with our team a mere six weeks earlier, had been especially caught up in the whirlwind of rearranging his life to leave his home, two kids, aikido dojo, and therapy practice in Marin to join us on the other side of the country.

At 6:00 a.m. just after sunrise on August 5, Joel, Richard, Jack, and Chris left for their first full day on base. After a short drive on the interstate highway, they pulled into the guard station for what would become a familiar ritual of crossing the threshold each day into the base and a different world. With men in uniform everywhere, neat well-trimmed grounds and buildings looking like they all dated back for decades, it was a surreal scene, reminiscent of a movie set.

Driving through the clean streets and manicured landscaping, they found their way to a parking lot near the Special Forces buildings assigned to them, where they were warmly greeted by Top Sergeant Ramon, who walked them down the hall to their rather drab interview rooms, each with three chairs, a desk, and an old army recruiting poster sagging on the wall. Richard and Joel were in one interview room, and Chris and Jack in another, meeting with the men, one by one. Little did we know what would be revealed this day.

We were assigned twenty-five of the best trained and equipped soldiers in the world, so-called million-dollar men, tough, highly skilled, committed, and well-trained in traditional military disciplines. Except for one skilled martial artist, these men were unfamiliar with the disciplines of self-regulation and self-mastery and types of inner transformational technologies that we would be introducing to them. All these soldiers were Caucasian males, middle class, mostly with roots in the Midwest and the South. Their ages spanned from twenty-two to forty-one, and they were diverse in their beliefs, philosophies, physical builds, and worldviews. Their average time in the service was ten years, ranging from a minimum of five years to twenty-two years. Though they had all passed exams that placed them at a college level, only four of them had graduated from college, two from West Point.

Our first soldier arrived unceremoniously wearing cut-off jeans, a stained T-shirt, and rubber sandals. He had a wad of chewing tobacco in his cheek and a Coke can in his hand to spit in. With a kind of blank expression, he introduced himself last name first, rank, and serial number and shook our hands. Richard and I (Joel) gave each other a quizzical glance and took our seats. At first impression, he presented as really fit from the waist up, with a classic American male physique, but didn't seem to have been working out to develop a lot of strength and flexibility in his legs.

We dove into the interview asking basic questions: "What have been your military training and specialties? How long have you served? What's your family status? Career goals?" It turned out he was single, had been in the service a couple years, and was eager to see some action and serve his country.

As we launched into deeper questions about his goals and expectations for participating in the program, we asked, "So, what do you hope to learn in this program?" He answered, "I don't know." Long pause. "And what personal goals do you have in participating in this program?" "Well sir, if it can help me build my strength and endurance, that would be a good thing." Then we asked, "So why did you volunteer for this program?" and with this he looked truly confused and responded, "Well, it wasn't so much a personal decision. Most of the guys on my team thought this could be a good opportunity to expand our skills, and we wanted to stay together and not bust up our team." Richard and I exchanged another glance, this time with a sense of dread. After a long pause, we asked, "Do you have any questions for us about the program?" To this he confessed, "Well, honestly, I'm not so sure what this program is all about, so I don't really have any questions. I guess I'll just see what you have to offer." He spit a thick brown ooze from his chewing tobacco quid under his cheek into his Coke can and left.

Richard and I leaned back and looked at each other with a kind of silent groan. As the morning interviews continued, the overall outlook was eerily the same. Some of the guys merely answered our questions with simple "yes sir" or "no sir" responses. We managed to tease out some questions from the guys who were curious: Will we develop extrasensory powers? Will our families be involved in any ways? Will we have to stop smoking or using chewing tobacco? Will we be spending much time in the field doing mission simulations?

Some of the men were reserved, some suspicious, and some genuinely courteous or friendly. Most seemed distant. We were clearly outsiders entering their realm, and they had very little information about us that would give us any credibility in their minds. Given how uninformed they were, they were understandably guarded, sizing us up and probing to get a read on who we were and where we were coming from as we entered their world.

At the end of the interviews, only two of the men had conveyed even a glimmer of a sense that they were excited about the program and looking forward to it. After preparing for years for this incredible opportunity to work closely with twenty-five volunteers who we had expected would be well briefed on the program, we were stunned! Based on our agreements outlined in our contract, we had devoted the past two and a half years to developing a robust program for highly motivated, well-informed, and fully engaged volunteers who were totally stoked to have such an incredible opportunity for personal and professional development. Michelle and I had prepared for this program like we would prepare to teach one of our graduate courses at the university. Yet after these interviews, we were all left with a sinking sense of deep disappointment and, to some degree, betrayal.

Meeting up afterward with Jack and Chris, it was clear that we were all getting the same read on the situation. These men had not been well briefed. It was clear that they were focused on practicalities, wanted to see results, and everything we brought to them was going to need to be relevant to their lives and missions. They likely wouldn't have a great deal of interest in theory or the fascinating research that might offer meaning and depth to the learning. Their priority was on results that would give them an advantage on the battlefield because their lives depended on it. If we were in their position and had their missions, we'd likely feel the same way.

On the drive home and into the evening, we processed the revelations of the day, sorting through the implications of working with twenty-five "voluntolds" rather than volunteers and how this would impact our plans. We would likely need to radically recalibrate our expectations, curriculum, and approach to training. We were truly blindsided, and it had never occurred to any of us that we'd be in this compromised position.

The distress of this was compounded by the discovery that, contrary to our contractual agreements, the build-out of the classroom, dojo, and lab had not even begun yet! This meant that rather than launching straight into the training as we had planned in a packed schedule with no space to juggle, some aspects of our training would be delayed by at least a week while the guys hustled to find the lumber, paint, wiring, and other supplies needed to build out the spaces.

As near as we could tell they didn't have a budget, a plan, or a materials list and were just winging it with the whole build-out process. Yet, we later came to appreciate the incredible resourcefulness of these guys in "acquiring" whatever supplies and resources were required. One of the men came in and proudly announced that he found some paint for the classroom. Jack responded, "That's great! Where'd you find it?" and with a shy twinkle, he simply responded, "You probably don't want to know the answer to that question, sir." These were can-do guys. If there was a need, and they had the mission and the motivation to fulfill that need, we could rest assured that it would be sorted out, one way or the other.

As we continued our interviews the next day, they had a bit of a different tone to them. It was clear that the men had talked among themselves, briefing each other on their own read of us from the day before. On this second day we mostly met with the older, higher-ranking men, and they were prepared to anticipate and respond to our questions at a higher level than the soldiers we interviewed on the first day. These men were much clearer on what they wanted from this program and had chosen to participate. They too were looking for practical value but expressed more sincere interest in developing their awareness and resilience and expanding their capacity to lead and perform. There was some sense that the program would enhance and expand their mental and physical capabilities. A couple of the soldiers half seriously asked about developing some cool psychic powers. But as our interviews progressed, we came to realize that even among the team leadership, there was only the vaguest sense of what this project was about, what they would learn, or what they should expect. We were aghast at how little they had been briefed.

As all this sank in, we stretched our minds to conceive of what an odd, novel, and disorienting situation this must be for these soldiers. Nothing like this had ever been attempted in their ranks. How could they in their wildest imagination anticipate what an odyssey this program would be, and what their participation would ultimately mean for them? It was vividly clear that we were all way out of our familiar areas of operations and that we were all going to need to be attentive, agile, adaptive, and skillful in discerning a wise and meaningful path through this new terrain.

On day three, we departed from our house at 0600 to drive to the base and meet up with the men on the neatly mowed lawn next to the cemetery to stretch and warm up before a morning run. This was a quiet pastoral setting for a workout, with morning bird songs flitting through the soft, filtered light streaming through the morning mists in the old oaks. Just stretching with the rising sun, we were already soaked with sweat as the heat and humidity of early August and sweet smells of freshly mowed grass enveloped us. It was an odd and poignant scene: twenty-eight buff, energetic guys stretching and warming up next to the low rock wall bordering neat lines of gravestones of fallen comrades. From a meditative perspective it was picture-perfect in the sense of wisely pausing to remember and take to heart the inescapable reality of our mortality as we begin each new day of our precious, fleeting lives and prepare ourselves to clarify what is most important and essential for us in this day to truly live on purpose, true to spirit, without drifting off into the wastelands of mindless habits. The men were in their prime, feeling invincible, and had the illusion of being prepared to grapple with whatever the world might throw at them. Strangely, in all the months that we observed this morning ritual of working out at the cemetery, no one would ever comment on the poignancy of this setting.

In our work with the teams over the months to come, we would participate in everything they did with one important exception—we weren't allowed to join the men to parachute due to liability concerns, which we could well understand. During a break Chris asked the jumpmaster, Sergeant Jordon, what it would take to teach him how to parachute like a Special Forces pro. Jordie, in his humorous, understated manner, beamed a wry smile and replied, "Just one shove, sir." We all got a good laugh out of that.

Mercifully, the weather shifted later in the day with a gentle rain and cooler temperatures. It was a welcome respite from the previous week of parboiling heat and humidity as the men prepared to launch into a physically grueling Army Physical Fitness Test (APFT) that involved a two-mile run, push-ups, sit-ups, and pull-ups, plus a stretching flexibility test. Over the course of the next six months, we'd repeat this test four times to measure any changes and improvements resulting from our training.

The mood was a mix of boisterous anticipation, seriousness, and camaraderie akin to the tone of athletes preparing for a sporting event or competition where everyone was hoping to do their best and wishing each other well. Throughout the morning they cheered each other on to score high so that it would be more difficult to surpass their scores later in the program. They pushed hard through the tests with confidence and determination. In the end nearly all their scores surpassed the army's maximum scores by an impressive margin.

After this intense morning of physical testing and a short break for lunch, the men suited up in full camo gear and boots to drive straight on into an even more grueling Special Forces fifteen-mile ruck march, each person loaded with a hundred-pound pack, an M16 (add eight pounds), and, for some, an additional M9 grenade launcher. Their goal was to cover the distance as fast as they could, racing against the clock, but not against each other in a test of personal endurance and strength. When they finished the ruck, they each had three shots to hit a bull's-eye the size of a gold coin at fifty meters. Their performance on this test would serve as a baseline to assess their progress and performance over the course of the program.

These guys were in their element, right at home in their camo, lugging their heavy rucksacks and carrying their weapons. They were calm, assured, intent, and at ease. They'd trained hard, and this mode was second nature to them. Compared to tests to come later in the program, and to their actual mission descriptions, this was a relatively simple, undemanding test.

It was our first moment of seeing the men fully suited up and in their natural state. A bit of a chill ran through us as we came face-to-face with their warrior spirits fully locked, loaded, and ready to rumble. For Jack and Richard, as former military, this was a familiar world. For Joel, this was new, uncharted territory.

Two and a half hours later, dehydrated and drenched in sweat, the men crossed the finish line. Standing in our unstained SportsMind uniforms, we were humbled by their accomplishment and somewhat self-conscious that we hadn't joined them in this ordeal.

As we mingled with the men at the firing range, Jack asked one of the officers if we could fire any of the weapons. The staff sergeant lit up with a smile, handed us each an M16, and proceeded to give us instructions for how to work the safety lock and shift from single shot to semiautomatic. "And this," he beamed, "is what you can call rock-and-roll, my friends. Light it up!" He was delighted to see us take a few shots. There we were, belly on the ground, M16 in hand, taking aim at the target, with weapons blazing around us and fire sparking from the muzzles of the guns. Joel thought to himself, *I am definitely not in Kansas anymore, or Seattle, or any other familiar realm that I have ever inhabited. I am a guest in this world, with a lot to learn and hopefully a lot to share.* With smug smiles, some of the guys came by to show us their targets, most with the center of the bull's-eye fully blown out.

It felt like we all crossed a threshold that day, as we entered deeper into their world, and they welcomed and included us. Jack had stepped fully into his role as team leader. Strong, determined, dedicated, hard driving, and demanding, he was learning to be more open, inclusive, and collaborative with all of us on the team. This would continue to be a learning zone for him, deep in opportunity and challenge. Richard, Michelle, Joel, Chris, Larry, and Horst all flowed with it, at times honoring Jack's experience and continually nudging him back toward a more inclusive, collegial mode of collaboration that was more our norm at SportsMind than the command-and-control mode that Jack was so accustomed to.

At home that evening, our attention turned to completing our preparations for the official launch of the program the next day, and each of us set off to fine-tune our portions of the program. Jack and Richard stayed up into the wee hours of the night finishing off some fine details. We admired their dedication.

We Begin!

Rising early before the sun the next morning, we loaded up our two cars and made the drive to the base. We were well prepared and acutely aware that, with this audience, it was difficult to anticipate what the reception and response will be.

After morning workout and breakfast, the opening session began in the dojo at 0900 hours. In addition to our core team, we also had Chris, Larry, and Horst, our two Special Forces teams, the battalion commander, Colonel Getty, and Colonel Barnes, the commander of the Special Forces Group. There was a somber, ceremonial sense that this truly was a historic moment. As we approached this threshold of lighting the fuse for this program to officially commence, there was a rich tone of anticipation and solemnity mixed with curiosity.

Opening the session with introductions to all our team members, Chris proceeded to give one of the most inspired presentations we'd ever seen him do, speaking with insight and passion, invoking the great warriors and traditions of the past, including the Japanese samurais, African Zulus, and Roman centurions, and illuminating the historical significance of our program and how the way of the warrior will be clarified and strengthened by our work together. With a dramatic flourish, he ceremoniously presented Colonel Barnes with a samurai sword on behalf of our team, and Barnes responded in turn offering our team a dagger from the Special Forces.

Colonel Barnes then stepped up to speak to the uniqueness of this program within the Special Forces and the extraordinary opportunity that such a training presents. He acknowledged that this was new and uncharted territory for the Special Forces to enter into and that this might be a glimpse of the future for Special Ops training. Concluding his speech with encouragement for each man to make the most of this rare opportunity and acknowledging that this training would carry the men into territory unfamiliar and even strange to them, Barnes said that he wanted everyone to give this a 100-percent effort to master the new skills and integrate them into their arsenal of warrior skills and strengths. Given the unease and lack of engagement that we had encountered during our interviews, our team was left to wonder how all this was landing for these guys.

Next up was Richard Strozzi-Heckler, wearing his *gi* and *hakama*. He told the men about the deep history and tradition of the martial art of aikido. The soldiers, all suited up in their new white gis with their army issue name patch neatly sewn onto the left breast, sat listening attentively on the mat, with a small group of officers and senior NCOs from the battalion headquarters sitting nearby in chairs.

About midway through Richard's presentation, Jack let loose an ear-splitting yell from the back of the room and came charging forward toward Richard, brandishing a butcher knife above his head. The intensity of his incoming attack led us all to brace for impact. This was certainly a convincing simulation. As Jack closed in for the kill, Richard adeptly stepped aside, grabbing Jack's knife hand and twisting his wrist in the *kote gaeshi* technique that sent Jack flipping head over heels to land on the mat. By twisting the knife from Jack's hand and putting it out of reach, Richard ended the first wave of Jack's attack, which next led to Jack leaping to his feet and aiming a kick at Richard's groin. Richard once again threw Jack to the mat. Undaunted, Jack continued with a volley of punches, grabs, and kicks, while Richard continued to blend, redirect, and deflect, demonstrating a variety of classic aikido moves.

On one long throw toward the edge of the mat, Jack picked up a hidden M16 with an affixed bayonet and with his tenacious Marine spirit came barreling down on Richard with a battle cry. Having led his company through two tours of Vietnam, Jack knew how to handle this weapon, and he charged toward Richard with a look of fierce determination. The drama of the engagement took us all by surprise, and there were moments when we were all holding our breath. Sensei Strozzi-Heckler stepped aside, evading Jack's lunge, guiding the force of his attack in a tight spiraling circle that brought Jack hard to the mat, with Richard in possession of the weapon. As Richard put the weapon aside, there was a momentary sense that this dance was complete, only to be shattered by Jack leaping up to begin a new cycle of attacks, grabbing at Richard's throat, only to be pinned to the mat. Jack battled on, struggling to reach the M16 inches beyond his grasp on the mat. His persistence compelled Richard to crank down tighter on Jack's arm until the pain finally led Jack to relent and tap the mat indicating that he had reached his limit.

This free-form combat, called *jiyu-waza,* offered an inspiring glimpse of the power, grace, and wisdom of aikido as a martial art. It was clear that both Jack and Richard were wholeheartedly committed to the intensity of this fierce play. When the attack was hard and fast, Richard yielded: he stepped aside and allowed Jack's own momentum to propel him to the other side of the mat. With other moves, Richard stepped in, blending with the force of the attack to guide and redirect it. This dynamic embodied energetic interplay and interfusion of awareness, intent, sensitivity, responsive force blending, spiraling, and rolling had the quality of call and response between the *uke*, the attacker, and the *nage*, the one responding to the attack, by embodying the many skillful methods of the art of aikido. The elegance, modulation, and dynamism of their pulsing interaction conveyed the beauty, power, and wisdom of the art as an inspiring example of differentiated individuals dynamically linked in fluid embodied communication.

The visceral intensity of this live simulation offered a sense of the immediacy of the potentially relevant applications of aikido. Richard's philosophy and style of teaching focused less on the mechanics of technique and much more on the deeper principles of grounding, centering, blending, sensing, and responding to the flow of *ki*, the subtle flow of vital energy that weaves all things and all beings into the seamless fabric of reality.

We would mirror this approach in the Mind Lab, teaching the basics of mind-fitness training, biopsybernautics, and meditation, starting with the most tangible and gradually moving to deeper, subtler levels of awareness and responsive control.

Family Night

At the end of the first week, our team hosted a family night welcoming all the soldiers and their families to gather, meet us, and be introduced to the nature, content, and spirit of the program. Our team, plus Anne, arrived early to set up the dojo with some tables with handouts, refreshments, and demonstration zones. After a humidly intense week of smelling sweat and snuff, seeing men in camouflage gear, and hearing rifle fire, we watched the men walk in the room hand in hand with wives and girlfriends, kids in tow. Seeing the men with babes in arms and even with some grandparents tagging along was quite a sight to behold. One image really stands out to us of Thorne, a tough, hard-driving, and formidable soldier, walking in all cleaned up, hair nicely combed, with his infant daughter cradled tenderly in his arms. Our hearts quivered to behold this.

The mood and dress of the evening was a bit like a church social or a high school reunion, with small gaggles of friends clustered together, kids whirling around, and the single men in small groups looking a bit awkward and out of place. Without their uniforms, rank strips and insignias, rifles, rucksacks, and snuff cans, these fit, clean-cut men were an ordinary-looking cross-section of all-American guys—the jocks, the geeks, the tough guys, the philosophers, all the many shades of masculinity, all mingling together with their families. We felt privileged for this opportunity to be in service to them and their families and grateful that the army leadership recognized the value of involving the families from the beginning.

Underneath the social awkwardness, cordiality, and sense of community, there was an undercurrent of concern, especially in the minds of some of the spouses and girlfriends. Our vision, plan, and intention for this first family evening was to quell those fears and to inspire and enlist the families to understand and embrace their partners in ways that would support them in making lifestyle changes that enhanced their health, well-being, and relationships. We also recognized that the families had a lot to gain from their partners participating in this training.

The evening opened with a warm welcome and discussion of our logo, composed of a pair of flying horses, with an ancient warrior's helmet and crossed light sabers. Underneath was the Green Berets' Latin motto *De Oppresso Liber* (Liberators of the Oppressed), coupled with *Vi Cit Tecum* (May the Force Be with You). The visionary scope of this program, with its deep roots in the mythos of Jim Channon's *Evolutionary Tactics* along with the imagery and symbolism of George Lucas's Jedi warriors, inspired high popular regard and respect within the local community for this program.

Given that our program was following on the heels of the notorious Project MKUltra—which had the sordid history of brainwashing, psychological torture, and unwitting dosing of soldiers with LSD, which had left the minds of some soldiers in ruins—this evening provided us with the opportunity to assure the men and their partners that this program was based on good science and research and authentic moral and ethical standards and was guided by credible, skilled, and caring professionals who had no plans to subject the men to mind-bending doses of LSD or other mind-altering drugs or to immerse them in any destructive mental conditioning. When we announced point-blank that we would not be dosing the soldiers with LSD or any other mind-altering substances, there was a noticeable sigh of relief, and some of the tension in the room evaporated.

After a series of minipresentations by Horst on basic concepts of health, fitness, and peak performance and by Richard on the principles of aikido and the tenets of warrior training, Michelle and Joel stepped up to offer a glimpse of some of the universally useful ideas and simple practices related to mastering stress, focusing attention, and optimizing mind-body that were core to this training program. We introduced some of the basic elements of personal mastery and advanced mind-fitness training, such as explaining "choice follows awareness," "you can only modify what you monitor," and "listen to (and respond to) the whispers, don't wait for the screams." It was heartening to see many heads nod and tensions melt away. Our session was designed to be as universally relevant as possible and to offer value, insight, and inspiration for as many people in the room as possible, even the older kids. We wanted the families and couples to leave inspired to continue to talk about and explore these themes together and to apply them in their lives.

Our session concluded with a demonstration of one of our biofeedback devices that measured levels of muscle tension and displayed those levels as a balloon rising into the air with increasing tension and descending with relaxation. The goal of the game was to avoid the balloons being blown up by incoming missiles on the screen through learning how to control the elevation of the balloon by consciously tensing and deeply relaxing.

This task was more challenging than might be expected, especially for anyone who was used to operating from a macho "I can power my way through any kind of obstacle" mind-set and approach to life. The game required deep, grounded, in-the-body wisdom and attunement to the vital synergy of intentional effort and letting go with ease. This was new territory and a new operating system for most of these men. We concluded our presentation with an invitation for anyone who was interested to join us for a test drive with the game during the social hour and mingling time that followed.

We instantly had a long line of volunteers, eager to take our biofeedback game for a test drive, mostly composed of kids, a couple of wives, and some of the soldiers. It was heartwarming to see the soldiers rooting their kids on and then giving the game a try themselves, only to be cheered on by their kids, taunted by their teammates, and in some cases humbled by their children, who bested their dads at the game.

As the only woman on our team, Michelle was a magnet for the wives, girlfriends, and curious, shy young daughters who were fascinated by her presence on the team. She welcomed questions about her story and how she came to gather the knowledge and experience to be designing and guiding advanced mind-fitness training for these Green Berets.

As we were packing to leave, Chief Kirby of Bravo Team stopped us at the door to say, "You have won all our respect. We are all on board now." We were all grateful and relieved. This memorable evening of including and honoring the families and significant relationships of these soldiers generated a potent sense and feeling of potential for this kind of wholistic, integral, fully human training.

Crossing this long-anticipated threshold of engaging the families to support the soldiers was a significant milestone for the Jedi Warrior program and a testament to these soldiers' intimate connections and how their well-being, capacity, and ability relied on those interdependencies. This evening also affirmed the powerful truth that both the inner suffering and the well-being of a soldier did not just affect him. His state of being impacted the lives, the health and well-being, of his family and community in ways that could uplift and heal or traumatize and devastate their quality of life.

THE WARRIOR MONK

Chinese Monks were often attacked by robbers. They developed a new fighting system based on using the force of the attacker against him. Likewise the soldiers of the FIRST EARTH will learn martial arts with the same ethical basis. NO EARTH soldier shall be denied the kingdom of heaven because they are used as an instrument of indiscriminate war. The conscience will be developed together with the ability to neutralize the opponent.

NINE

The Subtle Transformational Power of Aikido

The secret of Aikido is to harmonize ourselves with the movement of the universe and bring ourselves into accord with the universe itself. Those who have gained the secret of Aikido have the universe in themselves and can say "I am the universe."

MORIHEI UESHIBA, "THE MEMOIR
OF THE MASTER," AIKIWEB

Thirteen years earlier, on a magical late summer's afternoon in 1972, I (Michelle) was walking along a long, stony beach strewn with oyster shells, flocks of gulls flying overhead. I was on an inlet near the Cold Mountain Institute on Cortez Island in the remote northern straits of the Salish Sea in British Columbia. I came upon a bearded elder wearing flowing black robes and carrying a long staff. Looking like a mountain sage who had come to walk the beach, his bright, clear eyes caught mine, and I was moved to bow in greeting. We spoke for a while of the vivid beauty of that moment, and when I asked his name, he smiled, and with a touch of his heart and slight bow, he simply replied, "Alan Watts."

I'd been reading Watts's inspiring works on Zen and the nature of mind for a few years, so we shared some precious moments together, bathed in the golden rays of sunlight streaming across the Salish Sea and musing on the timeless wisdom conveyed in this ancient tradition. This fortuitous meeting ignited a spark for me to go to Japan and study Zen. Some months later, I booked passage on a freighter from North Vancouver to Tokyo to study Zen in Japan. This was to be followed by passage to Europe via the Trans-Siberian Railway to study with Krishnamurti the next summer in Saanen, Switzerland.

While living in Japan, I looked up a couple of old friends, Beth and Harold, whom I'd met while traveling in Asia some years earlier and who had invited me to stay with them if I ever journeyed to Tokyo. When I arrived, they invited me to accompany them when they went to train at the nearby Hombu Dojo in the Shinjuku district. This dedicated dojo was established by Morihei Ueshiba. Though I was touched by the spirit of this training and enjoyed visiting the dojo and watching the grace and discipline of the students training there, little could I imagine that, within a decade, an inspiring aikido demonstration by our friend Bud Cook at the launch of the First Earth Battalion would open the portal of possibilities to beam me straight into the middle of the modern-day Jedi Warrior program for the U.S. Army Special Forces, where aikido, often translated as the "art of peace," would play a prominent role. The martial art of aikido was integral to our design of the Jedi program as a discipline to test in embodied ways the deeper inner training and to then serve as a bridge to the spirit of performance these soldiers would bring to their missions.

Morihei Ueshiba is regarded by many martial arts masters as history's greatest martial artist. Practitioners of aikido refer to Ueshiba as O'Sensei (Great Teacher). Though barely over five feet tall, and so short that he was turned down when he first tried to enlist in the Japanese army, O'Sensei was virtually untouchable and undefeatable by any martial artist of any tradition in his time. He continued to grow in power, skill, and suppleness well into his eighties.

Ueshiba's unique style of practice and teaching was inspired by a triad of three spiritual experiences that gave him profound insights into the deepest nature and highest purpose of aikido. The first vision was in 1925, following O'Sensei's defeat of a naval officer's attacks with a *bokken*, a long slender wooden staff, without harming the officer. After the intensity of this close encounter, Ueshiba strolled out into his garden, where he was filled with a visionary experience:

> I felt the universe suddenly quake and a golden spirit sprang up from the ground, veiled my body, and changed my body into a golden one. At the same time, my body became light. I was able to understand the whispering of the birds and was aware of the mind of God, the creator of the universe. At that moment I was enlightened (and realized): the source of *Budo* [Japanese for the Spirit of the Warrior] is God's love— the spirit of loving protection for all beings. . . . *Budo* is not the felling of an opponent by force; nor is it a tool to lead the world to destruction with arms. True *Budo* is to accept the spirit of the universe, keep the peace of the world, correctly produce, protect, and cultivate all beings in nature.[1]

Ueshiba's second vision came to him in 1940 when he was engaged in the practice of *misogi*, a Japanese Shinto ritual of personal purification, which often involves immersion in icy cold water: "Around 2 am, I suddenly forgot all the martial techniques I had ever learned. The techniques of my teachers appeared completely new. Now they were vehicles for the cultivation of life, knowledge, and virtue, not devices to throw people with."[2]

Ueshiba's third awakening was in 1942 in the midst of some of the bloodiest fighting of World War II when he had a vision of the "Great Spirit of Peace." "The Way of the Warrior," he taught, "has been misunderstood. It is not a means to kill and destroy others. Those who seek to compete and better one another are making a terrible mistake. To smash, injure, or destroy is the worst thing a human being can do. The real Way of a Warrior is to prevent such slaughter—it is the Art of Peace."[3]

Over time, O'Sensei's teachings reflected the progression of his own evolutionary path and journey of awakening. His earlier style of training focused more on traditional Japanese martial arts and was much harder, focusing on strikes to vital points of the body and greater reliance on weapons work. He called his style *aiki-jujitsu*. As O'Sensei grew older and wiser and his vital spirit grew stronger, his spiritual understanding infused his practice and teaching of the martial arts. His technique became subtler, softer, gentler, and more focused on the sensing, control, and transmission of ki, the flow of subtle energy, and for a time was called *aiki budo*. He gave greater emphasis to what he called *kokyū-nage,* or "breath throws," which involved a deep attunement and blending with the energy and force of one's opponent, to skillfully harness the energy of their attack to throw them with minimal effort and maximal ease. When Ueshiba and his students joined the Dai Nippon Butoku Kai in 1942, the martial art that he developed finally came to be known as aikido.

It is helpful to consider here that the Western term *warrior* is somewhat neutral and amoral, simply implying someone who makes war. Translating the Japanese tradition of *budo* as "the way of the warrior" misses the deeper meaning. Budo is almost the opposite. Budo means the way of ending war and conflict. To practice budo in the samurai tradition implies dedicating one's entire life in service of peace, to the way of wise and loving protection, to stopping war and conflict, and to bringing the hearts and minds of ourselves and others to peace, balance, and harmony. Contradictory as it sounds, a warrior in this tradition fights fiercely to establish peace. Through disciplined training and cultivation of mind-body-spirit, practitioners forge their warrior spirit to increase their capacity to live in dynamic inner harmony to increase the joy and well-being of the world, not the pain.

Budo implies a way of life that embodies wise and loving protection of the peace and harmony that allows us and those we know to truly thrive and find the rare and precious qualities of peace, joy, and contentment in our lives. The cultivation of warrior spirit in the budo tradition involves developing mastery in hand-to-hand combat and weapons work, as well as cultivating skills in painting, calligraphy, flower arranging, and other forms of art.

Given that our dojo had not been built out when we arrived on base, the men had the opportunity to help build the racks for our *jos* (wooden staffs) and bokkens (wooden swords), set up a small alter, and lay out the mats for the new dojo. Richard brought a photo of O'Sensei, which hung ceremoniously at the front of the dojo as a reminder that this warrior art had a deep lineage and tradition to it. While some of the men had heard of aikido, none had trained in this discipline and its philosophy of combat and warriorship, thus our dojo provided a learning laboratory to explore new territory and domains of mind-energy-body-spirit in motion and in dynamic, fluid relationships. For these soldiers who had trained in a variety of hard, effective forms of hand-to-hand combat, aikido offered a novel, rich, and challenging opportunity to access extraordinary dimensions of martial skills and personal and universal power.

Outwardly, the basics of the art of aikido involved learning a series of embodied forms and moves, alternating between the roles of nage and uke. We learned *irimi,* to step forward to meet and blend with the energy of an attack, and *tankon,* to flow, blend, and redirect the force of an attack. Inwardly, we learned to relax and release unnecessary tension, to hold one point, centering ourselves in the *hara* point below the navel, an inner dimension of balance and of connection to the presence and movement of all things, and to bring peace and harmony to life by opening ourselves to be a conduit for the flow of universal life force energy or ki streaming to us and through us. We also learned various forms, or *katas,* of weapons work with our jo and bokken.

While the initial training was focused on learning the outer form of physical moves, that learning provided the scaffolding to begin to sense the inner power and spirit of aikido as ki, the flow of subtle energy that circulates within us and among us, weaving us into the seamless fabric of wholeness that encompasses all creation in all its dimensions. Ki is akin to "the force" in George Lucas's Jedi warrior tradition and mythology. Once one becomes sufficiently adept and in flow with the outer form of this art, then one can begin to more reliably sense, fathom, and direct the deeper, subtler, more powerful, and meaningful dimensions of ai-ki-do: the *do*, or way, of divining *ki*, the energy of intent, so you can *ai*, love and harmonize.

We admired Sensei Strozzi-Heckler and his skillfulness in blending with the men on the mat. He was a master in the art and an inspiring and gifted teacher. Still, he too was continually challenged to gather and hold the attention of the men in their training. There was often a layer of tension between the men sincerely applying themselves to learning and practicing the form, while also looking for an opportunity to nail Richard with a blast of macho smash-it-to-the-mat one-upmanship. Throughout the program, Richard was challenged again and again not to take the bait or get entangled into a competitive or combative stance with the men, to maintain his poise and center as the sensei and not let his switch get flipped to join the "who is the toughest dude on the mat" club. As a trained athlete, martial artist with military experience, and elder to the troops, Richard played a fine edge of pushing to show that he had what it took to keep up with our young bucks, and on numerous occasions he paid a heavy toll by pushing too hard and ended up with painful injuries.

I (Joel) recall that part of my unspoken contract with the men was that I would work out with them in the early mornings and grapple with them on the mat every day, and they would then come train with Michelle and me in our Mind Lab dojo in the afternoons. Though I had trained for the past twelve years in the martial arts traditions of t'ai chi and qigong, coming into this program, I had less than a year of actual aikido training under my belt, having trained a bit with Bud and Hirata Sensei at the Ki-Aikido Dojo in Seattle. With a structurally wonky knee, I was wisely cautious on the mat but still showed up every day and trained hard with the men. Though I was fit and strong and could hold my own with most of the physical training, it was clear to these guys that I was not a macho jock who was going to go head-to-head to compete with them and that doing some fancy move to knock my lights out would not score anyone any extra points. Free from the competitive edge that Richard and Jack danced on with the men, I sensed that I was respected for my chutzpah for simply showing up, suiting up in my gi, and stepping out on the mat to train with them. Though I sometimes ended up with a bloody nose or sprain in our sparring, I was generally warmly cared for in training with the men on the mat.

I was talking with Shultz one day after training in the dojo. There was a pause, and Shultz said tenderly, with a bit of a sheepish grin, "You know Joel, you are one strange bird in our nest. But you are for real and such a straight shooter with us, and we respect that what you and Michelle are teaching us might well save our lives or our missions someday."

The inclusion and vital presence of aikido as an integral domain of training for our Jedi Warrior program opened a portal of extraordinary possibilities far beyond the scope of traditional Special Forces training. It provided a tangible, embodied martial arts practice with direct application to being a warrior and opened the way to viscerally exploring and experiencing entirely novel modes of sensing and responding to attack, conflict, and relationship in general. Aikido also provided an entry point into the exploration of how we sense and work with the flows of energy that weave our individual whirlpool of embodied being into the larger ocean of energy and interbeing with all creation. Aikido offered a deeply penetrating sword of insight able to pierce and dismantle the conventional armor of cultural and military indoctrination and open a way to a mature and somewhat cosmic conversation regarding the deeper meanings and higher purposes of the modern-day warrior. We felt honored to have a clear contractual mandate to engage these soldiers in such an inquiry.

In the initial weeks of training, the men were awkward, clumsy, and way out of their comfort zone. These guys knew how to fight and to kill with their bare hands, but to relax, drop their center of gravity into their core, extend ki, and carefully attune to the momentum, energy, and intent of an attack in order to blend with that force and smoothly guide their opponent to an immobilized place of rest on the mat was completely new territory for them. Some were thrilled to master a new martial art, while others had trouble wrapping their heads around why they needed to train in this way or were simply ambivalent. Yet, gradually over days and weeks of unrelenting training, embodied learning progressed. One memorable day, about two months into the program, we were standing at the edge of the mat with Jack watching the men grapple and throw. We all marveled at how far these men had come in their learning and at their fluidity, grace, embodied ease, and exhilaration. Chuckling to himself, Jack mused, "Wow, look at that! It appears that radical transformation really *is* possible for these guys."

Introducing these soldiers to aikido was less about giving them skills for hand-to-hand combat and more about helping them see the boundless potential available in a radically expanded view of themselves. We wanted to change how they related to power and conflict and help them harness and direct these potent forces with better presence and love for the greater good, rather than settling for a fleeting moment of victory. Their missions were complex, exhausting, and demanding, and introducing them to a wide range of responses and options would be vital to their success and survival.

Over the course of our six months together, we trained the men in aikido for two hours daily on average, four to five days per week. We administered two tests in five months. In the first test, they had to demonstrate their understanding of aikido terms and their ability to sustain focus, to properly execute classic aikido moves under pressure, and to maintain attuned relationships with partners. They also had to demonstrate their ability to respond to unanticipated threats and to understand how aikido could be applied as a metaphor in life and work. The second test was offered on an invitational basis to the three most accomplished aikidoists from each team, plus the commanding officer. This test was far more technically challenging, extending to three grades of mastery higher than the initial test and involved advanced jo work in both solo and partner practice. All six individuals who took the advanced test were successful.

At this time, others who felt prepared could request permission from Sensei Strozzi-Heckler to take the second test.

Eventually, the remaining eighteen team members were invited to take the same advanced test. One declined, and sixteen successfully completed it. The element of choice in stepping up for this challenge was important. All in all, these men were far more advanced in their training when compared with a civilian population of practitioners who had trained for the same length of time.

In the wholistic spirit of the Jedi program, we also referenced three other martial arts—karate, capoeira (a Brazilian martial art), and escrima (the national martial art of the Philippines)—to illustrate how the principles of aikido apply in these other arts. The principles were continually referenced and woven into physical training, field exercises, and training in the Mind Lab. While this radically new form of martial practice was challenging for the soldiers to learn, the consensus was that aikido training improved physical and mental performance, increased their capacity to stay relaxed and centered in stressful situations, and played a significant role in reducing injuries.

A friend once met O'Sensei doing a *rondori*, free-style multiple attack demonstration that left seventeen big bruisers on the ground. After the session, she asked him what his secret was for disarming all these attackers without harming them. As she described, O'Sensei warmly smiled and giggled at her question saying, "A long time ago, I realized that every person was just my sister, my brother, my cousin. All these guys lying on the floor are my brothers, and you are my little sister." In that spirit, O'Sensei taught, "I am never defeated, however fast the enemy may attack. When an enemy tries to fight with me, the universe itself, the enemy has to break the harmony of the universe. Hence at the moment he has the mind to fight with me . . . he is already defeated. Winning means winning over the mind of discord in yourself. . . .How can you straighten your warped mind, purify your heart, and be harmonized with the activities of all things in nature? You should first make God's heart yours. This is a Great Love Omnipresent in all quarters and in all times of the universe. There is no discord in love. There is no enemy of Love.[4]

The Jedi Warrior Advantage

The spirit of the Jedi Warrior training is exemplified in another story about O'Sensei. O'Sensei was virtually unbeatable and embodied the wisdom of the dynamic responsiveness to the flow of changing conditions both on and off the mat. O'Sensei was once asked by his students, "Sensei, how do you keep your balance all the time?" The master laughed and responded, "Aikido, the art of peace, is not about rigidly trying to hold your ground and keep your balance. It is about losing it again and again and learning how swiftly you can return to the fluid center of dynamic balance. The reason you don't see me lose my balance is because I regain it so quickly that no one ever notices that I have wobbled!"

The realities of life and war are fluid, dynamic, and ever changing. It is a given that as we become aware of threats present in our environment, we will naturally gear up and depart from the "green zone" of our optimal state and shift into states of stress and arousal necessary to assess, resolve, or neutralize the danger. The profound advantage gained by our well-trained warriors was that they became equipped with the self-awareness and self-mastery skills and confidence necessary to adeptly regain their inner balance and optimize their condition. By applying their self-regulation skills, they quickly returned to their "window of tolerance," the psychophysical zone of optimal mind-body tuning. These skills would enhance their capacity as warriors to wisely respond to threats or dangers when they are present, and once those threats are resolved, to swiftly return to balance, to rest, renew, regenerate, and prepare for the next volley of assaults or their next mission. Through becoming ever more adept in the personal mastery skills necessary to optimize their psychophysical mind-body state and performance, our warriors could minimize the enduring trauma they would suffer or inflict upon others.

This six-month-long immersive training would provide our troops with a tremendous advantage over any less well-trained adversaries that they may encounter in their missions in terms of their capacities for self-awareness, self-healing, self-mastery, energy management, wise discernment, and responsive compassion necessary to develop strong enduring alliances. These advantages could have profound implications for the outcomes of their missions and their potential consequences for humanity over generations to come.

This is not mere theory. You practice it. Then you will accept the great power of oneness with Nature.
                                                    MORIHEI UESHIBA

How do people look when they are "whole"... together... in charge of themselves and in charge of their bodies? How do people look when they have coughed up all the pain buried deep in their psyche and deep in their muscle structure? How do people look when they are centered... grounded... and focused? How do people look when they <u>know</u> for a fact that the universe (GOD) has a positive plan for mankind? How do people look when they <u>know</u> they have an active role in that plan? Here are some clues!

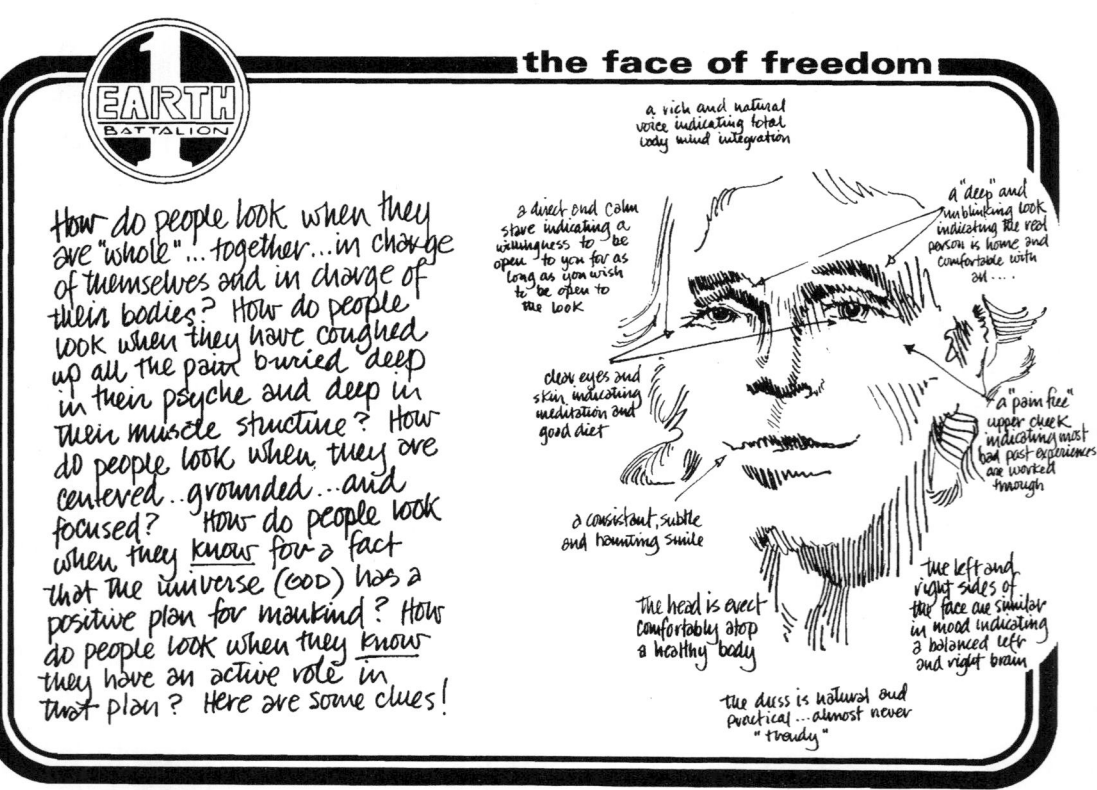

a rich and natural voice indicating total body mind integration

a direct and calm stare indicating a willingness to be open to you for as long as you wish to be open to the look

a "deep" and unblinking look indicating the real person is home and comfortable with an ...

clear eyes and skin indicating meditation and good diet

a "pain free" upper cheek indicating most bad past experiences are worked through

a consistent, subtle and haunting smile

the head is erect comfortably atop a healthy body

the left and right sides of the face are similar in mood indicating a balanced left and right brain

the dress is natural and practical ... almost never "trendy"

THE FIRST EARTH BATTALION

TEN

Caution! Entering Mind Field

The greatest thing in all education is to make the nervous system our ally instead of our enemy.

WILLIAM JAMES, *HABIT* AND
THE PRINCIPLES OF PSYCHOLOGY

Imagine walking down the hall to the Jedi Warrior Mind Lab. You come to a door that says "Mind Lab," and as you open it, the first thing you see is a large mirror straight ahead of you with a sign saying, "Caution! Entering Mind Field." The lab's central control pod is filled with hundreds of thousands of dollars' worth of the most sophisticated biomedical equipment on the planet. These various devices have been designed to create a learning laboratory where these fortunate soldiers can learn to radically expand their capacity to monitor, manage, self-regulate, and optimize their own mind-body nervous system. This highly advanced brain hacking is achieved by using a laboratory full of state-of-the-art technology to measure and then mirror back information to the soldiers about their own internal physiological state, thus helping them recognize the qualities, states, and strategies of mind that enhance or diminish their physiological optimization. This Mind Lab is the best that the Pentagon, and your taxes, can buy.

Here's an analogy to give you a sense for how advanced physiological self-mastery can be trained. As you envision entering the lab, imagine seeing a circle of soldiers intensely focused on toy cars racing around a track. They are competing to win the race, and the speed of their cars is determined by how well they can warm their hands by relaxing and increasing the blood flow. To accomplish this, they are using a thermal biofeedback device: Each soldier has a biothermal sensor taped to a fingertip that measures minute fluctuations in skin temperature to a hundredth of a degree. The sensor is plugged into a biofeedback device that offers a real-time display of the soldier's finger temperature and controls the speed of their race car. We explain that skin temperature reflects changes in the blood flow to their hands, which is controlled by the tension in their blood vessels. The autonomic nervous system, which is activated by stress, plays a key role in regulating blood vessel tension and contraction. The more these men are able to consciously and intentionally relax and quiet the activation of their stress response, the more the smooth muscles in their blood vessels dilate, the warmer their hands become, and the faster their race cars speed along the track.

Some of the men's cars are whizzing around the track. Those soldiers are laughing and having a great time. They are gaining a life-changing insight into how the mind-body works together and are seeing the potential for a deeper kind of self-awareness and psychophysical self-mastery. Other cars are stuck and stuttering. The men trying to control them are feeling strangely out of their league—incompetent and inept, not a common state for soldiers at this echelon of achievement and skill. They are cursing, feeling frustrated and totally out of control, without a clue for how to regain a sense of influence, let alone control, over their race cars.

In teeing up an exercise like this, we would begin by asking the men to consider, "When you relax, will your hands get warmer or colder? What do you think? And why?" Then we would explain that our hands get warmer when we relax, and colder when we become tense or anxious. The cardiovascular system works like a highly sensitive biological hydraulic system. The peripheral blood vessels in the fingers and toes are lined with sensitive smooth muscles, which are innervated by the sympathetic branch of the autonomic nervous system. When you are in a mental state of distress, the sympathetic nervous system is triggered, which activates a cascade of stress responses. This stress activation constricts the muscles lining the peripheral blood vessels, reducing blood flow to the hands and feet, cooling your fingers and toes, and requiring your heart to pump harder, which raises your blood pressure. Meanwhile, more blood is sent to your internal organs and large muscles to prepare you to fight or flee.

We introduced the notion that relaxation is what is left when you stop creating tension. When we learn to shift our mind state from distress to a calm, effortless, yet intentional state of aware presence and well-being, the neural activation of the stress response quiets down, and the clenched muscles in the blood vessels relax, allowing the blood flow to naturally increase. This increased blood flow warms the hands, perhaps leading them to tingle a bit, and the body relaxes. This relaxation response not only brings more blood to warm our hands, but it also brings more blood to the brain to sharpen awareness, focus, reasoning, and wise discernment.

The survival of soldiers deployed on a mission may well depend on how skilled they are in managing their minds and mastering their stress levels to self-regulate and optimize their psychophysical state. Their success or failure in this inner work will affect the lives of many others as well. The soldiers we were training were likely to be dug in doing surveillance in frigid conditions in remote and hostile territory for long periods of time, and learning to stay calm, focused, and able to control the blood flow to their extremities might also decrease their vulnerability to frostbite and increase their dexterity and precision in using the many instruments that they must rely upon to do their job.

For the soldiers in this lab race track scenario, their cars would speed along when they find their neural groove—relaxing and allowing more blood to flow to their hands until the critical threshold on the device is met and the circuit closes. The big challenge happens when they get competitive and try harder to win or to go faster. This flips the neural switch that creates more stress arousal, which in turn constricts the blood vessels, cools their hands, and causes their race car to come to a dead stop. The harder they try to win, the less control they have, and paradoxically, the more they lose.

Through this unique competition scenario, the soldiers learn to find a profoundly rare and powerful quality of inner balance. They are competing to see who can be most skillful and successful in generating this learnable but elusive blend of mind states. First, they need to generate a mental state of equanimity or letting go with awareness. At the same time, they need to also hold the intention to accomplish the task and win the race. If they let go and relax too much, they have no influence or control, and if they try too hard or tense up, they'll also lose control. When they find the right blend and balance of intention, attention, attitude, and effort, they access a whole new order of awareness, influence, control, and power and taste the sweet fruits of success and expanded self-mastery and mind-body integration.

Biofeedback Training for Jedi Warriors

Jedi Warrior training was centered on practices of mindfulness and meditation, which refine and develop awareness. To complement these mind-fitness practices we also used the power tools of biofeedback technology. The training relied on two primary domains: first is peripheral biofeedback, which uses a wide variety of devices to measure and provide feedback regarding a wide array of other physiological functions and systems. In the Jedi program the varieties of peripheral biofeedback training that we relied upon included muscle tension and relaxation levels (EMG or electromyography); blood pressure; skin temperature; electrical conductance of the skin (EDR or electrodermal response); and heart-rate variability (HRV), which is an excellent measure of stress levels and of the autonomic nervous system. There are also other types of peripheral biofeedback, such as ocular focusing related to vision and sphincter control for incontinence. The other domain of biofeedback training is neurofeedback, which measures and provides feedback necessary to influence the fluctuations of the subtle neuro-electric activity of the brain, which are associated with changes in levels of awareness, neural connectivity, and states of consciousness.

In biofeedback, sensors are placed on the body, which pick up various physiological signals, such as muscle tension, blood flow, skin temperature, heart rate, and brainwaves. The signal is then amplified and fed back to the person whose body it is coming from. Changes in the physiological state modulate the feedback signal that may be in the form of a tone that changes in frequency or loudness, a light bar or graph, a digital score, a computer game, a video clip, or a virtual reality display. For example, if you were using an EMG—which involves attaching sensors on various muscle groups, such as the frontalis muscle on the forehead or the trapezius muscles of the neck and shoulders—you would place a sensor over a muscle that is frequently tense. You would then use a monitor to amplify and feedback moment-to-moment changes reflecting subtle increases and decreases of tension; in this way you would quickly learn how to recognize and influence the levels of your tension or relaxation. When you visit a doctor's office you are likely to have some of these signals measured and recorded by the nurse or the doctor who then informs you about your physiological state, whereas in a biofeedback training context you are the one monitoring the display of ever-changing data streaming from your own body.

When biofeedback training is combined with methods of relaxation, concentration, mindfulness, meditation, and mind-fitness training, this larger bundle of disciplines can either be referred to as *cyberphysiology* or, as we often call it, *biopsybernautic* training. These terms speak to the interweaving disciplines that explore the interphase of technology, embodied awareness, biology, and psyche.

Biofeedback training opened up whole new horizons and dimensions of power and self-mastery for our soldiers, especially the tough can-do guys who were used to being in control on the outside but who were actually quite out of control on the inside. The lack of inner awareness and control leaves them more vulnerable when the pressures and complexity of their lives increase and push them out of their optimal window of tolerance. Biofeedback training made it clear that the inner game of true self-mastery is ultimately less about effort and powering through and more about learning the exquisitely subtle balance of intention combined with the essential presence of a receptive quality of mindful presence and even-mindedness. *Trying* to relax in an effortful way will never lead to success in personal mastery, self-regulation, and self-control. In practical application this means that once you master these skills, then even in the midst of extreme intensity and complexity you will be more optimally tuned, present, sensitive to change, adaptable, intuitively responsive, and more likely to recognize options, make wiser choices, and create the best outcomes in difficult or challenging situations.

Learning to let go while simultaneously maintaining focus and intention is the only way to successfully generate the mind states that will produce the desired physiological state. In the biofeedback world, this state is referred to as passive volition or doing without trying. In the martial arts traditions, this may be referred to as effortless effort or wielding the sword of no sword.

Introducing Biofeedback

We reminded the men that life is about learning, and all learning depends on feedback. If we are doing target practice, we adjust our aim by noticing the result of each of our shots. If we are playing an instrument, we listen to the quality of music and change our tuning and technique accordingly. If we are cooking, we adjust the ingredients and flavor of the food by tasting it. We rely upon feedback to refine our skills and reach our goals in any task and improve our performance. The same is true with regard to living and working in relationships. By attending to the feedback of our bodies, our relationships, and our environment, we can learn, grow, and become more successful and effective in accomplishing our goals in our lives. Yet, if the feedback signals are too subtle to notice, or if our awareness is not sufficiently trained or refined to access the stream of energy and information that comprises the feedback, our learning will not progress.

In mapping out the territory of psychophysical self-regulation and self-mastery for our soldiers, we explained that biofeedback training is likely the most empowering use of technology in our world. The implications and applications of biofeedback training are profound in that any physiological signal that can be measured and fed back to a subject in real time can be influenced or controlled. Taking to heart the notion that you can only manage what you monitor, biofeedback gives you powerful tools to monitor physiological processes that are otherwise too subtle to monitor.

To help the men understand how mind training to refine awareness synergizes with biofeedback technology, we guided them in the following mental simulation: Imagine a continuum before you with the most tangible waveforms of energy, information, and experience at the top ranging to progressively ever-subtler levels of experience toward the bottom of the scale. Then imagine that you draw a line indicating that everything above the line has a signal strength and clarity strong enough to register at your current level of awareness, while every waveform of energy information that lies below the line is too subtle to consciously discern, even though it may register at subliminal levels of intuition.

We explained that in this training we would rely upon the practices of mindfulness and meditation to refine awareness and rewire the brain to lower the threshold of awareness to encompass ever-subtler levels. In this way, the mind training would equip them with the skills necessary to gradually awaken to aspects of experience and dimensions of reality that were previously too subtle or elusive for them to bring into their conscious awareness and conscious control.

We explained to the men that as they observed the display of moment-to-moment changes within their body that the biofeedback device mirrored those changes through modulated sounds and graphics that correlated with increases or decreases in the signal strength. A profoundly intimate feedback loop is established between the physical dimensions of your being and the awareness dimensions of your being. We told them that through their own curiosity, awareness, and practice, they would come to realize two truths: first that their psychophysical state is constantly changing moment to moment at every level; and second that through mindful awareness of the data stream from the biofeedback, they could learn to influence and consciously change their physiological condition by learning how to change their state of mind. This is truly a demonstration of mind over matter. It seems that virtually any physiological signal that we can monitor in real time can be influenced by creating a feedback loop with our embodied awareness. The implications of this are most profound.

The Matrix of Responsive Awareness

With only six months to teach our soldiers advanced self-mastery skills, the inclusion of biofeedback training, rather than mind training alone, created a supercharged accelerator for learning psychophysical self-mastery. We shared with the men one of the most compelling examples of the profound advantages of biofeedback to hasten the development of intentional control of physiological systems. Colleagues Elmer and Alyce Green of the Menninger Foundation invited an accomplished yogi, Swami Rama, to their psychophysiological control laboratory. The swami was wired to two temperature sensors to measure the change of temperature and blood flow to different parts of the palm of his hand a couple of inches apart. Under rigorous experimental conditions, the researchers watched as the swami demonstrated his ability to perform a medical miracle by consciously altering his circulation to make one part of his palm nearly 17 degrees warmer than an area a couple of inches away. While the medical implications of such self-mastery were stunning, and the researchers were very excited, it was sobering to hear Swami Rama say that it had taken him nearly twenty-five years of intensive yogic training and discipline to refine this level of subtle awareness and self-control.

A graduate student at Kansas State University who had heard about the Greens' experiment decided to see if he could learn the same control using a thermal biofeedback device to accelerate his training. Within two weeks of biofeedback training, he had achieved the same degree of extraordinary psychophysiological control that the yogi admitted had taken him decades to learn!

As pioneers in the biofeedback field, Alyce and Elmer Green articulated the famous psychophysical principle, which states that "every change in the physiological state is accompanied by an appropriate change in the mental-emotional state, conscious or unconscious; and conversely, every change in the mental-emotional state, conscious or unconscious, is accompanied by an appropriate change in the physiological state."[1]

This understanding gives rise to a fundamental model that was at the core of Jedi Warrior training: the matrix of responsive awareness. In essence, Jedi Warrior was based on teaching responsive awareness skills to our soldiers (fig. 10.1). The core training was to expand our soldiers' range of personal mastery and awareness by helping them understand and embody the wisdom that "you can only manage what you monitor" and "control follows awareness." The foundation of this work was developing mindful awareness. The matrix of responsive awareness has four interwoven dimensions:

1. **Personal** is about knowing and owning the awareness and power that flows to and through the matrix of the portion of the universe that we identify with as our self.

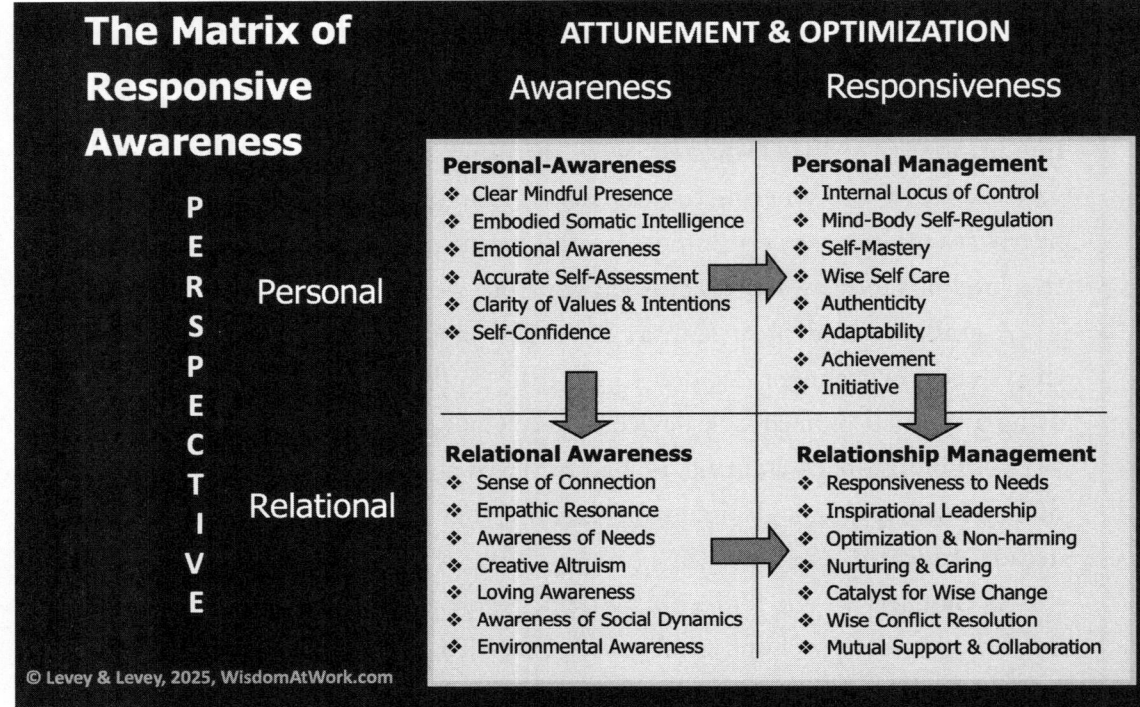

Fig. 10.1. Matrix of Responsive Awareness

2. **Relational** is about how we participate in the flow of energy and information that is continually informing us about the nature and status of our social and environmental fields. As our awareness and wisdom grow, the intention to optimize all conditions within this relational field also grows. Within this relational field there are no impermeable boundaries, only boundless fields of interrelationships formed by the flow of energy and information.

3. **Awareness** is clear, knowing, mindful presence. It has an infinite range and is about learning to recognize the actual nature of current reality with ever-greater lucidity at ever-more inclusive, subtle, and expansive dimensions.

4. **Responsiveness** is about living on purpose, continually clarifying

what is important to us and what we value, need, and desire for ourselves, for others, and for our world. Responsiveness is about managing the flow of our attention, choices, and actions to realize those outcomes. This is about how we respond to the energy and information that flows to us and through us from the relational field of interaction we share with other people and beings and from the natural and built environments in which we live. This is about learning to source the deepest wisdom and clearest guidance available to us to inform and guide our responsiveness to ultimately bring the greatest benefit and best outcomes for all involved.

Basic training in the disciplines of self-regulation begins in our infancy with the intimate blending of awareness and responsive influence as required to coregulate and soothe ourselves in bonded relationships with our caregivers. In our early years, we learn to calm and comfort ourselves, to walk and talk, to regulate our bowels, to play with others, and to engage in many other embodied skills. The quality of care we receive during this vulnerable, formative stage of our development, when key pathways in our nervous system are developing, determines how we will later attune ourselves to dance, make love, fight, use weapons, and create beautiful music or art. It also has a great impact on how we learn to self-regulate and care for our needs and for the needs of others later in our lives and determines how we empathically attune and develop mutually thriving and nurturing relationships.

At advanced stages of self-mastery, curious, motivated, and disciplined individuals can access and explore more refined and powerful applications of these principles to encompass vaster, deeper, and subtler domains of awareness, relatedness, and responsive interaction. The potential scope of this learning is boundless.

Spectrum of Self-Awareness, Self-Regulation, and Self-Mastery

In mapping out the territory of psychophysical self-regulation and self-mastery for our soldiers, we explained that biofeedback training is likely the most empowering use of technology in our world. The implications and applications of biofeedback training are profound in that any physiological signal that can be measured and fed back to a subject in real time can be influenced or controlled. Taking to heart the notion that you can only manage what you monitor, biofeedback gives you powerful tools to monitor physiological processes that are otherwise too subtle to monitor.

Jedi Warrior training relied on two primary domains to biofeedback training. First is "peripheral biofeedback" which uses a wide variety of devices to measure and provide feedback regarding a wide array of other physiological functions and systems. In the Jedi program the varieties of peripheral biofeedback training that we relied upon included: EMG (muscle tension and relaxation levels); blood pressure; skin temperature; electrical conductance of the skin (EDR); and heart-rate variability (HRV), which is an excellent measure of stress levels and the autonomic nervous system.

The other domain of biofeedback training is "neurofeedback," which measures and provides feedback necessary to influence the fluctuations of the subtle neuroelectric activity of the brain are associated with changes in levels of awareness, neural connectivity, and states of consciousness.

When combined in synergy with various inner mind-fitness practices of mindfulness, meditation, and creative visualization, biofeedback training is supercharged to accelerate the development of greater interoceptive awareness, self-mastery, and somatic intelligence. The Jedi Warrior biofeedback protocols were designed to develop awareness, skill, mastery, and confidence at progressively subtler and subtler levels in order to wisely integrate this embodied awareness into daily life, work, social interactions, and missions. Here is a glimpse of the progression of psychophysical training at the heart of Jedi Warrior, from the most tangible and measurable domains to the most subtle and elusive.

Voluntary Physical Movement

The soldiers we worked with were well trained in basic physical training, yet their training was not very scientifically informed or technically sophisticated. As described in chapter 9, our SportsMind fitness trainers Larry Burback and Horst Abraham, plus Richard Strozzi-Heckler with his aikido training, opened many new horizons for these very physically fit men and introduced them to wiser and more effective ways to inhabit their bodies. While the physical training carried on throughout the program, it also laid a foundation for training in much more subtle domains of embodiment. These outer practices of fitness training and martial arts provided a testing ground to refine and affirm the more subtle internal training that we focused on in our Mind Lab sessions and during the encampment. The biofeedback and mind-fitness training were further enhanced and refined through introducing practices of mindful movement, such as mindful jogging and exercise.

In our initial training we invited our aspiring Jedi warriors to engage in a simple experiment. "Look at your hands. Then, with your mind, select one finger on one of your hands. Now, lift this finger up to touch your nose. Then pause to reflect: How did I accomplish this? How did my mental awareness and intention lead to the mobilization and precise deployment of thousands of nerves, muscles, bones, and ligaments to be orchestrated so precisely and guided through my vision and inner senses to accomplish even this simple task?" Though we inhabit and move our bodies every moment of our lives, we generally do so with little or no awareness or understanding of how this miraculous process actually works.

Neuromuscular Awareness and Control

The next level of psychophysical self-mastery training was to increase awareness and mastery of the neuromuscular system, which is a part of the voluntary nervous system, accounting for our ability to move most of our muscles at will. That said, while some people have learned to wiggle their ears, others have not. Similarly, many people have learned over time to inhabit their body with extremely high baseline levels of muscular tension, causing a host of neuromuscular disorders ranging from tension headaches to backaches and chronic muscle pain.

During our first week of training in the lab, we introduced our soldiers to EMG biofeedback. Through measuring the levels of tension in these regions and feeding that information back to the men, they were able to easily learn to increase and decrease their tension levels at will, combined with a variety of powerful meditative methods for learning to monitor, manage, and optimize levels along a continuum ranging from hypertense to deeply relaxed. This initial level of self-awareness and personal mastery training provided a strong foundation of confidence in their ability to change the state of their bodies through changing the state of their minds. New horizons opened for them of freedom from unnecessary tension and pain and of embodied well-being, relaxation, recovery, and resilience, which led to optimal performance in many physical activities that involved the neuromuscular system.

For example, many of the men had assumed certain postures and ways of inhabiting their bodies that maintained extremely high levels of physical tension, like body armor they had become so accustomed to that they were no longer consciously aware of how much energy was being drained maintaining this maladaptive tension. As we connected the men up with the

EMG instruments, they could instantly see how much tension they were holding in certain muscle groups, and they came to appreciate how tiring, painful, and inefficient that was.

As an initial strategy in working with the EMG biofeedback, the men began by tuning into their baseline levels of muscle tension in various muscle groups. We then challenged them to sense what inner moves or methods worked best to increase their tension levels by 50 percent, for example to go from 10 microvolts (mv) of tension up to 15 mv. We then invited them to bring their tension levels back to their baseline level and to oscillate with increasing the tension and then relaxing back to baseline, again and again.

Following their initial success with this, we asked them to increase their tension by only 25 percent (from 10 mv to 12.5 mv) and then oscillate back down to baseline (10 mv) and back up again, noticing how it felt and noting the difference between the baseline reading, the 50 percent increase, and this 25 percent level.

We then challenged the men to drop back down to their baseline level (10 mv) and to explore and discover the inner moves necessary to lower their baseline tension level by 10 percent down to 9 mv. When they were able to do this, their challenge became to increase their tension back to their initial baseline and to notice and feel the difference.

Over the days to come, we would continue to refine awareness and control to help the soldiers gain access to progressively subtler levels or depths of relaxation, challenging them to see how much tension they could release and how deeply they could relax. Whenever they reached a point where they seemed to be as relaxed as possible, we then had them bring their subtle interoceptive awareness of their body to hover at that threshold and to focus on sensing the very subtle fluctuations of slightly increasing tension or deepening relaxation so that they could begin to integrate these deeper and subtler levels of awareness and self-mastery into their embodied daily life. Through this kind of synergistic training, the men quickly developed awareness, skill, and confidence in being able to sense and change their levels of tension, as well as learning to bring their tension levels down as low as 0.5 to 2.0 mv.

We would then bridge this exploration in the lab into the physical fitness sessions by building in time for deep and total relaxation following their more intensive fitness-training sessions. In a relatively short time, all the men were able to access a much higher level of awareness, a much deeper state of relaxation, and a far greater awareness of optimal states of muscle tension in performing embodied activities.

Realizing that many of these soldiers compensated for previous injuries in their daily lives, Joel shared the story of Eddie, a veteran and former clinical patient he had worked with in the medical center who had lived with intense neuromuscular pain for decades and relied heavily on alcohol and drugs for many years to manage his chronic pain. After running Eddie through similar neuromuscular-training protocols, Eddie developed confidence and skill in recognizing and releasing tension and managed to work his tension levels down to the point where he found himself sitting and talking with Joel at 2 mv of tension and realized that he was completely pain free—for the first time in many years!

Noticing that his pain was totally gone, Eddie, a tugboat captain at the time, exploded into a fit of anger, slamming his fist on the table and swearing like a sailor, saying, "Why the hell didn't someone teach me this sooner! I've suffered for so many years, and now here, in an hour my pain is completely gone. If I had learned this in my twenties, I wouldn't have suffered so damn much over all these many years." Hearing this, many of our soldiers realized how fortunate they were to be learning these vital life skills in their twenties and thirties.

Courage and Communication

At the end of a long day of biofeedback training with the Bravo Team, we were cleaning up the lab and noticed that Shawn had lingered on after all the other team members had left. Standing close by the door, he was shuffling around nervously as though trying to find the courage to ask someone out on a first date. Sensing that he was staying on for a reason, we checked in. "Hey Shawn, what's up? Anything we can help you with?" He seemed relieved to be acknowledged and somewhat shyly replied, "Um . . . I'm just wondering . . . What do you guys think of us?"

We were both a bit taken aback. This was a first big test. How completely honest and authentic would we be in responding to vulnerable "make it or break it" questions like this with the soldiers? After a momentary pause, Joel took a deep breath, checked in with himself, and stepped in: "Honestly, Shawn, I'm surprised how much we really like you guys." Whoosh! It felt like a big breeze of fresh air had blown through, clearing the clouds in the room, and Shawn brightened and beamed back, "Yeah, I'm surprised how much I like you guys too. I guess hippies ain't all bad!"

The courage Shawn brought to launching his question was inspiring, and Joel's courage in responding truthfully in a sincere and unguarded way reflected the kind of mutual care, curiosity, risk-taking, and honesty needed to humanize one another and go beyond preestablished stereotypes on both sides. Through opening channels of communication, we could ease tensions and increase trust and build working alliances dedicated to a larger set of shared objectives. There would be more tests like this to follow, and we were off to a strong start.

Autonomic Nervous System

In the Jedi Mind Lab, after an initial phase of training with EMG and the voluntary nervous system, we progressed to the next most subtle level of mind-body integration, interoceptive awareness, and self-mastery—the autonomic nervous system, which regulates our psychophysical responses to stress. To accomplish this, we used a variety of sensors and methods: real-time feedback of blood pressure; EDR, which is related to sweat gland activity in the skin and measured in lie detector tests; HRV; and thermal regulation related to blood flow and stress responses, described in the race-car competition. This domain of self-regulation training was perhaps the most tangibly important for the soldiers that we worked with, as awareness and control of these functions would determine their ability to recognize and recover from stress and return to their window of tolerance and optimal state of being. This autonomic learning would also help our soldiers learn to keep their hands and feet warmer in the freezing conditions they would encounter in their area of operations.

Visits from Colonel Getty

Our Mind Lab was known as a strange attractor on base, and we were often a first stop for curious visiting dignitaries and top brass who had heard of our program. Colonel Getty prided himself on the Jedi program and had a deep personal interest in learning as much as he could from us. He regarded the Mind Lab and time with us as one of his favorite refuges. He would often come to hang out with us in the lab for hours, leaving with armloads of books and biofeedback devices to take home and work with on his own time. He understood well the transformational power and value of this training and was deeply committed to reducing suffering and the causes of suffering within his sphere of influence.

Colonel Getty was fond of bringing visiting colleagues to the lab. The blood pressure biofeedback device was the most popular instrument because most of the senior officers had concerns about their blood pressure, yet very few had the inner skills for managing it. Hooking up with the blood pressure biofeedback instrument made it vividly clear that blood pressure is not only constantly changing from moment to moment, but also that feedback and awareness training can teach people to influence and lower its level. When the officers experienced firsthand the potential for greater self-optimization and self-mastery, they frequently engaged us in deeper conversations about the vast array of extraordinary human potentials and the disciplines necessary to realize them.

One day Colonel Getty gave us a heads-up that the general in his chain of command was planning to be on base and was looking forward to meeting us and touring the lab later that week. We put some time and effort into sprucing up the lab and preparing for his visit, but the general never showed up, and Colonel Getty never called. We were disappointed to miss the opportunity to thank the general for his support of the program and to show off a bit for him, and we were curious about what had happened that had scrubbed their visit.

When we met up with the colonel the next day, Michelle teased him, "So Colonel Getty, what happened with your visit to the lab with the general? We had the lab all spiffed up and sparkling for you and the general, and I even went so far as to give Joel a haircut and trimmed his beard, and you stood us up. What's with that?" Colonel Getty apologized saying, "I'm so sorry to stand you up. There was an unexpected incident in the European field of operations early yesterday, and the general needed to stay focused on that. He's postponed his visit for now." And then beaming a big smile, the colonel laughed, looked tenderly at Joel, and said, "Honestly Joel, you could show up with a robe and a turban on, and I'd still love you." We were speechless and deeply touched by his disarming warmth, friendly humor, and unabashed affection.

Some months later, at the Christmas party hosted by Colonel Getty and his wife, we were approached by a woman who introduced herself as the wife of one of his close staff members. With great sincerity she thanked us for all the help we had given to her. Having never met her before, we asked curiously what kind of help she had received from us. To which she replied, "Oh, didn't Colonel Getty tell you? I was suffering greatly with severe Raynaud's disease, and my doctor had scheduled me for surgery to sever the nerves in my hands that were cutting off the blood flow and causing so much pain and danger of gangrene. Colonel Getty learned of my predicament from my husband who works on his staff. He reached out to me saying he might be able to help me, and then shared what he had

189

learned from you in your biofeedback lab, teaching me how to use the thermal biofeedback and relaxation exercises to increase the blood flow to my hands. I was so successful in learning to warm my hands with my mind that my surgeon said the surgery was no longer necessary. He was amazed and said he had never seen anyone learn to do this before. I'm so grateful for your help, and I'm thrilled to be able to thank you in person!"

Neurofeedback: Training the Central Nervous System

Proceeding on to even more subtle levels of embodied awareness and self-mastery, we progressed to training with neurofeedback. This modality attaches sensors to the skull to measure and provide feedback on the extremely subtle fluctuations of our brainwaves, the electrical activity generated from various regions and networks in our brains. Neurofeedback is especially helpful for refining our awareness of very subtle changes in our mind-brain states related to changes in our state of consciousness.

During the intensive neurofeedback training, the soldiers were in the lab with us for seven days, five to seven hours each day, in six-man teams. There were also three follow-up sessions of three hours each. Our daily neurofeedback sessions involved filling out a questionnaire regarding food intake, drink, nicotine, caffeine, or any other substance intake and sexual activity in the preceding twenty hours. We also administered mood inventories to assess the mood and mind-set of each soldier at the beginning and end of each training session. Then the men buddied up to apply the neuro-sensors to their skulls and to check for proper impedance readings before each soldier hooked into the network in a small, darkened, sound-isolated training module.

The Jedi Warrior neurofeedback training had two phases to it. The first was focused on individual neurofeedback training, which helped each of the men tune in and "get their heads on straight," guided by the tones generated by their mind-brain states. During the training sessions, each soldier listened to electronically synthesized tones through headphones that were modulated by the intensity and power of increases and decreases in the alpha brainwave frequencies. Tones for signals from the right hemisphere were heard in the right ear, while tones from signals generated by the left hemisphere were presented to the left ear, thus creating a profoundly intimate feedback loop between one's own awareness and one's ever-changing brain-body state. With training it became exquisitely clear that the flow of energy and information streaming to and through the nervous system was changing moment to moment and that with curiosity, openness, and awareness, one could learn to influence that flow.

Insights from the EEG Lab

Joel and I (Michelle) sat at "Alpha Control" in the core of the lab, surrounded by the training rooms monitoring the brain waves of each of the soldiers, and we had intercoms to be able to communicate with the soldiers in each room. Over the course of our training, gigabytes of data were gathered from the left and right occipital lobes of each soldier's brain in the beta frequencies (associated with the busy thinking mind that processes details), alpha frequencies (calm, clear, attentive presence of mind), and theta frequencies (a dreamy, visionary mind state or creative awake awareness, for those trained to be lucid in subtle states of awareness). Having collected baseline EEG measurements during the middle of the first month of the program in a variety of conditions—with eyes open and closed and during an auditory vigilance task—we later compared those baselines with the soldiers' EEG scores on day one and day six of the intensive training.

While getting one of the captains prepped for an initial neurofeedback session, I was in the midst of attaching several brainwave sensors to his scalp when I was presented head-on with a surprise encounter. The captain was semireclined in his chair in a very relaxed and receptive mode as his scalp was being cleaned and groomed to assure optimal contact with the sensors. Looking up at me, he suddenly asked in a somewhat dreamy voice, "Michelle, were you one of those antiwar peace activists and protestors demonstrating in the streets during the Vietnam War days?" Boom! My heart skipped a beat, then seemed to speed up as blood rushed to my likely flushed face, and I felt my electrodermal response spike momentarily. OK . . . here it is, another moment-of-truth opportunity. Centering myself, I took a deep breath and got very present, not knowing where this would go.

"Yes, you bet, Captain, I was definitely out there back then, actively taking part in many of those antiwar demonstrations." Hearing this, he seemed to relax even more deeply and nodded, giving me a broad smile as he responded disarmingly, "That is one of my favorite periods of history."

History! I suddenly felt like a dinosaur. It had been such a pivotal time in the awakening of my social consciousness and values formation and was still so vividly present in my memory. This unexpected and collegially relaxed response from a member of the armed forces once again under-scored the power of truth and spontaneous, uncontrived authenticity. We had both demonstrated our commitments to be honest and vulnerable in a potentially polarizing situation and experienced the power this commit-ment had to melt barriers, actual or perceived, and open a space of shared humanity, closeness, trust, and mutual care. Another gift from the EEG lab that I hadn't anticipated but was very grateful for.

A State of Calm Intensity

There are a wide variety of neurofeedback protocols to encourage the devel-opment of different states of mind-brain tuning that target different mixes of EEG frequencies generated by different regions of the brain. For exam-ple, to quiet the ruminating mind, we focus on quieting the beta frequen-cies, and to increase access to creative and meditative states, we work with various blends of beta suppression and alpha-theta enhancement. For Jedi Warrior, we focused on a neurofeedback protocol that encouraged greater power in the alpha brainwave range, between 8 and 12 cycles per second.

This state opened the psychoneuromatrix to access a rare and treasured quality of alert yet relaxed awareness capable of noticing the rich mix of various inner and outer experiences that arise and pass in the open space of the mind moment to moment. The soldiers came to describe the target alpha brainwave range as a state of "calm intensity," which seemed a most fitting and appropriate description. This alert, relaxed awareness was vital to building the men's confidence, self-mastery, sustainability, resilience, and capacity for success and had profound mission applications for remaining alert and attentive for long periods of time in their reconnaissance-based missions.

As one of the soldiers noted, "This neurofeedback and mind-fitness training helps us get into the state of calm intensity that we need to perform at our best. I used to think this state of mind just came out of the blue, like grace now and then, but here I'm learning how to turn on the quality of mind and brain that gets me into this state whenever I want. I thought I had great control over my body before, but it was superficial control. This is real core training that works from the mind-side out into physiology and into performance."

Michelle recalls another memorable moment of neurofeedback training that arose during a session on the fourth day of training with one of the teams while sitting in alpha central, monitoring the brainwaves of each soldier in their training pods. We'd noticed that Chief Harner in pod three was way off his game, and his usual stellar levels of power had totally crashed. During a pause in the action, I (Michelle) went back to check in on him, announcing as I knocked on the door to his pod, "Hi Chief, can I come in? I'd like to check and see if any of your sensors might be loose."

Checking all the sensors, I confirmed that they were all still perfectly attached to his skull. "Everything looks OK, Chief. Any ideas for what's going on for you today?"

"Yeah, I hate to admit it," he replied, "but I had a real blow-out argument with my wife before I left for the base this morning, and I'm still really upset. This brainwave biofeedback training is a fierce mirror for how my mind state affects my physiology. I can feel how high my blood pressure is, and I hate to admit it, but when I'm angry, I can't get my brain to work worth a darn. My brain power is down nearly 80 percent over my average yesterday, and I just can't focus. It's a good thing I'm not out on a mission with a lot of anger or fear jamming my circuits. I'd be a sitting duck with a mind like this. Any suggestions, coach?"

Sitting down with him for a few minutes, I shared several strategies for generating forgiveness and getting the mind focused in the here and now. "Experiment with these strategies and see what happens," I said, turning to head toward the door. After flashing a thumbs-up to each other, I turned down the lights and closed the door.

Back in the control room, we watched to see what would happen. With fits and starts, Chief showed some success and then slipped back into a less-coherent or stable mind-brain state. We were really rooting for him and were hoping that his efforts would prove successful. Finally, there was a big burst of alpha and theta brain wave activity, and his readings skyrocketed to a higher level than we had seen on any previous day. During the next break, we clicked on the intercom to check in, "This is Alpha Control to Chief. Do you read?"

"Chief here, read you loud and clear."

"Great comeback, Chief. You're off the charts and set a new high for yourself. What kicked in for you?"

"It's not too hard to describe," he said. "After trying that forgiveness practice you taught me, I finally just slipped into a space where I felt really close to my wife and could feel her close to me. I was able to connect with the love I have in my heart for her. When I just stayed with that feeling, the power and amplitude of my brain waves were off the charts. This is powerful stuff we're working with here, and I'm beginning to understand that the mind and brain are incredibly responsive . . . and I'm learning that I can shift my energy and tune into whatever quality of mind state I choose."

"Good to have you back on board, Chief. You're beginning to discover the internal control panel and the internal moves that will make it or break it for you if you go out on your mission. Unfasten your seat belt and let's launch into the last session for today. Imagine what is possible and stretch toward it. Alpha Control over and out."

Phase Two Neurofeedback

With this as our foundation, we then moved into the second phase of training, which involved shared neurofeedback. In this phase the men were able to not only hear their own neurosynch tones, but to also hear the tones of their buddies' brains and see their digital scores as well. The measurements displayed were a quantification of the quotient of neural amplitude (power) and duration (stability) of the EEG spectral activity at any given moment for each neural site.

Our guidance to them was to explore how deeply synched up and tuned into each other they could become, using real-time feedback, which provided a moment-to-moment indication of when they were moving into neural synchronization and when they were drifting out of synch with each other. Their task was to notice what brought them back into synch and what pulled them away from it. This type of shared neurosynch training was, and still is, an uncharted frontier of neuropsychological research and training. Jedi Warrior was likely the first time that shared neurosynch biofeedback had been applied in a professional training situation.

The various regions of the brain are all harmonic oscillators. To perform any task requires a deep attunement and synchronization of different regions and circuits of our brain that enable us to coordinate our seeing, sensing, and movement with our intention and attention to accomplish our goals. The same principles apply in any complex task that requires coordinated group activity, but at this level we need to expand our awareness to tune in not only to ourselves but to also deeply attune to the flow of energy and information linking us with other people. This may apply in the dynamic flow of collaborating to cook up a family dinner, plan the launch of a complex business project, or carry out a dangerous military mission. Our language is filled with idioms that reflect this understanding, such as "getting on the same wavelength," "putting our heads together," or "making beautiful music together." Each of these phrases could translate into a direct correlation with synchronizing the electrophysiological activity and frequencies of our brains.

Neurofeedback training develops entrainment and resonance between all the oscillating regions of an individual brain, and shared neurofeedback develops the entrainment and resonance of macro-oscillations linking two or more human brains. Such shared feedback has the potential to strengthen empathic attunement and more effective cooperation and synchronization in performing collaborative tasks.

Energy Awareness

As we refined awareness and self-regulation to even more subtle levels, we also worked with a variety of practices for refining our sense of subtle energies and directing their flow. Within the Jedi Warrior training protocol, this level of training involved practices of energy sensing and healing and sensory enhancements, as we'll describe in detail in chapters 12 and 13. Interestingly, the interest in energy-healing methods, rooted in aikido and the somatic sciences, was surprisingly high, especially among the medics who appreciated that they needed as many effective methods as possible on hand—especially if they were to be deployed for long periods of time with limited medications and no chance of resupply.

A glimpse of this dimension of our embodied being is offered by our mentor Joanna Macy who lucidly observed the following.

We consist of and are sustained by interweaving currents of matter, energy, and information that flow through us interconnecting us with our environment and other beings. Yet, we are accustomed to identify-ing ourselves only with a small arc of the flow that is lit, like the narrow beam of a flashlight, by our individual subjective awareness. We don't have to so limit our self-perceptions. It is as plausible to align our identity with the larger pattern, interexistent with all beings, as to break off one segment of the process and build our borders there.[3]

This level of training was validated by decades of research at the Menninger Foundation, Stanford University, Princeton University's Princeton Engineering Anomalies Research (PEAR) Project,[4] and numer-ous other prestigious institutions around the world. These institutions have already begun to investigate and document the impact experimental operators have on various quantifiable, measured external things, such as computer functions, when they focus conscious attention and intention on a device and receive moment-to-moment feedback from the targeted device. Most interestingly, this research demonstrates that when these operators, who are adept at measurably influencing distant biological or electronic sys-tems, are asked to describe the inner moves and mechanisms they employ to influence their distant targets, the terms they use are identical to those used to describe how they might change their own internal physiological state with their mind. The profound implication of this mind-expanding research is that it seems that the so-called distant targets of our intention, attention, and prayer are actually part of our body—nonlocal, yet inti-mately accessible to us.

Over the past sixty years, thousands of well-controlled scientific stud-ies on the nonlocal effects of the mind consistently demonstrate that the same qualities of mind—attention and intention—that enable us to cre-ate changes in our own bodies, if properly directed, can make measurable changes within and beyond our bodies. The growing evidence is profoundly compelling, and the data suggests that even ordinary, untrained people have the latent ability to develop and demonstrate extraordinary abilities, many of which challenge our cherished mental models and assumptions regarding the nature of mind and reality. This trend in research is rapidly and radically expanding the dimensions of scientific inquiry and challenging researchers to become ever more adept in both the inner and outer sciences.

The implications of the military's long history of research into remote viewing and remote influence via subtle energies on distant, nonlocal biological and technical systems through the focus and power of the mind are intriguing. Barbara Brown, a respected researcher from the UCLA psychiatry department, has astutely suggested that

> if mental activity truly originates from our brain cells, then it is logical to assume that psychic phenomena also use these same brain cells. We assume this because psychic activity involves a change in mental activity; otherwise, it could not be integrated, stored, recalled, and communicated by human means. Telepathic information must have entry into the universe of the brain cells where the 'picture' of the information is developed. Even if the psychic information gets into the brain supernaturally, it must go through the ordinary channels of brain processing to get out of the brain to be communicated to other people. This means that there is a neurophysiological impression of the psychic experience. If that impression is there, then we should be able to find it. If biofeedback can be used with this brain indicator to bring psychic abilities under voluntary, predictable control, this will be one of the most explosive discoveries that biofeedback can make.[5]

One stellar example of extraordinary energy awareness with measurable effects is our colleague Mietek Wirkus, who was participating in some research on cell metabolism at Walter Reed Military Hospital in Bethesda, Maryland. Mietek is one of the world's most respected, gifted, and scientifically studied energy healers in the world. As a child in Poland after World

War II, Mietek would accompany the local doctor in caring for sick people in pain. The doctor had few supplies, but he found that his patients would often feel better, and their conditions would improve, just by having young Mietek sit with them and hold their hand.

Through prayer, meditation, and what Mietek describes as the healing love of Christ, along with years of training with elders who had developed their own healing gifts, he learned to deeply sense and transmit the healing energy of love. When bioenergy therapy was approved in Poland to supplement ordinary medical work, Mietek became one of the first professional bioenergy therapists to work in the Polish medical centers, performing detailed diagnoses and treatments for hundreds of people each week. After immigrating to the United States in 1985, Mietek and his wife, Margaret, settled in Bethesda and trained thousands of physicians, nurses, and other helping professionals.

This brought Mietek to the attention of researchers at Walter Reed who were measuring the impact of bioenergy healing on the calcium uptake of cell cultures. After working with the cell cultures for a short while, the cells became so sensitized to his energetic presence that they would begin to alter their metabolism the moment he entered the hospital lobby some floors below the actual laboratory. One time when Mietek was visiting family in Poland, something emotionally activating happened just before he was scheduled to do a distant healing session. In this highly activated state, Mietek's energetic impact on the cells back in the lab at the army hospital thousands of miles away was surprisingly more powerful and significant than in any of the sessions he had conducted back at the laboratory in person!

While we can certainly measure and validate the temporal correlation of intention, transmission, and the level of actual impact, the mechanism of the transmission of subtle energies across vast distances remains elusive. Such is the case with thousands of similarly inspiring experiments. The implications of these powerful nonlocal bioenergetic effects are highly relevant for military intelligence, as well as for those involved with healing, prayer, and energy work, and we were fortunate to have a charter to introduce this work within our Jedi program.

Mental Formations

There are seemingly infinite levels to the mind, yet upon examination all of these are mere displays of creative potential arising in the mind space of awareness as perceptions, sensations, and mental formations, such as thoughts, images, intentions, and states of consciousness. As the power of our concentration grows sufficiently strong and is directed to carefully observe and investigate these subtle mind states, one of the most profound and liberating insights is that, though these images and sensations seem very compelling and often bind and define us, they are actually ever changing, insubstantial, and dreamlike. These experiences vividly appear in the mind for only an instant, and then they immediately vanish without leaving a trace, like a handprint in water. These mind states are experienced as binding and solid because of what Einstein referred to as the "optical delusion of consciousness," which leads most of us to misapprehend the nature of mind states and to mistake or confuse our thoughts and beliefs as actual reality.

Once carefully observed with penetrating insight, we can release these many old, binding habits, which have defined and constrained us for decades, and our mind begins to become more clear, open, and malleable, giving rise to new degrees of freedom and creative redefinition of ourselves. Once this level of insight is reached, one is faced with a profound question: If I am more than and not defined by my thoughts, narratives, and stories, then who, or what, or how am I in actual reality? This is where the journey of awakening becomes most interesting as the range of possibilities and potentials available to us from this point on become vast.

Using a wide variety of awareness and meditation techniques, our soldiers learned to observe, influence, and manage the activity of their minds. The implications for them of glimpsing or realizing this level of insight were both profound and elusive to grasp. Learning to regard thoughts as mere daydreams lacking any inherent power to cloud one's clear direct perception of reality opens the mind to greater freedom and to encountering reality in a more direct, intimate, and undistorted manner.

At this level of subtle mind awareness and influence, the profound discipline of lucid dreaming—where the dreamer becomes aware they are dreaming and uses the dream realm to train in extraordinary mindfulness and skill—becomes available. Though this domain of mind-fitness training is worthy of exploration, it was beyond the scope of our Jedi program.

Awareness Itself

As training progressed from the most tangible to the most subtle levels, we came to the most essential and foundational dimension of awareness or mindful presence itself. Our friend and colleague Jon Kabat Zinn, a pioneer in introducing mindfulness to a wider mainstream audience, wrote the following in his foreword for the British Parliament's *Mindful Nation UK* report.

> Basically, when we are talking about mindfulness, we are talking about awareness—pure awareness. It is an innate human capacity that is different from thinking but wholly complementary to it. It is also "bigger" than thinking, because any thought, no matter how momentous or profound, illuminating, or destructive, can be held in awareness, and thus looked at, known, and understood in a multiplicity of ways which may provide new degrees of insight and fresh perspectives for dealing with old problems and emergent challenges, whether individual, societal, or global. Awareness in its purest form, or mindfulness, thus has the potential to add value and new degrees of freedom to living life fully and wisely and,

thus, to making wiser and healthier, more compassionate and altruistic choices—in the only moment that any of us ever has for tapping our deep interior resources for imagination and creativity, for learning, growing, and healing, and in the end, for transformation, going beyond the limitations of our presently understood models of who we are as human beings and individual citizens, as communities and societies, as nations, and as a species.[6]

As we gain higher levels of mastery over the habitual tendency to identify with or reify our mental formations and learn to quiet the turbulence of the mind, we begin to glimpse and then gradually come to abide more deeply in the open, nonreactive quality of awake, loving, selfless presence that is limitless in expanse like the sky. Accompanying this realization is a quality of wonderment at this sublime level of being that leads to a sense of connection and reverence for all life, a great humility in the face of the mysteries of existence, and a natural dedication if not devotion to courageously stand for the good of all, even if this means risking one's own life. To us, and to many of our most inspired teachers, this is where we come to know the true heart of the warrior spirit.

Axioms of Biopsybernautics

In order to convey the most essential principles of extraordinary mind-body mastery, we developed a useful set of pithy axioms to help our soldiers remember and keep in mind the core principles of advanced biopsybernautic training.

- **Make your nervous system your ally—instead of your enemy.** As you learn to listen to, befriend, and work with the innate, natural intelligence of your mind-body-brain, you are better able to quickly recover from mishaps and to martial the power, strength, and intelligence you need to harmonize your nervous system, to rise again refreshed, renewed, and resilient to meet the next waves of changes and challenges that will inevitably come your way. When you are out of harmony, your mind and nervous system are highjacked by mindless, reactive habits, and you are functioning out of control, putting yourself and others in danger. Having deep confidence that your body knows how to heal and that your nervous system is your ally offers you a priceless and profound sense of strength, confidence, and potential.

- **Recognize and stop the war inside first—then proceed.** When wars and conflicts erupt within us, our mind-body is hijacked by unconscious, reactive forces that overtake and undermine our intelligence and dissipate our power and strength. Learning how to recognize the early warning signs of inner conflict and stop the war inside before it escalates and overwhelms you will prevent the inner conflicts from spewing out, affecting others and causing more unnecessary damage and destruction. If you are to liberate others from oppression, learn to free yourself first, and then proceed.

- **Warrior up! This work takes courage.** Jedi Warrior training requires a special kind of courage. It is not for the fainthearted. To find power, you will have to own, embrace, and understand your joys and sorrows, your strengths and vulnerabilities. To find peace you must own, embrace, and understand everything within you that is turbulent or at war. To find wisdom, you must seek to deeply question your ignorance, arrogance, and misconceptions. Ultimately, your greatest power lies in wisdom, compassion, and deep connection.

- **Your most primary resources and power tools are attention, intention, and attitude.** These are your three primary mental superpowers. Knowing how to wisely monitor, manage, synergize, optimize, and deploy your attention, intention, and attitude is vital to this training and to your success in virtually every moment and every field of operations in your life.

- **You can only manage what you monitor.** This is how awareness and intention work together. Mindful clear presence is your core skill and strength. It is what allows you to monitor flows of energy and information and wisely deploy your resources to skillfully respond in order to optimize the systems that you are monitoring. In the absence of monitoring and awareness, you have no capacity for intentional influence or skillful management.

- **Control follows awareness.** When you are mindful you have access to choice, agency, intention, and influence. When you are mindless and functioning on autopilot or driven by unconscious habits, you lose touch with your life, your power, and your self-determination, and mindless habit energy takes control of your life. Reclaim your life from the marauding demons of mindless habit.

- **What gets fired gets wired. Where attention goes, neural firing flows, and neural connection grows.** Mind fitness is embodied and hardwired into your neural pathways. As your mind changes, your brain changes. As you train your mind, you change the structure, functioning, and capacity of your brain. As you learn to understand how this works, you accelerate your learning and turn transient states of experience into powerful enduring traits. This gives you a huge advantage over others who have not developed themselves in these ways. With the rare privilege of accessing this learning comes the responsibility to help others to learn and practice these skills, so that they in turn can help others to learn and practice these skills.

- **Go to ground.** Ground and find strength in the stillness in the midst of turbulence, peace in the midst of chaos, and clarity in the midst of confusion. The force *is* with you—always. The more you learn how to access the enduring treasury of the deepest dimensions of your being, the more profoundly resourced and capable you will be. Once you learn to open this inner portal, no one can take this inexhaustible reservoir of strength away from you.

- **Call in your allies.** Remember, you exist within a vast matrix of deep and meaningful relationships. You are continually informed by the flow of energy and information streaming to you and through you from others, even if you are physically distant from them. You are always deeply connected. Cultivate and deepen these vital connections. Within this seamless wholeness you have access to virtually limitless resources and reservoirs of strength and inspiration. Learn how to access them at any time and in every circumstance.

  As a first step, envision being in the presence of an inspiring mentor or mentors. Imagine them looking kindly upon you and reaching out to take your hand. As you hold their hand, envision that you can breathe in their strength, wisdom, inspiration, and blessings and radiate back to them your gratitude and appreciation. As you reach out to them, envision them reaching out to hold the hands of their mentors, who in turn hold the hands of their mentors, in an infinite succession back through time, lineages, and ancestors. As you breathe in, sense that you receive from them all, and as you breathe out, radiate and extend your gratitude rippling back upstream to them all. This is one of countless such practices to help you call in your allies and access the vast treasury of inspiring resources that is available to you at all times.

- **You are part of the wisdom lineage.** Ripples of impact flowing through time from generation to generation, to you and through you in an endless cascade. If you think this training is just about your personal development, you are missing the point. Remember: the wisdom, power, and blessings that have informed and inspired this program have cascaded down through wisdom lineages of awakening beings since the dawn of humanity. As it flows to you, take it to heart, make it your own, and then let it flow through you on to others and through them to others, in an endless cascade. Think in terms of ripples of influence and benefit for generations to come because you had the privilege and good fortune of this rare and precious opportunity to participate in this program. Let your learning be truly dedicated to the benefit of all.

Confidence and Shifting the Locus of Control Inward

As our soldiers learned these self-regulation skills, they became measurably more self-empowered, self-confident, discerning, and less reactive. This is often indicated on psychological tests that point to a shift from an outer locus of control—where people feel powerless, victimized, or less in control of their lives—to an inner locus of control—where people are more capable and confident in their ability to make choices and be more in control of their lives.

Properly understood and taken to heart, these disciplines extend in profound ways into the entirety of our lives. We have seen many times that when people discover and find within themselves the power to influence the subtle inner working of their bodies, it often opens whole new avenues of personal choice, power, and confidence in their daily lives, work, and relationships. This can open for people even after a brief encounter with biofeedback where by learning to increase their skin temperature by a half a degree they see the possibility of having more agency and control in their lives. The awakening of such a deep confidence in the power of one's own agency to shape the inner conditions of one's own life may be expressed in many ways: for example, the courage to take an unpopular stand, to question or challenge orthodoxy or authority, to rise up and occupy a wider realm of possibilities, or to say no to someone who has dominated or overshadowed one.

Toward the end of our program, we had a visit from a research team from the NIH (National Institutes of Health) who had heard some wild stories about our program and were interested to learn more about it. We were happy to show them around the lab and share some of the data that came from our research. Looking around our lab at all the tech we had for doing deep cyberphysiology and biopsybernautic training, one of the visitors asked, "How do you justify the incredible expense of all the time and technology involved in this program?" We replied, "In a word, to build the confidence of the men we are training."

That response was met with a quizzical look. "Can you say more about confidence and why that is so important for these soldiers?" We smiled and explained:

"Certainly. Supposing your job required you to be prepared to say good-bye to your family some morning, then go to work and be notified that you were being shipped out on a mission to a distant land, and your family would have no idea where you were deployed. You are loaded into a plane, flown deep into enemy territory, and parachute in the dead of night, falling HALO* with a hundred-pound pack, to dig in for as long as you can to send out reconnaissance info for as long as you can. You are so deep into hostile territory that you are not expected to come out alive.

"Wouldn't you want to know that you had the necessary skills and confidence you needed to carry you through that deployment without succumbing to the dreaded inner enemies of self-doubt and fear? Wouldn't you want to have confidence that, whatever arose, you had access to an arsenal of ever-renewing inner resources and skills to manage your mind-body in ways that would optimize your chances of mission success and survival? And wouldn't you want to know that not only are you equipped with these skills, but that your whole team also carried these resources and capacities within them?

"So, yes sir, we have all this technology and training to teach these men confidence that regardless of their circumstances they had the personal

---

*In a HALO (high altitude low opening) jump, the parachute jumper exits at a higher-than-usual altitude (between 15,000 and 35,000 feet) and opens the parachute at a lower altitude.

power and skills to take care of themselves and each other and fulfill their mission in the best ways possible."

Our response gave rise to a lengthy dialogue regarding the nature of this training and how such transformational inner work serves to deepen awareness and shift the locus of control in people's lives toward more skillful and empowered ways of living. People who have lived their lives assuming others have power over them are likely to feel victimized by circumstances and exhaust themselves blaming others and outer conditions for their unfortunate circumstances. But as people develop sufficient skills, confidence, understanding, personal mastery, and a sense of agency necessary to assume greater ownership for their own responses to the outer conditions of their lives, they make a measurable shift toward a more empowered internal locus of control, even if they are still embedded within toxic social systems that have deleterious impacts on their lives.

The profound insight of Victor Frankl came to mind regarding our human capacity for living with an internal locus of control, even in the most harrowing of human circumstances. Frankl, who was a prisoner in the Nazi concentration camp at Auschwitz, once wrote: "Between stimulus and response there is a space. In that space is our power to choose our response. In our response lies our growth and our freedom. . . . Everything can be taken from a person but one thing: the last of human freedoms. . . . The one thing you can't take away from me is the way I choose to respond to what you do to me. . . . The last of one's freedoms is to choose one's attitude in any given circumstance." Having endured great suffering and great abuse, Frankl spoke to the grace, power, courage, and dignity that we can bring to even the most horrific human conditions, writing, "Man is that being who invented the gas chambers of Auschwitz; however, he is also that being who entered those chambers upright, with the Lord's Prayer or the Shema Yisrael on his lips."[7]

Our aspiration in guiding Jedi Warrior was to help our soldiers find their version of this kind of profound and enduring presence, dignity, deep confidence, faith, dedication, and inner strength necessary to face the dangers of their missions and to wisely navigate the VUCAA nature of their lives. May we all have the curiosity, courage, commitment, opportunity, and wise guidance necessary to explore these farther reaches of human potential.

> *You have brains in your head.*
> *You have feet in your shoes.*
> *You can steer yourself*
> *any direction you choose.*
> *You're on your own. And you know what you know.*
> *And YOU are the one who'll decide where to go.*
> DR. SEUSS, *OH, THE PLACES YOU'LL GO!*

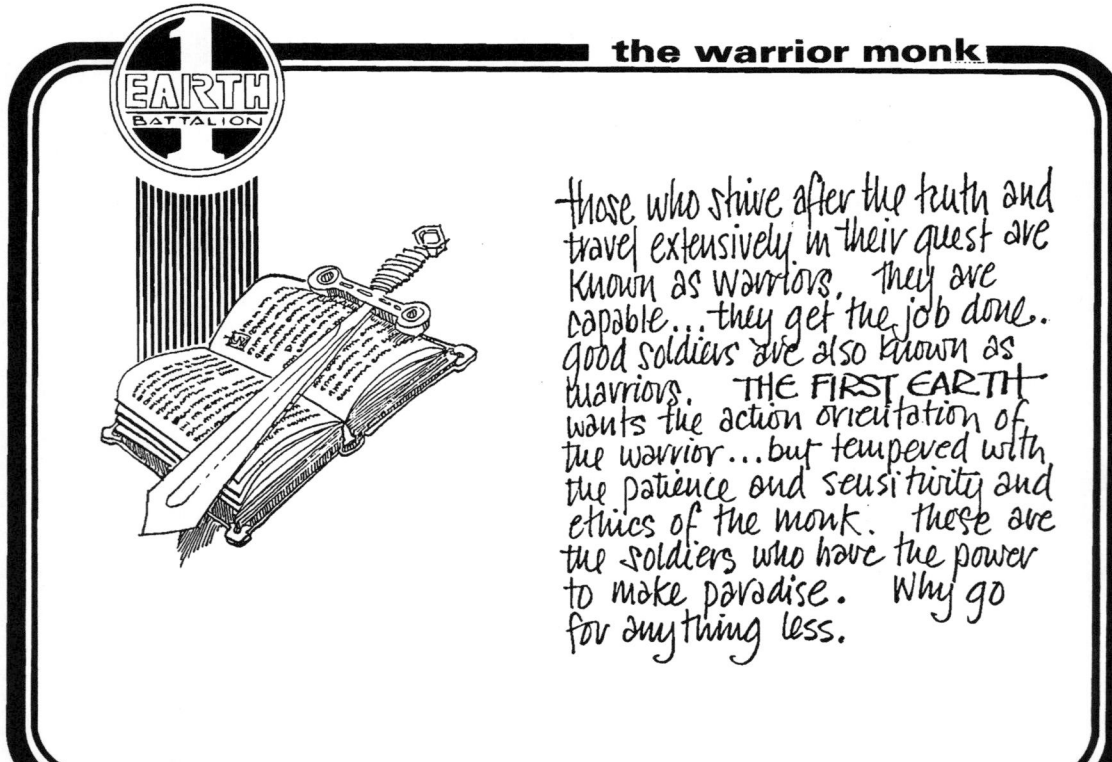

the warrior monk

those who strive after the truth and travel extensively in their quest are known as warriors. they are capable... they get the job done. good soldiers are also known as warriors. THE FIRST EARTH wants the action orientation of the warrior... but tempered with the patience and sensitivity and ethics of the monk. these are the soldiers who have the power to make paradise. why go for anything less.

THE FIRST EARTH BATTALION

ELEVEN

The Encampment Begins

Now and again, it is necessary to seclude yourself among deep mountains and hidden valleys to restore your link to the source of life . . . The Divine is not something high above us. It is in heaven, it is in earth, it is inside us.

MORIHEI UESHIBA, "ART OF PEACE"

Waking up on the morning of September 8, we felt like we were on the edge of a high cliff, about to leap into unknown terrain. We enjoyed a long tender snuggle appreciating that for the next month we would be staying in separate cabins as part of the discipline for the encampment, a continuous immersion in focused mind-body-spirit training spanning fifteen to twenty hours per day for an entire month. This would be the longest, most intensive phase of our Jedi Warrior training, and we both felt a rich mix of excitement and trepidation regarding the possibilities and challenges awaiting us in this month to come.

No one in the Western world had ever guided, or experienced, a meditation "retreat" like this with twenty-five Special Ops soldiers, let alone one that was a full monthlong in silence. We decided to call this immersive training period an encampment since the term "retreat" traditionally does not have positive associations within the military! It was also being held away from the military base in a somewhat remote and humble Boy Scouts

Camp up in the mountains of New Hampshire near Mount Monadnock.

While all of the other aspects of Jedi Warrior training took place in settings and scenarios that were somewhat familiar to our soldiers, the encampment offered a radically novel environment and would serve as a crucible to discover, refine, and affirm the essence of personal power, presence, and courage for these men. It was designed to provide a rarified, intensified, learning laboratory that had the power and potential to reveal the deepest fears and vulnerabilities of these soldiers as well as the greatest strengths, extraordinary special forces, and highest potentials of each of these men. This unrelenting 24/7 psychophysical experience would require truly extraordinary discipline, courage, humility, patience, strength, nonreactivity, endurance, and dedication from each soldier, and this intensity of presence would need to be ceaselessly reaffirmed each moment of each day, lest one might drift off into the sinkholes of the wandering mind. This challenge course promised to reveal the myriad of ways these strengths of character were present, and absent, in the lives of these men, and would illuminate their true priorities and the degree of their dedication to courageously face the intensity and complexity of their most noble light and most terrifying darkness.

While our original plan for this vital phase of training was designed for twenty-five men who were eager, curious, and fully engaged, it was clear that not all our men were so wholeheartedly dedicated. We wondered how this kind of intensive mental training and exploration would translate to immersing the men into an environment that was so utterly unfamiliar and where the success of the process would be reflective of the level of engagement that each person brought to it. We were also aware that due to a delay in the building out of workspaces, we had lost two weeks of preparatory training that would have laid a much stronger foundation and sense of understanding.

The drive through the luminous autumn foliage was magical, and we both savored the precious moments of delight in simply being alone together amid this vivid autumn beauty. The weeks before had been full to the max, and we were working insanely long hours most days of the week. This drive would likely be our last time of just being and talking together without being "on" and holding space for this encampment. The preciousness of these moments alone together was palpable. And while there were certainly maps of the territory, the complex and widely varying nature of our mission offered a rich blend of excitement and apprehension. We both pondered how our own teachers might guide such a "retreat." Talking about this together, it seemed clear that we needed to be well prepared and also ready to respond to the emerging unique needs, circumstances, challenges, and opportunities of the encampment, moment to moment to moment.

Driving through the gate into Camp Wanocksett, we were inspired by the natural beauty of the setting for such an immersive program. As we pulled in, we met two young privates who worked in the mess hall on base. They had also just arrived and were beginning to unload the food supplies into the dining hall. We had engaged a colleague of ours to be the main cook, nutritionist, and menu planner, and she was grateful to have helpers in the kitchen with her. Barbara had been a cook at the Insight Meditation Center in Barre, Massachusetts, not far from the base, and was used to cooking healthful and delicious meals for retreatants. IMS was the foremost mindfulness meditation center in North America at that time. Barbara's job was to optimize the nutrition for our meals and to also bring a mindful presence to how the food would be prepared and served during our month of intensive training.

One of the young privates commented that he didn't know how to cook vegetarian food, and when we said that there was supposed to be some meat, fish, and chicken, which had been ordered as well, they checked the food order documents and came back to inform us that these orders had not been delivered. As we talked with them it was clear that they were clueless about what this encampment was about and found this one of the strangest postings they had ever been deployed on. All they knew was that this was their assignment for the next month, and they were looking to us for leadership.

We parked and searched out the cabins where we'd be staying, Joel in the cabin with Jack and Richard, and Michelle bunking with Barbara. We spent the day exploring the site, walking the trails, transforming one of the meeting halls into our meditation "zendo," planning our teachings, and getting a bit of rest. This felt like the calm before the storm.

The Troops Arrive

The men rolled in the next day in a small convoy of camouflaged vehicles. They unloaded in a boisterous spirit curious to see where we'd be for the month. The afternoon was spent with the men settling into their cabins and exploring the forest and lakeside. It was a day of open space to relax and orient to their new surroundings.

We gathered the next morning for muster at 6 a.m. amid the mist wafting in from the pond, to stand in ranks at attention as the flag was raised. As Sargent Flynn called out his command, the men snapped off a salute to the flag. Jack, Richard, Michelle, and I stood to the side and flashed a glance as if to say, "this is certainly a novel way to begin a meditation retreat!" After some stretching and warm-ups, the men broke off into their three running groups: the Wolves, the fast and fit, were mostly the younger guys; the Poodles were the middle group; and the Stallions were the older men. The groups headed out through the mists and the rising sun for a good long run, followed by breakfast.

After breakfast, we gathered in the main hall to begin the practice. The rows were neatly lined with wooden meditation benches that the men had made themselves and carved with their team numbers. At the predeparture orientation briefing, Jack had invited them to also bring a power object that had meaning for them to place on the altar we would cocreate together in the hall. Upon entering we noticed that a collection of medals, knives, photos, dog tags of fallen friends, and other special items had already been assembled and carefully arranged in places of honor on the table up front designated for this purpose, consecrating our meditation hall as sacred space.

The mind field of our collective presence resounded with a rich and complex mix of tension, curiosity, and apprehension. For some of the men, the atmosphere in the room was charged with a heightened sense of excitement, sort of like taking off for their first parachute jump. For others, the tension held a sense of cold aloofness, perhaps even anger at being sent off for a month for this kind of immersive training that they could barely comprehend. We were struck by a feeling of great potential—both for engagement and for resistance.

We began by framing the mission of the encampment. "Today we embark on the first of thirty days of a mission that has the power to change your life. This mission involves securing and safeguarding a most precious yet vulnerable asset—your wakeful awareness—from being captured by the unrelenting forces of your unruly mind. Only when you are in the presence of this awareness do you have choice, power, or control in your life. Without it, you are lost."

"We encourage you to regard the threshold we are about to cross into this encampment like you would regard your first HALO jump, and to meet this moment with a deep honoring of whatever fear or excitement may be alive for you. If you don't feel some excitement, and some fear, you haven't understood the gravity, potential, and power of this new and very foreign field of operations that you are dropping into.

"This mission will most certainly test your courage, your determination, and your strength of character. Along the way, you will likely catch glimpses of peace of mind, mental clarity, insight, and inspiration. And you may also at times be assailed by moments of intense doubt, boredom, frustration, regret, sadness, loneliness, or rebelliousness. The perimeter of this encampment provides a safe zone to encounter, understand, and perhaps befriend your inner enemies. Though we can offer guidance and encouragement, keep in mind that no one can do this work for you but yourself. Whatever you experience, own it, examine it, question it. Your responses and reactions are mirrors of your own mind. Notice how all these experiences will arise and pass, come and flow. Remember that no experience, no matter how intense, will remain for long, and that no changing experience can fully define you. You are most essentially the awareness that will know and name all the different experiences that may arise in your mind."

We then asked the men to drop in for a few moments to notice what was alive within them and to name it. A barrage of words and images let loose: curious, open, frustrated, don't care, whatever. Murphy flatly said, "I'm honestly not sure why we have to do this!"

Joel stepped into it. "Let's look at this. To appreciate the value and relevance of the training that this encampment offers to you, pause for a moment, and imagine reaching out and holding in one hand all the moments of your life when you were fully present, mindful, and vividly awake to what was going on within and around you. In these moments of mindful presence, you were able to recognize options and discern wiser choices. If your eyes were open, you were *seeing*. If someone was talking to you, you were *listening* and attuned to the people in the conversation. If you were eating, you were vividly aware of the tastes and textures of the food. If you were walking, you were mindful of movements, sensations, and attuned to your surroundings. If you were thinking, you were aware of the nature of your thoughts."

Joel then gave examples of mindlessness: "Now, in your other hand, envision reaching out and holding all the moments of your life when you were *mindlessly* going through the moves, letting habits of mindless inattention rule and dominate your life. All those moments when your eyes were open but you weren't seeing, those moments when you were eating or drinking but didn't taste a bit, the moments that you were walking or driving and totally lost in your thoughts, unaware of your body or location.

Imagine getting in touch with all the moments where you were mentally absent, checked out, when you deserted the command of your precious life. In these moments of mindlessness, you relinquished your power of discernment and choice, and unconscious mindless habits dominated your life. Consider all those moments that passed by unnoticed, unlived, never to be fully known. Pause for a moment now to compare the proportion of the moments of your life that you hold in each of your two hands and put your hands into a gesture that represents the relative balance. As you do this, notice what thoughts, feelings, or aspirations you're mindful of."

We asked the men to call out an estimate of what their assessment was for the percent of their life that they were fully present and awake to their lives. A few estimated 30 to 50 percent. Most were between 10 and 20 percent. And a few were around 5 percent. Some just didn't seem to care.

Joel continued, "Having done this exercise with thousands of people around the globe, when people are honest with themselves, on average, most admit they are mindful and present with what they are experiencing for only 5 to 10 percent of the time. Let's be generous and say that you are fully awake and present to your life 20 percent of the time. That would mean that if you live to be one hundred years old you will have only fully lived twenty years of your entire life. Is that good enough for you? If you have a child that is ten years old, and you were only present for them for two years of their life, would that be good enough for you? If you were to spend thousands of dollars on good drinks and food, and other enjoyments, and only really showed up to enjoy 20 percent of the total satisfaction available to you, would that be enough? Or do you want more? And if you do want more of your life, are you willing to train for it and develop the powers of the mind and the neural integrity necessary to maintain and sustain higher levels of awareness? With this deep, personal, inner work, no one can do this for you, and no one can make you do it. This is an inside job! You've got to want it to get it.

"So, consider, if this 5, or 10, or 20 percent is your baseline or default capacity for showing up fully, courageously, and wholeheartedly for your life, then what are the implications of this for you going out on a mission, or in developing and maintaining relationships, or in any other arena of your life?

"While such reflections are humbling, if you take them to heart, this kind of deep reflection can give you a good kick in the ass to get it together, to train hard, fully show up, and reclaim your life from the powerful habits of mindlessness that dominate most of our lives. If your mission is really to be a liberator of the oppressed, this is where that liberation begins— by mustering the courage, the discipline, and the dedication necessary to develop your capacity to show up and to free yourself from the domination of mindlessness habits that have captured 80 or 90 percent of the territory, and the time, of your life.

"This encampment offers a rare opportunity to learn how to fight back against these powerful, unseen, and unconscious forces that unguarded will rob you of your life. Whatever hardship you endure, or whatever kind of resistance you might have to work through here, can and will make you a better soldier, a better person, and a more effective mentor to others whom you may teach as a trainer in the future."

Some heads were nodding; some eyes were rolling. One of the guys called out "Hua!" Someone else groaned. And so we began.

Joel added, "Let's get to work. As we begin, I'd like to remind you of the three essential elements common to all the countless methods of mind-fitness training. These are: attention, intention, and attitude. To optimize your practice, remember to be mindful and monitor each of these constantly throughout the day, as they are the three primary gauges on your mental control panel."

Joel proceeded to explain in detail what comprised these three elements.

- **The first essential element is attention.** Attention is the quality of mindful presence or awareness that you bring to each moment of your experience. Wake up and be here now! Be aware of what is present within and around you in this moment.

218

- **The second essential element is intention.** Intention is the quality of mind necessary to sustain the focus of attention. Intention allows you to live, and work, and train on purpose. Pause for a moment to clarify the intention you are bringing to this moment. Why are you here, what is your motivation and highest intention for engaging in this training? Notice that this intention has two dimensions to it. One is very personal. What do you want to learn, develop, or realize? And at a more expansive level, what is your intention to be of greater service or inspiration or value to others?
- **The third essential element is attitude.** Attitude is an important quality of mind that determines the quality of your practice. The attitudes that you choose will either supercharge or sabotage your practice. To optimize your practice, experiment with bringing a deeper sense of curiosity, openness, acceptance, and care.

Joel offered some further advice to the men: "When you notice that your attention is fading into mindlessness or wandering off into thinking or distraction, come back to focus again. If you are drifting or unclear about what you are doing or why you are doing it, clarify your intention so you can focus your awareness on purpose and gain greater mastery over your mind. And if you notice that your attitude is deteriorating into bitching and moaning, feeling frustrated, or doubting yourself, do what you can to shift toward attitudes that give you strength, boost your confidence, focus, or even joy in the practice. In general, optimizing attitudes will be in the directions of curious, open, accepting, patient, and caring awareness. I promise you that if you wisely monitor and manage these three essential elements carefully, your practice and training will swiftly progress. If you ignore these important factors, you will most likely flounder, get bored or frustrated, and likely feel like you are wasting your time. The choice, moment to moment and day to day, will be yours. Understood?"

A few heads nodded, there were a few thumbs-up, and a few guys groaned, having endured Joel's instructions. From here we moved into the initial meditation instructions:

"Your assignment is to stand guard on your mind, to protect and maintain your mindful presence of mind. To accomplish this, we will begin with anchoring your awareness in the ever-flowing changing sensations and rhythm of your breathing. We focus on the breath for several reasons. Twenty-one thousand, six hundred times a day, more or less, we inhale and exhale, so the breath is always with us and easy to find and focus upon. Respiration is an unusual function as we can consciously control our breath, and our autonomic nervous system will also regulate our breathing without any conscious interaction from us.

"To begin, simply synchronize your breathing with a short phrase, mentally saying *here* as you inhale and *now* as you exhale. If you like, it can also be helpful to synchronize your inhalations and exhalations with a simple movement or gesture, slowing raising a hand or both hands as you inhale and letting the hand(s) lower as you exhale. Breathing in *here* with the hand lifting, breathing out *now* with the hand lowering. If you like, think 'wax on, wax off' like in the Karate Kid movie."

A peal of giggles and guffaws rippled around the room, but some took the challenge to heart and did their best not to be dissuaded by their more dubious teammates.

Joel told them that to accomplish this seemingly simple task and maintain focus, they would be learning to recognize and overcome the habits of mental dullness and distraction. As they learned to understand, subdue, or even befriend these powerful mental habits, their confidence would grow, and the power of the practice would deepen, opening new horizons of insight, choice, and potential. He reminded them that they were the only ones with the power to affect these qualities of mind; no one else could do this work for them. Once they realized this, they would no longer delude themselves into thinking that others had the power to make them happy or angry.

"Keep in mind that if you can't maintain your awareness continuously with a focus on the breath, it is unlikely that you will be able to attend to anything else going on in your life with continuous, sustained awareness. OK, is everyone clear on the practice? Let's experiment with this for five minutes, and then we'll check in to see if there are any questions to fine tune the technique."

An awkward semisilence followed for an interminable five minutes, punctuated by self-conscious peals of giggling, with some moments of silence in between. It was clear that we were stepping into alien territory and that some of the men were self-conscious and uncomfortable.

At the end of that time, Joel rang a bell and invited questions, clarifying some points of the practice. He continued, "As we begin, we want to train for quality, not quantity. To accomplish this, we'll just sit for short sessions with the goal of developing and increasing our capacity to be present, to notice when the mind wanders or our attention fades, and to come back to awareness again and again. It's kind of like surfing or skateboarding. There is a kind of internal balance that is elusive to find at first, but as you begin to get the hang of it, you can stay on your board, or maintain your awareness more continuously before you drift off or fade out and need to reboot again."

One emerging concern was the incongruity of sitting in the meditation hall with an M16 by their side, which had begun to feel uncomfortably obvious to everyone, and the question arose of how to address this. According to military protocol, soldiers were required to either keep their weapons with them or ensure that they were being carefully guarded by military personnel, yet the presence of such weapons clearly felt out of place in this space. We explored possible options, and a creative, though unorthodox, possibility emerged. Our team agreed to check it out during lunch and report back with our findings when we regrouped for the next sitting.

"OK." Joel brought the session to a close. "Let's take a short break now and meet outside on the lawn by the pond in ten minutes to take the next steps together. During this break, remember to keep and protect the silence, and see how mindful you can be in moving, walking, going to the toilet, or whatever you are doing."

Walking Meditation

We gathered in a small field by the pond to introduce the men to walking meditation. Michelle explained, "Mindful walking begins with mindful standing. Consider, how many people who are standing on this planet right now have no awareness at all that they are standing, or even that they inhabit a body. They are just lost in their mindless thoughts, completely out of touch with the reality that is present to them right here, and right now."

Michelle invited the men, now in this moment and place, to bring awareness into their body and notice what it feels like to simply stand still and be aware of their body occupying a space filled with countless sensations and pulsations. She invited them to sense how they were embedded within their surroundings, supported by Earth, held by the air and space, here in each other's presence, and with the trees, birds, and animals all around them.

Michelle guided them through the mechanics of walking meditation: "We discover that every single step is made of a sequence of smaller microsteps. So, let's break this down. To take a step you need to shift your weight to one foot. Let's do that. And then, from here, move through the sequence of lifting the other foot, moving it through space, and then placing that foot on the ground. And now shifting your weight to that foot and lifting, moving, and placing the other foot. Shifting, lifting, moving, placing. Shifting, lifting, moving, placing. As you walk, guard your mind. Distractions will arise and try to steal your attention. Be vigilant and disciplined and hold your ground. Do not let thoughts capture your attention and drag you off to get lost in your fantasies, memories, or mental narra-

222

tives. With each step there is a sense of arriving—here, now, here, now. You aren't trying to get somewhere or reach a destination. You are simply learning how to fully arrive with each step—here, now. See if you can muster the curiosity, openness, discipline, and courage to stick to this and to fully and continuously show up and stay present and awake to this flow of mindful moments, without slacking off, drifting off, going mentally limp, and losing the vibrant clarity of your awareness."

Michelle advised them that when they noticed their attention was starting to drift, to focus back to the breath and sensations in the body of shifting, lifting, moving, placing. If a thought had completely captured and carried them away, she advised them to stop walking, refocus awareness, renew intention, and begin again. She warned them they would be humbled by how challenging and awkward this simple exercise was and encouraged them to find the treasure in it.

"Millions of people have walked this path before you with inspiring results, so have confidence that you too can be successful. With practice, you will begin to develop a powerful continuity of awareness that will overpower the distraction that has dominated your life," she advised them. "Classically, this practice is done by picking a walking lane about as long as a bowling lane. You walk the length of this, mindfully turn around, and walk back for however long your session is. This keeps you from wandering aimlessly around or getting caught in the idea that you are trying to get somewhere. While you may practice in this mode during formal sessions, the encouragement is to practice mindful walking as you walk between buildings or on the trails here on site."

Imparting these instructions reminded us of the many traditional meditation centers in Asia that provide walking meditation paths where there's a skeleton at one end to remind practitioners that with every step they are approaching their death, encouraging them to wake up and embrace their life fully now. At the other end of the walking path is a Buddha statue whose peaceful presence reminds the meditators that with each mindful step they make, they are moving closer to awakening to their innate wisdom, courage, love, compassion, and power. The practice is simple: mindfully walking the aisle, reaching the end, turning around, and walking back, again and again, awakening more deeply with each step.

Michelle continued, "As you explore this practice, remember, this isn't about hypervigilance or extreme effort. It is more about curiosity and about simply and intentionally relaxing into a quality of mindful, deep, clear presence that is always available to you as your deepest ground of being. Even in your deepest sleep, there is a dimension of mindful presence available to you if you know how to access it and to be lucid within your dreams or deep sleep states. It is as though through the force and power of your continuity of practice, you develop a profound neural connectivity and integrity that allows energy and information to stream through your nervous system with less interference and with greater fidelity and coherence. With practice, over time, your mind becomes clearer, more coherent and diamond like, more like a laser and less fragile and dull like graphite or coal.

"As your capacity grows, you realize that the qualities of aliveness that you are seeking do not lie out there someplace but are latent within you all along. In many ways, this kind of cultivation is more about remembering the deepest ground of your being and returning to it. If you learn to reliably access and mine this treasure, it will give you strength, endurance, and insight that surpass your ordinary capacities and will give you an advantage over others who have not been as fortunate to train in these ways.

"Given the nature of your missions, it is not unlikely that someday, having access to these inner resources may give you an advantage that may save your life, mission, or sanity, or prevent some inattention, misstep, misjudgment, or accident that would have likely happened if your mindless habit energy had taken over as you moved through the world."

Looking out at the field, some of the men were deep in the exploration, inhabiting their bodies and exploring the nuances of each micromovement and step with a deep sense of wonder and discovery. Some were hardly able to take a conscious, mindful step without wobbling or stumbling. Others were just aimlessly looking around, kicking rocks, and walking about seemingly clueless or defiant. Out beyond the field, it looked like someone was out in the bushes, peeing on a tree. Sighing deeply, Joel thought, *This is clearly going to be a different meditation retreat than we have ever guided in the past.*

And so, the morning continued with another sitting meditation session and another walking meditation session before lunch. As lunch approached, we reminded the men that eating too was part of the seamless continuity of training the mind and encouraged them to be curious with every micromoment, every movement, sensation, and perception involved with eating. We told them there would be an unstructured time following lunch for thirty minutes, and then we'd gather with our gis on for aikido on the beach at 1400 hours.

At lunch we did our best to be models of mindful eating—slow, steady, and really present with each bite, setting our forks down between bites while we chewed and tasted our food. Others around us were experimenting with mindful eating, while some wolfed their food down and shot out of the dining hall as swiftly as they could. All the while, our minds were running a parallel track listening for guidance on how to adjust most wisely to engage those who were yet to get any traction in the practice.

Finishing our meal, our team regrouped to consider the novel proposal that had come forward earlier about how to take care of the M16s during our meditation training sessions. Our Special Forces troops were known for their out-of-the-box thinking and brilliant skill and ingenuity in finding ways to get things done by whatever means possible. Someone had suggested that since there were two authorized uniformed soldiers working in the kitchen, perhaps we could find a secured place there where the M16s could be stored under their watchful eyes each morning and guarded until it was time for the teams to collect them again at the end of the day before heading back up to their hooches at night.

The privates helping in the kitchen pointed out that there was a walk-in Hobart freezer, currently turned off and not needed, that could be locked for this purpose during the day while they were on duty. And so, a uniquely uncommon solution had been found that worked to everyone's satisfaction.

Aikido

While Michelle stayed on to help Barbara and the kitchen crew figure out creative and nourishing ways to work with the provisions they had available, Joel went back to his cabin to prepare for the evening teachings and get his gi on for aikido practice with Richard. He recalled that first afternoon, walking down the lane to the beach, jo in hand, and feeling both a deep fatigue and relief at the mere thought of having a couple of hours free from guiding and facilitating, to be immersed in the beauty of nature and just be a student for a while, as Richard stepped forward to facilitate.

The lake was still, save for the rippling tracers from the geese and ducks paddling about or landing with a splash, and the expanding rings of ripples from the feeding bass. This dynamic stillness reflected the brilliant crimsons and oranges of the gorgeous autumn foliage and the wispy clouds in the blue sky. Richard stood closest to the water's edge, with the rest of us facing and taking in the glorious view of the lake and forest behind him. Standing there in our white gis we seemed strangely incongruent with the glorious riot of colorful foliage all around us, yet there was a deep sense of naturalness in our embodied presence. For the men, the opportunity to return to a familiar embodied practice seemed like a comforting balm.

In the natural splendor of our outdoor *dojo*, Richard was really lit up. He began, "Today we practice blending not just with our uke, but also with the energies of nature, of earth, the sky, the water, the winds within us—and around us." His teachings offered a fresh attention to the natural world and the ways that ki-energy flows interfuse and weave us deeply into the fabric of the environment and the matrix of life. Weaving our way through the eight directions *jo kata*, blending the energies of all the directions together, we were serenaded by a chorus of many migrating birds, under the watchful eye of a curious eagle in the tall crag of a tree near the lake. We concluded with a quiet meditation sitting there on the beach. For a moment, we all seemed to share a great sense of tranquility.

Evening, Day One

The evening session began with another twenty-minute meditation session of mindful breathing with awareness of the breath synchronized with "here, now" and the movement of the hands. It was quieter than expected, punctuated by a few snores. Toward the end of the meditation, we invited the men to open their awareness to be mindful of whatever images, thoughts, feelings, or sensations in their bodies were alive for them in that moment.

At the end of the meditation Joel rang a bell and offered some commentary: "We're focusing on the breath to develop mastery of attention because it's an embodied experience that is ever present, continuous, changing yet relatively stable, and its signals are strong enough to always find, yet subtle enough to refine your awareness. There are amazing ancient and modern sciences around the power of breath to focus the mind and shift our states of consciousness, and gradually we will explore more of this together."

He explained that they were learning to turn a fleeting or occasional *state* of mind, such as a moment of lucid awareness of the rhythmic sensations of breathing, into a more enduring *trait* of mind, and to do this they needed to sustain mental focus long enough to create a structural change in the neural networks of the brain. Such neural rewiring will only come about through focused, intentional practice over time. He asked them to remember the axiom of biopsybernautics: "Where attention goes, neural firing flows, and neural connection grows."

Joel reminded them, "With any learned skill such as marksmanship or playing music, mastery develops over time. Some say that mastery begins to emerge after ten thousand conscious, mindful repetitions of an action. If that is the case, then ten thousand breaths would be equivalent to breathing with full awareness for almost the entire waking portion of a day— without being carried away into distraction or sinking into mental dullness and losing your focus.

"That said, please keep in mind that ten thousand is used here as an analogy. In the Tibetan warrior-monk tradition, the basic training involves one hundred thousand repetitions of at least four different sets of methods of mastery, just to gain entry-level access necessary for progressing to more advanced levels of mental-fitness training. That is, four hundred thousand reps! So, for comparison with your training here, if you engage with it, it can lay a strong foundation, but this will still be quite a basic introduction to the vast potential yet to be realized."

Ben blurted out, "So how long do we have to practice to be able to levitate or walk through walls?" He seemed quite serious in his question, which was refreshing in that moment. "Ben, thanks for being willing to even consider how far reaching and powerful these methods of mastery can be. Let's just say that with our practice here, we are approaching the edge of this ocean and beginning to step into this ocean up to our ankles. There are indeed much deeper waters to explore, but we need to lay a strong foundation first. Regarding farther reaches and frontiers of potential, time will tell by how deeply you train."

A story comes to mind of one of our teachers, Kalu Rinpoche, who had encouraged us as we were first considering getting involved in developing this program. Rinpoche was once invited to speak to a group of consciousness explorers and one of them asked him, "Rinpoche, you are a great yogi and have spent more than a decade in deep, solitary mental training and meditation. Please tell us, can you walk through walls?" "No," Rinpoche replied, "I don't walk through walls." "Do you levitate or read people's minds?" "No" he again replied, "I don't levitate or read people's minds." Somewhat frustrated, the questioner said, "Well, if you are such a realized and accomplished yogi, what is your greatest miracle then?" Rinpoche smiled, bemused by the questioner's sense of curiosity, and kindly replied, "My greatest miracle is that I practice unconditional love and compassion for all beings."

Joel advised the soldiers that as their concentration gathered strength and power, and the flow and continuity of their awareness became more clear, continuous, and stable, they would be better able to mindfully surf the waves of their breathing without distraction. Then they could cease the synchronized movement of the hand with their breathing and eventually the synchronization with the phrases as well. "Simply allow your awareness to stay in touch with the changing flow of sensations that each breath brings," Joel continued. "The movements and the words are like training wheels to support you in catching the wave, and once you are steady in the flow of awareness and sensations, you can let go of the movements and the phrases.

"We are clearly embarking into new terrain that few of you have ever dreamed of. As your guides on this journey, we want to make sure that you are well equipped to move into the deeper, more challenging levels of your mental frontiers without getting overwhelmed, frustrated, or losing confidence in your ability to successfully master this training.

It's easy to just blow this mind training off as nonsensical or irrelevant to your Special Forces training, but if you run the simulation of being out on a mission, dug in, needing to remain silent, still, awake, and effectively engaged for days or weeks at a time in hostile territory and physically challenging conditions, this encampment is like a laboratory or incubator in which you can develop and refine these methods of mastery. And, if you should find yourself captured, imprisoned, or worse, then this kind of training will also protect you from the most dangerous of tormentors—the demonic forces of your own untrained, undisciplined mind. So, heads-up, it is likely that this training will push just about every reactive button that you have and will require immense courage, commitment, and discipline to stay with it. To give you strength, remember that you are not on this journey just for yourself; you are training in order to be a soldier, a husband, a father, a friend, who is better equipped to meet the dangers, challenges, and opportunities of whatever missions life brings to you. The level of engagement that you bring to this training will be up to you. Only you will know how fully you are showing up and training hard, or if you're mentally checked out, lost in mindless fantasies, or snoozing through this whole encampment. Moment to moment and day to day, this will be your choice, and we cannot mandate or make that choice for you."

And so, the practice began and would progress through the days to come, with starts and stops and some wobbles along the way. As always, about 20 percent of the men were fully engaged, and about 20 percent were withdrawn or checked out, some with an edge of defiance. The others were oscillating, inhibited a bit by their recalcitrant peers. Our job was to do the best we could to keep nudging them all in the right direction and to offer a structure and support system that would optimize this training. As you can imagine, we were all challenged.

Homework

During the second evening of the encampment, Joel offered the following encouragement and homework to our meditators-in-training. "The goal of the encampment is to wake you up to your life so that you'll be better able to bring that clear, wakeful presence to your work, mission, and all the other aspects and relationships in your life. Without wakeful presence, mindless habit rules your life.

"Some of you might say, 'But Joel, I'm already awake. Here I am. I'm not asleep or snoring!' But are you aware that you are awake? That's the question," said Joel. "So, here's how this works, if you take this training to heart and train hard here this month, it will be like you are on guard duty 24/7 for every waking moment of the day. It begins with the very first nanosecond of the day when you have enough presence of mind to smile to yourself and say, 'Ahhhh, I am aware that I am awake.' That is the moment you begin your training for the day. Ideally, this will be before you even get out of bed! For some of you, this awareness might not happen until you are in the shower or walking to morning muster or at breakfast. And for some, you might find that you have sleepwalked through your entire morning on autopilot, without any self-reflective, self-determining awareness—until you walk back into this hall for the first session of the day, and we ask you, How many of you remembered your homework?"

Joel then told the men that whenever that first wakeful moment occurred, they needed to go through five important steps:

"The first is to notice that this wakeful, clear, mindful presence is available to you, that the lights of awareness are on and shining in the clear sky of your mind. You are aware that you are awake. Second, once you have established yourself in this mindful presence, then pause for a few moments to turn your mind toward gratitude for the gift of another day of life, another day of opportunity, another day for learning, another day when your eyes can still see and your ears can hear, when your arms and legs are still working. Some people go to bed and don't wake up the next day. . ."

Joel urged them not to take their good fortune and privilege for granted and miss the opportunity to give thanks that they weren't injured or sick and that their family and team members were all safe and free. He emphasized that this practice of gratitude would saturate their nervous system with essential nutriments and healthful neuropeptides to energize and optimize their lives and practice.

"If you want to take this gratitude to a higher level, then actually take a further step to imagine that your gratefulness echoes back to whoever or whatever you are grateful for with a wave of thanksgiving," Joel taught them, adding, "The First Nations people understood that we live in a universe that functions in the spirit of reciprocity, and to them no gift was ever received without some gesture of giving thanks back to the source of that goodness."

Continuing with their homework assignment, Joel explained that the third and vital point was to begin each day with the awareness of death and impermanence. In his famous *Primer of Bushido: The Way of the Warrior*, Diado-ji Yusan wrote, "The idea most vital and essential to the warrior is that of death, which warriors ought to have before their minds day and night, night and day, from the dawn of the first day of the year to the last minute of the last day of it. . . . Think of what a frail thing life is, especially that of a warrior. This being so, you will come to consider every day of your life your last and dedicate it to the fulfillment of your obligations."[1] Cultivating the courage to welcome and take to heart this ever-present reality of death each day would help them to stay true to what is most important to them in fulfilling their missions, Joel said. One warrior tradition teaches that we should keep death with us as an adviser who sits on our left shoulder throughout the day.

"Now, on this foundation, turn your mind to listen for and clarify your intentions for this precious day. This is the fourth point to remember upon awakening. Clarify: What are your priorities today? How do you want to live? What is most important to remember and stay true to today? What qualities of being do you aspire to bring alive and embody in order to fulfill your missions for this day? Sourcing this clarity will give you the power to live your life on purpose and not just mindlessly wander through the day haphazardly, propelled by the momentum of mindless habits and impulses that dominate and rule most people's lives."

Joel told them that as warriors they had an obligation to wake up, be fully present, and continually remember what's important to them and to those they served and to stand strong, determined to guard their mind in order to fulfill their mission. "This encampment provides a rare learning laboratory for you to burn this wakefulness in through practicing it again and again, to get this fully locked and loaded now so that when you need to tap this strength in combat, you'll have ready access to this power of presence," he said.

The fifth step is to always remember that though this practice is self-directed and at times solitary, they would always have backup and a network of support to draw from. "Bring to mind everyone and everything you draw strength from—all your mentors and role models and all those you deeply trust. Reach out to them with your mind, your heart, even your hands, and draw in their strength and wisdom energy. Radiate and extend to them your gratitude and blessings," Joel advised. "You are deeply connected to these sources of strength whether they are near or far. Simply rest in this sense of deep connection, receiving and radiating with each breath to strengthen and steady you. In this way, remember that meditation is the practice of deep connectedness, deep relatedness. You never meditate alone. Having affirmed these vital connections, carry this strength with you into your practice, and to whatever missions await you."

Joel counseled them to go forth and meet the day being mindful to stay aligned with their intentions and to closely monitor and manage their progress with as much continuity as possible, moment to moment throughout the day. "As you guard your attention, seek to protect and maintain the integrity of this lucid mindful awareness by being vigilant to notice whenever mindless habits of dullness or distraction invade your mind, capture your awareness, and drag you off into the vacuous wasteland of mindlessness. Whenever you wander from the intention you set in the morning for how you want to live today, notice the excursion, and return to mindful presence. Keep coming back to your intention over and over throughout the day. This is your primary mission during this encampment."

In his closing reflections for the evening, Joel remarked that instead of freeing hostages from somewhere behind the Iron Curtain, they were learning to free themselves from being taken hostage by mindless, habitual, reactive patterns. "Remember this. Stay true to this. Keep liberating yourself from the tyranny and domination of your mental habits. Return to awareness whenever mindless habits or distractions invade your mind and carry you off."

It was difficult to gauge how the men received this information, as they filed out under the dark starry sky, stopping for a snack in the mess hall before settling into their bunks for the night. Back at their cabin, Richard, Jack, and Joel discussed how challenging it was to read the energy of the group as a whole. For now, they agreed to just proceed as planned, watch the signs, meet up, and adjust as necessary.

The next day, after morning muster, a mindful run, and breakfast, we gathered in the hall for the first meditation session of the day. Joel began as promised asking, "OK, so how many of you remembered your homework this morning?" A wave of groans rippled around the meditation hall as about half of the men had totally forgot about the assignment. The other half had self-congratulatory grins on their faces and seemed to delight in having remembered when so many of their teammates totally forgot. A few jabs were exchanged.

Joel took a poll asking, "So how many remembered while you were still in bed? How many before you left your cabin or tent? How many of you remembered during morning muster? On the run? At breakfast? Or when you entered the hall here?" There was a smattering at each of these times, and a significant number who hadn't remembered at all.

"You really get a humbling visceral sense for the power of this practice when you find yourself having gotten out of bed and launched into action, a full two to three hours into your day, having completely forgotten about establishing this deep, strong, definitive intentional start. At such a time, one is wise to pause to consider: How is it that I could have been so active, and perhaps interactive, yet lacked the mindfulness, self-reflective wisdom, and power to show up with a conscious sense of presence and intentionality?

Who has been living my life thus far today? How strong and dominating are my mindless habits? This sequence of simple, yet profound contemplations has become a life-affirming daily practice for the thousands of people we've worked with over the years."

We proceeded to review the morning meditation practice and slowly moved through each of the four stages: first tuning into an embodied awake presence, then activating our potential for responsive gratitude, remembering the ever-present reality of death, and finally clarifying our intentions for the day to live "on purpose," rather than being overcome by mindless habits. As the early morning session concluded, Joel encouraged everyone to be disciplined in maintaining the presence of these rare qualities of being in as many moments, breaths, steps, and activities as possible in this new day. Leaving the meditation hall in silence, we moved forward into a day of alternating sitting and walking meditations, with aikido in the afternoon. In this way, the first days of the encampment unfolded, establishing a rhythm and flow of practice.

Uprising

In the weeks leading up to the encampment we had done our best to set clear expectations for the intense nature and purpose of the training. We had reviewed the ground rules before heading out for the encampment, and all program participants had affirmed their understanding of them and their intention to show up fully for this training. We had taken them at their word and had prepared accordingly.

While we had anticipated some resistance, we had no idea how strong this would turn out to be until after we had arrived at base camp. Prior to this encampment, we had guided many meditation retreats that were attended by individuals who willingly signed up to explore the inner workings of their minds and bodies and participated with a genuine sense of excitement and personal motivation. Generally speaking, most of these people appreciated that such an experience required a special kind of heroic courage, yet they felt truly privileged to have this unique opportunity for awakening to deeper insight and cultivating freedom from conscious and unconscious habits and conditioning that diminished the quality of their lives.

Some of the men, it turned out, had taken our pre-encampment briefing with a grain of salt and an attitude of "It can't be that tough" or "I can deal with anything these damn civilians might throw at me." For others, however, the anticipation of a whole month immersed in silence, sitting for hours a day in the dojo of their own mind, was terrifying.

Over the weeks before the encampment several men had come to see us privately to discuss their trepidations. Jackson stayed on at the lab after a training session and confided in us that he had once spent some days dug into a hide site and needed to be still, silent, and alert, and he had a pretty rough time with this. "And now," he said, "you're telling me I'm going to be dug in with my own mind, with no escape or outlet for a whole month. I'm afraid I'm likely to explode or go fuckin' crazy." It became clear that he was not alone in his apprehensions.

That said, such concerns are not only natural but are also appropriate. Parachuting out of a plane, diving underwater on a dangerous mission, taking a dose of psilocybin or ayahuasca, developing an intimate relationship, or attending a silent meditation retreat are all activities that can be highly dangerous to the well-fortified, yet vulnerable defenses of our ordinary, conditioned egoic identity with its implosive and sometimes explosive self-defense mechanisms. The relaxing, widening, or dissolving of these boundaries can bring us to the threshold of ego death, the death of our habits of identity, and out of terror we are likely to defend ourselves from this at all costs.

As our men arrived, settled into the rhythm of the encampment, and began to practice and comprehend the discipline expected of them, it became increasingly clear that a wave of apprehension, unrest, and rebelliousness was rising up. For some of the soldiers, the challenge of understanding and mastering their minds in new ways was exhilarating, and they were leaning into this intensive training with gusto, really challenging themselves to be in the flow of awareness moment to moment. But for others, the value of these possibilities remained elusive, and they vacillated between feeling bored, bewildered, lost, restless, or resentful.

The tension building in the psychosphere felt like the thunderous winds of an approaching tornado. The air was charged with an unnerving sense of unease that became increasingly palpable in the first few days of the encampment. This tension was fueled by three unexpected developments that had compromised the original design for the encampment. First was realizing just how far out of their comfort zone the intensity of the encampment discipline had pushed some of the men who blamed us for not better informing them. This was surprising to us because we had vividly described the expectations for the encampment, and the men had all agreed to this.

Second was the added unexpected distress caused by both the unfamiliar vegetarian diet and Jack's decision to prohibit nicotine. Given that a retreat of this nature is already austere, it is wise to minimize any additional stressors—such as a radically different diet and addiction withdrawal. We had objected to Jack's adamant stance on nicotine, motivated by his own desire to kick the habit, but he wasn't willing to budge on this. Both the imposed diet and nicotine ban had caused considerable physical discomfort and imbalance for the men, creating tension and resentment, which manifested in the practice. Realizing that at least one of these factors could have been avoided was particularly frustrating for the two of us.

The third more subtle and complex factor was growing tension and fracturing both within each team and between the two teams. Even though all the men had committed to honor a set of shared agreements regarding their conduct during the encampment, this wasn't playing out as had been agreed. The fault line lay between those who were sincerely motivated to dive into the training and those who were resistant or disruptive to creating a shared practice space in which the practice could be optimized, at least for those who were self-motivated enough to get with the program. To us this defiance seemed to reflect a deep fear and lack of courage to show up fully and to look deeply into their own minds,

As it turned out, the Alpha Team leaders were engaged and supported the full participation of their team members; consequently, there was far less resistance from members of that team. On the other hand, some of the Bravo Team leaders resisted the training, which then rippled down through the team's chain of command, making it difficult for team members who wholeheartedly wanted to dive into the practice to engage without defying their team leaders. Talking privately with many of those men in interviews during the encampment, we were saddened to hear that their teammates had taunted and shamed them when they tried to break ranks and get into the practice. Since the members of each team were bunking together, and to varying degrees grumbling together, the self-reinforcing loops were strong. There didn't appear to be a clear path to break out of the loop and participate fully for those who were caught in it.

As one of the senior officers would later muse:

When faced with the intensity of the actual encampment, many of the soldiers were unwilling or unable to keep their agreement to abide by the rules. The dynamic of deception, dishonesty, and disruption that this caused for the mental training at the encampment was a truly great loss to the soldiers. During this time the training team, and the leadership of each team, were forced to examine their initial assumptions and reframe a more realistic view of what was possible in training these soldiers.

Training effectiveness generally corresponded directly with the maturity of the individual. . . . A majority of the soldiers openly disobeyed the rule against talking. . . . Every man had given his word that he would follow the rules prior to leaving Ft. Devens. Once at the training site they decided that their word no longer applied. The logic was appalling but short to disciplinary action I could see no other way of altering their behavior.

After about a week of training, the disparity between the expectations of the training team and the attitude of the soldiers reached crisis proportions. Trainer morale sagged visibly. The training team decided to adjust their expectations and made several attempts to get the soldiers back into the training. . . . These changes caused two groups to form with the soldiers; one group which wanted to go as far with the training as they could and another group who participated as little as possible. With one exception the group willing to go forward contained the majority of the older, more mature soldiers.

While an actual hurricane was moving up the East Coast in our direction, these multiple factors all combined to create a perfect storm of challenges for the two of us and for Richard, as guides and facilitators for the encampment. All this tension finally came to a head on the fifth day of the encampment. Richard described this moment as follows:

A dark thunderhead of tension arrives with the men as they file into the meditation hall. They're sullen and withdrawn, hiding behind masks of indifference. The usual horsing around is replaced by an explosive silence; my chest tightens in response. I inhale deeply, straightening myself on the sitting cushion. The men take their seats and stare blankly at nothing.

Freeze-out.

This is the "I will give you nothing" game. It's near the end of the first week of the retreat and all the pressures of the previous two weeks, or perhaps since the program began, have been compressed into this small space. It feels as if a sudden noise or movement will combust the room.[2]

Unwittingly, Jack stepped up to light the fuse saying:

In the weeks before the retreat we briefed you about what would be required in terms of the silence, no-smoking rule, diet, and intensive meditation practice. You gave your word to follow the procedures, but now that the idea has become a reality most of you, as far as I can tell, have continued to talk among yourselves, the smokers have continued to smoke, and there's a minimum, if any, effort toward the meditation practice. We need to talk about this, and we need to know what you're going to do to make it right.[3]

The men received Jack's scolding with stony silence. He then proceeded to fan the smoldering flames, saying, "We expected more from you as Special Forces soldiers." The men bristled, and a surge of tension filled the room as he completed his comments saying, "If you are the best the army has to offer . . ." He shrugged and raised his hands in a gesture of loss for words.

Jack's words and tone flipped the switch. Kaboom! Bedlam followed, and the room exploded with a barrage of accusations, many voices shouting at once, a few men leaping to their feet to speak with reddened faces, shaking their fists or shouting "fuck you" pointedly to each member of our team. They were angry about the silence, angry about the food, angry about the Asian teachings related to the meditation and martial arts, angry about our authority or judgment of them. The blame was clearly all on us in this initial barrage, and it was delivered with force: "Joel doesn't know how to reach the men and make the teachings relevant," "Richard is confusing us doing aikido when this is supposed to be a meditation retreat," "Jack's need for control compromises trust."

Richard held his ground and responded with surprising steadiness: "Look, guys . . . you're simply sitting quietly with yourselves here and then this rage pours out of you and you blame us. What's that about? Take responsibility for your own anger and quit laying it on us. . . . I'm tired of your resistance. Making us your problem is missing the point. I think this anger is in you all the time, it's just coming out now because you're not distracted by the rest of your life."[4]

In his book *In Search of the Warrior Spirit*, Richard described how Rollins snapped back at his comments, saying, "No, it's not natural to sit in silence like this. Anyone would get upset over this. I hardly ever feel like this. This situation is making me angry."

Richard replied, "The anger is yours . . . Maybe if you're more aware of it, it won't interfere with your mission, or family life." It was clear that Rollins and some of the others just didn't want to be doing this kind of intensive inner practice; it was completely foreign territory for them. These men were way out of their comfort zones and spooked by feeling so out of control, and Richard was clearly frustrated by their lack of willingness to own and take responsibility for their own emotional feelings and reactivity, without blaming others, even though all this was right there staring them all in the face.

As we opened to and braced for the barrage directed toward our team, we also had an underlying concern that these men would miss the opportunity of a lifetime to gain insight into and mastery of their emotional volatility and reactivity. Without this training, their lack of mastery could lead to great suffering for themselves and others, by compromising their relationships and even the outcomes of their missions. Even in the best of circumstances, this was hard training, and it was unclear if these men had the willingness, discipline, interest, or dedication to dive into these mysterious waters and not end up frustrated and feeling like the training was a waste of time. It was also clear that our team was struggling to communicate these potential benefits to the men in a way that they could grasp.

Amid this intense exchange, some of the older, wiser soldiers sat quietly, gazing on like wizened elders observing the emotional outbursts of young children acting out. Their still, silent, observing presence brought a steadiness into the room that was subtle yet palpable. Rader leaned over to Richard at one point saying, "Sit tight. They just need to vent and get this out. Don't take it personally."

Harner chimed in to say, "I'm concerned that all this stuff is going to get in the way of those of us who really want to take advantage of this time and opportunity to train. We all knew what was expected of us here, so let's get on with it. It's not going to kill you. Let's get on with it!"

James stepped up and in a thoughtful measured voice suggested, "What if those of us who are serious about this training stay in tents or hooches away from the others. That way we won't be bothered or pulled into the socializing, and we can get into the practice. Perhaps we'll have a positive effect on everyone if we do that." His comments triggered a wave of gestures and looks rippling through the silence. He had just spoken the unspeakable in suggesting that the men break up the teams and let go of the formal chain of command.

This suggestion lit up Harley, the Bravo Team leader, who said, "No way! That doesn't work for me. I'm responsible for my men, and I won't have any control at all if they are sleeping all over the place, and we aren't all together as a team."

A voice from the back of the room half groaned, "Hell, why not just give it a try?"

Someone else suggested that we could give this a try and report in once each day to the team's top sergeant, so he knew where everyone was staying: "It's not like we're going to run off somewhere."

Jack countered that assumption saying, "I'm not so sure some of you might not try to leave." To which the company commander weighed in saying, "Yeah, I'm not so sure either."

The explosive outburst had blasted through a layer of tension that had been hovering over us for days, and the impact on each of us on the training team had landed hard. Nonetheless, it was a relief to get it all out on the table so we could start moving toward some open dialogue that might help resolve our predicament. Exhausted and relieved by the release of tension, we ended the session with the decision that the teams would go back to their quarters and sort it all out and then come back to us with a proposal that they were all willing to stick to.

We gathered outside for a while afterward to debrief. Jack, feeling rejected, disappointed, and frustrated, glared at Michelle, pointing his finger at her. In a harsh tone of voice commanding obedience, he barked, "And you, keep quiet, no speaking with any of them." Some of the men had sought out guidance from Michelle, reflecting on their meditative experiences and the feelings this whole process had brought up for them. They had entrusted her, as a teacher and empathic listener, with their confidential communications. This seemed to have aroused some jealousy in Jack who hadn't been taken into their confidence in this way. "Jack's intense command-and-control style and dictatorial, finger-pointing words reverberated painfully and traumatically inside me," Michelle recalled. "I was stunned at being silenced by a team member in this way. We were all pretty shaken."

Walking back to our cabin that night, under a canopy of stars, serenaded by a hoot owl and chirping crickets, each of us seemed to be silently integrating the intensity of the evening. Back at their cabin, Richard and Joel crashed on the couch while Jack made some tea. We talked deep into the night considering how we might adjust our expectations of the men and adjust our teaching style to meet them where they were at. Richard, speaking like a concerned elder brother, encouraged Joel to simplify his teachings and bring them down to a level that the men could more easily grasp, saying, "Joel, at times your style of teaching is just way over the men's heads. You need to bring it down to where they're at. They aren't your graduate students. Simplify. Give them the basics. They need to feel some success to build their confidence for exploring this new terrain." Touched by Richard's insight and kindness, Joel took his words to heart.

Richard pointed out that the encampment immersion and our whole program in general were designed to equip these men with the wisdom, strength, and courage to assume greater authority and responsibility for their own lives, and this collided with and challenged the most sacred of all military institutions—allegiance to the chain of command and the sense of dedication to one's team. His insights helped to illuminate the explosive set of polarizing conditions that were at play in our midst.

The encampment highlighted this dynamic tension between the modern warriors' allegiance to the institutional chain of command and their own inner freedom, choice, authority, and autonomy in assessing the circumstances they encounter, and making decisions congruent with their own personal values, desires, and moral compass.

Richard observed:

Our entire program asks these guys to take emotional and spiritual risks that are entirely new territory for them. Instead of having them leap out of planes we're asking them to leap into new psychological parts of themselves. This is novel ground, and it makes them feel vulnerable and out of control. They aren't supposed to feel vulnerable and out of control, so they try to hide it and blame others and the environment for their anxiety. They become rowdy and loud, as they did tonight, and attempt to overwhelm us with sheer force and volume. They tell us that as outsiders we can never understand a Special Forces soldier or the loyalty he feels for his team. They shout that we will never be able to "smoke them" (present them with something they are unable to do). They blame us and abdicate responsibility when things aren't going right. "If you were doing your job right,' they tell us, 'things wouldn't be so crazy now." They do everything they possibly can to smokescreen and defend, from themselves and us, any likelihood of being vulnerable or out of control. As the program has progressed the litany "It's not manly to be weak. It's not the way of the S.F. man" is becoming a frontline defense against what we're teaching.[5]

The next day, the teams met, worked through various proposals and scenarios, and came to us with their plan. The men would divide themselves into two groups—those who were motivated to fully engage in the practice and training and those who were still resistant—and bunk separately. This would allow the men who wanted to train to maintain and deepen their discipline and would create a separate zone for the troublemakers so they would not distract those engaged in the practice 24/7. The ones who were not fully engaged would focus on the discipline of not being overtly disruptive and belligerent, which would be a welcome relief. Everyone would attend the instructional sessions in the mornings and the evening's teaching and reflection sessions. Everyone would engage in the physical training and aikido practice. The teams accepted responsibility for enforcing discipline as needed within their own ranks.

As we all signed off on this, it felt like a turbulent storm was beginning to dissipate, revealing a clear sky. Released from tension, we were free to move forward and still have a successful and productive time of intensive training. Compromised though this arrangement was, we had successfully worked together and avoided a full-on mutiny. Time would tell if the resistance would endure through the entire encampment, or if it would gradually fade, allowing more of the men to explore the deeper strata and more subtle dimensions of their selves and be drawn into this rare and radical opportunity to mine the depths of their innate potentials.

> *Let us meet the monsters in the wilds beyond our fences and learn another way of framing the problems that trouble us. Let us wait in silence longer than we are used to, and meet the universe halfway.*
>
> BÁYÒ AKÓMOLAFÉ

EARTH 1 BATTALION

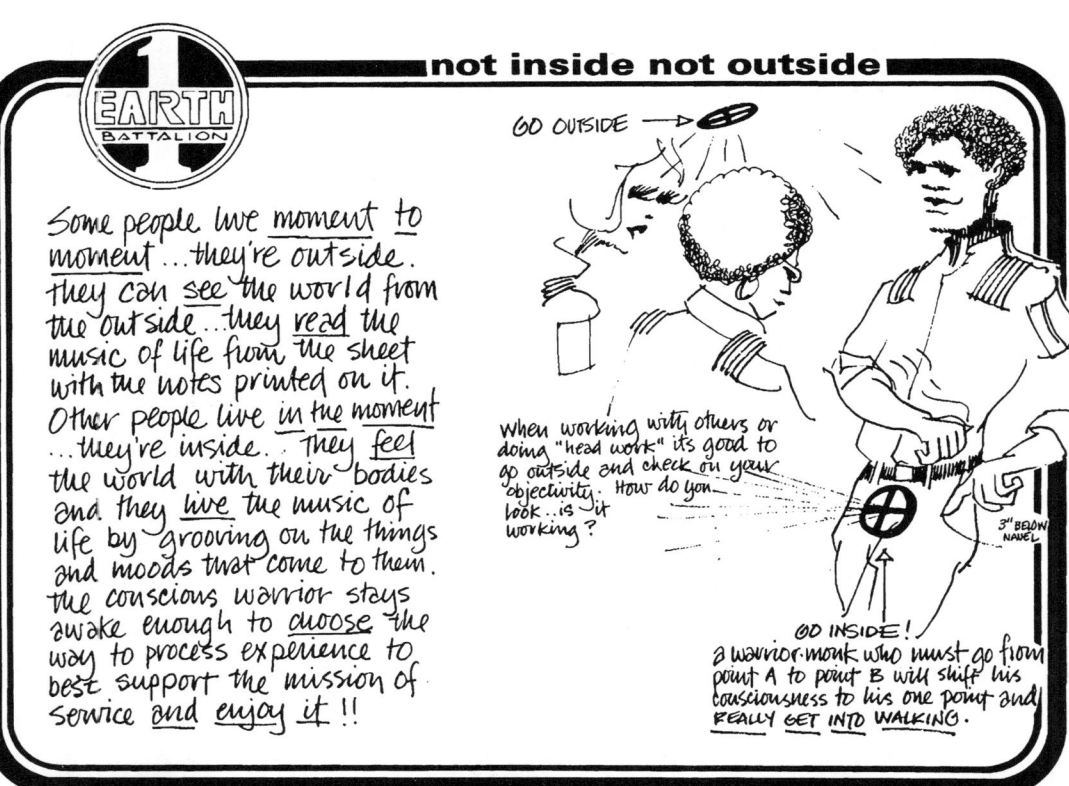

GO OUTSIDE ──▷

Some people live moment to moment ...they're outside. They can see the world from the outside... they read the music of life from the sheet with the notes printed on it. Other people live in the moment ...they're inside. They feel the world with their bodies and they live the music of life by grooving on the things and moods that come to them. The conscious warrior stays awake enough to choose the way to process experience to best support the mission of service and enjoy it !!

When working with others or doing "head work" its good to go outside and check on your objectivity. How do you look ...is it working?

3" BELOW NAVEL

GO INSIDE!
A warrior-monk who must go from point A to point B will shift his consciousness to his one point and REALLY GET INTO WALKING.

THE FIRST EARTH BATTALION

TWELVE

Mastery and Mystery

*If you bring forth what is within you, it will save you. If you
do not bring forth what is within you, it will destroy you.*

GOSPEL OF THOMAS

The stakes of this encampment were exceedingly high. Each of these men
would decide whether this would be an exhausting month of tortuous
confinement and frustration or a liberating and empowering month of
self-discovery.

Imagine being deployed on a critical mission deep behind enemy lines.
You are flown in by stealth in the dead of night, leap out to free fall thousands of feet into the darkness, parachuting HALO silently through space
in the dark of night, and opening your chute just above the treetops, hopefully landing intact and unscathed. Using only night vision goggles, you
would then search in the dark to find the members of your team who survived the jump and find a hide site to dig in close to your target zone,
gathering and transmitting as much information as you can until you are
captured, killed, or find some miraculous way to exfiltrate to safety. During
the days, weeks, or months of your mission, you would need to be able to
remain quiet, often motionless, alert, and attentive for long stretches of
time.

Immersed in such intense and challenging circumstances you are almost certain to encounter your most feared enemy—the powerful legions of "inner enemies" assailing you as fear, self-judgment, distractibility, arrogance, self-doubt, worry, and agitation. If these inner enemies don't destroy you, they will potentially leave you mentally and physically compromised and vulnerable to any outer enemy's intent to vanquish you. Either way, if you embarked on this mission, you and those who have issued the orders that have sent you into this situation know that the odds of you making it out alive are slim to none.

While you are equipped with the best technology available and have trained extensively in all the mission critical skills necessary to do your job in terms of physical performance, imagine that up to this point in time you've had little explicit, scientific training on how to optimize your states of mind and their powerful impacts on your physical performance, subtlety of perception, capacity to clear and focus your mind and make wise and critical decisions. How would you most wisely prepare for deployment on such a mission? What inner skills, strengths, and preparation would you need?

In the Crucible

In ancient times, various holistic sciences were developed by highly evolved beings to enable their own evolution and that of others. These subtle arts were created through the linking of individual minds with the universal mind. They are still taught by traditional teachers to those who display virtue and desire to assist others. Students who seek out and study these teachings further the evolution of humankind as well as their own spiritual unfolding. The student who ignores them hinders the development of all beings.

LAO TZU, *HUA HU CHING*
(NEW YORK: HARPER ONE, 2009), 54

The experience of silence, stillness, and spaciousness that the crucible of the Encampment provided was perfectly designed to create a contrast medium in which deep fears, reactive patterns, blind spots, and unconscious impulses would be illuminated. It also offered a space of psychological potency with the potential to reveal a treasury of powerful human strengths seldom glimpsed or realized in a lifetime. Yet, to discover, awaken, and reliably access these treasures great courage, commitment, and discipline were required.

Stillness reveals everything in us that is restless, agitated, and wants to bust out and move. Silence clarifies and highlights the incessant noisiness of our inner narratives. Spaciousness vivifies even the most subtle sense of contractedness, tension, narrow mindedness, and lack of tolerance that reside in our bodies and minds. Austerity or simplicity intensifies our awareness of desire, insufficiency, the wish to indulge, cut loose, party, and acquire more. . . . Peacefulness calls forth and illuminates all the warring, conflicted, agitated latencies for unrest within us. Discipline confronts us with our unruliness, lack of discipline, and defiance.

Stillness, silence, spaciousness, simplicity, peacefulness, and discipline illuminate any tendencies within us that are disturbed by simply being with whatever is arising in the moment without reactivity and without a compulsive need to change it. Properly understood, rare and noble qualities provide a crucible for us to discover and develop the power to reveal our capacity for profound personal power, peace of mind, well-being, self-mastery, and confidence.

With this vivid contrast available, our encampment psychonauts had the rare opportunity to understand what the mind-body complex is and how it works and to refine their awareness to resolve and burn through impediments, liberating themselves from reactive tendencies that defaulted to narrow-minded, delusional, torturous, suboptimizing modes of being, which could become their most dangerous enemies in life or on the battlefield. Here, they could also gain greater access to more powerful and capable modes of being that would be their greatest allies and sources of strength. The goal was to awaken the special kind of courage required to stand strong in the clear presence of mind capable of recognizing both their deepest fears and unconscious impulses, and the mind-blowing brilliance and power of their true spirit.

As we develop the courage, curiosity, and capacity to stay with and deepen into the disciplines of meditation, we increase our ability to burn through and purify the mindlessness, restlessness, impatience, and reactivity that dominate the conditioned mind and find a greater sense of natural ease, inner strength, confidence, and well-being. Taking this insight to heart we invited our band of warrior-monks to appreciate the trepidation that is likely to arise for anyone who approaches the threshold of an experience that would involve diving into deep silence, stillness, and austerity.

We explained that as we find the courage to take our seat for meditation with clear intent and a sense of dignity and presence, to sit in the midst of the raging fire and heat of our reactivity and avoidance, and simply be brave enough, still enough, open enough, and awake enough to bear witness to the creative display of energies that constellate as the flow of our experience, we find the light of clear, spacious awareness naturally shines forth, embracing and illuminating whatever arises in this multifaceted field of experience.

The terrain of experience that opens during such an encampment retreat is inconceivably deep and unfamiliar to the uninitiated. As we were once preparing to enter a one-year silent meditation retreat, our teacher, Gen Lamrimpa, who had spent more than seventeen years in solitary retreat in the Himalayan mountains, reminded us, "as you go deeper and deeper into your practice, and refine your awareness to more and more subtle levels and degrees of sensitivity, you will become aware of levels of experience that you were previously completely unaware of." Dilgo Khyentse Rinpoche brilliantly observed that "the more you listen, the more you will hear. The more you hear, the more and more deeply you will understand."

In this encampment, the men would discover that as they dove deep into silence, they would inevitably confront the profound psychological constructs that underpin their perception of self and reality. The more they immersed themselves in silence, the more apparent it would become that their understanding of a separate "self" and "others"—their very concepts of identity and independent existence—were merely mental constructs.

Ego Death

We told the men that they may find themselves at a liminal crossroads where they would choose to either continue living out the ordinary, familiar, habit-driven life of their personalities or cross a threshold into a vast, deep, mysterious, and all-encompassing dimension of being. At this threshold there is the unnerving sense that if we go any deeper into the stillness, silence, and spaciousness, we will certainly die, if not physically then at least in terms of ego identity. Here there is no certainty of resurrection and no assurance of who or what might emerge on the other side. The alternative is pulling out of the deep dive into the meditation and assuming, again, the habits that define our ordinary identity. If we do pull away from this threshold, though, we may be plagued for life by an uneasy wondering or regret that we just didn't have the courage or capacity to make the big leap and break on through to the other side to see what, or who, is there. This profound sense of regret is the ultimate sense of FOMO, fear of missing out.

In the mystic wisdom traditions, there are many versions of the quote, "if you die before you die, then when you die, you won't really die." This means that for those who cross the threshold and shatter their limited sense of separate self and die into the boundless, nondual, unitive dimension of their being, there will be less, or no, fear of actual physical death. This view is supported by considerable research with people in palliative care who explore the use of meditation and psychedelics in coming to peace with their approaching death. This is also akin to the prayer, "Yea though I walk through the valley of the shadow of death I will fear no evil," which reflects a deeper quality of courage, peace, faith, and strength that is available to those who have in a sense already died and been reborn. Many contemplative disciplines encourage their practitioners to actually simulate death and regeneration multiple times each day. This can be as simple as experiencing going to sleep each night as an analogue for dying and waking in the morning as a rebirth. This can also be found in walking a labyrinth, departing from the enticements and attachments of our outer world to come to rest in our universal center where we are renewed and go forth with fresh guidance as we emerge inspired to reenter the world.

The profound implications of this deep transformational work for modern-day warriors are that those who muster the courage necessary to explore the farther reaches and deeper frontiers of their human psyche-spirit will be more likely to live their life as a force for good in the world. This is the essence of the message of Channon's *Evolutionary Tactics* manual.

In the final analysis, fully a third of the men made unexpected forays into nonordinary states of experience during the encampment. These excursions led to many questions as the soldiers sought to understand and integrate their shifts in consciousness. We explained that when our culturally conditioned brain and mental operating systems are functioning in an ordinary mindless, distracted, ruminative, or reactive default mode, our DMN (default mode network) is fully engaged. In this mode, we lose touch with reality as it is and live lost in delusions woven of misconceptions and misapprehensions of reality. Just as we may easily mistake the illusion of a solid ring of light created by someone spinning fire, we misapprehend the illusions spun by our whirling minds, which distort our perceptions of ourselves, others, and the world around us.

Delving deeper into the methods of the encampment, honing our awareness and mastering attention, a remarkable transformation naturally begins to emerge. Through mindful presence and discernment, coupled with curiosity and stillness, subtle portals of perception begin to open, liberating us from our misapprehensions. Shifting our brain states by refining our awareness, the illusion of a separate self dissolves like a cloud melting into the sky, and we glimpse the true nature of ourselves and our world.

Crossing this threshold in consciousness is a kind of "apocalyptic" revelation, as the veils of delusion that have maintained the illusion of our ordinary identity and culturally biased worldviews melt away. As we go deeper into the contemplative practices and our minds grow calmer, clearer, and quieter, our concentration strengthens, the whirling circuits of our DMN quiet down, and our wisdom eyes and hearts naturally open. We come to abide within a more boundless, lucid, loving quality of being, intimately interwoven with all things and all beings, that utterly transcends the boundaries of ego and separateness.

Wordsworth offers a glimpse of this in this quote from his poem "Lines Written a Few Miles above Tintern Abbey":

> *And I have felt*
> *A presence that disturbs me with the joy*
> *Of elevated thoughts; a sense sublime*
> *Of something far more deeply interfused,*
> *Whose dwelling is the light of setting suns,*
> *And the round ocean and the living air,*
> *And the blue sky, and in the mind of man;*
> *A motion and a spirit that impels*
> *All thinking things, all objects of thought,*
> *And rolls through all things.*

Though crossing this threshold can be daunting as it entails the dismantling of familiar structures and the experiential death of our ego, for a timeless moment we are in a sense reborn into a wider, wiser, humbler, and more peaceful and powerful way of being. As we become more adept in our contemplative practice, we become ever more familiar with these sublime and powerful states of being, integrating them into our identity and way of living.

Aldous Huxley, a renowned explorer of human potential echoes this: "The man who comes back through the door in the wall will never be quite the same as that man who went out. He will be wiser, but less cocksure, happier, but less self-satisfied, humbler in acknowledging his ignorance, yet better equipped to understand the relationship of words to things, of systematic reasoning to the unfathomable Mystery which it tries forever vainly to comprehend."[1]

Beginner's Mind

If your mind is empty, it is always ready for anything; it is open to everything. In the beginner's mind there are many possibilities; in the expert's mind there are few.

SHUNRYU SUZUKI ROSHI,
ZEN MIND, BEGINNER'S MIND

Our soldiers appreciated the wisdom of "expect nothing and be ready for anything." This meant that they needed to develop a healthy respect and realistic view of the dual interweaving paths of mastery and mystery. We invited them to explore this more deeply with the following contemplation:

Pause for a moment and reach out with both hands. Imagine that in one hand you can touch or hold everything that you fully understand, have certainty about, or have mastery over. With your other hand, reach out and touch or hold everything that is mysterious and defies your full comprehension, mastery, or control.

Then, sense the relative proportion of what you hold in your two hands. Ponder what this means for how you live your life, set your priorities, and creatively sculpt a life based on assumptions, worldviews, and identities that are each merely cognitive approximations conjured up by your own mind. As you strive for greater mastery and a deeper sense for the vastness and power of mystery, how does this inform how you prepare yourself for the challenges of your missions and chart your path through life?

We explained that in our conversations with astrophysicists, they often reminded us that we can only measure about 5 percent of what actually exists in the entire universe, and the other 95 percent is mysterious. We can't measure it. We really don't know what it is composed of. Though we may refer to this mystery as dark energy or dark matter, the entire physical, measurable, perceivable universe is like a wispy cloud floating and pulsing in an inconceivably vast ocean of mystery. Even Edward Deming, the father of Total Quality Management, which relies on extensive measurement of complex dynamic systems in manufacturing, wisely mused that "98 percent of what is important cannot be measured."

Taken to heart, these notions inspire us to appreciate how thin the ice of the measurable, known, familiar world is, and how mind-bogglingly deep and incomprehensible the many dimensional oceans of existence are. A humble appreciation for these mysteries can offer a more realistic view of reality and great power, presence, and potential for how a warrior is able to bring intuitive wisdom to the complex and mysterious circumstances they encounter.

Sweeping and Sittings of Strong Determination

As the men progressed in developing their concentration, we introduced the powerful insight meditation practice from the Vedana Vipassana tradition taught widely in Thailand, Burma, and Sri Lanka and often called sweeping. This practice is a fierce warrior training discipline in that it shows how difficult it is to hold the ground of your awareness in the body without being carried away by the powerful forces of distraction and dullness.

This style of meditation is very popular in the West as well as the East. The practice came down through a lineage from U Ba Khin, a former accountant general of Burma. He passed this lineage on to seven other teachers, including John E. Coleman, a former MI6 operative who carried these teachings back to the United Kingdom, and S. N. Goenka, who is the most well known of these teachers. We were fortunate to study and practice with Goenka, Robert Hover, and Ruth Denison, who were all among the lineage holders, and also learned this powerful practice from Rina Sircar, whom we mentioned in chapter 6.

As we introduced this meditation practice to the soldiers we offered the following advice:

Having focused your awareness with mindful breathing, let's direct the beam of concentration deep into the body now, using a technique called sweeping. This is a powerful and very useful practice to have in your mental toolkit that will help you to clear stress and tension, heal after physical trauma, and gain a deep insight into the nature of your mind and body. It involves sweeping your awareness throughout your body like an inner radar scan, part by part, in a continuous flowing beam of awareness. We'll begin at the top of the head and slowly scan down through the entire body to the tips of the fingers and toes, at which point, simply return again to the top of your head and keep sweeping in a continuous flow of awareness through the body for cycle after cycle.

After guiding the men in sweeping the beam of their awareness slowly through their bodies, we explained:

As you sweep your awareness through your body, be open to whatever comes to your attention. If what you encounter is pleasurable or painful, let those feelings flow into and through your awareness of the present, ever-changing moment. Let your mindfulness pass through your body like a warm wave passing through an ice field, allowing any places of holding or tightness to release. Let your mindfulness sweep through your body like a magnet passing over a pile of jumbled iron filings. With each pass through your body, sense and feel your energies beginning to align and to flow more smoothly and harmoniously, dissolving tension, removing congestion, and revitalizing you at every level of your being.

After a few days of practicing in this way, we introduced a potent and challenging aspect of this style of practice—special sessions called "sittings of strong determination." During these sessions the men were encouraged to be mindful of any impulses that might arise to move and to challenge themselves to override their reactive impulse and instead to remain perfectly still. "If there is an itch, sit with it. If a mosquito lands on your arm or if a fly crawls up your nose, experience those sensations fully, without letting your default reactivity mindlessly take control to swat the fly. Do you have the discipline and courage to sit through this or not? If not, then notice what is more important. This kind of practice helps to illuminate and expand our window of tolerance and nonreactivity and to strengthen our courage, compassion, and confidence."

Having sat through many long silent retreats in this style of practice, we knew from our own deep visceral experience that this is a fierce and humbling warrior-training practice, and we were curious to see how our soldiers would respond. The practice of deep stillness would surely amplify awareness of every little reactive impulse to avoid or push away physical discomfort, and it can also reveal great strength, courage, and freedom.

As usual, some of the men simply ignored our instructions and fidgeted around, some tried and struggled with this and couldn't see the point, and some found this a powerful training tool for developing greater awareness, disciplined self-control, and personal mastery in taming mindless, reactive, or impulsive action. We reminded the men, "The key point here is to remember that you always have a choice, and that the freedoms offered by that choice are only available if you are fully aware of your experience in the moment. To react? To check out? To endure? To investigate? Each mind moment is composed of different mental factors that may be at play. These may include curiosity, mindfulness, aversion, anxiety, peace, sleepiness, restlessness, equanimity, or compassion. In moments that you are mindful you always have a choice for how you compose or modify your state of mind." We would return to this challenge from time to time throughout the encampment, with varied responses each time. Some would actually declare sittings of strong determination on their own.

Nature of Mind

As the encampment progressed, the soldiers' minds became calmer and clearer. Many came to glimpse the potential to liberate themselves from the tyranny of becoming entangled or defined by their thoughts. One simple, yet profound method that we introduced was to be mindful of thoughts as they arise and distinguish the nature of the thought by noting either that "this is a story that doesn't need to happen," when a negative scenario comes to mind, or "and this is a healing story," when a more encouraging thought comes to mind.

The encampment offered a rare opportunity to explore, understand, and discover the nature and potentials of mind. We explained that, in essence, mind has two primary dimensions: the relative mind, which is composed of the constantly changing perceptions, sensations, and mental formations of thoughts and mental images, and the ultimate mind, which is the subtle essential nature of mind, a formless, colorless expanse of boundless awareness. While most people spend their lives completely lost in the ceaseless display of ever-changing experiences, which are like whirling clouds in the sky, precious few ever discover the treasure and power of the ultimate nature of mind, which is more like the imperturbable vastness of the sky itself.

Sadly, since most people don't understand the true nature of their minds, they don't use them very well. Thus, we behold a myriad of misguided and short-sighted decisions, policies, and actions playing out in our world, creating devastating cascades of unintended consequences that harm and destroy lives, communities, economies, and our environment. For wisdom to prevail we need a clear view of reality to guide our decisions and actions. For this it's essential to have a deep comprehension of the profound synergy and interdependence of these two aspects of mind, the relative and the ultimate.

In understanding the nature, potentials, and powers of our minds, it's helpful to understand that it's not that thoughts and mental formations are unreal, it's just that they are transient shimmering displays of the creative potential of the mind—dreamlike appearances that are vivid yet vaporous. They arise in the clear space of our knowing awareness and then immediately vanish within that same open, clear dimension.

To catch a glimpse of how this works, be still, look into your mind, and notice how thoughts and mental images emerge from the clear, sky-like awareness. Notice how these mental formations appear vividly for an instant, and then vanish like fireworks in the sky. As a thought arises, focus your attention to see if you can find the source or origin of the thought. Where does it come from? Where does it go? How amazing it is that so many people allow themselves to believe in and be defined or imprisoned by these ephemeral thoughts, even though they are completely insubstantial.

Properly understood, the powerful inner technologies of the contemplative sciences offer us the means to free us from being defined by these vivid, yet insubstantial shimmerings of thoughts and beliefs. It is liberating to realize that thoughts are merely thoughts, and beliefs are merely beliefs. No thought or belief can fully encompass or describe the true nature of reality.

If our primary mission is to liberate ourselves so that we can liberate others, we must muster the courage to investigate, question, and dismantle illusions and delusions that have defined us for our entire lives. Having been embedded in the psychological, familial, religious, and social systems of our upbringing and culture, which have shaped our sense of ourselves and our world for decades, it can be terrifying to expand our well-forged identity and worldview to embrace a more realistic view of ourselves and the nature of reality itself.

Traversing the Four Dimensions of Mindfulness

Another practice that we relied upon during the encampment was a simple yet profound practice of traversing four dimensions of mindfulness through nine phases, woven into two stages. Once you learn the architecture and flow of this practice, your sessions can be very brief, moving through each stage rather quickly, or you can be very thorough, diving deeply into each phase and lingering there as long as you like. The four dimensions of mindfulness are:

- **First dimension:** Mindful of perceptions—the flow of sights, sounds, and impressions streaming to you and through you from the world around you
- **Second dimension:** Mindful of the flow of sensations and pulsations in the body
- **Third dimension:** Mindful of the flow of thoughts, mental images, and mindstates
- **Fourth dimension:** Mindful clear presence, resting in awareness

In the first four phases of this nine-phase practice, practitioners mindfully observe and appreciate the uniqueness of each of the four dimensions of experience by differentiating each dimension as they meditate through them. In the fifth through ninth phases, the four dimensions are integrated.

We suggested to the soldiers that as they moved through the nine phases it's helpful to mark the transition between each phase by softly sounding *ahhh*. This quiet vocalization serves to mark the shift in the focus of attention at each stage. In practice, we told them that as they moved through each stage, they could explore that stage for as long as it was easy to maintain their interest and mindfulness, and then, when their focus began to wane, they could move on to the next stage. What follows is the guidance we provided them.

With the sound *ahhh*, open the field of your senses to welcome whatever sights, sounds, or sensory impressions are streaming to you and through you from the world around you. Be mindful of how each sensory experience comes and flows, arises and passes, within the clear, open space of awareness.

With a second *ahhh* now, remain deeply grounded in the awareness of the space around you, and open the field of your mindful presence to embrace the changing flow of feelings, sensations, and pulsations streaming through your body. Notice how all these changing experiences come and flow, arising and passing within the clear, open space of awareness.

With the third *ahhh* shift your mindful awareness to focus on the movements of thoughts and mental images streaming in the clear space of your mind like so many clouds or winds passing through the vast sky undisturbed by their movement. Be mindful of how each of these mental formations comes and flows, arises and passes, within the clear, open spaciousness of awareness.

Up to this stage, you have been observing the flow of changing experiences. Now, with the fourth phase and another *ahhh*, it's like you are turning the mind around to look straight back into itself. Let your awareness open as though it is mixing with space and simply rest here in the clear presence of mindful awareness, the most subtle, clear, and essential dimension of your being. Here you come to rest in the spaciousness of awake awareness, within which all the changing experiences come and flow, arise and pass. After a lifetime of chasing after changing perceptions, sensations, and mind states, discovering and becoming familiar with the open, clear formless dimension of space-like awareness can be quite liberating. Knowing how to access and find rest here in the deep essential dimension of your being can be deeply reenergizing, nourishing, and insightful. If you notice that you have become entangled in any thoughts or feelings, with a smile and an *ahhh* cut loose from that entanglement and come to rest again in this open, clear awake awareness. Simply remain in this open sky-like awareness for as long as you can, becoming ever more familiar with this elusive and powerful dimension of your being. Be vigilant to notice if you wander off, and whenever you do, just keep coming back again and again.

Now, having focused specifically on the uniqueness of each of these four dimensions of experience, we begin the integrative phase of this practice incorporating and including each dimension as we go.

Moving on to the fifth stage now with an *ahhh*, remain deeply grounded in and connected to the subtle dimension of quiet, clear, open, mindful presence, and as you do simply observe how the activity of the mind begins to stir, shape, arise, appear, and dissolve. Whatever thoughts, feelings, images, or mental formations may arise, simply notice them without becoming entangled in them and allow them to arise and dissolve on their own, within the clear, open space of awareness.

As we move to the sixth stage of the practice with the next *ahhh*, remain deeply grounded in the dimension of mindful clear presence as you expand your field of awareness to once again welcome and embrace the flow of sensations, pulsations, and vibrations within your body as they arise and pass within the clear, open space of your awareness. Allow these physical sensations and pulsations to comingle with whatever mental formations may also arise within this open, clear awareness.

As you arrive at the seventh phase now with an *ahhh*, open to an integrative awareness of remaining deeply grounded in the mindful, clear presence that incorporates your mental and physical experience and expand your field of awareness to once again welcome and embrace the flow of sensory experiences streaming to you and through you from the world around you. Allow whatever sounds, sights, smells, or impressions arise for you to vividly appear and then dissolve into the clear, open space of awareness.

With an eighth *ahhh*, experience the integration and unification of all of these dimensions of your being, embracing the full spectrum of your experience in its many varied waveforms, frequencies, and nuances.

And now, if you like, with a ninth and final *ahhh*, sense how your body sitting here is embedded within the seamless fabric of reality that encompasses all things and all beings. Envision that you can generate a wave of influence radiating from your wholeness to dedicate and transmit to others any of the positive feelings or qualities of being that have been cultivated, refined, and activated through this practice. Imagine that you can dedicate all this positive energy like streams of light that flow into the continuum of your being, that you might be more fully present as your journey of awakening continues. Envision that you can allow the light or energy of these positive qualities to ripple out as a wave of support and encouragement to each of your team members, to all your loved ones and friends, and to beings everywhere that they too may be well and awaken to the true full dimensions of their wholeness.

As the session ended and lunch approached, Joel encouraged everyone to integrate awareness of these levels of experience throughout the day and practice integrating each and all of these dimensions into a seamless whole.

Gasshuku

After lunch, Richard and Joel met to discuss the upcoming *gasshuku*. As Richard described it, *gasshuku* is a Japanese word referring to a time of intensive immersion in aikido training in the dojo. While our gasshuku would only be for a single day, such sessions could last as long as a week or a month. Joel had some reservations about disrupting the meditation training with too much agitating movement, but Richard made a wise and strong case for helping the men integrate their awareness with dynamic action, and the aikido training certainly was a skillful vehicle for this.

Richard spoke to his high expectations and hopes for this day as an opportunity to advance the action of realizing the potential for modern day warriors who truly embodied their deepest values in service of a higher purpose in the world. To Richard, "the key word here is embodiment. *To embody and live out our deepest values* is by definition an urge to call the spirit into the flesh; it's a yearning to experience our ideals as a living expression. This means . . . that if we hold compassion as a virtue we will not only think compassionately, or think that compassion is a good idea, but that we will *be* compassionate." To him this was "something quite different from a behavioral response to an ideological belief. It means to experience, within oneself, the cellular and muscular version of compassion."[2] We respected Richard's depth of wisdom regarding somatic integration and the vital role of learning to embody and live true to our mental ideals, and he was a master of creatively guiding people into the direct experience. From his own experience training in martial arts and in All-American Track and Field, pre-Olympic, and Central American Games sports competition, Richard had a passion for embodying integrity and loathed the hypocrisy of decoupling high ideals from our embodied experience in our daily lives.

Though the gasshuku day got off to a strong start and offered value, it highlighted the continuing rifts among the men in being willing to fully engage in the training. Richard's enthusiasm and sincerity was palpable. He pushed hard to help the men be aware and viscerally connect with the deep sensual wisdom of their bodies and the deeper intuitive embodied intelligence beyond their intellect and thinking minds, but the men met his offerings with a range of disregard, rejection, belligerence, and just out-right lack of comprehension of what he was talking about. Their responses ranged from, "I have no idea what you are talking about when you say, 'Imagine your brain is in your belly and sense what is happening from here,'" to edgy, thinly veiled dismissals that conveyed, "Fuck you, Richard! No way am I playing along with your program." Knowing the treasures that were being offered and simply trampled over by many of the men, Joel's heart went out to Richard and so empathically resonated with his frustration and disappointment.

Surprise Visit

Much to our surprise, Colonel Getty arrived unannounced one day. Officially he was visiting the encampment to see how things were going, but unofficially he was following up on the rumors that had been in the wind that there had been some mighty challenges. Getty's a straight shooter, and a real fan of our work. It's due to his courageous and visionary leadership that we were all there together. He lobbied hard for this program to be funded and made available to the Special Forces community, knowing that this kind of deep transformational mind-body training is the next frontier for the evolving field of Special Forces training to promote the vision of "wholistic soldiers." He had seen what happened to soldiers in war who lacked deep inner preparation and training, and he was determined to make sure that he made these rare resources available to his men. His vision was that these soldiers would someday be trainers for others, and he was heavily invested in the success of this program. He understood all too well that the modern military relied too much on developing new technologies and weapons while investing little in developing the human potential of the soldiers themselves.

His visit came as a surprise to us all and the men were startled to see him suddenly appear unannounced. In one interaction Colonel Getty encountered Travis and asked, "Hey Trav, what's that on your face?"

Travis beamed a wide smile and rubbing the stubble of his unshaved face replied, "Well, sir, I was just exercising my beard."

Getty smiled back and, with what may have been a wink to Joel (the only bearded guy on site), said, "Well, OK then, just make sure you're not turning into a hippie."

"No, sir," Travis replied.

It was surprisingly heartening to have the colonel on site with us and to sense how warmly regarded as a mentor and role model he was to these men. To some he was even a healthy and inspiring father figure. As usual, his presence commanded respect, yet he was also inclusive and collaborative with the senior team leaders in a very mutually honoring manner. Seeing him interact with the soldiers, we were reminded that these men enjoyed a special quality of camaraderie with one another. They were clearly part of this unique, elite fraternity and had a manner of banter and conduct that was not available for us to share.

With the colonel's visit, our team was hopeful that his presence or influence would be the nudge, or kick in the ass, needed to get the men on board for the encampment. His presence, though powerful, was low key. Before he departed, he held a surprisingly brief meeting with Jack and the team leaders, and then rode off into the sunset and back to the base. When we asked Jack why Colonel Getty didn't meet with all the men, he merely said, "He spoke to the team leaders about tightening up their attitude." We all looked at each other with a bit of a shrug. Time would tell what the impact would be.

Connecting with More of Ourselves

As the encampment continued and our practice deepened, we realized it was time to expand the view of interdependence. We began with this notion, offered many years ago by microbiologist and contemplative science researcher Francisco Varela, that if a living system is suffering from ill health, or suboptimized in any way, the remedy is to be found by connecting it with more of itself.[3] Pause for a moment to consider what it would mean for you to connect with more of yourself. Be mindful of what images, themes, and relationships come into awareness. In evolutionary terms, survival, health, and vitality are found in the most robust, diverse, interconnected, mutually nourishing, and symbiotic environments and fields of interrelationship, such as whole systems design, all-star teams, thriving social networks, rainforests, and permaculture farms. Contrast this with systems characterized by hierarchy and isolation, such as authoritarian governments, monocropping, and factory farming, all creating more fragile collapsing systems.

Speaking to the courage required to fearlessly embrace ourselves through meditation practice, our mentor Joanna Macy, a true embodiment of the wisdom warrior spirit said:

> See how we are called to not run from the discomfort, and not run from the grief or the feelings of outrage or even fear. If we can be fearless to be with our pain, it turns. It doesn't stay. It only doesn't change if we refuse to look at it. When we look at it, when we take it in our hands, when we can just be with it, when we keep breathing, then it turns. It turns to reveal its other face. And the other face of our pain for the world is our love for the world, our absolutely inseparable connectedness with all life."[4]

Given the extreme and extraordinary nature of jobs and missions of these soldiers, it was clear that their chances of health, survival, and success in their missions would be in large part a measure of their capacity to access as many supportive inner and outer resources and allies available to them. We wanted them to have confidence in their capacity to tap their deepest sources of strength, resilience, and regeneration even in the most challenging of circumstances.

After a time of reflecting deeply on each of these questions, we invited everyone to refocus their attention by being mindful of the sensations of breathing in and breathing out for a little while. When they had dropped into a depth of concentration with this, we offered this guidance:

"Now notice how each breath, drawn in, absorbed into our body, and exhaled is a continual reminder that we are more like flow-through tea-bags in a boundless ocean of energy and information, than impenetrable fortresses walled off and separated from each other and the world around us. We literally share the breath and the energy information that flows with all breathing beings. As we increase our capacity to observe the flow of inner and outer experiences without turbulence and distraction, it becomes apparent to us that we are intimately interconnected and interwoven with the lives of all things and all beings. We exist like waves, whirlpools, or currents within a vast ocean, or like clouds or storm systems in a great sky. Though we may be labeled with a certain name, our true nature is inseparable from the larger ocean or sky."

We told them that with each breath we breathe in and absorb millions of atoms that have streamed through the bodies of countless breathing beings of the past, and that in a sense we truly do breathe with "all our relations" as the First Nations people would say. "We breathe with the trees, with the birds and the bees, with the eagles and polar bears. We breathe with the salmon and the whales who live on Earth today—and with all creatures great and small who have ever walked, or flew, swam, or crawled upon our Earth in ages past. We breathe with our allies and enemies, with the rich and the poor, the kind and the cruel, the wise and the ignorant, the greedy and the generous peoples of our world. We breathe with those living now, with all our relations from the distant past, and with all those breathing beings of countless generations yet to come, or who will ever breathe in this world. As you take this image to heart, be mindful of who comes to mind that you are sharing your breath with and can draw strength and inspiration from."

The Mind-Bomb Question

After some time of silently resting in the flow of our breathing in this way, the ringing of the bell sounded the conclusion of the meditation, and we were bathed in its sonorous tones intermingling with the sounds of frogs and crickets in the night. As the resonance became more subtle and melted into silence, Joel asked, "Are there any questions or reflections?" Danny commented that he'd never thought about or experienced breathing in this way before. Stan noted that for a few moments it felt like he just vanished, melting into the vastness of flowing breath, awareness, and energy.

Then, after a long pause, Ben slowly, and somewhat tentatively, raised his hand, stammering a bit to articulate his thoughts. Looking at him we could sense, and almost hear, the gears of his mind grinding away as he tried to wrap his head around the implications of this theme of deep interrelatedness that we were exploring. With a voice reflecting both his insight and his cognitive dissonance, he spoke somewhat haltingly, half questioning himself and half questioning the universe, wondering aloud, "But Joel . . . if what you're saying is really true . . . if we're all really so deeply connected, like parts of the same body, then how could we ever kill anyone?"

Ben's courageous question landed like a meteor in our little zendo, sending out shockwaves echoing through the corridors of our minds, slicing into the depths of our shared silence, and striking into our hearts. After a thoughtful silence, Joel responded, blending with the power, depth, and potency of Ben's question. "What a profound question, Ben! Let's consider this together, sitting with this question in mind for a few quiet moments and noticing what arises as we do. If we are all this deeply connected, then how could we ever kill anyone? Welcome whatever comes up without editing or pushing anything away, and be mindful of the images, thoughts, and feelings that arise for you."

After a short while of quiet reflection, Joel invited the soldiers to discuss this question in small groups, so that everyone had the opportunity to give voice to their views. The question was hyperrelevant, and the room was abuzz with voices and animated gestures. After some time, we drew all the men back together to discuss as a group and listened deeply to their various points of view shimmering like a cloud of pixels coalescing into an emergent picture.

We mentioned Jim Channon's role leading search-and-destroy missions over three tours of duty as a battalion commander in Vietnam with 319 days of combat in a way that he only lost one man and never killed an innocent civilian. Channon believed that he had created a nearly invisible platoon with extrasensory paranormal sensitivities that allowed them to detect enemies hiding in thick, triple-canopy forests. Returning home from this intense and prolonged experience, Channon was certain that the warriors of the future would need a much more robust and multidimensional skillset than the army had ever envisioned. Our being here, with the rare privilege of participating in this encampment was, in many ways, the opening of the door to the inner armory of potent inner technologies that Jim envisioned the First Earth Battalion warriors would need to accomplish their missions in the VUCAA world of the twenty-first century.

The key point that emerged through our dialogue was a deep recognition that to take a life in a manner that one would regret could create a moral injury that could potentially debilitate that soldier for life and in some cases could be worse than having been killed oneself. Most of the men had glimpsed the devastating impacts for this kind of deep, invisible, and enduring wounding, if not in their own lives, then in the lives of family members and friends. Some of these soldiers still carried wounds from killing farm animals they had raised and grown to love as kids, as a modern-day initiation into "being a man" by being willing to endure the deep trauma of being forced by an authority figure to slaughter a being they had loved and cared for.

One example of this was a former army sniper who had sought guidance from us during a corporate leadership workshop we had offered for a large software company. Now in his civilian life, he and his wife had just birthed their first child, and he was struggling to find a way to open his heart and reawaken his capacity for empathy so he could feel genuine love for his baby girl. His heartache, shame, and struggle in freeing himself from his years of successfully shutting down his empathic senses so that he could kill those he targeted had left him wounded and imprisoned in a stark and lonely realm, and though he longed for greater intimacy and love in his relationships, he was afraid that those aspects of his humanity might have been permanently lost or sacrificed.

There was a sobering realization dawning for us all that to take a person's life was a profound choice, with potentially immense and lifelong consequences not to be taken lightly. In some cases, it would be unwise not to kill or at least immobilize someone who was intent on doing harm. In other cases, a myriad of options would be worthy of consideration. There was clearly no simple answer to such a sincere and profound, point-blank question, "How could we ever kill anyone?"

Deep in reflection, we talked late into that starry night, searching for the personal and collective wisdom necessary to discern the profound implications of Ben's question for each of our lives and for the missions awaiting the men if they were to deploy. The Dalai Lama was once asked what to do if someone were to burst into the room with a gun and threaten to kill everyone. He thoughtfully replied, "First shoot him in the leg, then take his gun away."

Sitting there together bathed in flickering lantern light, we wondered, "How many other circles of human beings had sat together under the stars throughout the ages, huddled around campfires, talking late into the night, sharing their discoveries, raising powerful questions, questioning assumptions, considering options, searching for wisdom to clarify their purpose and guide their lives?" The main point we all came to was that we would all be wise to contemplate this question, take it to heart, wrestle with it, and be ready when the time comes to respond as skillfully as possible to the circumstances we find ourselves in, with as much clear presence as we can muster to inform and guide our actions.

As our dialogue came to a natural sense of completion, we noticed our lanterns and candles had burned low and realized it was nearly midnight. There was a profound sense of peaceful vibrancy in the space we occupied together. It felt like we had stepped through a portal together into the realm that Martin Luther King Jr. described when he said, "In a real sense all life is inter-related. All men are caught in an inescapable network of mutuality, tied in a single garment of destiny. Whatever affects one directly, affects all indirectly. I can never be what I ought to be until you are what you ought to be, and you can never be what you ought to be until I am what I ought to be. . . . This is the inter-related structure of reality."[5] Dr. King's wisdom is echoed by his contemporary, Father Thomas Merton, who wrote, "The whole idea of compassion is based on a keen awareness of the interdependence of all living beings, who are all part of one another, and all involved in one another."[6] This realization was vividly palpable to us all.

Stepping out into a clear night we all held this thread of open awareness. There was a crispness to the air, vibrant with the bright light of myriad stars yet completely still save for the swooping shadows of bats. Bathed in the serenade of the hoot owls and frogs, not a word was heard as we walked off into the night to sleep, dream, and hopefully awaken to continue our explorations of these ineffable reaches of our humanity and human potential with the coming dawn.

Reading the Field

One crisp sunny afternoon, surrounded by the brilliantly colored foliage of a New England September day, I (Joel) and the soldiers gathered on a sandy beach. Dressed in our white aikido gi, we looked like a band of monks. We were there to refine their awareness of the subtle energy fields that radiate from and surround all things and spent hours fine-tuning the qualities of attention necessary to discern the flow of energy.

First, we paired up for a drill where one person was the transmitter and one the receiver. The challenge was to see if we could sense when our partner was holding the open radiant palm of their hand behind our back at the level of our heart or if their hand was near the sacrum. It was fascinating to see how many people noticed differences in their experience and awareness in pairing with different partners.

Later we spread out and "dowsed" the beach, using our hands as sensors, searching for a cast-iron skillet that Richard and I had buried early in the day. What an odd sight our white-clad troop would have been for any passerby! We learned to "listen," to deeply feel with our usually ignored subtle senses. We caught glimpses of ourselves as continuums of energy awareness woven into the universal fabric, living in relationship and in balance with all things. A few of the men seemed particularly gifted for this kind of subtle discernment.

Sitting on the beach debriefing the afternoon's training drills, it was clear that some of the men were really lit up with excitement and delight at glimpsing an expanded spectrum of awareness. Walter described how his grandfather had a gift for water witching and finding the best places to dig wells for their community. Others shared stories of aunties or uncles who had a gift for healing with their hands. It seems that while this wasn't a domain that most of the men had explored, it was at least on their radar as a bundle of human capabilities worthy of consideration and exploration.

At the same time, some of the other men seemed dejected and felt inept. Having not experienced anything meaningful, they felt like they were just pretending and not getting any direct discernible insights. This frustration mirrored some of the early days working with biofeedback training in the lab when some of the men couldn't yet make the conscious connection between the quality of their attention and the changes taking place in their bodies. Yet, with patience and engagement, it didn't take long before the signals and states of mind that were previously too subtle to recognize became discernible on a deeper level of refined awareness. Through the combination of the meditation and biopsybernautic training, the threshold of their awareness gradually expanded to subtler levels.

With these subtle energy awareness exercises, I found myself wishing we had a special bioenergy feedback device at the encampment that the consciousness research lab at the university where I had worked had obtained from mind scientists in the Soviet Union. Our Soviet colleagues had worked on the research described in the classic book *Psychic Discoveries behind the Iron Curtain,* and my research team had secured this device through an exchange of psychoactive pharmaceuticals that were difficult for the Soviet researchers to obtain in those times. This feedback device would light up and make a beeping sound whenever one was successful in extending ki energy toward it. It was quite an oddity and made for many lively conversations with colleagues and guests to the consciousness research laboratory. It would have been so interesting to have this technology available to work with our troops.

The afternoon's exploration opened the way for a deeper conversation about expanding the range of our senses both to be more receptive to sensing fields of energy information, as well as being able to transmit energy in a meaningful way.

We discussed and experimented with some aikido healing practices, working first with ourselves, holding our hands over a part of our body that had been injured or was in pain. Most of the men were surprised that they were able to sense some meaningful feeling and transmission with this. We then had the men pair up and extend their ki with a healing and helping intention to a partner. While this was clearly a bit awkward for some of the men, after a couple of pairings, most everyone had something meaningful that they noticed, even if it was challenging to describe in words. As it turned out, the medics were the most lit up with this work and were excited to learn more. They had an instinct for how important this kind of highly portable, on-demand treatment option could be in a battlefield operation, especially if their meds were running low.

I stepped up for a few minutes to demonstrate a practice I had learned that would be especially helpful if someone was going into shock or had just experienced a trauma. With one of the medics as my helper, I put my right hand on the medic's belly, just below the navel, and left hand at the crown of his head, and described the practice of letting the ki energy flow, circulating from the right hand through the subject's body up and out the crown of the head into the receptive left hand. I told a story of hiking in Mexico and coming across a woman who had fallen from a rock face. Finding her lying at the base of the slope, white with shock, I stepped in and did this same energy technique with her. She quickly regained consciousness, and the color returned to her face and extremities. She was able to stay alert and conscious until the EMTs arrived. My story was compelling, and some of the men seemed eager to give this a try.

Sam, one of the medics asked, "Is there any good science that confirms what we are experiencing with all this energy stuff?" This led me to share my discovery of the pioneering work of Robert O. Becker, M.D., on the dual nervous system, which clarifies the biological basis for our capacity to sense subtle energy fields and for intuitive intelligence.[7]

According to Becker, the brain sciences have classically focused almost exclusively on only half of the nervous system—the neurons. The neuronal system works on an alternating current (AC) with neurons either on and firing, after they reach a certain threshold of stimulation, or off when thresholds of stimulation necessary for activation have not been reached. The neuronal nervous system functions like an inconceivably vast digital computer comprised of billions of neurons.

The neurons are surrounded by a crystalline gel latticework of perineural or glial (as in "glue") cells that regulate the formation and functioning of the neurons. This glial nervous system, sometimes called the deep nervous system, not only surrounds all the neurons in the brain but also comprises a hypersensitive bioantenna that envelopes all the neurons through the entire body. This superconductive crystalline lattice is sensitive to the most subtle fluctuations in both internal and external fields of energy information and continuously registers variations in voltage power, fluctuations in current strength, and any differentials in the flow and current direction. These subtle waveforms carry vast amounts of information, and each ripple in the field or in "the Force," conveys meaningful energy information. This subtle system equips organisms with the capacity to continuously monitor and adapt to the constantly changing influences streaming to and through it from the natural environment. These findings stretch our minds to appreciate and tune in to the exquisite sensitivity of our bodies as multidimensional antennae embedded within and attuned to our larger body, the cosmos, which includes all things and all beings.

Since our capacity to consciously tune into these subtle senses is relative to our capacity to quiet the extraneous noise in our mind-body created by physical tension and mental turbulence, learning how to quiet and focus our minds to listen deeply is essential. Through the various contemplative practices that help us tap into the stillness, silence, and spaciousness of mind, we open our awareness to access a boundless sphere of energy and information for guidance and inspiration. Such attunement to the ever-present wealth of subtle energy information that streams to us and through us in each moment widens the aperture of wisdom available to us through our intuitive glial-based sensing.

In explaining this to Sam, I remembered Channon's deep regard for the brilliant work of Buckminster Fuller, who once wrote:

> My own working assumption of why we are here is that we are here as local-Universe information-gatherers and that we are given access to the divine design principles so that we can therefrom objectively invent instruments and tools . . . because human beings, tiny though we are, are here . . . as local Universe problem-solvers in support of the integrity of an eternally regenerative Universe. . . .

I am confident that humanity's survival depends on all our willingness to comprehend *feelingly* the way nature works.[8]

In the dappled light on the beach, as we delved deeper into the subtle levels of attunement required for these aikido energy practices, the surface of the lake beside us was still, reflecting the vivid colors of the autumn foliage, yet quivering with moiré patterns of bass surfacing to feed on insects and with dragonflies skimming the water. In this splendor, we were certainly learning to "comprehend feelingly the way nature worked." An occasional wave of wind wafted across the water, as if to remind us that we are constantly bathed in waves of information that, though invisible to our primary senses, are continually informing us. Through this training we too were learning to find stillness within motion, clarity within turbulence, and beauty within the chaos and heartbreak of our world.

Sitting on the beach meditating after the aikido session finished, I was mindful of a vision of these men out on dangerous missions in the future, remembering this timeless moment on the beach in their white gis, and drawing strength and inspiration from this memory. In this magical space of awareness, the wisdom of the great aikido master Koichi Tohei, in his book *Aikido: The Arts of Self-Defense,* came to mind:

Remember that you live always under the protection of some mysterious force. This force is nature. Therefore, true self-defense does not stop with defending oneself against others but strives to make oneself worthy of defense by nature herself. It respects the principles of nature. . . . When your mind and your acts become one with nature, then nature will protect you. . . . Let your mind be as merciful as nature which loves the smallest tree or blade of grass. Let your mind be strong with sincerity that can pierce iron or stone. Repay the forces of nature, work for the good of all, and make yourself a person whom nature is pleased to let live. This is the true purpose of training.[9]

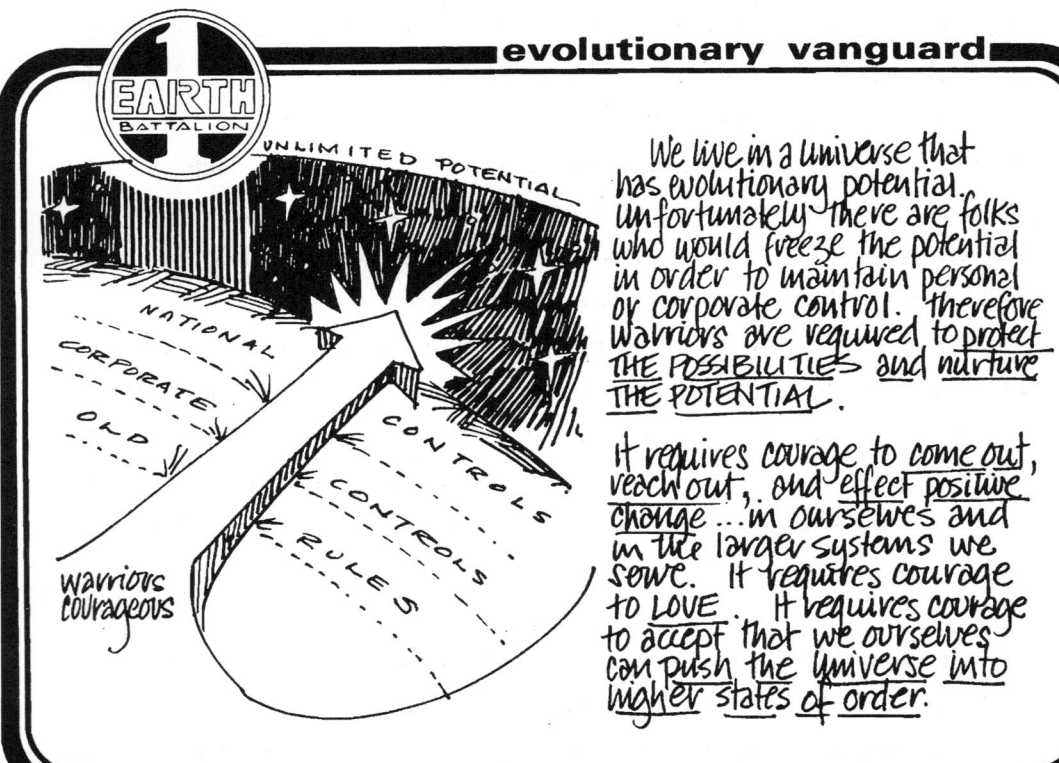

We live in a universe that has evolutionary potential. Unfortunately there are folks who would freeze the potential in order to maintain personal or corporate control. Therefore warriors are required to protect THE POSSIBILITIES and nurture THE POTENTIAL.

It requires courage to come out, reach out, and effect positive change... in ourselves and in the larger systems we serve. It requires courage to LOVE. It requires courage to accept that we ourselves can push the universe into higher states of order.

THE FIRST EARTH BATTALION

THIRTEEN

Taking the Practice to Heart

We all likely know the feeling of making popcorn and wondering, at times, if it's ever going to pop. We felt like that a bit at the encampment. At about two weeks into the encampment, things started to pop, and we were both approached at various times by several of the men individually, each seeking an opportunity to talk privately in a one-to-one interview.

One day after lunch, midway through the training, James came over to me (Michelle) in the dining room looking concerned. "Can we talk?" he asked earnestly. We stepped aside out of the main thoroughfare to a quieter area. James proceeded to describe what was happening to him and asked my advice. "All my life," he said, "I've either been very high or very low . . . but starting a few days ago, I've been feeling balanced in between, not up or down, just really *eeeven*." He stretched out the pronunciation of that word as if it were a troubling medical condition or disease diagnosis. "I've never felt like this before. Do you think something's wrong with me?" He was sincerely puzzled by this sudden strangeness.

"No, don't worry," I replied, trying to reassure him. "This is OK. There's nothing wrong with you. What you're experiencing, though unfamiliar, is very understandable. You've been eating such a different diet here than the one you're used to. It's not only vegetarian and quite wholesome, but it's also been very low in sugar, and all the meals are really balanced nutritionally. Also, the meditation practices you've been doing have created a more calm and balanced mental state as well. So, all of this lifestyle change has contributed to generating a more even-keeled state of being, both mentally and physically. No wonder it feels strange! This is to be expected—and perfectly on target."

I was inspired by his candor. "I'm so glad you came over to check this out with me, James. Thank you for your authenticity, courage, and trust in being willing to share this with me, and no worries! Please put your mind at rest and continue with your practice just as you've been doing. You'll soon start to feel more comfortable and at ease with this new way of feeling. You might even start to enjoy it and find that it gives you more sustained levels of energy and high performance." I smiled encouragingly.

His facial expression looked relieved and his body visibly relaxed, as he thanked me for allaying his concerns with helpful input and perspective. I felt honored, touched, and encouraged by his trust and willingness to be so vulnerable and open with me in such a forthright way.

Soon after this, Paul, one of the sergeants, approached me (Joel) saying, "I need to check my 'maps' with you." "Sure," I agreed. "Let's meet after lunch down at the point by the lake."

As I approached the lake spot designated as our encampment "office" for having one-on-one meetings with participants, I saw Paul sitting cross-legged on a rock, looking over the lake. He looked like a Taoist sage from an old Chinese tapestry, only he was wearing camo gear and had an army-issue rucksack and a can of Copenhagen snuff in his shirt pocket with a wad in his cheek. The forest was ablaze in a glory of autumnal hues and bird songs. I leaned up against a rock next to him and we sat quietly for a few moments, looking out over the still lake with moiré circles from feeding fish and insects, mindful and appreciative of the beauty and serenity we beheld.

Then Paul began to speak. "You know, in a very strange way, this time here in silence has been the toughest training and duty I've ever pulled. That really surprised me! It's taken heroic effort just to hang in here and really face myself and not turn and run, or just check out. I've never felt this vulnerable and defenseless, and I've never faced an adversary as elusive as the invasive habit patterns of my own mind.

"Until this encampment, I never realized how out of control my mind is, and how difficult it is to stay focused, how hard it is to accept some of the choices that I have made in my life and the actions I've taken that I regret . . . It's difficult to understand or accept some of the things I think and feel at times. But I'm beginning to understand that it is all changing, moment by moment, and I'm learning to just keep my mind, or my heart, open to the flow without needing to turn toward distraction or just dull myself and space out.

"It takes incredible commitment to stay awake, to stay focused, and just stay with what is going on moment to moment to moment. The first week was really intense. I was angry and frustrated a lot of the time, and it was certainly easier to blame you guys, than to take responsibility for my feelings myself. At times I thought I'd just totally fail this course, and my first response was to blame you, or blame others for my own failure. It's like what you are teaching us to do just seems like an impossible task—to find peace in myself or to tame my wild mind.

"But as I've settled down into the discipline, it seems to be working, and I must admit I am seeing signs of progress . . ." Paul's voice trailed off, eclipsed by the honking cries of a flock of geese circling over the treetops and then splashing down into the pond just a stone's throw from where we sat. He continued:

"At the beginning of this encampment, some of the stuff you were talking about seemed strange and totally abstract to me. All this stuff about subtle dimensions of awareness, the flow of energy and information, the historical and universal dimensions of what you are teaching, all this seemed at best philosophical, at worst sort of flakey or New Age. But I have to admit that as I wrestle with myself and get deeper into these mind mastery practices, I'm discovering that you have actually been talking descriptively not metaphorically."

Paul laughed. "It's like you were describing to us colors, tones, or frequencies of experience that I wasn't calibrated to register or to be aware of before. Kind of like one of those Mongolian overtone singers who's hitting notes that seem like they are in completely other orders or dimensions of sound.

"I guess my mind, or my brain, or whatever it is, was just too dull or too noisy or too out of focus to notice those more subtle things or elements of my existence. Or honestly, maybe I just didn't want to believe they existed because if they did, I might feel more stupid, disoriented, or out of control.

"I've been struggling to keep an open mind and to apply myself to the disciplines we've been practicing here. But you know, there's nothing else to do while we are here, and I have been curious about this kind of mind training. This kind of training is really sci-fi, and if what you are saying and teaching is really true, then maybe it's worthwhile. So, I've been being more disciplined and challenging myself to stay with it and kind of kick myself in the ass when I slack off. I'm surprised to say it's really starting to work for me, and this is pretty exciting and also a bit scary. The discipline is paying off, and as I get into it, I'm surprised to say that this path of practice seems very scientific, well-reasoned, and honestly seems pretty spiritual to me.

"The more I learn to quiet and focus my mind and balance my energy, the more in control I feel. But it is a kind of control without so much effort. Strangely, that also means I feel more balanced when I feel out of control, which means I don't lock down or leap in and make things worse. I can just sort of step back, be mindful of the turbulence, and then see a way through without escalating the chaos. Given what guys like us have been known to do when we get out of control, I find this very comforting, and my confidence in myself is really growing."

Paul paused for a moment, his eyes moist, trying to compose himself. The dragonflies chased each other like fighter pilots dipping into the pond, sending a mini-tsunami of tiny ripples across the water. He continued: "At the same time, my faith in God or whatever that universal reality is, has really deepened here. I would have never expected that, but I've started trusting it enough to reach out and pray again." I noticed that both of our eyes were moist at this point in our conversation. "It's really difficult, if not impossible, to put all this into words," he said, "but I had to try to explain this to you."

We looked deep and long into each other's eyes and then self-consciously turned to watch the dragonflies skimming the surface of the lake for some quiet moments.

"Thanks for believing in me and having the patience to put up with all the flack some of us have launched your way, Joel. You must have wondered sometimes if we'd ever get with the program." Standing up, he offered a half bow and a thumbs-up as he turned, kind of shyly, to walk mindfully up the path, saying over his shoulder before he turned into the wood, "Keep the faith, Dr. Wiz."

Twelve years later, after a succession of assignments in Europe, Somalia, and the heartbreaks of Desert Storm, Paul wrote to us from the Middle East. "Greetings friends and teachers, I'm over here training Special Ops troops, and had a few questions on that meditation you taught me, you know the one about filling your heart with love and sending supportive strength and energy to others." He closed his message by reminding us, "Space connects everything and everyone! Paul."

Paul was not alone in these reflections, and many of the men shared similar insights and revelations in their interviews with us, especially in the later weeks of the encampment. I had one very potent and surprising conversation with one of the senior team leaders who had been very resistant about the program since the beginning. He explained to me (Joel) a shift that had taken place within him.

"The encampment has really taken me by surprise. In the beginning I really didn't see its value and thought this was a total waste of time. Your language and these techniques are just so foreign to me and beyond anything I've ever encountered in my life or training before. But as we have all sorted out the issues, and released the tensions between us, I've been surprised that I've been inspired by learning to control my wild mind and to find a deeper peace and power within myself than I have ever known before.

"A few days ago, as I was walking, I just cracked open. This was a biblical moment, and I was filled with a depth and vastness of being that shook me to my core. I don't know how to describe it but whatever that view of myself, my life, my potential, my purpose was that was given to me in that vision, it is so powerful and so compelling to me that I just want to leave everything, to pursue and realize it completely. But if I were to follow that course, take that turn in the road, it would completely shatter everything I have established in my life—my work, my marriage, my values.

"It's like I have seen what it is like to make the leap, yet, I'm standing here at the threshold holding on, feeling that if I do make the leap, I'll never be able to return to my old way of being, my sense of self, or my old way of living. I'm thinking I'll just try to set this vision and knowing aside and try to get back to this when my kids are out of school, or when I retire, or . . ." His voice drifted off, and his eyes filled with tears, which he allowed to flow. "After all the shit I've thrown your way during this training, I needed to bring this to you, and honestly say, that I'm grateful, that I welcome your perspective on all this, and that I'm really not sure how to proceed or what to do with what I have been given."

I was deeply touched and surprised by the courage and vulnerability it took for him to seek me out and share this with me.

Bathed in the golden light of the late afternoon we talked for a while longer as the geese swam slowly by and the swallows swooped to ruffle the glassy surface of the lake. Our soulful moments together concluded with a warm handshake and a recognition of each other as fellow explorers of a vast mystery that called us both to humbly fathom its depths. This was clearly a pivotal moment in his life, and I was so curious how it would inspire and guide him as his journey continued.

There is a line in the Psalm of David (16:8) that is often used as a contemplative focus for reflective meditation. One Kabbalistic interpretation that we've received translates this verse as, "When I bring myself into balance, I behold the Divine before me all ways." In such moments when we come into dynamic flow and balance through specific practices, or in moments of spontaneous grace, we glimpse the true nature of ourselves and reality more deeply. In developing a more intimate relationship with this true nature, we source the guidance we need to live in harmony with and in service to this larger reality that we are integral to. It's worth repeating Joanna Macy, whose wise warrior spirit echoes this insight:

> We consist of and are sustained by interweaving currents of matter, energy, and information that flow through us interconnecting us with our environment and other beings. Yet, we are accustomed to identifying ourselves only with that small arc of the flow that is lit, like the narrow beam of a flashlight, by our individual subjective awareness. But we don't have to so limit our self-perceptions. . . . It is as plausible to align our identity with the larger pattern, inter-existent with all beings, as to break off one segment of the process and build our borders there.[1]

Such a view offers great peace, great power to guide our lives, and this vision is at the heart and core of the Jedi Warrior spirit and the noble spirit of the First Earth Battalion.

Can We Extend the Retreat?

A few days later Chief Harner approached us as we left the dining hall saying, "Hey, can we find a time to talk? Some of us team leaders would like to find a time to meet with you, Richard, Jack, and Michelle, sometime soon to discuss an important question." We decided to meet later that afternoon, in the meadow by the lake.

Sitting at our outdoor "office" by the lake under the dappled light of a maple in her full autumn glory we spoke in soft tones so as not to draw the attention of the other men. Harner spoke first:

"We have been talking within our teams about our experience here at this encampment, and it's clear that many of us were slow to get with the program and didn't really engage with the training here. The value of this opportunity was not clear to many of us up front, and as a result, many of us didn't fully apply ourselves to it as diligently as we could have.

"Now, as time has passed and we're more engaged, we realize that we really wasted a lot of valuable time and missed some very rare and important opportunities that were offered by this encampment. What we are learning here is so different and far beyond the kind of survival training that we are used to, and we can really see how what we're learning here could be really helpful to prepare us to do well in the long haul with our missions.

"Our goal in talking with you now is to ask you if there's some way for us to either schedule another encampment during this program and 'leave the kids home,'" or perhaps to extend this encampment longer to make up for the time we wasted?"

We looked at one another stunned by this unexpected and disarmingly sincere request. We clumsily thanked the men and said that we would give this some thought and see if we could find a way to expand the encampment, saying that, given the already packed schedule for the remaining months of the program and the approach of winter, we couldn't at that moment envision when another opportunity would be, so we had better make the most of whatever time we had left with it now. We were clearly taken aback by their courage to bring this audacious and radical proposal to us. This was a significant moment and turning point in the program.

Samurai Game

In the spirit of integration, we devoted an evening toward the end of the encampment to play the Samurai Game, an intense and challenging leadership and team-building simulation that was developed by George Leonard. At SportsMind, we had relied upon this simulation exercise in our work with thousands of leaders, and teams in many mainstream organizations.

Framed in the context of a game with a medieval samurai spirit, its participants are challenged to embody and enact the disciplined living code of bushido, the way of the warrior. The game provides a portal to enter and immerse oneself in a novel, totally alien form of interaction, governance, and consciousness. During this time two teams engage in a series of symbolic battles that call forth the resourcefulness, decisiveness, dignity, skill, integrity, respect, and personal commitment of the combatants. The pace stays fast and unpredictable with highly uncertain outcomes, playing out in different ways each time the game is played. This simulator of the Samurai Game provides an opportunity to leap into an alternate reality and to look back and see one's own life in "the conventional world" with a newfound vividness and broader perspective. Although set in the context of war and battle, the Samurai Game invites participants to deeply question the option of war and see its senseless antiquatedness in today's world. The game offers a rare nonlethal window to glimpse the intensity of combat in a visceral way—combat that has left so many people wounded or traumatized over countless centuries.

To play, the group is divided into two armies, in our case the two teams, Alpha and Bravo. Each army elects a *daimyo*, or clan chieftain, who then appoints a second in command, the sentry, and a ninja who serves as a spy or assassin. Jack and Richard played the role of co–war gods, who are capricious, unfair, and arbitrary. For example, if a war god notices a soldier looking at him, he can put that soldier to death, merely by saying, "You die!" In that case, the soldier must instantly fall to the ground, with eyes closed, to be carried off to the "graveyard" for a ritual burial. Once a player has been killed, he must lie in the graveyard until the game concludes.

As the game played out between our two teams, a succession of "battles" was waged, each highlighting the necessity of maintaining an intensified awareness of what was taking place in every corner of the "battlefield." These battles took the form of exercises pitting soldiers from the two teams against each other in encounters requiring skills of endurance, agility, balance, surprise, energy awareness, and, to some degree, good luck. In one of the battles, Jan and Geo were challenged to hold their arms straight out in front of them, without dropping their arms below their shoulders. Whoever moved or dropped their arms below that point would instantly die. After holding their ground nearly motionless in a standoff for over twenty minutes, our war gods turned benevolent, praised their noble effort and declared a tie. Other battles required contestants to stand on one leg while clasping their hands together above their heads to see who could stay balanced the longest or staring each other in the eye without blinking—or smiling.

The evening concluded with the Bravo Team clearly shining bright as the winner, and we sat together for some time to debrief and reflect on the insights from the game. Most agreed it was just fun and surprising to have a new kind of interactive, challenging but enjoyable experience together. Some reflected on how different playing this game would have been before the deep practice of the encampment, which all agreed brought a greater sense of depth and self-mastery. One combat veteran movingly commented that "it sure is a luxury to go to war, get killed, and then rejoin the living. There's a lot of men I know who didn't have that second chance."

Picnic Interruptus

As the Gut Check approached, we shifted our training schedule. After breakfast, the men would all load up with their eighty- to ninety-pound packs, plus their M16s, and we'd head out with a packed lunch for four to eight hours of rucking together. During these long days we would hike in silence for forty-five to sixty minutes, then sit and meditate silently for twenty to thirty minutes, and then continue with this alternation of hiking and sitting throughout the whole day. Sometimes we'd pause to reflect on what we had noticed in the world around us and within us, while we walked, and then we'd go back into silence.

On one of these mornings, Joel was called aside with a question from one of the men. When he returned, the call went out to load up and head out on the trail. Joel went over to pick up his pack and could barely lift it off the ground. He realized that all eyes were on him, with one of the guys saying, "Aww come on, Joel. We thought we'd load you up like we are today and see how that rides for you." We all shared a big laugh as Joel unloaded the heavy stones that had been smuggled into his rucksack.

Later that day, in a beautiful grove by a small pond in a remote yet public natural area, we were deep in a sitting meditation phase of our walkabout when a car unexpectedly pulled over and parked nearby. Everyone remained still and on high alert. A young couple got out of the car, tenderly embraced with a big kiss, and went to the trunk of the car, pulling out a blanket and a picnic basket. Closing the trunk with a thud, they headed our way, chatting and playfully flirting, completely oblivious to our circle of camo-clad soldiers, sitting on their rucksacks with rifles at their side.

As the lovers approached, the woman cooed, "Oh yes, this will be a lovely place for lunch and a snuggle," and with that they rounded a small cluster of bushes and literally stepped right into the middle of our circle. Our men held their ground of stillness, silence, and spaciousness. No one so much as blinked an eye. A pause and then the young lovers let out a shriek of disbelief at having encountered such an incomprehensible mind-boggling scene and fled back to their car. Throwing their gear in the backseat, they swiftly sped away with a spray of dust and gravel down the dirt road.

Our men held it together until the car had left, and then Randy began to laugh, triggering spasms of laughter that knocked most of us off our seats. Someone commented, "That boy thought he was going to get some poontang, and I guess we right ruined his whole day." Yet, amid the chuckling, few words were spoken, and as we quickly composed ourselves and returned to silence, there was an unspoken recognition that someday out on some mission, their lives and success might depend on their capacity to remain as still, silent, and invisible as possible, so that people entering into their presence would simply pass by without noticing that they were there.

After this close encounter, we hefted on our packs and continued on our way, climbing a hill, traversing a dense forest, and then crossing a marshy area filled with migrating geese. From time to time a ripple of giggles would spill over us as we replayed in our minds the bizarre scene by the pond, and then we'd return to stillness, silence, and spacious presence with only the sounds of our footsteps and the wild geese remaining.

Returning to camp in the crimson glow of sunset with high wisps of lacey clouds, we were serenaded by migrating mallards swooping in to land in the lake for the night. We feasted again in silence in the mess hall on a simple yet hearty harvest meal of fresh squash, brown rice, tofu, and stir-fried veggies.

And so, the subsequent days rolled on: breathing in, breathing out; sitting, walking; sitting, walking; waking, sleeping. With each passing day, the men learned to hold strong to the unassailable fortress of clear, open, all-encompassing presence that is the stillness within motion, the silence within sound, and the spaciousness within all constriction. Slowly, slowly, the men were shifting their default base camp to this higher ground, to take refuge here and now and to guard and preserve it.

Heart Power

In our weeks of practice together we had all learned to listen more deeply, and the quality of clear, listening presence in the hall where we gathered

290

was profound. Our soldiers were approaching a critical threshold where the mental armor and cultural conditioning that had previously served to dehumanize them, to "other" some individuals or groups of people and regard some others as "the enemy," was becoming more permeable.

Reading the energy of the group, it seemed a wise time to introduce a new order of mind-training practice associated with the cultivation of care, kindness, well-wishing, and compassion for ourselves and others. These "heart-centered practices" would come to be valued and relied upon by the men and were sometimes referred to as doing "that heart thing."

While these meditations have deep and ancient roots in various contemplative and wisdom traditions, the forms that are most often used and adapted in these contemporary times come from the contemplative traditions of loving-kindness and compassion. In these postmodern VUCAA times characterized by high levels of stress, tension, anxiety, depression, burnout, trauma, substance abuse, and PTSD, these practices have been widely studied in hundreds of respected universities and medical centers around the globe and shown to be profoundly beneficial, both in resolving or healing these conditions and in preventing them from arising. These heart-centered practices have been shown to be extremely beneficial for military personnel and veterans.

In combat settings where one is constantly on high alert and in a state of hypervigilance, fear and distrust of others becomes a default setting for the mind. While this may be useful and tolerable for short periods in times of danger and intensity, if one feels that one is under constant assault and this becomes one's default mode of moving through the world, the impact of the load of cortisol and hyperactivation can have debilitating impacts over time, contributing to severe anxiety, rage, violence, and PTSD. The capacity of those suffering from PTSD to relate to people prosocially with empathy, kindness, and love is eroded. This can lead to a sense of alienation, loneliness, lack of self-worth, depression, substance abuse, abuse of others, and even suicide.

Stanford University, Seattle VA Medical Center, and many other institutions have studied the beneficial impacts of LKM (Loving-Kindness Meditation), CM (Compassion Meditation), and SCM (Self-Compassion Meditation) on military personnel and veterans for decades. Affirming the wisdom of including these practices in a military training program, the Compassion Cultivation Training (CCT), initially developed with Stanford University's CCARE (Center for Compassion and Altruism Research and Education) program, combines traditional contemplative practices with contemporary psychology and scientific research to help people live a healthier, happier, more resilient, and compassionate life.[2] This CCT protocol, which has been offered to traumatized veterans, involves an elegant progression across six steps, each of which strengthens different psychological and neurological capacities.

1. Focusing the mind and developing mindfulness skills.
2. Cultivating loving-kindness and compassion for a loved one.
3. Cultivating loving-kindness and compassion for oneself.
4. Extending compassion toward others embracing our shared humanity.
5. Extending compassion toward all vulnerable and suffering beings.
6. Activating and supercharging compassion practice by envisioning gathering and transforming the pain and sorrow of self and others.

From our own work directing clinical programs, we were inspired by the beneficial impacts of these practices for patients suffering from a wide array of stress and trauma-related conditions. Thus, we were confident of the value of integrating these methods into our Jedi Warrior training.

As we were entering the last leg of this monthlong encampment, the men had been away from and out of communication with their loved ones for three weeks. We sensed that many of the hearts in the room were a bit softened and that it was time to open this portal of heart-centered practice.

We began the evening's meditation session with a short while of arriving in the present moment, mindfully welcoming whatever was present—the sensations of inhalation and exhalation, the fullness of the belly, the sounds of the birds and insects outside, the memories of the day, the longings of the heart. Taking this as our foundation, we turned the meditation toward a classic form of loving-kindness or *metta* meditation. We reminded the men that this kind of practice requires great courage and a commitment to go beyond the narrow boundaries that we usually constrain our awareness and kind regard to.

In practice, one first turns one's attention to someone for whom it is easy to feel love and caring, ideally someone where your relationship is not too complicated and where it's easy and natural for you to wish them well. Holding this person in your thoughts while repeating the following phrases, you let the words call forth the feelings behind these phrases: *May you be safe and at ease. May you be healthy and strong. May you be happy. May you be free from mental and physical suffering.* We asked the men to repeat these phrases again and again, going for the feelings the words invoked, as they held this person in mind and extended these wishes to them.

Having primed the pump of warmhearted feelings in this way, we now asked them to turn these thoughts and wishes around and direct them toward themselves: *May I be safe and at ease. May I be healthy and strong. May I be happy. May I be free from mental and physical suffering.* We asked them to repeat these phrases over and over, using the words to find and generate the feelings behind the words.

Michelle once had the opportunity to sit a three-month silent retreat focused on this practice. During this time her teacher frequently reminded everyone that even if they spent the entire three months just learning to open their hearts and minds to sincerely wishing themselves well, it would have been a worthwhile investment of time and effort. How else, she pointed out, can we ever deeply and genuinely wish others well if we can't find that kind of warm regard toward ourselves?

Turning our minds toward loving-kindness and compassion, it is likely that this will also create a contrast medium that illuminates all the ways and places within the mind and body where we are hard-hearted and close-minded, where we harbor negativity or ill will, shame, regret, or hatred, or are less than loving, caring, and kind. Over time and with practice, these heart-centered meditations will illuminate, clarify, and burn through these occlusions and open our hearts to the power of regarding others with greater love and kindness. Given the wounds, traumas, regrets, and shame that most people carry, this kind of meditation is clearly warriors' work, requiring great courage, patience, and forgiveness.

We continued, "With the next step, turn your thoughts toward a stranger, or someone you've seen or met but don't really know well. You might not even know their name. Perhaps it's a person you see on base, a clerk in a store, or a neighbor you've seen down the street. In the same way now, hold them in the focus of your awareness, as you find the feeling behind these phrases: *May you be safe and at ease. May you be healthy and strong. May you be happy. May you be free from suffering.*"

We next asked them to recall someone they regarded as an adversary, someone toward whom it was difficult to open their heart and mind, and to repeat these phrases with that person in mind. We challenged the men to find the courage to hold this person in their awareness in this well-wishing way and to appreciate that if this person were safe, well, at ease, and free from trauma and suffering in their lives, they likely would not be a threat to others.

We then asked them to widen the circle to include all beings: "To all those near and far away. All those old and young. To those close to you and to those you regard as more distant. To those it is easy to include and to those who are challenging for you. To all those in the East and in the West. Those to the North and to the South. Those above and below. To all the human beings and to all the nonhuman beings who share this world with you. Let your mind and heart extend to them all equally with the feeling behind the phrases: *May all beings be safe and at ease. May all beings be healthy and strong. May all be happy. May all be free from suffering.* Continue for as long as you can, repeating these phrases again and again. Use the words to awaken the feeling and meaning behind the words."

Finally, we once again returned to simply resting mindfully in open, clear awareness and noticing how this sequence of contemplations had come alive within them. As the bell rang to signal the end of the meditation, we invited the men to review the sequence of stages in this meditative protocol so that they would remember them. "We began by arriving, taking our seats, settling in with mindful breathing and open awareness. Then with the loving-kindness practice, we began with someone it was easy to extend these wishes to and to feel the meaning behind the words. And then to ourselves. Then on to include strangers, and next to adversaries. Finally, we expanded the "blast radius" of this meditation to include all beings. And then to wrap up, in the spirit of integration, we just sat with open awareness for a while to sense how this practice landed for us, what was alive and aglow within us now." This review seemed helpful and was appreciated, especially by those who liked to have clear guidelines and protocols to follow in their own practice.

In closing, we asked the men if they had any questions for clarity or reflections to share on the practice. "What had meaning? What came easily and what was challenging? What would you like to remember or explore more deeply?"

There was a sense of deep quiet, and the men seemed a bit shy to respond. Finally, Sam simply said, "I'm surprised, but I kind of liked that meditation." A number of heads nodded. Some discussion followed, talking about how it was awkward and uncomfortable for some to hold themselves in the focus of this practice. Others talked about struggling to really include some individuals, or groups of others who were challenging in the practice. We spoke to the value of beginning this practice where it is most easy, and then exploring ways to widen the field of view to include more and more beings, human and nonhuman, especially those who were either neutral to us or more challenging.

In this way, we pointed out the great courage it takes to engage in such a practice and to wrestle with everything that arises within us that is less than loving, caring, kind, or inclusive, and how a practice like this one, focused on loving-kindness, is likely to make us aware of all the ways that we constrict, shut down, and exclude or are biased, and narrow in our view of the world, leaving us feeling less empowered, more alone, paranoid, defended, or vulnerable.

We also discussed how findings from fields related to evolutionary biology and interpersonal neurobiology are providing evidence that our evolution and development relies on "the survival of the kindest" and the most prosocial, connected, and inclusive, rather than on the outdated misinterpretation of Darwin's work on natural selection that has relied on the myth of the survival of the fittest, which is too often misconstrued as the most dominating or intimidating. This *metta* meditation is certainly a practice that increases our personal capacity to function at higher levels of strength and well-being and in groups, teams, communities, and organizations in which this quality of regard is taken as the norm, there is generally a much higher sense of mutual trust, support, synergy, camaraderie, and collective success.

Like every other evening, this final session of the day was followed by an optional interlude when hot drinks and snacks, or milk and cookies, were offered to the men in the mess hall before they retrieved their M16s from the Hobart freezer and went off to their cabins to sleep, or to accept our standing challenge to return for the optional but encouraged "night owl meditation session."

Death from Above

Returning to our zendo after the evening refreshments, we settled in and took our seats, enveloped in the warm glow of soft lantern and candlelight.

These night owl sessions were unique in the encampment as they were completely silent and self-guided with no instruction offered other than a single ring of the bell calling everyone to attention at the beginning of the session and another bell at the end. These sessions were also unique in that this was the only session of the day when the men sat in the meditation hall with their M16 automatic rifles on the floor next to them, a sight that we had all grown strangely accustomed to by now.

Looking around the room in the soft light, we realized that there were more men present at that session than had ever come back for the late-night sit before. It seemed that something in this heart-centered meditation had captured their attention or offered some deeper meaning to these men. With the ring of the bell, we all dropped in. There was a deep, clear stillness present in the room.

I (Joel) recall that after about ten minutes into the meditation, I opened my eyes to look around the room. Jim and Jon had nodded off. Tad and Shawn were touching their hearts and appeared to be deep in the practice As my gaze turned to Danner, sitting to my right, I noticed him sitting, as always, straight, still, and solid, like a wizened ninja, wearing a black T-shirt with a skull-and-crossbones logo emblazoned with the motto "U.S. Army Ranger—Death from Above." Sitting there like a formidable samurai, with his M16 on the floorboards beside him, he was a sight to behold. He was clearly deeply dropped into this meditation. Looking closer, I noticed that glistening on his cheeks in the candlelight were tears streaming down his face and dripping off his broad square jaw to dampen the skull and crossbones on his T-shirt. In the presence of this collage of colliding images, my thinking mind was stunned. I observed with wonder the embodied paradox of such vulnerable strength and courageous presence.

I sensed that the power of the authenticity present in the meditation hall was warping space-time to open a portal of possibilities that had not yet been glimpsed in this encampment up to this point. Sitting there it felt as though we were all suspended in motionless free fall within an infinite depth of clear, still, presence. I experienced this palpable presence filling the room. There was a lucid sense that this meditation on loving-kindness had truly been taken to heart. I felt a deep, rich mix of humbled gratitude.

After ringing the bell for the conclusion of this sitting, most of the men left to go off to sleep. A small group of us continued to sit, deepening into the liminal expanse together. After another ten minutes, one by one, the men silently gathered their gear and stepped out into the night, M16s in hand. Sitting there, cracked wide open, I continued to sit on late into the night, fathoming what had emerged and was present.

Walking back to my cabin, musing on the potent themes and images of this memorable evening, the image of Father Thomas Merton's famous epiphany while walking down the street in Louisville, Kentucky, came to mind. Merton wrote:

> At the corner of Fourth and Walnut, in the center of the shopping district, I was suddenly overwhelmed with the realization that I loved all those people, that they were mine and I theirs, that we could not be alien to one another even though we were total strangers. It was like waking from a dream of separateness, of spurious self-isolation in a special world. . . .
>
> This sense of liberation from an illusory difference was such a relief and such a joy to me that I almost laughed out loud. . . . now I realize what we all are. And if only everybody could realize this! But it cannot be explained. There is no way of telling people that they are all walking around shining like the sun.[3]

Looking out upon the people walking down the street, Merton's heart and mind were blown wide open.

> Then it was as if I suddenly saw the secret beauty of their hearts, the depth of their hearts where neither sin nor knowledge could reach, the

core of their reality, the person that each one is in God's eyes. If only they could all see themselves as they really *are*. If only we could see each other that way all the time. There would be no more war; no more hatred, no more cruelty, no more greed. . . . I suppose the big problem would be that we would fall down and worship each other.[4]

Courageous Heart: The Transformational Warrior Practice of Tonglen

In the natural progression of practice, it was clear that the next step would be to introduce the heroic practice of *tonglen,* or "taking and sending." It is a heart-centered practice that requires tapping great courage in order to overcome the powerful forces of fear, self-centeredness, and delusion. Its objective is to open the heart-mind to a more genuine engagement of compassionate responsiveness for ourselves and toward others who are vulnerable or suffering. This radically transformational method, at the heart of the bodhisattva warrior teachings of the Mahayana tradition, is not for the fainthearted and requires a rare blend of wisdom, courage, and compassion.

Tonglen is based on seeing ourselves and all things as dynamic, interdependent fields of energy and information, devoid of any separation, within a boundless expanse of wholeness. Within this vast view we establish a sense of spaciousness within our body as though the whole interior dimension of it is filled with space, which is continuous with the space around us. We then establish a locus of transformation in the most subtle dimension of our being, in the region of our heart center. You can conceive of this as residing in your "heart of hearts" or within some deep, pure, quantum dimension having infinite transformational potential.[5]

In practice, we first begin by affirming the vast stores of strength we have available to us and bring to mind the constellation of inspiring beings from whom we draw strength and inspiration. Receiving waves of inspiration and taking it to heart, we radiate our gratitude, thus grounding ourselves in a deep sense of boundless resource-fullness. We then deploy our mindful awareness to scan for any sensations, vibrations, thoughts, or feelings of discord, suffering, or pain within or around us. Upon noticing any suffering or pain, we envision gathering the energy of that suffering, mounted on the waves of our in-breath, into the locus of transformation in our heart of hearts, where the discord or suffering is instantly and completely dissolved or resolved. This gives rise to an upwelling of compassion and comfort that overflows from our heart with the out-breath and shines forth as waves of compassionate light. In essence, this breath of fierce compassion courageously seeks out and gathers in suffering, transforms it, and with the exhalation, radiates compassionate energy.

In many ways, our practice of aikido established a strong foundation for this practice in teaching the men how to refine their capacity to sense, blend with, and transform the energy of an incoming attack or aggression and to respond with a fluid, embodied, and benevolent spirit of engagement.

In some variations of this practice, we may also merge our heart center with an idealized embodiment of universal compassion. For some this might be Jesus or Mother Mary, for others, Quan Yin, or another embodiment of great compassion. Through merging our hearts with this great being's heart, we are guided, inspired, and empowered to find the skill and courage to engage wholeheartedly in this practice. In so doing, we hold the confident view that whatever suffering is encountered is completely transformed without leaving any trace or residue.

A colleague who was a Christian theologian wrote a brilliant paper inviting readers to conceive of the possibility that this meditation was embodied by Jesus on the cross, when he gathered the sins and the latencies for sins in the future into his sacred heart and purified them, radiating and dedicating the energy of his compassionate salvation back to all. The universal spirit of tonglen is lucidly expressed by Francesco di Pietro di

Bernardone, a wounded combat veteran and traumatized prisoner of war during the Crusades who found his way to this kind of radically transformational practice after suffering great hardship and a year of imprisonment while at war in the Middle East. He is known to us today as Saint Francis of Assisi. His heartfelt prayer conveys the spirit of the practice of tonglen:

> Lord, make me an instrument of your peace; where there is hatred, let me sow love; where there is injury, pardon; where there is doubt, faith; where there is despair, hope; where there is darkness, light; and where there is sadness, joy. O Divine Master, grant that I may not so much seek to be consoled as to console; to be understood, as to understand; to be loved, as to love; for it is in giving that we receive, it is in pardoning that we are pardoned, and it is in dying that we are born to Eternal Life

We explained that the meditation is encouraged to naturally and organically expand in widening circles, letting any worries, fears, aches, or pains open our heart-mind to commune with and transform these sufferings within ourselves and within the hearts, minds, bodies, and souls of all beings who may also be afflicted with such sufferings. The meditation naturally expands and evolves to encompass any individuals or groups of beings who may come to mind who are vulnerable, inflamed, suffering, or misguided or who are in danger or may cause danger for others. You simply and selflessly breathe in the heat, the tension, the intensity of the suffering and pain of their torment, to be resolved and dissolved within your heart of hearts, opening your heart to radiate coolness, relaxation, comfort and healing in whatever form is needed, flowing back with the exhalation to wherever the suffering came from.

As we find the courage to go deeper into this practice we realize that it is true to the warrior spirit. It can open the door to a profound mode of stealth "quantum activism" motivated by compassion where we can reach into the larger body of life to gather the latencies of disease, aggression, ignorance, or meanness, and neutralize those seeds of potential so they are less likely to manifest in our lives and world. In this way we learn to defuse harmful tendencies embedded within the field of potentialities and encourage the emergence of beneficial ones.

It is said that tonglen is a practice that once learned continues to deepen and grow naturally over time as one's wisdom, courage, compassion, and spiritual power increases, culminating in full awakening where all that remains is a boundless, selfless presence of wise, compassionate responsiveness. [6] Who could have imagined a radical transformational practice like this being an essential technology in the inner arsenal of Special Forces mind training?

Extraordinary Brain Power

As many of the men dropped deeper into the practice, they began to "pop" with new, often liberating insights. Though anyone may, in a fleeting, rarified moment of grace, glimpse extraordinary states of consciousness, these glimpses are likely to fade as the entropy of old habits of perception and conception reassert themselves. Many people pursue activities or life paths designed to offer many such glimpses, but even though they get high, they come down again, back to their ordinary state. To truly free ourselves from limiting habits and reliably access, integrate, and abide within more wise and powerful ways of knowing and being requires dedicated mental training over significant periods of time.

Intensive mind training leads to neurological and cognitive changes necessary to establish enduring new traits. This means that these extraordinary human potentials and states of being can only be reliably accessed by those who are personally motivated to train hard to realize the fruits of their practice. Like professional musicians who devote hours to studying and practicing their art, rewiring their musculoskeletal systems and refining their awareness through the brain-sculpting power of neuroplasticity, we too can develop extraordinary, enduring creative capabilities that those who lack the commitment and discipline seldom realize.

Having trained hard ourselves over many years and many long retreats and having coached thousands of people in sports, medical, corporate, and educational arenas, we had glimpsed what was possible for people who seriously engaged in these practices, and we certainly wanted our warriors to experience this themselves. Each of these men faced their unique set of challenges to find the interest, motivation, and courage to engage in this journey of awakening, and we were challenged to find the skillful means to guide each of them toward these portals of possibility.

Insight regarding the transformational power of our Jedi Warrior mind training is illuminated by the research of Richard Davidson at the University of Wisconsin. Richie, as he is widely known, has been a pioneer in neuroscientific study of contemplative science and extraordinary human health and human potentials for many years.

In one series of studies, Richie and his team flew an elite group of virtuoso-level meditators from the Himalayas in India and Nepal and from France to their lab in at the university. Once at the lab, they were each requested to engage in a series of different modes of meditation while in the laboratory's brain scanners, running state-of-the-art tests. The astounding results from this study were mind-blowing. Davidson's research illuminated how the brain frequency and power of these highly adept meditators were remarkably different from ordinary, nonmeditating people. It was as though they were running completely different neural operating systems. One of the most significant findings in these highly experienced meditators was that they produced levels of high-frequency gamma brainwaves never recorded before.

Gamma is the most powerful and most coherent waveform that our brains can generate and is in the 35 to 100 Hz range. While we all generate brief bursts of gamma during *aha* moments, when we find something we were looking for or solve a complex problem, these bursts light up the brain for a mere half a second. We may also generate gamma waves when we coordinate different regions of the brain that are involved with integrating seeing, smelling, and muscle movements, such as bending down to smell a fragrant flower. What was most striking with these high-level meditators was that even when they were not actively meditating, their brains were ablaze with gamma. Daniel Goleman, former science editor for the *New York Times* and author of *Emotional Intelligence,* describes these meditators:

> What was stunning was that the Olympic-level meditators, these are people who've done up to 62,000 lifetime hours of meditation, their brainwave shows gamma very strong all the time as a lasting trait, just no matter what they're doing. It's not a state effect. It's not during their meditation alone, but it's just their everyday state of mind. . . . Science has never seen it before. We also find that in these Olympic-level meditators, when we ask them, for example, to do a meditation on compassion, their level of gamma power jumps 700 to 800 percent in a few seconds. This has also never been seen by science.[7]

The research indicates that the extraordinary gamma brainwave power is fueled by a mind filled with compassion. Compassion is the impulse to actively reach out with our body, our speech, and our mind to relieve suffering, protect others, and resolve the causes of suffering. Gamma waves in the brain reach out to connect and integrate different regions of the brain into a larger, integrated state where the uniquely differentiated regions and functions are linked into a powerful synergy that allows energy and information to flow unimpededly through the nervous system, and new, emergent properties and creative potentials to emerge.

As Goleman describes:

> We have to assume that the special state of consciousness that you see in the highest-level meditators is a lot like something described in the

classical meditation literature centuries ago, which is that there is a state of being which is not like our ordinary state. Sometimes it's called liberation, enlightenment, awake, whatever the word may be. We suspect there's really no vocabulary that captures what that might be. The people that we've talked to in this Olympic-level group say it's a very spacious sense. You're wide open. You're prepared for whatever may come.[8]

With our Jedi Warriors in mind, envision how the powerful presence of a warrior, fueled by compassion rather that hatred, would be dedicated to courageously defending living beings, their habitats, resources, and sources of well-being. Those individuals described in the classical literature as bodhisattva warriors are remarkable beings who, by definition, are devoting their lives to realizing their highest potentials in order to inspire and guide others to realize their own highest potentials.

These beings may assume a variety of forms or lifestyles, as actual warriors, teachers, medical providers, firefighters, habitat protectors, leaders, or just ordinary people. At their core they live with a fierce dedication to courageously recognizing, resolving, and liberating themselves from any inner states that diminish their full presence, power, and love. At the same time, they are dedicated to developing and perfecting whatever strengths and noble capacities that they have, for the benefit of all beings. Anyone who aspires to live with such a dedication must increase their compassion. This requires mustering the courage necessary to recognize, investigate, and resolve everything within us that is lacking in compassion.

In designing Jedi Warrior, we set our sights high based on what we knew was possible and based on agreements with our colleagues in Special Ops. We had assumed that those fortunate few who would be volunteering for this special training program would feel deeply privileged to be selected to participate, highly motivated to engage wholeheartedly in these six months of intensive training, and totally intrigued and excited by the extraordinary potentials that could be realized through such immersive wholistic training.

We were excited and modest in our expectations, understanding that our six-month program only offered at most 1,440 hours of training and practice as compared to the 62,000 hours noted above. We were clear from the outset that the outcomes realized would mirror the degree of engagement of our soldiers in the precious time we had together. And so they did.

Deepening Neural Impact

The training protocols we relied upon during the Jedi encampment took into consideration a wealth of research confirming that the enduring neural changes associated with intensive mental training can be amplified, accelerated, supercharged, and firmly established in a two-phase, six-factor manner.

The first phase is *activation*. Activation means to generate within ourselves an actual experience and feeling of a useful mental state that we wish to strengthen. This could be to activate mental focus, patience, nonreactivity, gratitude, and so on.

Having activated this desired mental state, we then move to the second phase of *installation* where we burn this mental experience into strong, new, and vibrantly accessible neural networks that allow us to call upon these strengths as enduring traits integral to our quality of our being.

The installation phase has six important factors. The first factor is *duration*. How can you prolong, savor, and allow a positive or useful experience to soak deeply into your neural networks? The longer you can keep those neural circuits activated and lit up, the more likely they will begin to grow more neural connections.

The second factor is *intensity*; the more intense the experience, the better. There's a famous statement by neuropsychologist Donald Hebb who first wrote in 1949 that "neurons that fire together, wire together." More recently, Dan Siegel has stated this as "where attention goes, neural firing flows and neural connection grows." This means that the more intensely you can activate the specific neural networks related to the mind state you are intent on strengthening, the more likely these experiences will be woven into the dynamic ever-growing fabric of your brain.

The third factor is the *felt sense of embodiment*, which means that we feel the quality of being we are cultivating as it lives in our body with a sense of meaningful emotional resonance. The more we can bring this experience into our body in a way that is reflected in our facial expression, our posture, or the tone of our voice, the more neural regions will be activated to remember and encode this embodied experience into our neural architecture.

The fourth factor is *novelty*. Your brain functions like a highly sophisticated novelty detector, constantly seeking for interesting facets of the ever-changing flow of experience. The more you can engage an open, curious "beginner's mind" that has a sense of freshness and wonder, the more deeply your experiences become encoded into your neural networks.

The fifth factor for developing and strengthening the neural matrix that allows valued states to become enduring traits is to find *meaning* or *salience* in the experience. The more relevance and meaning you attribute to the experience, the greater the impacts on the neurons that carry the flow of that experience through your brain.[9]

We relied on all five of these powerful strategies during our Jedi training program and are delighted to say that, over the years since our program ended, the efficacy of these strategies has been confirmed by many rigorous studies of human learning and neuroplasticity. Frequently remembering and taking these principles and practices to heart will help you bring the strengths and superpowers of mind and brain that you have glimpsed as transient states into enduring, accessible, and integral traits of your character.

Further insight is gleaned when we consider the learning cycle where we first mindfully *observe* what is going on, and then *reflect* upon the meaning of what we observe. This ripens *insight*, which guides and informs our

307

choices and *actions.* When each of these elements are attended to, learning takes place, but when we add a sixth supercharging factor, *dedication* or *commitment,* the learning is deepened and accelerated. To the degree that it is authentically present in our minds within the learning cycle, wondrous results are more likely. To the degree that it is lacking, the gains will certainly be more modest and less likely to endure.

It is interesting and important to note that in many ancient wisdom traditions, great care is given to nurturing the causes and conditions necessary to ripen the potentials latent in deep transformational practice. The power of a mind-training technique lies not so much in the method itself, but in a deeper contextual field of influences that can either diminish or activate the full potentials of a specific method of practice. Classically, mind states of focus, intentionality, faith, devotion, dedication, commitment, sincerity, selflessness, and so on are recommended to supercharge one's practice.

A glimpse of this wisdom is found in the Arabic word *kushu.* Kushu translates literally as "humility." The actualization it conveys is said to lie in the quality of the "presence of our hearts." Kushu is regarded as the essential quality of mind for us to bring to our prayers and meditations. In the absence of this quality of wholehearted intention, on-purpose presence, and dedication, we are merely going through the moves of mind training with little enduring power or potency to be realized through our practice. A similar word in Hebrew is *kavanah,* which literally means "intention" or "sincere feeling, direction of the heart." Kavanah is most often used to refer to a worshiper's state of mind and heart, his or her sincerity, devotion, intention, and emotional absorption during prayers. Such sincere, humble, heartfelt dedication guides and fuels our inner practices. To the degree we bring this forth, the power, depth, and transformative potential of our mind training will be greatly enhanced.

Speaking to the enduring value of training the mind, Matthieu Ricard, microbiologist and long-term contemplative, who was a subject in Davidson's research explains:

The reason why we emphasize mental training is the realization that although outer conditions are important contributive factors to our well-being or suffering, in the end the mind can override that. You can retain inner strength and well-being in very difficult situations, and you can be totally a wreck where apparently everything seems perfect. Knowing that, what are the inner conditions for well-being and suffering? That's what mental training is about, trying to find antidotes to suffering and to afflictive mental states—antidotes that let you deal with the arising of hatred, for example, to dissolve it before it triggers a chain reaction. Mental training is gradually going to change the baseline. It is the most fascinating endeavor we can conceive. Mind training is the process of becoming a better human being for your own sake and for the sake of others.[10]

Integration: The Calm before the Gut Check

In an ancient text about the progress of meditation over the stages of its practice, the great Indian sage Tilopa wrote, "In the beginning, mind is like a torrent rushing down a gorge. In the middle, it flows gently like the river Ganges. In the end, it's like a stream returning to the sea."[11] And so, it had been for us here, each in our own way, at our cloistered forest encampment far away from the army base.

The silence, stillness, and spaciousness of the encampment had gradually opened to allow the more subtle overtones of noble, clear, and continuous presence to emerge into awareness. Gradually over time, there was less restlessness and more stillness, less wandering gazes, and more focused awareness, less snoring and more of a vibrant sense of clear wakeful presence. There was less fidgeting, groaning, and nodding off, and a greater sense of peace, well-being, and flow, perhaps even a fleeting sense of the actual privilege of participating in this noble endeavor. The vibe shifted gradually from feeling like enduring an interminable detention in a strict study hall, to feeling more like an exciting adventure with new vistas every day in an actual monastery or dojo for engaged and motivated novices.

As the practice progressed and deepened over the days and weeks, we gradually moved through stages of refinement. From focusing on the continuity of awareness in breathing, walking, and eating, we moved into the cultivation of ever more subtle awareness, distinguishing the arising and dissolving of thoughts in the clear space of mind. We progressed from simply sensing the flow of sensations associated with inhaling and exhaling, to noticing the moments of stillness at the fullness of the breath cycle—and in its emptiness. We learned to refine our listening inner awareness to notice how the rhythm of the heart-beat-pulse modulated and interfused with the cycles of inhaling and exhaling.

Subtler still, we explored and realized how gossamer mental formations coalesce as patterns of appearance in the space of awareness like diaphanous fireworks that vividly display their vibrant aliveness for a brief instant, only to dissipate and fade into the empty, clear openness of the sky-like, clear mind. The men learned to observe mental formations of thinking, imagination, and feelings arise and disintegrate in spacious awareness without becoming entangled in or dominated by the often-powerful impulse to embellish those dreamlike mental experiences and without trying to inhibit them.

From there we proceeded to challenge and guide the men to awaken the courage necessary to allow empathy and compassion to emerge as a natural response to the presence of suffering in their lives and world. This was uncharted territory for some of these men who had years of intense conditioning as soldiers successfully dampening their empathic awareness of feelings. Helping these tough and tender soldiers tap the courage to embrace their feelings and shared humanity more deeply was awkward, sometimes terrifying, and often quite healing and liberating.

A vital element of this exploration was the unexpected discovery of the value and power of self-compassion. Many of these men carried wounds and traumas embedded deep within their bodies and minds. These wounds were not only from the missions they had been deployed on, but often from very difficult childhoods, life circumstances, and choices in general. Many of these men had deep resentments and deep regrets that shackled them, so the discovery of the potential benefits of a good dose of self-compassion was most useful.

The practice space of the encampment provided a learning laboratory environment in which the men could safely examine these old wounds with curiosity, openness, kindness, and acceptance, shining the light of compassionate awareness into them. This could allow a release or resolution of the rage, sadness, grief, guilt, and shame that they carried, lightening the burdens that had weighed them down for decades. For some it was clear that the traumas they carried were not merely their own, but ancestral legacies that had been passed on to them and unknowingly embedded within their minds, bodies, nervous systems, identity, and worldview, like hidden filters that dampened or colored their lived experience in each moment of their lives.

In the absence of such a rare opportunity, the heaviness of these embedded traumas would likely remain, forever ignored, denied, and buried deep within their bodies and psyches, ready to surface in reactivity whenever those latencies were triggered. Such reactions could lead to self-harm, harming others, or compromising missions in the future, so becoming more aware of and able to neutralize these unconscious reactive patterns was of great value.

While the encampment started with a tense, pressurized, and explosive tone, it mellowed over time, and a greater sense of natural ease and flow encompassed our days. The men learned that they had access to a many dimensional arsenal of vital tools that offered greater peace, power, ease, humility and confidence. They discovered that they could reliably access a state of "calm intensity," which they valued greatly. All this newfound territory was hard won by the effort, patience, practice, and whatever levels of dedication each of the men could find.

In the final analysis of the encampment, one of the senior leaders reflected:

> Most of the men reported that the encampment was useful to them. All men recommended more preparation during future programs. Personnel should be prepared from the start of the program for the lifestyle changes expected during the encampment. I still feel that a ban on smoking, alcohol, and talking would be beneficial. To make the encampment more effective, each man should live by himself, and the team should only come together for meals and a daily discussion. Physical training and aikido should continue during the encampment on an individual basis. Some of the men will be able to go further than others so the cadre and contract instructors need to plan for this.[12]

Like the image we evoked in the opening pages of this book of many hands reaching out to pick an apple, it was clear that what each of the participants in this encampment had experienced was uniquely their own retreat or advance. We had all progressed on the path in our own ways. Some had worked hard, made it up above the clouds and fierce winds of their noisy minds, and truly caught a glimpse of broader vistas. Others sensed promise and potential yet to be realized and held a thirst or curiosity to return and explore these realms more deeply. Still others had some beautiful walks in the gorgeous autumnal beauty of the forest, a good rest, and a month of deep reflection and life review. And some perhaps still wondered why we had come and devoted an entire month to such elusive pursuits.

These men had trained hard, and they were now about to embark on a mission that would stretch and test them to their limits individually and as teams. We all wondered how the lessons learned and the inner technologies gained at this encampment would translate into the arduous arena of the brutal Gut Check.

> *When a complex system is far from equilibrium, small islands of coherence in a sea of chaos have the capacity to shift the entire system to a higher order.*
>
> ILYA PRIGOGINE, NOBEL LAUREATE IN CHEMISTRY

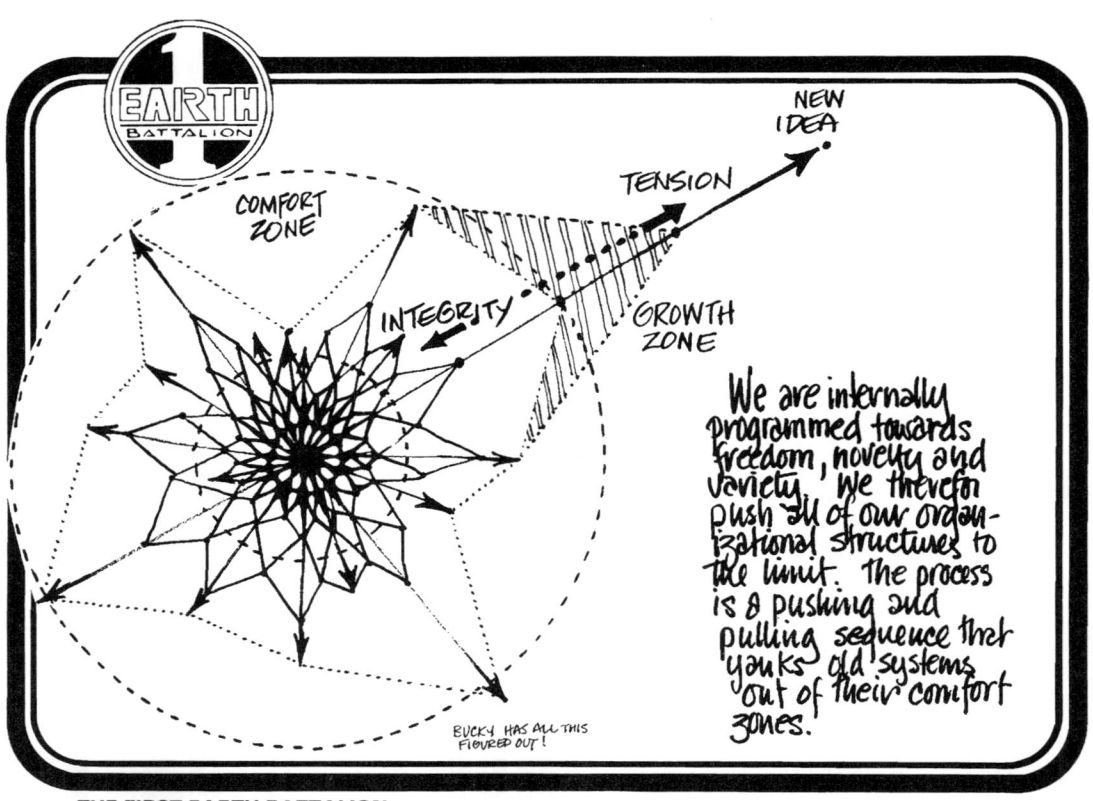

THE FIRST EARTH BATTALION

FOURTEEN

The Gut Check and Maritime Operations

At night fall, the men prepared their parachutes, loaded their rucksacks onto an awaiting troop carrier plane that would take them to their drop zone, and boarded. As the big bird lifted into the sky, the mood was subdued.

They knew that no other teams had successfully completed this Gut Check gut orienteering course that they were embarking on, and there was a sense of excitement and trepidation in the air. Simulating an actual mission, the men would fly to the drop zone and jump HALO in the dark of night, falling silently for thirty thousand feet and then opening their chutes just above the treetops somewhere in the most rugged terrain of Pennsylvania. Once on the ground, they would hopefully find each other and assemble their teams, get their bearings, find the trail, and set off on the first leg of this arduous trek.

The Gut Check provided a real-world, challenging way to assess the impact and value of the mind-body training our soldiers had received during the encampment and the program in general. Would it make any difference in their capacity under stress over a prolonged period of time? In the army's own words, "We wanted to determine whether the combination of optimal diet, efficient, though spare, cardiovascular conditioning, and intensive mental training (i.e., the encampment) would enable these teams to pass an arduous mission-related test of proven difficulty, which no other special ops teams had ever successfully completed in the past."

This post encampment Gut Check test was designed to determine:

- The ability of the men to move long distances with mission loads while maintaining security. Within this objective, the following was to be closely monitored: sleep and rest management, energy management, diet, self-healing, and willingness to help other team members.
- The ability of the men to remain alert for several days while under stress.
- The ability of each man to monitor himself and take appropriate actions to ensure continued effectiveness.
- The effectiveness of interpersonal communications.
- The ability of the men to respond to rapidly changing situations without losing time fighting the problem.
- The ability of the men to avoid injury. This will come from the improved balance, coordination, and agility gained through aikido, as well as from the increased sensitivity to the messages their bodies are sending (i.e., fatigue, stress, etc.).

The Gut Check was a strenuous test, difficult and tiring, used by the battalion commanding officer as a reliable measure of the soldiers' individual and team physical endurance and mental toughness. Note that numerous other teams had attempted this test, and all had failed, due to injuries or breakdowns in conduct among team members.

The troops had to cover nearly one hundred miles carrying heavy rucksacks (sixty-five to eighty-five pounds) and complete the course within seventy-one hours. The course included one leg of thirty-eight miles in twenty-four hours. The terrain was a remote, mountainous region in Pennsylvania with features such as the infamous Heartbreak Hill with temperatures ranging from freezing to a rainy 50 degrees F.

Each team received a partial and barely legible map of only one leg of the course at a time. A checkpoint was indicated with no other information provided than an outer time limit to complete that leg of the course. The teams did not know how many legs or checkpoints there would be and were only provided with rations if they made the checkpoint on time as a full team. If they missed the time as a full team, they would be without food or water for the next leg of the test. Each team had to complete all segments of this severe orienteering-style course as a full team. Keep in mind that this was in the predigital age, so these soldiers had no access to digital maps, apps, navigation, or drones. They were navigating "old style" with only compasses and paper maps.

After the monthlong encampment, both of our teams were able to successfully complete the entire course, making all the checkpoints, with no injuries, and became the first two teams to successfully complete this test. Our training team was inspired and relieved by these results, and the soldiers had a sense of significant accomplishment and recognition for what they had achieved. According to the battalion commander, the results of the Gut Check included:

- **Food.** Healthier food choices of a high-carbohydrate diet rather than standard issue LRP (Long Range Patrol) freeze-dried rations did make a difference, and many soldiers reported a noticeable difference in their ability to maintain a steady, strong energy level.
- **Injuries.** Despite the physical challenges of this arduous test, only considerable soreness after the exercise was reported. A reoccurrence of a preexisting knee injury, surfacing late in the exercise, was the sole injury.
- **Self-healing.** Fifteen percent of the soldiers reported some success in employing mental self-healing techniques to promote faster body healing on this long march. In one instance, a trainer noted a successful self-healing process that, in the trainer's opinion, saved that soldier from needing to be medically evaluated.

- **Endurance.** Despite the prolonged isolation of the encampment and the stressful training the soldiers underwent, not only was the soldiers' endurance reported to be high, but it was also determined to be the best ever for some soldiers. Those reporting higher endurance levels consistently had healthier diets.
- **Team cohesion.** Both teams successfully completed the course without any significant injuries or team meltdowns. No other teams had accomplished this before.

Returning home triumphant from the Gut Check, the men enjoyed a long weekend with their families and friends. In the weeks to come we continued with our daily schedule of working out, practicing aikido and MOS soldier skills, and training in the lab.

That Heart Thing

Afterward we debriefed Danner, one of the oldest and most experienced men on the team. He reflected on his experience on Heartbreak Hill—a long steep climb to what appeared to be the crest, which upon arrival turned out to be just a resting spot for another even steeper and longer climb. No wonder this particularly intense stretch of the course bore that name. It was even more of an ordeal on limited rations and carrying such heavy loads.

We asked him, "So, what kept you going on those long climbs?" With a tone of calm surprise, he replied, "You know I'm kind of surprised to say it, but that heart thing you taught us during the encampment really helped me to find the energy I needed when I started to lose energy or be overwhelmed by pain or exhaustion."

Michelle inquired more deeply, "So, just to make sure I'm understanding you correctly, can you describe what you mean by that heart thing?"

Danner beamed a big smile and replied, "You know, that practice where you breathe in the pain, the exhaustion, or the doubt, transform it in your heart, and then blast out some kind of strength or healing energy back to wherever the pain or the fatigue came from. I had plenty of my own physical pain to work with, and that technique was super helpful for that. But what really gave me the strength to keep going and push through when it was really hard was when I used my own aches and pains, exhaustion or fears, to open my awareness to how much the other guys on my team were hurting, and that reminded me to extend my ki and my strength to the others and light them up. Doing that actually filled me with the strength I needed to keep going. I even made up some of my own focus phrases for myself and the other guys on the trek, like: *may you stay strong, may you rise above the pain, may you come through this shining.* That was a new set of moves for me, a real surprise, and valuable discovery. I'll remember this when I need it in the future."

We were heartened and inspired by Danner's description of how extending positive energy and care to others gave him strength. Interestingly, we had witnessed the power of this strategy twice before in our work as mind-fitness coaches with Cheryl Merrick and Estelle Grey, who had set a long-standing record for the RAAM, the Ride Across America, and with Ed Eliason, an Olympic gold medal archer. It seemed clear that extending sincere positive energy to others is a surefire way to energize and strengthen ourselves.

Maritime Operations

Sitting around the dinner table at home together, our trainer team savored an autumn harvest meal of wild rice, baked squash, and tempeh, with a side of roast, and the opportunity to be back in the warmth and comforts of our home, enjoying delicious homecooked food and the attention of Shaba, our sweet four-legged companion.

After dinner, Jack and Richard started packing and gearing up for the maritime ops exercises, while we were getting ready to fine-tune and calibrate our state-of-the-art multiperson neurofeedback synchrony system for the upcoming phase of training. This would be a historic event as, to the best of our knowledge, no other labs, universities, or research centers on the planet had ever created or used such a collective brain-hacking system before to train subjects not only to sense and control their own brain states but to then synchronize their brainwaves with each other. While Joel was in some ways sorry to miss the adventure of the maritime ops, he was also just as glad to be home and excited by the inner adventures that awaited us and the teams as we opened the neurofeedback portal into new and unexplored realms of personal and collective potential.

Upstairs in their rooms, Jack and Richard were packing wool socks, rain gear, down jackets, and sleeping bags and preparing for the cold, rough weather on the New England coastline. Larry had also arrived and had spread out his gear on the couch in the living room, excited by the opportunity to share a rough-and-tumble extended ops adventure with the soldiers, rather than just be training on base.

The next morning, we all assembled on base as the men went off to the airfield to board the choppers that would take them north to the Atlantic seacoast of Maine for ten days of intensive maritime operations training. In addition to military skills training, this exercise would provide an opportunity for our soldiers to test some of the aspects of their self-regulation training under actual mission conditions, especially their ability to warm their extremities both while camping in the chilly autumn north and while on and in the ocean during training exercises. For some of the soldiers, they would experience how profoundly useful these inner skills could be. For others, these skills hadn't quite landed yet.

Camping out on the rugged, wind-swept coast of Maine, our two teams, along with Jack, Richard, and Larry, were having a frosty, soggy time. Maritime operations involved ten days in the great outdoors, with most days spent in wet suits in Zodiacs on rough seas or in the sea itself. Richard, Larry, and Jack played minimal teaching roles during this time, other than guiding some workouts and martial arts. Mostly, they were on board in solidarity, to participate, learn, and connect with the men.

The cold, stormy days offered long ocean swims, rescues, Zodiac ocean navigation, swamped boats in heavy seas with dead engines, men overboard, dangerous launches and landings, some injuries, and a late-night exercise lost at sea, trying to find a safe landing at camp. One team, cast adrift with a dead engine was rescued by a local lobster boat, whose captain stoically towed them to safe harbor up the coast. During this time, many of the men succumbed to the weather and came down with colds. All in all, these maritime exercises offered a rich mix of mission-related circumstances that mirrored for each man and each team how their habits, reactive patterns, relationships, equipment, and new skills functioned under stress.

Returning home again to the comforts of shelter, central heating, and family, they all relished a long weekend to rest and renew themselves.

Deep Dives in the Mind Lab

During the time the teams were deployed for maritime ops we returned to the Mind Lab to do some systems checks and calibrations with our neurofeedback system in preparation for the next level of advanced neurofeedback training described in chapter 10. It was strangely novel for us to be quietly in the lab together without the soldiers around, and we realized that we hadn't had a moment like this before, other than late at night after a lab run with the teams.

During these days Colonel Kenneth Getty joined us at the lab several times, swapping out books and biofeedback gear he had borrowed to inspire his own study and inner explorations of psychophysiological sciences and picking up new books to study. With the teams away for the maritime ops, he was more at ease, and we spent long afternoons in dialogue and exploration, sharing stories and research and guiding him to a deeper comprehension and skill with using the various biofeedback devices and the contemplative sciences. We were inspired by his thirst for learning, his depth of presence, and his deep care for those within his sphere of influence. He was truly an exceptional leader and guiding light, and each encounter and conversation we shared was mutually enlivening.

Ken was fascinated by a passage we had written in one of our training manuals that described how "patterns of energy and mind weave together into the subtle and gross body influencing the coherence and circulation of energy, our biochemical balance, and physical functioning associated with both health and disease. These formative patterns of mind may arise due to mindless habits and social conditioning, or they may be intentionally cultivated. Each method of mind training will generate a unique energetic, biochemical, and neurological signature." We spent quite some time exploring the meaning and implications of this, discussing how each method of mind training had its specific effects and impacts.

Ken also brought forth deep questions and themes to explore. He was wonderstruck by how a subtle change of mind state could create measurable changes in the body and fascinated by the implications of this experience of "mind over," "mind within," or "mind as" matter. We examined his questions of: "How deep and how far can this exploration go, and how far reaching are the impacts?" Ken was deeply interested in both the tangible, easily accessible aspects of biofeedback, as well as the more mind-blowing aspects of this training.

In this vein, the research emerging from the Princeton Engineering Anomalies Research Lab (PEAR) was of particular interest. The project had been established in 1979 by Robert G. Jahn, the then dean of engineering. PEAR conducted formal studies on two primary subject areas, psychokinesis and remote viewing—two topics that had been of great interest to the military and intelligence community for many years. After working with secret experiments for the Department of Defense at Stanford, demonstrating that the mind could indeed change or influence matter and even bend laser beams, one colleague of ours bowed out of the program when the targets began to cast more ethically dubious shadows. Exploring the implications and applications of mental activity and intention directed toward "nonlocal" targets, sometimes at a great distance from the "operators" is, and was, profoundly worthy of deep reflection and ethical discernment.

We discussed the implications of thousands of scientific studies that confirm that our minds have both local effects within the boundaries of our skin and nonlocal effects that extend far beyond. Strangely, it seemed that the military has actually invested more in studying the nonlocal effects of mind at a distance than the powers of the mind within the body for self-regulation and healing. Just as our minds can reach into our fingers or toes or to an aching or injured part of our body, it seems clear that, with proper training, our mind can reach out into the seamless fabric of reality beyond the boundaries of our physical body and identity. To the degree that this view is true, then our mind and intentions can reach out to touch, influence, bless, heal, or perturb anyone or anything distant from our physical body.

Though there is no definitive explanation for how this works, there is little doubt that the mind is capable of generating influence at a distance, and considerable military research has generously funded this research for decades. While the mental power and skill necessary to do this reliably appears to be learnable and universally available, few people have had the interest, discipline, guidance, and confidence necessary to develop much mastery in this realm. Yet, even to conceive of these potentialities is quite profound and significant in a world that is increasingly networked, programmed, and filled with many exploitable vulnerabilities whose function could be disrupted by minute fluctuations in electronic circuits.

After timeless afternoons immersed in such conversations and contemplations, Colonel Getty would leave with new books and research papers to explore and biofeedback equipment to continue his personal studies, and we'd be left to muse on how profoundly different it would be to have twenty-five soldiers engaged in the Jedi Warrior training program with the same energy, enthusiasm, and thirst for learning as the good colonel.

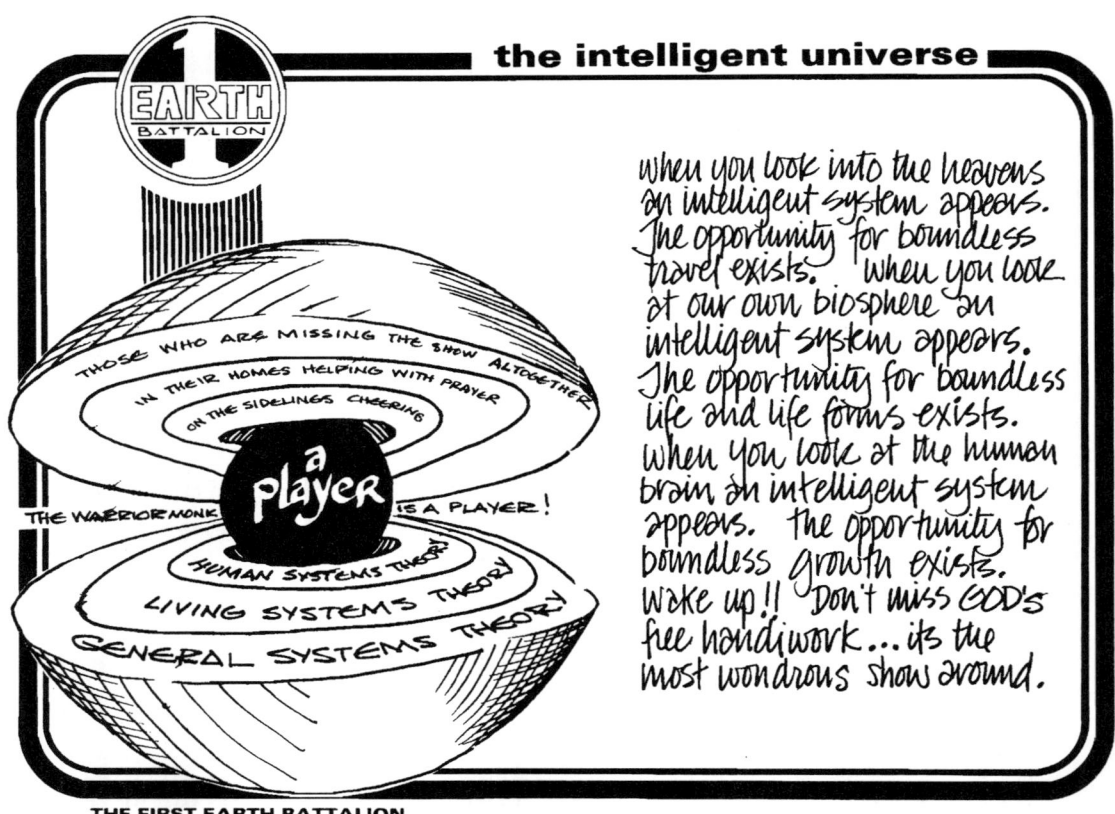

EARTH 1 BATTALION

THOSE WHO ARE MISSING THE SHOW ALTOGETHER
IN THEIR HOMES HELPING WITH PRAYER
ON THE SIDELINES CHEERING
a Player
THE WARRIOR MONK IS A PLAYER!
HUMAN SYSTEMS THEORY
LIVING SYSTEMS THEORY
GENERAL SYSTEMS THEORY

when you look into the heavens
an intelligent system appears.
The opportunity for boundless
travel exists. When you look
at our own biosphere an
intelligent system appears.
The opportunity for boundless
life and life forms exists.
When you look at the human
brain an intelligent system
appears. the opportunity for
boundless growth exists.
wake up!! Don't miss GOD's
free handiwork...its the
most wondrous show around.

THE FIRST EARTH BATTALION

FIFTEEN

Awakening Warriors

Over the course of the program, we had the good fortune to host a diverse array of luminary guest presenters who guided our teams in deeper inquiries into new dimensions and expanded potentials for themselves as awakening warriors. Here is a glimpse of some of these meaningful close encounters.

Samurai Spirit

In mid-October, just before the teams left for maritime ops, the respected elder, George Leonard, joined us for three days of training. George was a man of great stature, a rich blend of Japanese samurai spirit and European Renaissance man. He had lived a many-faceted life, having flown as a combat pilot in the South Pacific during World War II and served as an intelligence officer during the Korean War. George had authored six significant books on social and individual transformation and was an accomplished musician, playing clarinet and piano, and had composed a musical. At forty-seven years of age, a time when many athletes bow out and retire, George began his practice of aikido. At the time of his visit to the base, George held the rank of *sandan*, third-degree black belt in aikido, which he earned at the age of fifty-two. He and Richard had worked and trained together for years and were codirectors of the Aikido of Tamalpais dojo in Marin, along with Richard's former wife, Wendy Palmer.

George was a strange attractor who had connections with all of us working on the SportsMind team. We had trained with George at his dojo, and our work was deeply inspired by his writings. Jack had studied Leonard Energy Training with him, Bud was inspired by his work, and for Chris, George was a bit of a hero.

During his time with us, George taught all the aikido classes, which offered Richard a rare opportunity to be on the mat training with the men as a fellow student of aikido, rather than in the role of teacher. As an elder aikido master, George's grace, fluidity, and power in the art of aikido was an inspiration for our young bucks and offered a glimpse of how strength and vitality could be maintained in elder years. Many commented on how inspired they were that this man who was twice their age could move with such fluid grace and power.

George skillfully blended his aikido instruction with a deeper dive into what it means to be a modern-day warrior, inviting us all to reflect on the relevance of this term and frame of reference in how we define ourselves as individuals, leaders, team members, and modern-day warriors in service of a greater good.

Richard astutely observed that George's presence had an unexpected impact on the men, saying that he "gave them a clearer sense of who we were as a training team. We became more real in their eyes. We weren't simply those guys from the West Coast trying to stuff strange exotic teachings down their throats. For the first time they saw us as part of a larger community of extraordinary people who are authentically committed to awareness work, much as they are to their own practice."[1] Throughout the classes, talks, and informal conversations, George succeeded in drawing the men into a series of meaningful discussions about the warrior theme, while our previous attempts to open this conversation had most often been met with reluctance if not disdain.

At the beginning of George's first class on base, he asked, "How many of you feel that Rambo represents the Special Forces soldier?" His question evoked a ripple of laughter and wry amusement from the men.

"How many of you enjoyed the movie?"

Nearly all the men raised their hands, opening the way to a rich conversation of the many ways that the Hollywood image of Rambo was entertaining but lacked realism in the minds of the men. Their main gripe was that they never saw Rambo humping a hundred-pound rucksack like them. George then invited them to define their own view and vision of an "ideal warrior." This invitation evoked a rich barrage of qualities including dedication, service, loyalty, determination, steadfastness, and calm intensity in the midst of pressure. At the top of the list were service and self-mastery, reflecting the dedication required to continually improve oneself. One soldier, Shepherd, commented, "It's not only improving our skills, but also it's improving ourselves, being the master of ourselves."

Jack added, "The warrior is also aware of his limitations. It's not that the warrior doesn't have any holes; it's that he's aware of his holes."

This inquiry drew us deeper to discuss the difference between the kind of agile, fluid, responsive self-mastery that we cultivate on the aikido mat and the opposing qualities of reactive rigidity and aggression.

"So, it seems to me that the warrior virtue of service, especially offering the service of protecting others, could also be a justification for your job," observed George. "Does that mean that service can justify a violent way of life?"

The men leaned into this question, discussing the need for them to be capable of violence when their job required it, based on the belief that they were acting in service of a greater good. It was clear that these soldiers weren't looking for violence, but they were willing to die to protect each other and defend their country. It was also clear from this discussion that a higher order of discernment is often needed to assess the assumptions behind the phrase "for the greater good."

This drew us into a rich and moving exploration of what had called these men to enlist in the first place, or to re-up for a second tour of duty. For some, they were inspired to carry on family traditions of service to their country through the military service. Others talked about how events in the world led them to leave well-paying jobs to enlist to serve their country.

Dunham lit up with fervor saying, "Yes, and we're here to protect our right to sit here and talk openly about all this. We protect the rights of those intellectual long-hair hippies in Berkeley or wherever, even here in Harvard Square, who talk down the country and badmouth us. Our job is to serve our country by protecting these freedoms. Maybe our mission will be to put our lives on the line someday, maybe not. But in the meantime, we're here to serve and protect those rights."

Rader spoke about the devastation of the recent big earthquake in Mexico, saying, "They could have used us down there. We could have really helped. We just want to be part of the action. It doesn't have to be a war. We just want to put our skills to good use wherever it may be needed."

This reminder of the role of these Special Forces troops to serve in disaster situations really struck a chord for these guys and led to a cascade of ideas. In moments, the dialogue morphed into mock planning for such a mission, calling out the elements involved based on the location and size of disaster. How big a unit to parachute into a remote area to provide medical assistance, support local authorities on the ground, rescue people trapped under debris, provide security from looters, create shelters, and provide food and water. These men knew how to assess, plan, organize, and rapidly deploy, and they were used to working round the clock for days at a time to meet their objectives.

Witnessing the energy and enthusiasm of these soldiers envisioning such a mission, our hearts were warmed, as this conversation echoed so much of what Jim Channon had envisioned for the First Earth Battalion, whose mission was to deploy to places of great ecological or social disruption to offer needed assistance and protection.

At one point, Jack spoke up to say, "After my second tour in Vietnam, I realized it was not in the cards for me to die a quick and glorious death. I was going to live. So, what was I going to do about that? How was I going to face and deal with living? That was stage two in the warrior game for me. I was going to live, and I wanted to live as a warrior. So, I figured I better start planning to live a good and meaningful life."

Knowing Jack, it was clear that for him, "living a good and meaningful life" was not about fame, fortune, and fancy toys. For him it was about wholehearted courageous engagement with life, to make a meaningful and beneficial difference in the lives of those within his sphere of influence.

The scope and vision of our training program was expansive to say the least. Our contract required us to delve into territory that had never been explored with Special Forces troops before, and we had an explicit mandate to go there. If you hold the example of the Rambo-esque archetype of a modern-day warrior in one hand, and the vision of O'Sensei's vision of aikido as "the art of peace" in the other, we were aiming for a middle way closely akin to Channon's vision of the attributes of the warriors of the First Earth Battalion.

George's presence in our midst was ennobling for us all, and his teachings framed the wisdom and disciplines of warriorship in ways that blended both the gritty personal and the more universal aspirations of the warriors' life. In our days together, both on the mat and in dialogue, George shared elements of what he would later codify as "The Modern Warrior: A Manifesto." This pithy set of aphorisms was inspired by his study of aikido, the teachings of O'Sensei, and the wisdom reflective of his own lived experience in combat and in daily life. Notice how each point resonates for you:

1. The Modern Warrior is not one who goes to war or kills people, but rather one who is dedicated to the creation of a more vivid peace.
2. The Modern Warrior honors the traditional warrior virtues: loyalty, integrity, dignity, courtesy, courage, prudence, and benevolence.
3. The Modern Warrior pursues self-mastery through will, patience, and diligent practice.

4. The Modern Warrior works to perfect himself or herself not so much as a means to achieving some external goal as for its own sake.

5. The Modern Warrior is willing to take calculated risks to realize his or her potential and further the general good.

6. The Modern Warrior is fully accountable for his or her actions.

7. The Modern Warrior seeks the inner freedom that comes from the study of aesthetics, culture, and the wisdom of the ages.

8. The Modern Warrior respects and values the human individual and the entire web of life on this planet. To serve others is of the highest good. To freely give and accept nourishment from life is the warrior's challenge.

9. The Modern Warrior reveres the spiritual realm that lies beyond appetites and appearances.

10. The Modern Warrior cherishes life and thus conducts his or her affairs in such a manner as to be prepared at every moment for death. In this light, he or she is able to view all complaints, regrets, and moods of melancholy as indulgences.

11. The Modern Warrior aims to achieve control and act with abandon.

12. The Modern Warrior realizes that being a warrior doesn't mean winning or even succeeding. It does mean putting your life on the line. It means risking and failing and risking again, as long as you live.

Context Is Everything

Another guest presenter was Mike Blondell, a combat veteran who served in the Navy SEALs and embodied a quality of strength, dignity, and grace that was disarming. His inspired work with "Context Training," a reflective and confrontational personal growth training that was popular in the '80s, invited courageous soul searching to bring awareness to the often unconscious emotional patterns, triggers, attitudes, and beliefs that sabotage or ennoble people's lives. Mike was a master of his art and an admired member of our SportsMind team. His skill in making this work accessible to many people who have never dreamed of engaging in this kind of transformational process had a gritty elegance to it.

Mike was a large 220-pound man, with a bright smile and a generous belly hanging over his belt. Initially Jack, as a newer member of our SportsMind team, raised concerns about inviting Mike to teach in this program, noting that he didn't physically model the values we were seeking to instill in the men in terms of physical training and appearance. But as Jack and the men would quickly discover, Mike's huge heart far outweighed his belly.

Mike really modeled what it meant to establish and hold a presence before the room with a profound sense of dignity and poise that commanded the men's attention. They knew he was a former SEAL, and they were curious what he was bringing to this program. Mike stepped up to the flipchart and wrote a single word: INTEGRITY. "So, what does this mean to you?" he asked.

After the first assault of crass comments—"Hell, if we had that we wouldn't be SF" and "Are you sure you spelled that right?"—Mike rolled with it and turned to beam and smile at them like a wizened elder, saying simply, "OK, anybody ready to go deeper?"

Slowly, tentatively, some deeper musings emerged. Mike took each comment to heart with a generous acknowledgment for each voice and wrapped up this opening exchange saying, "OK, so can we all agree that integrity is the consistency of our thoughts, words, and actions?" Without much effort, everyone bought in to this. "Then let's look more closely at where in our lives we are out of integrity."

As we slipped into deeper waters in the days to come, our team of trainers joined the men in an exploration of psychological strengths, vulnerabilities, and emotional values. Mike's mastery guided us to focus the beam of our individual and collective attention to illuminate and clarify an arsenal of potent themes, including integrity, honesty, accountability, engagement, commitment, and the vital role that the presence or absence of these qualities played in our lives.

Along the way, Mike made it clear that this kind of deep inquiry is vital to a warrior's life work. To ask such questions in an honest way requires great courage. His Special Ops experience tested in combat, blended with his depth of care and presence, was disarming. He generated a potent space of challenge, safety, and support for these men to penetrate into deeper layers of their hearts, minds, and souls than most of them had ever explored before. Coming on the heels of the encampment, this inquiry offered an opportunity to give voice to many of the realizations that the men had come to but hadn't had a space to discuss and integrate their insights in dialogue with others.

Reflecting on this work from an aikido perspective, Richard noted that

early in the training Mike evoked ire by telling the men that they were avoiding important emotional issues with their machismo and bravado. He went on to say that if they didn't deal with these issues there was no way they would reach their full potential. They booed, hissed, and yelled, until finally Dunham, red-faced with clenched fists, stormed up from the back of the room. I was sure that he was going to take a poke at Mike, and I was fully prepared to intervene. As he angrily crashed to the front Mike calmly took a step toward him, quietly facing his charge. It was the ideal illustration of the power of the aikido *hanmi* stance—he was neither on the offense nor on the defense, he was simply being present. The rest of us sat in silence, riveted to our seats. Dunham stopped in a fury, about two paces in front of Mike, and began yelling in his face. Mike simply and profoundly just stood there, neither retracting nor fighting back. It was one of the best aikido-in-daily-life techniques I have ever witnessed. In a few moments Dunham quieted down, and after looking at Mike in silence for a few minutes, muttered something under his breath and returned to his seat.[2]

After this close encounter, Mike simply rode that wave observing, "That was a perfect example of integrity. What he was feeling on the inside was what he expressed on the outside. What he presented to us is what was true on the inside. That's consistency in thought, word, and action. Integrity."

When Mike first made it clear that this training would involve sharing their feelings, beliefs, values, and attitudes with partners and with the group as a whole, there was a sense of massive constriction and pulling away. Davis was really triggered by this notion of sharing and let loose with a deeply moving tirade about how he was raised to be a soldier and taught by his father that men never openly share their feelings, adding that "even now to hear the word *share* makes me want to throw up." He continued at length in a long, deep sharing of the many reasons he was unwilling to share.

As Mike skillfully and surgically guided the men layer by layer deeper into recognizing, probing, and cutting through the attitudes, beliefs, and defense mechanisms they had relied upon to shield their vulnerability, gradually, one by one, the men opened up in ways that then invited others to engage and step forward. No one in the room could defend themselves from being moved by the powerful force of such authenticity and humanity being revealed by those who had the courage to step forward to share so deeply.

Over the days of Mike's workshop, he moved us into pairs to reflect on questions such as: What is important to you? Where in your life have you paid a price for not being honest? What commitments have you made and what has kept you to honor or dishonor them? When one partner answered, the other was instructed to simply repeat the question and not get into dialogue about it but to keep going deeper as the time allowed.

This aspect of the training was an event that, in part, fulfilled William James' call for a moral equivalent to war. Although physical life and death were not an issue, an emotional life and death were certainly close at hand. For many of these men, this encounter was as frightening as facing hostile fire. Jumping out of a plane, no matter how many times it's done, will involve a risk, but this week there were much greater risks taken while standing in front of their friends and teammates. I saw again that sharing our humanity makes it possible to lift ourselves to higher ground. Opening ourselves emotionally, we can go beyond ourselves in the same way that an act of heroism or sacrifice in a physically dangerous situation can bring forth something inside of us, something that we didn't know was there.[3]

This inquiry followed our team home each evening, spilling over into our evening meal conversations as we continued to reflect together upon these themes and the potency of this work for each of us, for our work together as a team, and for the men. We realized that this penetrating inquiry and deeply personal and shared honesty would have been well placed much earlier in the training and that it could have served to create a deeper bond among the men and with us and a stronger foundation for the entire program. If this work had been done earlier in the program, then when it came to issues like the men making commitments and agreements regarding their conduct in the program and not following through, everyone would have understood that meant to do "whatever it takes" to stay in integrity.

Deeply Touched

Mike Blondell was a perfect example of many professional soldiers or athletes whose training had taken a toll on their bodies. Our men didn't complain, and they compensated well for the wounds, tensions, and traumas they carried. Most just assumed that they would have full-on active years of physically challenging service and that by their early to mid-thirties they would likely just move on to a less physically demanding job.

As a skilled bodyworker and teacher of somatic healing arts, Richard recognized that it would be of great value for these men to have the opportunity to receive the benefits of structural alignment and deep tissue work and had done a bit of this work on some of the men during the program with good results. He invited his friend and colleague Randy Cherner to join us on base for a week to offer personal body work sessions for the men.

While this was a precious gift, rarely provided to soldiers, most of these men had never been touched by another man in a noncombative, nonsexual, healing, and caring way, and there was clearly some awkward discomfort for all involved, including Randy.

As the individual sessions progressed, word quickly spread among the men about the value of this work with a litany of testimonies emerging regarding increased range of motion, easing of pain, and the resolution of physical glitches. After a session with Randy the day before, one of the team sergeants expressed bewilderment and amazement to wake up the next morning looking at the eastern wall and window of his bedroom. For years he had not been able to sleep on his left side due to an injury sustained in a rough landing from a parachute jump. After a single session with Randy, the stiffness and bracing he had endured for so long cleared enough to offer an expansion of his view, comfort, and range of motion. One surprise that emerged from this wave of work was a great interest and enthusiasm on the part of the medics to get trained in how to carry some of this hands-on healing wisdom into the field without needing to add any weight to their heavy packs.

As Richard wisely observed in his book *In Search of the Warrior Spirit:*

A few weeks ago when I walked into the space where Randy Cherner was doing bodywork, I had a momentary fantasy of seeing one end of the room piled high with the armor released from his work. I imagined well-forged breastplates, layered shoulder pads, neck braces, shields, face masks, leg tubes, swords, and lances lying in a silvery, cluttered heap. I further saw that each piece of armor was also an attitude, a way the men positioned themselves mentally and emotionally, as well as bodily, to the world. The vision made me smile because I knew the power of this bodywork, and of Randy's touch. But the joy that spawned the smile came from knowing that the discarding of this dense and heavy armor would expose their hearts. And it was today that I saw this heart: a tender

335

heart, iron strong with dignity, fearlessly inviting the world in. Randy's bodywork, the flexibility and stretching exercises, the encampment, Mike Blondell, the daily aikido training, the brain synchrony training, all have become the alchemical elements that fired the seed of warrior fearlessness.[4]

The Capoeiristas

Walking into the dojo one morning, we were greeted by the twang and haunting resonance of the *berimbau*, a single-stringed instrument at the heart of capoeira practice. This signaled the long-anticipated arrival of Bira Almeida, Richard's esteemed capoeira teacher and dear friend. Richard had great admiration for Bira and regarded him as one of the best fighters he had ever met. Bira's reputation as a two-time heavyweight capoeira champion of Brazil, a master musician with his own samba band, and friend of some of the most beloved musicians and artists in Brazil had set some high expectations for the men. Given Richard's stories, the men likely expected a slick, tanned, muscular dude straight off the beaches of Rio. Yet at first glance, Bira with his thick glasses, uncombed curly hair, and beaming smile seemed a bit of an odd duck in our pond.

In a short while, bathed in the warmth of Bira's effusive greetings and strong handshakes connecting with each of the men, the room and spirits brightened up, smiles shone forth among the men, and a great curiosity arose. Though we're in the aikido dojo, we were training in capoeira that day, the Brazilian martial art that's performed in the spirit of play, accompanied by music, chant, and the rhythms of clapping hands. Dressed simply in white pants and T-shirts, we gathered round in a circle as Bira played his berimbau. Bira plays and sings with a voice that carries the joys and sorrows of ancestors trained in this ancient art, and these melodious haunting sounds soaked deep into each of us, conveying a sense for the struggles and redemptions of the capoeiristas of the past. The rhythms and songs convey how to play in the *roda*, the circle where pairs of capoeiristas test their martial skills.

Capoeira developed among the Brazilian slaves as a way to train in powerful martial arts under the guise of dance and singing. Its power and force were veiled to elude a sense of threat, but when applied in a fight, it was formidable and disarming against any opponent.

Bira took his place in the circle, and one by one invited each of the soldiers to step in to the roda "to play" with him. The play is a dynamic, novel, unexpected, fun, and challenging form of martial training. Bira's power and grace, his warm-hearted grin and swift, effortless moves in evading and responding to the men invited each man to open his awareness, inhabit his body, and blend with Bira's attacks. As the mat soaked with sweat and T-shirts flew off, it seemed that a layer of tension and effort melted in the field of the play, finding a fluid rhythm and pulse.

Bira had trained long and hard for many years, passing through a succession of trials, ordeals, and initiations. At each level he mastered different inner and outer strengths and burned through countless layers of doubt, fear, and personal and ancestral trauma. In his book *Capoeira, A Brazilian Art Form: History, Philosophy, and Practice*, he describes his journey through various levels: Playing in the Dark, open to explore and learn from the emergent nature of the art without anticipation. Then, Playing in the Water, where there is a growing sense of mastery of the fighting form and fluidity of the art. Next comes, Playing in the Light, a stage where he challenged all of his limits through fighting with other capoeiristas and other martial artists.[5]

After lapsing into a deep depression, going to graduate school, and setting aside his practice for three years, Bira awoke one day filled with a vivid sense of what was missing in his practice and a renewed inspiration to resume his training. Following his guidance to emigrate to the States and continue his training there, he entered what he called "the stage of Playing with the Crystal Ball," a phase where all the physical training was deeply in place and the focus was now on reading the mind of his opponent and finding the optimal place within the play.

Bira describes his realization upon reaching the final level of his evolution as a capoeirista:

> Then I reached the last level which I call "Playing with the Mind." The opponent must do what your mind silently orders him to do. Such control has no other purpose than to help your opponent, even your enemy, to evolve and to reach a universal harmony through the Capoeira way. There is a rhythm to life and to the universe. In doing Capoeira, you can play to find it, to attune to it. As long as you are true to this rhythm, you cannot fight a false fight. The rhythm is joyful and gay; it is filled with life's imbalances, but it transforms them. It takes the unpredictability of the world and allows you to move on it.[6]

In his book *In Search of the Warrior Spirit,* Richard remembers a time with Bira at a panel discussion exploring the topics of nuclear war and the difference between the warrior and the militarist, where Bira objected to the idea of a meaningful comparison between modern warfare and the true nature of a warrior.

> A fight in the Capoeira context is an important process of self-understanding because when one confronts a serious opponent he's also confronting himself in a situation that uncovers his weaknesses and strength. I believe that the fight in this context is a step toward self-discovery, and consequently personal growth. This is an individual process that cannot be extended to a level of millions of people fighting with contemporary war artifacts, or to a massive extermination of human beings in a nuclear confrontation of nations. I think that a nuclear war is also a comfortable kind of war. The person who is pressing the buttons does not suffer the fear of actual fighting. Certainly

there's fear of retaliation, but it's very different from the feelings that come during a personal confrontation. Think about the time when weapons were spears, swords, and clubs. You see your opponent running down a hill with a sword in hand. You can only rely on your own skill to defend the blows, or on your legs to flee. For the individual fight, the issue assumes a different perspective. At the moment you are fighting, your opponent becomes yourself. You confront your fears, your strength and weakness, your life itself. You do this without involving anybody besides your opponent and you. I have been involved in thousands of fights in my life, so I know what it is to feel this kind of thing inside. You know you must win. But to win means to win with yourself.[7]

The timeless days with Bira served to ignite a spark of new moves, rhythms, and possibilities for what embodying the warrior spirit could mean for each of us.

Saying Yes to Our Belonging

As part of our preparation for the Jedi Warrior program, we had consulted with Brother David Steindl-Rast, a beloved elder Benedictine monk who is among the most revered of modern contemplatives. We were leading a retreat at Esalen and had asked if he would be willing to come and spend a few days on base as part of our visiting guest program. Brother David followed an annual cycle that for many years led him to live in silent contemplative retreat at the Abbey at Big Sur, California, for half of the year, and to spend the other half of the year actively engaged in traveling, teaching, and service in the world. Since one of the mission objectives in the army's contract with us included "developing a greater sensitivity to spiritual orientations," we knew that Brother David, as a wise and inspiring teacher, would have a lot to contribute.

Little did we expect that he would begin his visit with the men on base with the opening words, "When I was a soldier in the Nazi army . . ." We were all stunned. Conscripted as a teenager by Hitler's troops when they invaded Austria, Brother David had the opportunity to experience military life firsthand. When the war was over, he realized he was at a crossroads. When asked how it was that he came to choose a life as a monk, Brother David laughed and told us his story.

"A friend loaned me *The Rule of St. Benedict*, and when I read it, I thought, *This is the way of life I have been looking for.* But where was there a monastery or community where such a way of life was lived and practiced? Saint Benedict had been dead for fifteen hundred years! Someone suggested that I should visit Mount Saviour Monastery. Well, I said, I'll take whichever comes first, the right monastery, or the right girl! When I visited Mount Saviour, I knew within a few hours that this was it. That was in 1953, and I'm still a member of this community." Rather than finding the right woman to be his wife, he found the right circumstances to enter a contemplative life of prayer and meditation and made the commitment to live his life within the rigor and discipline of the Benedictine monastic order.

Brother David surprised us all as he pointed out the similarities between serving as a soldier in the military and serving as a monk within the hierarchy of the church. Each had a mission to participate in and served a larger good than self, and each was often bogged down by hierarchical chains of command. As Brother David spoke, our men leaned in and listened.

Though elderly and not large of frame, Brother David had a commanding and engaging presence that expressed authenticity, authority, and wisdom. Many of the men on our teams had left the church years ago, having witnessed the hypocrisies of their religious leaders or been turned off by discrepancies and unsavory church politics within the faith communities in which they had been raised. Brother David's presence and conversation, however, was not about religion. It was about spirit and the mystery that infuses our lives and world with sacredness and meaning. As he taught and they listened, a deep quiet descended in our midst.

Brother David invited the men to consider just why they loved to do what they did. "What is it about jumping into the sky and soaring for thousands of feet that thrills you? What is it about being out in the extremes of nature for long periods of time, enduring hardships and finding the inner strength, inspiration, and guidance that you need to overcome all obstacles? What is it about being dedicated to your brothers-in-arms and willing to endure extreme dangers to protect them and fulfill your mission? What is it about being willing to lay down your life to defend and protect your nation and its people, to live and die for something greater than yourself?"

Brother David went on to say, "I take the time to feel gratitude for all that I have. There is so much to be grateful for—our health, our families, that we have food to eat and a beautiful world to live in, that we have friends and children who are healthy." Laughing with a joyful sincerity he confessed, "I could spend my entire day just being grateful!"

As our time together continued, Brother David asked the men about their own spiritual longings. Most of the men raised their hands noting that they had been raised in Christian denominations, while there were also a few agnostics and atheists. Tom, one of the most outspokenly skeptical members of the teams, said that he was an atheist and challenged Brother David with "What do you mean by God anyway? How do you know if you're leading a spiritual life?"

Brother David responded to the challenge unruffled, saying that spirituality is fundamentally about experiencing a sense of our belonging and connectedness with another living being, with nature, with a community, or with the whole mystery of the world and universe in which we live.

"Do you ever feel any of these feelings?" Brother David asked Tom, who softened a bit at Brother David's direct question. "I feel very connected to my newborn son, and of course, I'm really connected to and committed to the members of my team. After the birth of my son, this feeling of connectedness has really deepened. It caught me by surprise, and I feel a lot more from my heart. This has really been one of the most moving experiences

I've ever known. It fuels my own motivation for the kind of man and father I want to be and the kind of life I want to live and make possible for him."

"Then from my point of view, you are living a very spiritual life," Brother David responded.

"Yeah, if you look at it this way, I guess I do feel that my life is pretty spiritual," Tom reflected, half to himself and half to Brother David. The potency of this interplay between Brother David and Tom shifted the energy in the room, bringing us all to a powerful peace and focus of attention.

"Ethics is how we behave when we decide that we belong together," Brother David reminded us. He added, "And to the extent to which we have given room in our hearts for gratitude, we all have a share in this spiritual reality, by whatever name we may call it. All that matters is that we enter into that passage of gratitude and sacrifice, the passage that leads us to integrity within ourselves, to concord with one another, and to union with the very source of life."

This quality of exploration continued through the morning, with many of the men discovering, owning, and honoring a deeper sense of their own innate spirituality and the ways it was reflected in their lives. Brother David reminded them that few people on Earth had made a commitment to give their lives for the good of other people or were willing to die for a cause greater than their own.

"If you drive to go beyond yourself, then I hope you can see, as I do, that fulfilling your role and mission as a soldier can truly be a vehicle for honoring and worshipping in a sacred way. If you take this sacred trust to heart, then this profession that you have chosen can be an authentic expression and fulfillment of your highest spiritual values and aspirations."

The room was silent as his words soaked into the hearts and minds of these men. Never before had we seen them so open and unguarded, so focused and respectful to one of our instructors or guests. Brother David had recognized that their sense of belonging to and connectedness with a larger whole, their impulse to reach beyond the bounds of the ordinary personal self, was a sacred and spiritual yearning. The soldiers felt affirmed in the deepest core of their being—a place some of them had been out of touch with for a long time. In a gesture of respect, many of them approached the front of the room to shake his hand and pay their respects. They, in turn, recognized Brother David as a warrior of the heart, and this would forever inspire them in their own aspirations.

Through Brother David's compassion, warmth, and humor, the men opened to sense levels of insight and self-discovery that had rarely emerged during elements of our training in which they were more guarded. In the nonjudgmental space of his loving acceptance and humanity, they let many layers of their armoring fall away. It was as though he were gently helping them to discover a profound and unalienable birthright—that each and every one of them, regardless of the stories they held about themselves or the "transgressions" of their lives, was a spiritual being.

By affirming their commitments to one another and dedicating their lives to the betterment of a larger cause, their work as warriors had become ennobled. For many of these soldiers, who had left anything resembling a church or community of faith long ago, this was a profound and moving realization. Having fled their churches of origin, many had been told that they were sinners, doomed for eternity to pay for their sins. In response, some had assumed a stance of "What the hell—if I'm damned anyway, then I'll be good at it!" Yet, for some, under this "in your face" facade was often a lingering fear that, perhaps, they were adrift with no hope of redemption.

The mirror that Brother David held up to the men gave them the possibility of beholding their own divine reflection. In this possibility, some of the men were able to discover within themselves the dawning of faith and a connection with spirit that was rare to find even in church. Looking around the room while Brother David spoke humbly of his own experience, shared his wisdom, asked deep questions, and listened with empathy and understanding to the men's replies, we noticed that many of the men were moved to tears. In nearly five months of training, this had never happened.

At the end of the session, we drove home with Brother David, who himself was quite moved and inspired from his day with our men. He was clearly a man who regarded everyone as a portal for the love and presence of God to manifest in the world—a brother or sister in search of their true identity in spirit. As a contemplative of many years, Brother David's grasp of the inner sciences and technologies was profound, and we had many wonderful and deep conversations sharing insights from our various long contemplative retreats and studies with great masters from many traditions. Despite Brother David's obvious spiritual stature, he was able to share his wisdom with a clarity and simplicity that would touch and affirm even the simplest and uninitiated of minds.

That night at supper we had the grace of his presence, and the opportunity for Anne, Catherine, and Shaba to join our circle. We stayed at the dinner table talking late into the night, sharing stories from our adventures to date with the men and hearing of Brother David's inner and outer travels and the teachings he had received and given. Our evening time together offered a rare glimpse of the spiritual life and discipline of a contemplative monk and insights into that way of living in community.

As we cleared the table, Brother David was at the sink before anyone else, beginning to wash the dishes. Despite our protests, he insisted on continuing his devotions and service to God and humanity in this manner. Once he finished with the dishes, he set to work meticulously scrubbing the sink and scouring out the stains in the grout between the tiles. This image has stayed with us for years in a profoundly inspiring way. He shared with us his joy in even the tiniest act of service and led us to feel that to deprive him of the privilege of performing this holy task would in some way be unkind.

At the end of his stay with us, we drove Brother David to a small Benedictine hermitage in the New England countryside, a couple hours' drive from the base, where some members of his community lived and practiced, dedicating themselves to a life of contemplation. Brother David warmly introduced us to his brothers in spirit, speaking briefly and appreciatively of the precious time and adventures we had shared. We took our leave from them with some reluctance and let the profound impact of Brother David's visit soak in.

A couple of months later, as we neared the end of our time on base, we asked the men to pause and reflect on the question: "If you were deployed on a dangerous mission in which you might be dug in doing recon for long stretches at a time and you could take with you only one of the guest presenters from this program, whom would you choose?" Much to our collective surprise and delight, nearly all of the men chose Brother David, citing his "authenticity," "inner strength," "you could depend on him to carry his own weight," and "wisdom." It was clear that his presence had been a bunker buster for the heart and that the lives of these men had been changed forever by their encounter with this humble, selfless soul.

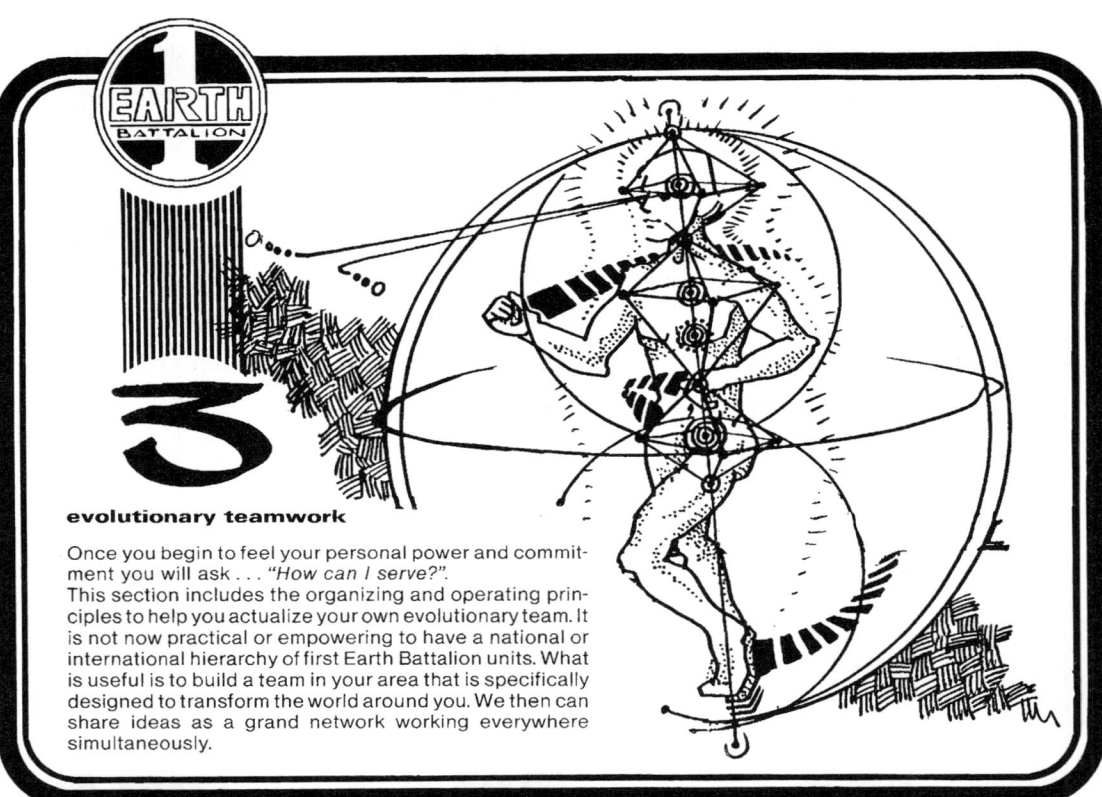

evolutionary teamwork

Once you begin to feel your personal power and commit-ment you will ask . . . *"How can I serve?"*.

This section includes the organizing and operating prin-ciples to help you actualize your own evolutionary team. It is not now practical or empowering to have a national or international hierarchy of first Earth Battalion units. What is useful is to build a team in your area that is specifically designed to transform the world around you. We then can share ideas as a grand network working everywhere simultaneously.

THE FIRST EARTH BATTALION

SIXTEEN

Winter Operations

As the end of the program approached, there was one more grueling mission simulation exercise to be accomplished. Given that the two A-Teams we were working with were preparing for missions that would be run in rugged, high-altitude, cold, snowy environments, the final test for the entire program was the winter operations exercises to be held high in the mountains of Utah. The five-week winter warfare field operation was jointly planned by our team and the Second Battalion staff. Spanning most of January into February, winter ops was comprised of three modules: an intensive ski training, a short survival exercise, and a major winter ops mission simulation exercise.

Working together with Colonel Getty and his staff, winter ops was designed as an opportunity to further test and evaluate the progress of our soldiers and their teams toward realizing many of the goals of the program. This arduous deployment into a harsh, remote, and challenging environment was crafted to assess the ability of our men to perform with greater endurance and overall mind-body mastery, while reducing injuries by managing their energy and mastering stress in the learning laboratory of the dangerous cold weather conditions of the high Rockies.

The battalion's goals for winter ops were to measure the soldiers' performance in mission-related terms such as: the ability to reach their target while carrying a hundred or more pounds of gear swiftly and safely through deep snow and rugged terrain and then dig in and stay hidden and undetected at that site, while reporting accurately, and in a timely manner, on the movements of "troops" and supplies they were observing in the area of operations. To date, no other teams of Special Forces had ever been deployed on such a difficult mission simulation or been required to travel as far or stay hidden on site for as long.

In preparation for the approaching winter operations, we were skiing together in a public ski area with John Q. Public and the hot shots from the local region. Decked out in their finest camouflage gear and army issue skis, our pack of soldiers were an odd sight on those New England ski slopes. With fresh snow, clear skies, and moderate crowds, we were all enjoying the runs. Cueing up in the lift line, one smart-ass kid jeered at the guys, "Hey, do you guys like killing?" In the blink of an eye, one of our lads responded with a sharp, clear response, striking direct to the heart, "Hey kid, do you like cancer?" Kaboom! Surprising to some who are prejudiced and steeped in preconceptions, these were men with courageous hearts, willing to give their lives to protect a larger good that they believed in.

Throughout the winter holidays and early January, Jack and Richard trained hard in preparation to join Horst and the men for this grueling winter ops exercise. They both expressed excitement and trepidation at participating in this harsh, high-altitude ordeal. The day before their scheduled departure, Richard was all packed and ready to go when he decided to treat himself with a drive into Cambridge to see some friends and train at Kanai Sensei's dojo with other black belt aikidoists. He trained hard on the mat that day but took a bad fall that left him hurt. He pulled it together to get back on the mat and push on, only to be thrown hard again, experiencing searing pain as a large muscle running the length of his thigh tore. Barely able to walk, he managed to get home, humbled and disappointed that he would not be able to participate in the winter ops.

The next morning, we all rose early to bid farewell to Jack and Horst as they drove to the airfield to travel with the men. Over breakfast, we talked about how to make the most of this upsetting change of plans and decided that Richard would help us to plunge into the daunting mountain of data we had collected and begin to sort it all out.

As our teams arrived in the Rockies, they were well aware that they would be under tremendous scrutiny during their winter operations maneuvers. Given that winter ops field tests had occurred on an annual basis for many years, there were many measures for comparing the performance of our men to past successes and failures. As the last mission simulation for our teams in the Jedi Warrior program, winter ops would serve in many ways as a final test of how our whole training had impacted them.

During the first segment of winter ops, the soldiers worked closely with our SportsMind ski wizard Horst in a weeklong intensive ski training that produced significant results. All the soldiers made fast progress in developing their skiing skills, especially the beginners. By the end, all five beginner skiers successfully tested at high intermediate competency level. One skier with no previous experience at all completed the course as a solid beginner. The rest of the skiers were already rated as intermediate or expert skiers, and in most cases, they advanced two levels of expertise in their skills. Except for the reoccurrence of one soldier's chronic shoulder separation and wrist broken in a pre-ski training incident at Fort Devens, there were no injuries sustained by our twenty-five team members during the entire time of winter exercises. In contrast, there were seventeen injuries reported for members of other battalion teams in a ski program that was far less challenging and intensive.

Following the weeklong strenuous ski training, with no recovery time built in, our two teams were immediately transferred to the field exercise. This intensive operation involved traversing 30 kilometers, or nearly 19 miles, of snow-covered mountainous terrain, at altitudes ranging from 7,500 to 8,500 feet, carrying extremely heavy loads. As part of the mission simulation, they traveled only at night, crossing dangerous, avalanche-prone areas with snows ranging in depth from four to eight feet. Upon arriving at their target site, they dug into their hide sites and remained hidden and undetected for a full ten days, while successfully sending out abundant and accurate reports. They successfully exfiltrated to their extraction site, reaching it on time, and offered what were described as "superb debriefs" for the battalion staff.

Commenting on the men's condition at the end of winter ops, the battalion commander, Colonel Getty, said, "I've seen at least 150 teams come back from these kinds of exercises, and they are always surly, cynical, and generally wiped out. These teams didn't look tired, sleep deprived, fatigued, or annoyed. They were high spirited." The battalion operations officer observed that "upon exfiltrating, these soldiers recovered extremely quickly and gave the best briefings I've ever heard."

In relation to the program goals, the following inspiring findings were reported:

- First, endurance was very high across the board: despite extremely challenging conditions for troop movement (deep wet snow, precipitation, large elevation changes), all members of both teams were able to keep up and carry their full loads.
- Second, the men exhibited a "superior ability to manage energy and master stress," as evidenced by the complete absence of new illnesses or cold weather injuries over this extended time of cold weather deployment.
- Third, these soldiers showed an ability to remain alert even after periods of intense, prolonged physical exertion or boredom, as evidenced by the teams' detailed reconnaissance reports.
- Fourth, the experimentation with a high-performance diet resulted in decidedly higher energy levels and fewer digestive problems.
- Fifth, virtually no injuries (breaks, tears, strains) were sustained on either of our teams during the exercise, and in premission training no injuries were reported, as compared with seventeen injuries to members of the other battalion teams who were involved in less extreme training.

- Sixth, and very importantly, team cohesion and team spirit remained strong despite the prolonged and extremely stressful circumstances of these field operations.

This arduous operation was considered an extremely successful demonstration of the benefits these soldiers realized from our unique wholistic model of Jedi Warrior physical- and mental-fitness training. Throughout winter ops, these soldiers demonstrated a level of personal mastery and degree of self-regulation skills higher than ever seen before, without compromising "their strong instincts for daring and aggressive action." The commanding officer pointed out that in the light of the challenges and hardships other teams had faced during winter warfare operations in previous years, our teams had achieved unprecedented results in this year's exercise during even more extreme conditions.

One of the most telling of all the results was the extremely rapid recovery time the men reported, along with their lack of injuries. This depth of embodied skills was attributed to the success of the advanced physical training, aikido, biofeedback, and mind-fitness training they had pursued over the preceding five months of immersive learning and practice.

The *Trojan Warrior After-Action Report* noted: "Simply stated, with solid fitness, one can control fatigue. With a high level of balance and coordination, there will be less overextension of the body parts. With less fatigue and less overextension, there will always be fewer injuries and faster recovery times. In a combat mission, or simulation, injuries can be translated as 'casualties' when it comes to winning and surviving on the battlefield."

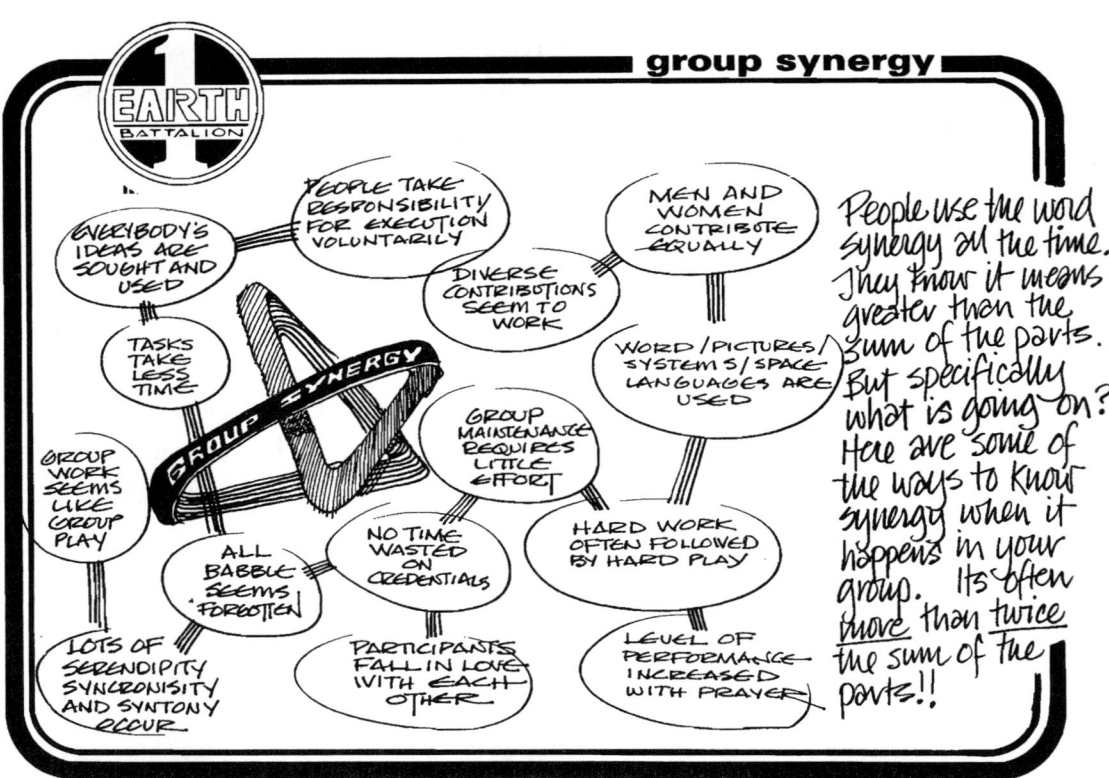

THE FIRST EARTH BATTALION

SEVENTEEN

A Wealth of Lessons Learned

Over the course of the six months of Jedi Warrior, we collected hundreds of pages of data and spent tens of thousands of dollars processing the data to document the results and impacts of this transformational program. While some of the program goals lended themselves to easily quantifiable objective measures, assessing our progress toward some of the other goals was more elusive. In the final analysis, the data we gathered was ultimately based on our progress toward achieving the goals stated in the contract and spanned a wide spectrum from the simplest to the more complex and from objective to deeply felt subjective measures. Though many of the most meaningful and profound aspects of this remarkable sequence of experiences remained elusive to quantify, they do make for an inspiring story.

Following the conclusion of the program, our team took a much-needed month of R&R to return to our homes and regenerate. During this time, we traveled to Hawaii to rest, reflect, and revitalize after these six-plus months of grueling work. While there, we also visited with Bud Cook and Jim Channon, both of whom had played such important roles in the program's coming to be, and clarified lessons learned.

In the months that followed, we pored over, organized, and compiled our impressions and data points and summarized our findings, results, and recommendations into a massive report called *Trojan Warrior After-Action Report*.[1] This report offered a glimpse of the breadth, depth, impact, paradoxes, and potentials—both realized and yet to be realized—of the Jedi Warrior program (referred to in the report as the Trojan Warrior program). According to this final report: "The Trojan Warrior program was a clear success. This is validated by the results of the objective tests, the subjective evaluations of the soldiers and the training team, and the outstanding performance of the two teams in field exercises."

The executive summary concluded that "the successful completion of the Trojan Warrior program has placed the Army in the forefront of human performance technology development. By validating, in a controlled, measured manner, the holistic approach of mind, body, and team training, the Army has demonstrated its commitment to providing soldiers with the very best training that is available." It also affirmed that "by applying the insights gained from this pilot program along with appropriate funding, support, and more rigorous participant selection, future programs will likely deliver performance results far beyond those realized in this initial test program and will likely provide fundamental training elements vital for the development and capacity of the entire Special Operations community."

As the program concluded, one of the senior officers whose work was vital to bringing this program online astutely observed:

Like many other educational experiences one may acquire, I found that the benefit I received from this program was directly proportional to the effort and thought that I contributed. We made mistakes during the execution of this program, and we will have to correct these problems before going on; however, significant gains were possible and, I feel, achieved by those who applied themselves. In the future this training program, or its successor, will produce a more stable, sophisticated, physically and mentally capable soldier than we have today. To accomplish the types of missions facing Special Forces in the years ahead without highly visible and embarrassing failures, we must begin now to train our soldiers to be better, more responsible, and capable individuals and soldiers."

The report placed the program and its outcomes within a larger context, reminding the readers that "the recommendations that we and our military collaborators distilled from our experience to offer to the Special Forces community, were intended to articulate both short and long-term applications within the Special Forces and were based on the results of the program as well as the philosophy regarding holistic training methods and the military environment." The following recommendations were made:

With appropriate funding and support, future programs will deliver performance results far beyond those realized in this initial test and will become a fundamental training element for all the Special Operations community. With that as our goal, we have prepared a series of recommendations that will best serve the short and long-range interests of SOCOM (Special Operations Command) and the Army in general. The following reflections and recommendations are based on the results of this program and our philosophy regarding emergent human technologies and the military environment:

The modern battlefield has become exceedingly complex and extremely demanding of the individual soldier's ability to adapt, respond, and recover.

Training methodologies that focus only on limited aspects of human potential will create limited soldiers who will face a battlefield of unlimited dangers.

The advanced concepts, methods, and material technologies necessary to train for optimal human performance are available and have now been clearly validated as effective and applicable to the military.

Our military forces will stay on the leading edge of modern warriorship by continuing to develop soldiers who can think clearly, act decisively, and optimize their physical efforts by drawing upon substantial reserves of psychophysical and emotional energies, to reduce the military mental health crisis of rampant suicides and self-destructive behaviors among men and women deploying to and returning from combat missions.

The results of the program speak for themselves and identify many of the gains that the men achieved in their physical and mental fitness. Many of the program's accomplishments cannot currently be duplicated anywhere else in the Armed Forces. Levels of development that were targeted and not achieved in this six-month program would clearly be reachable given proper attention to the lessons learned here. The clear message from this work is that it is possible to enhance soldier performance well beyond previously set limits. The methodology and technology necessary to realize greater achievements are available and await only a steady and determined application and support.

Another senior officer concluded the following:

The training program was effective and produced many of the enhancements specified in the contract's Statement of Work. Throughout the training program the contractor personnel acted in good faith and attempted to deliver instruction designed to produce the specified results. Army personnel undergoing the training cooperated to varying degrees in the program and in large part were responsible when the desired results were not achieved. Training of this type should have a future in the Special Forces due to the gains in individual and soldier effectiveness possible.

The attitude our soldiers exhibit during training will determine the degree of success. If they approach the training as they approach a normal army school, we will not achieve the full potential for the training. This training is designed to produce changes in lifestyle rather than imparting knowledge for future use. In this regard it differs completely from most formal schooling our personnel have attended. Once an individual develops a negative attitude toward the training, he will close his mind to everything that follows. Our greatest challenge in the future will be to find ways to prevent the closing of our soldiers' minds.

Let's look more closely now at the some of the nitty-gritty data and results of this historic and pioneering training program, but first, let's hear from some of the men as they reflect in their own words on their firsthand experiences.

Voices of the Awakening Warriors

The soldiers' own comments in our debriefs at the end of the program reflected the wide range of attitudes and experiences during the program. For some, their participation in the program was the highlight of their military career, if not their life as a whole. For others, it had been a prolonged ordeal to be endured. One of our warriors wrote:

> The Trojan Warrior Program has probably been the most enlightening of my military career of 15 years. The subjects taught in this course should be mandatory for anyone who is to be awarded the privilege and responsibility of leading soldiers, especially Special Forces soldiers.
>
> The biopsybernautic and meditation, where the student stops trying to analyze and just "accepts," leads quickly to a drastically increased awareness and understanding of self, those around us, and the problems each of us must cope with. The changes which occur are all desirable and frequently astounding. None of us need to learn tension or stress, we're saddled with these daily. But, for me, and most people I know, relaxation and true self-knowledge is beyond price. It cannot possibly be anything other than an aid in life or mission.
>
> The encampment phase of the training is one highlight of this training. If all concerned are prepared properly and cooperate, gains even greater than those experienced by myself and a few others will be forthcoming. It is an essential part of the training and should include alpha-enhancement (neurofeedback training) to "polish" the result.
>
> The fitness program, instead of merely "keeping us in shape" has

radically changed the way we use our bodies. We have found better, more efficient ways to fitness, and they work. Speaking for myself, for the first time, I have learned to enjoy running. Due to this change in attitude and a substantial change in running style, my speed over distances up to 10 miles have increased dramatically. If this were the only benefit to this course, I would feel the money well spent.

Strangely, Aikido has tied it all together, while allowing our bodies to relearn balance, grace, and fluidity or, in some cases, learn them for the first time. All this while teaching unarmed defense. The future of every member of the Special Forces can be changed for the better by the techniques and philosophies learned in the Trojan Warrior Program. It should be continued.

Another reflected:

When we began this project, I dealt with each day and its ups and downs with a state I liked to believe was intense but was probably closer to rage. I was certainly in physical pain much of the time and I would suspect often in psycho/emotional turmoil.

I am approaching the other end of the project and I'm not sure I can even quantify those specific subjects that were of value through the last six months.

I am not the same person. My style or behavior or perception has been modified significantly enough to produce some major changes in the way I react to most stimuli and in how I am perceived by others.

What follows is some notes on which things have made an impression upon me. Some general comments first.

Everything we have seen was presented in an acceptable if not outstanding manner . . . and a student shares a healthy part of the responsibility for what he learns or fails to learn. I felt the required reading, written assignments, and seminar discussions were and are a continuing requirement.

There were times when a subject could have been explored further but scheduling prevented it, and I think that flexibility should be built into the next iteration. I was, on several occasions, appalled at the lack of knowledge exhibited by some of my contemporaries and I suspect a more thorough screening and selection process is required.

One of the team leaders offered this cogent note on aikido:

Many of the men did not fully comprehend the potential for self-defense inherent in the art of Aikido. The army hand-to-hand combat techniques are probably effective, but aikido, if studied seriously, offers much more in the realm of self-defense. Aikido offers many mental, physical, and psychological enhancements which are not available from simple hand-to-hand combat. Other martial arts are available; however, Aikido offers a choice between a direct and indirect approach that is not as obvious in other arts. Thus, I recommend continuing the study of Aikido.

Insights Regarding Mind-Fitness Training

In our debriefs, one of the senior members of one of the teams recommended the following:

Since physical performance is the logical starting point of this program, it is also the place to introduce meditation. Starting with meditative running and relaxation regimes following runs will ease the soldiers into the practice without the pitfalls of sitting still techniques. Once these techniques are mastered, the still practice can be introduced. Emphasis must initially focus on the recuperative and healing techniques to maintain a clear sense of the function and purpose for the soldiers. After mastering this level, the practice can branch into meditation as a way of gaining greater control over the mind. My recommendations for future meditation training depends on the method of selecting detachments or individuals for future training programs.

If detachments are selected as they are constituted, then it will be necessary to split up the detachment for the more advanced levels of instruction. There will be a few individuals who are not mature enough to make much progress and these individuals will make it impossible for the others to progress if they are not separated and trained separately. If other methods are used to select trainees, then it may be possible to keep the detachment together during meditation training. Regardless of the method of selecting future trainees, meditation training is an important part of this program which leads to a more effective individual when the individual fully participates in the training.

Composite and Team Comparison Data: Overall Improvements and Outcomes

In the final analysis, it was concluded that the program significantly enhanced individual soldier capabilities and confirmed that many new and valuable mental and physical skills and strengths were developed, which directly contributed to increased performance, success, and survivability on the battlefield.

While there was a very wide range of individual progress realized, on average the final assessment was that the soldiers' abilities across the program goals increased by 75 percent from where they started. The average individual improvement for each of the contractual goals listed below is based on a combined analysis of the soldiers' own evaluations, objective test measures, and our training team's observations. Zero would be the baseline at the beginning of the program.

PHYSICAL ENHANCEMENTS

Improving overall physical fitness	109%
Managing energy	86%
Understanding effects of nutrition on performance	150%
Controlling pain and promoting healing	55%
Fine-tuning physical performance	85%

PSYCHOLOGICAL ENHANCEMENTS

Managing stress and shock	85%
Increasing mental abilities and resources	100%
Coordinating mind, body, and emotions	65%
Clarifying key values (accountability, etc.)	70%
Preparing for death better	20%

TEAM COHESION ENHANCEMENTS

Strengthening team	50%
Broadening spiritual base	60%
Strengthening leadership skills	40%

ENHANCEMENT OF
MISSION-SPECIFIC ABILITIES

Remaining alert and motionless	70%
Self-regulating temperature in extremities	40%
Extending sensory awareness	80%
Resting and rapidly recuperating	100%
Monitoring and managing energy, gaining endurance	90%

The data above is a composite of the combined performance enhancements and achievements of both of the two teams over the course of the Jedi Warrior program. A closer look at the data collected from the two teams offered a telling insight. When the results and achievements from each team are compared, the data revealed that members of Alpha Team realized 63 percent greater value from their participation in the Jedi Warrior program than Bravo Team.

This radical difference was both revealing and skewed. It was revealing in that the overall attitude and engagement in the training by members of Bravo Team were dampened by the attitudes and lack of enthusiasm of the team's leadership. The data was skewed in that some members of Bravo Team realized more value than they admitted to themselves or was revealed on the various tests and data gathering. Analysis of the "lie scales" on the psychometric tests showed that members of Bravo were less likely to answer the questions on these instruments honestly. Most of the objective data points to much more significant gains and accomplishments than the men would self-report.

The findings reflecting the significant differences between the two teams were evident in analyzing the psychological profiles of their team members. The psychometric data from Alpha Team generated a profile that was more inner directed, honest, and able to acknowledge and report potential internal and external dangers. The data from Team Bravo indicated that this team's members, overall, were more dependent on authority, less able or willing to recognize potential dangers, and far less open and honest with themselves and others. It is important to keep in mind that such generalizations about the two teams must be taken in context as each team had a mix of team members who were enthusiastic, as well as some who were less engaged.

Enhancement of Physical Capabilities

The Army Physical Readiness Test (APRT) measured the soldiers' endurance, strength, and flexibility. We ran this test four times throughout the program and added pull-ups and the stretch box as additional measures. The addition of pull-ups gave a measure of upper body strength related to mission skills necessary for climbing and carrying heavy rucksacks. The stretching tests helped to illuminate increased range of motion and suppleness, which help to prevent injury.

For the initial APRT stress test we had the opportunity to rely upon a control team for comparison, while for the rest of the program no other control groups were used, though we did make implicit comparisons and projections with other Special Forces teams who had engaged in similar tests or tasks in the past, as in the case of the Gut Check and winter ops. The measures of individual performance that we gathered were as objective as we could muster, supplemented by careful observations by members of our training team, anecdotal information, oral and written feedback from the soldiers, and the assessments of officers from the teams.

Our goals in physical training and testing were:

1. To maintain the men at their already high levels of fitness
2. To improve in their areas of weakness
3. To improve the overall team fitness rather than simply focus on the highest individual performance levels

Though our soldiers entered the program with ARPT scores that were already surpassing maximum standards, their scores continued to increase in each category throughout the program. These improvements were accomplished without specifically training for those measures and were realized in a variety of training conditions.

Alpha Team entered the program with an average 21 percent above army's maximum scale by age groups for push-ups, 12 percent above maximum for sit-ups, and 2 percent above for the two-mile run. Bravo Team averaged 12 percent above for push-ups, 1 percent above for sit-ups, and 3 percent below for the two-mile run. Many of the individual scores were considerably higher than the high averages. For example, five of these soldiers consistently did 90 push-ups in the allotted two minutes, and one repeatedly busted out over 100, hitting a high of 120 push-ups toward the end of the program. During our training, both the youngest and the oldest soldiers increased their scores for push-ups, sit-ups, and pull-ups by over 20 percent.

We also collected extensive laboratory data on measures of endurance and strength over a range of motion. These measures included a variety of blood chemistry elements, changes in lean body mass, and leg strength as measured on Cybex equipment. We found:

- Significant changes in lean body mass and body fat ratios that were reflected in extraordinary performance in the field
- Total reduction in cholesterol and HDL:LDL ratios indicated enhanced fitness in the blood transport system
- Increases in HDL levels indicated a definite increase in endurance
- Gain in the balance between opposing muscle groups, which can play a key role in reducing and preventing injuries

Biopsybernautics

Through the combined and synergistic training in mindfulness, meditation, mind fitness, and biofeedback, the soldiers developed greater awareness and self-mastery necessary to self-regulate and optimize the ordinary and subtle workings of the mind-body.

Approximately 70 percent of the soldiers reduced their baseline muscle tension between 100 percent and 500 percent. All soldiers learned to reduce their muscle tension by at least 25 percent.

The soldiers learned to warm their hands by intentionally increasing peripheral blood flow on a range of 3 to 25 degrees. Approximately 10 percent of the soldiers reported success and confidence in applying these skills to warm their hands during the frigid maritime ops and winter ops exercises. This also reflects a significant indicator of the ability to self-regulate by quieting hyperarousal associated with distress and to move back into the window of tolerance to rest, renew, regenerate, and redeploy with vigor.

Most soldiers learned to increase the presence and power of their alpha frequency brainwaves. This can be correlated with:

- Decreased vulnerability to debilitating anxiety and apprehension
- Greater mastery of attention and the "calm intensity" necessary to establish and maintain alert, relaxed, and sustained mindfulness
- Greater skill and confidence in mastering stress
- Reduced incidence of depression, paranoia, obsessive compulsive ideation, and so on
- Enhanced mental clarity, mental stability, and perceptual acuity

Neurofeedback Training Results: The Brain Power Advantage

Our data collections for the neurofeedback training were extensive and the findings included:

- Increased levels of alpha power, associated with greater mental focus and mindfulness, in both hemispheres of the brain for at least 70 percent of the soldiers.
- Increased alpha power in at least one hemisphere of the brain was measured for twenty-one of twenty-four soldiers.
- Notable increase of EEG alpha during eyes-open conditions and a significant increase in right hemisphere alpha during all training conditions. This can be correlated with enhanced capacity to remain awake, alert, and attentive without drifting off target into distracting thoughts or mental dullness.
- At least 90 percent of the soldiers reported being able to consciously

alter their mental-neural states to increase or decrease their alpha scores with neurofeedback at will.

- Fifty percent of the soldiers reported confidence in generating alpha mind-brain states outside of the lab.
- Sixty-three percent were able to subjectively correlate their inner attentional states with increases and decreases of alpha brainwave state.

All the soldiers were successful in learning to voluntarily enhance the amplitude and frequency of their alpha brain waves when they were provided with auditory and digital feedback. The data showed a vast variation in the depth of learning that varied from person to person, ranging from 5 percent to 280 percent increases in power and skills.

Disparities and Insights

Careful analysis of the data collection forms and surveys showed that in numerous cases Bravo Team members had initially written higher ratings on their questionnaires, which had then been erased and written over with lower ratings. The disparity was quite pronounced though the origin of the alterations remained unknown. The results in terms of some of the skewed data collected indicated that Alpha Team had 640 percent greater improvement on physical training as a result of this training as compared with Bravo Team; 1600 percent greater performance on mental and emotional training; 160 percent greater performance on team cohesion; and a 406 percent greater enhancement of their Mission Capability.

Given that the objective measures from various tests, plus the observational assessments of both the battalion leadership and our training team, indicated that both teams actually had much more similar levels of accomplishment, this skewed data was confounding, to say the least.

Further insight is gained by considering that shortly after the neurofeedback training, we asked each soldier to score themselves for the enhancement of physical, mental, emotional, and team factors as listed on a questionnaire. Their scores indicated the percentage of self-reported increases associated with their participation in alpha enhancement neurofeedback training as compared to the level of each factor prior to the neurofeedback sessions. These ratings are telling in terms of actual learning and the soldiers' attitudes toward learning:

PERCENTAGE OF ENHANCEMENT FROM BASELINE

	ALPHA TEAM	BRAVO TEAM
Mind-body Integration	90	29
Ability to Consciously Relax	93	16
Power to Change State of Mind	49	33
Power to Focus at Will	21	51
Trust of Team Members	64	0

Leadership and Brain Power

When the EEG brain power measurements of the two teams were compared, a stunning insight emerged that has huge implications for the impacts of the mind states and attitudes of leaders on the psychophysical performance and capabilities of their teams. The data showed that the collective brain power and neural learning of Alpha Team was strikingly greater than the collective brain power and learning of Bravo Team. This difference between the teams was so significant that when we showed the data to a neuro-savvy colleague, with years of personal neurofeedback experience, he took off his glasses, scratched his head, leaned back, pointed to the lower line of the data chart for Bravo Team, and half seriously asked, "So . . . am I right that this team was on drugs?" We all looked at each other with a bemused smile.

Given that the Bravo Team leader had for much of the program dampened the engagement and participation of many of his team members, it was sobering to see how both his and his team's negative attitude correlated with their diminished collective brain power. The attitudes of the leadership of Alpha Team, which were much more favorable, supportive, and encouraging of wholehearted engagement with the program, contributed to Alpha Team's striking collective brain power advantage over Bravo—or likely over any other teams they might encounter in combat.

We have often shared these insights and this data set in our work with senior leaders in large global organizations to help them recognize the profound importance of learning to be mindful of and wisely manage their own attitudes. A leader's internal state of being is constantly influencing members of their teams, broadcasting as a kind of social contagion that either uplifts or diminishes the well-being, performance, and effectiveness of team members. Time and time again in our work over decades, we have witnessed that when senior leaders have a profound change of mind or heart, almost instantly, a shift may take place, and new degrees of freedom and potential begin to emerge through members of their teams, even if those team members are not physically present with the leader. Such transpersonal effects are well acknowledged in the fields of interpersonal neurobiology, transpersonal psychology, social psychology, social contagion theory, and evolutionary biology.

Mind the Gap

Overall, there were substantial increases in the abilities of these soldiers compared to where they started. That said, there was general agreement that far greater advancements could easily be realized if we were to take to heart the lessons learned and apply those lessons to future training. In writing our final report, the assessment of our training team was that compared to what we believed was achievable in our program elements (100 percent) we had accomplished the following level of enhancement:

Physical fitness (endurance, flexibility, strength, etc.)	85%
Biopsybernautics (biofeedback, neurofeedback, mind-fitness training, etc.)	50%
Aikido (applied mind-body integration)	95%
Psychological orientations (emotional intelligence, attitudes)	45%

This gap, between what was realized versus what we believed was possible, indicates our team's assessment of how much farther these soldiers could have reasonably improved if each participant had been fully engaged and committed to this path of deep transformational learning and if the army had been committed to the follow-through necessary to support and sustain this transformation.

Given this was a mere six-month training program, we could reasonably expect much more from these soldiers if they dedicated themselves to years or even decades of disciplined psychophysical training. Many of our own teachers have immersed themselves in intensive training retreats spanning three to nearly twenty years and realized extraordinary results. Imagine, what might be possible for future programs with highly motivated soldiers?

Recommendations for Future Programs

Our lessons learned through the program led to a potent set of short- and long-range recommendations founded in the recognition that we live in an increasingly VUCAA world. This increasingly challenging environment places exceptional pressure on individuals to adeptly adapt, respond, recover, and learn. These recommendations were based on the following insights:

- Training methodologies that focus only on ordinary, limited aspects of human potential will create a limited soldier who must face and respond to a battlefield of limitless dangers.
- The concepts, methods, and technology necessary to training for

optimal human performance are available, and this program clearly validated them as highly effective, relevant, and applicable within the military.

- For our military forces to stay on the leading edge of modern warriorship, we must continue to develop the capacity of soldiers to perceive and think clearly, respond and act wisely and decisively, and optimize their mental and physical resources over short and long time frames of military engagement.

Short-Term Recommendations

Within this Special Forces Group, we recommended immediately following this program with a second program that is streamlined and focused on the ultimate goal of developing a cadre of qualified and inspiring trainers for Jedi Warrior disciplines. There are currently not enough qualified trainers to successfully conduct follow-on programs. Within the Special Operations Command Headquarters, the recommendation was to host a six-day demonstration training at Fort Bragg to offer a direct experience of this holistic training for a select audience of influential attendees. This special session would offer a rich and inspiring selection of elements from biopsybernautic training, high-performance fitness, and mind-fitness methods for optimal performance in VUCAA conditions.

Long-Term Recommendations

We recommended providing a similar training to other SOCOM units where a high degree of integration of mental, emotional and physical skills is crucial. We further recommended developing a portion of the training as a screening process for the Q Course (i.e., the Special Forces Qualification Course) or for similar key entry points or thresholds for advanced levels of Special Forces training. This recommendation emphasizes the importance of devoting greater attention and discernment to selecting Special Forces soldiers and to the potential for integrating elements of the Jedi Warrior training that "could improve the selections process and ultimately reduce the potential for compromise or failure in future missions."

Posttraining Recommendations

To keep the learnings and strengths realized in the program alive, we recommended that upon completion of the training each team should continue to study aikido and to study and practice meditation. During periods when equipment is not being used for training, those teams should also refresh their skills using the biofeedback equipment. Meditation retreats should be scheduled on an annual or semiannual basis and be about one week long.

Selection of Individuals and Teams for Future Programs

Drawing insights from lessons learned in the Jedi Warrior program, our colleagues from the battalion side recommended that the chain of command should select the individuals and detachments to attend training in generally the same fashion as teams are selected. They further recommended that each individual must volunteer for the training and should be interviewed by the training cadre in advance of the training. The interview would allow the cadre to discuss the training in detail, answer questions, and evaluate the training needs of the individual.

In the future they thought it might be possible to put together training detachments from a pool of newly arrived personnel (within ninety days of each other). These detachments would go through the training cycle, and if they developed into effective detachments, they would be available to replace existing detachments that had become weak or ineffective due to attrition. One of the qualities this training offers is the ability to quickly assimilate a replacement, especially if he is already trained in this manner.

Encampment

In reviewing the data and taking to heart the lessons learned from the encampment, there was a strong consensus that the encampment was a very important phase of the Jedi Warrior training. As familiar lifestyle patterns were disrupted, the ensuing disorientation gave way to redefining personal and team identities better aligned with these new circumstances. As the deeper strengths and weaknesses of each soldier and each team began to emerge into personal and collective awareness, each soldier had to regard himself and his team members in a new and more genuine manner.

During the meltdown phase the members of Alpha Team began to talk to each other in an honest, direct way. They discovered their similarities, their shared goals and aspirations, and began to deal with their differences. Almost to a man, they later spoke of the encampment as the phase of the training when they began to bond as a team. As a newly formed team, having so little in terms of team cohesion to begin with and thus little to lose, they were willing to take the risks that eventually bonded them together as a high-performing and cohesive team.

Bravo Team on the other hand began the course with an impressive record, exemplary reputation, and strong team identity and pride. They had an image to preserve and protect, and in the face of issues raised regarding their conduct during the encampment, they experienced greater difficulty in the process of disintegration in order to rebuild themselves at a higher level. The men in Bravo Team exhibited less tolerance for the differences among them, and the leaders were thrown into panic and defensiveness when they thought they were losing control. Unlike the Alpha Team, it seemed that the members of Bravo Team had so much difficulty during this period because they felt they had more to lose.

Though the performance of Bravo Team was very high to begin with, the team members individually and collectively seemed to have difficulty in holding the possibility that they could become even better. This mental block made them much more invested in maintaining the status quo than Alpha Team, whose disorganization made them much more available to change and significant personal and team growth and development. These differences are readily apparent in reading the subjective evaluations and comments from the soldiers throughout the program.

The members of Alpha Team were clearly more enthusiastic about and engaged in their personal and team development throughout the program than the members of Bravo Team. Alpha Team saw the program as a privileged opportunity rich in benefits and possibilities for each individual and for the team as a whole, while Bravo's members were more likely to regard the program as an inconvenience or imposition to be tolerated or endured, or an obstacle to be overcome or defended against. Most regarded this opportunity as offering little value and was worthy at most of a ho-hum level of engagement. Those individuals on Bravo Team who were personally excited about the program and the opportunities it offered for their personal and professional development were in a very difficult position, as their engagement was often discouraged or even ridiculed by some of their leaders and team members.

In our debriefs, one of the captains remarked:

The final analysis leads us to consider that in future programs it might be far more effective if new teams were formed and bonded through the training, rather than enlisting existing teams that may be burdened with history or reputations to uphold. This isn't to say that Bravo Team didn't gain a considerably greater team dynamic and cohesion from the program as evidenced in many reports and measures. In fact, they became even stronger by confronting their weaknesses and dealing with them. But the sustained defensiveness regarding their team's image and reputation rendered them more vulnerable and less available to change and growth that would have increased their overall performance and effectiveness. Unwittingly, it seemed that they had turned their team unity and identity into an excuse to deflect their effort and attention from realizing their full potentials for development and growth, rather than a catalyst to boost them to even greater levels of capability and success.

Additionally, one of the ranking officers observed:

Training effectiveness generally corresponded directly with the maturity of the individual. . . . Most of the soldiers openly disobeyed the rule against talking. . . . Every man had given his word that he would follow the rules prior to leaving Ft. Devens. Once at the training site they decided that their word no longer applied. The logic was appalling but short of disciplinary action I could see no other way of altering their behavior. . . . With one exception, the group willing to go forward contained the majority of the older, more mature soldiers . . .

During future training, the encampment should take place near the end of the training. It should rely upon all prior training and prepare the detachments for their final exercise. As addressed earlier . . . training in meditation and various techniques of practices need to occur well in advance of the encampment. Soldiers must be well prepared for the encampment to ensure maximum training values . . .

In summary, the encampment provided an excellent setting for each individual to gain a foundation in the practice of meditation. . . . Yet we failed to derive the maximum benefit from the encampment. . . . Given the knowledge that we now have, if we heed the lessons learned this time, the next encampment should be very successful!

During the encampment, nearly one-third of the soldiers reported "extraordinary experiences and insights of a profound personal nature." In speaking about these experiences with team members, some were met with ridicule, others with sincere interest and validation. We discussed many of these experiences with the men in our one-to-one check-ins and helped them to incorporate these glimpses of an expanded and more multidimensional view of themselves into their identity, worldview, and frames of reference and reverence.

One of the team leaders made the following comments during the encampment:

> Insights that I gained about myself and my teammates were valuable. . . . For myself, the extent of my distractions and the resulting draining effects were quite insightful. Also, the effects of leading and dealing with individuals was more extensive than I thought. As I was already somewhat aware, my "trying too hard" consistently resulted in useless if not harmful tension. On the positive side, I found that concentration and calmness (and the resulting enhanced performance) can be gained by something as simple as taking some time and focusing on one event (such as breathing). I also found that I thought I was operating at 90 to 95% optimal performance, but I realized that I may not even be operating at 50%. This has really widened my scope of looking at things. Finally, I learned much about the attitudes of my teammates and their personal codes of discipline.

Voices of the Soldiers' Families

Considering all the data that we gathered, the most meaningful feedback on the program for us came from the soldiers' spouses, partners, and children. Their comments came to us in conversations, notes, or letters, as well as from a survey conducted toward the end of the program. Many family members of the men shared deep gratitude that their partners or fathers were more mindful, present, caring, emotionally balanced and available, less stressed, and less physically and emotionally abusive at home since their participation in this training.

Among the responses we received, some wrote that they valued the nutrition and fitness classes and that they observed a greater overall well-being in their partners as well as a greater ability to relax and sleep. Relationship enhancements that were noted included: "Learning together, share, having fun with it." "More understanding in the relationship." "I feel like I have a friend and partner in our relationship now." "My dad used to come home from work and knock me around the house. Now we hang out and talk and do stuff together. He's much more fun to be with now. I feel like I have a father again." There was also a sense from their comments that while we had made many positive impacts, we could have gone deeper and given more time to some of the learning themes.

A Green Light for the Next Program?

Based on the program results, General Stevens and the Special Operations Command gave an enthusiastic go-ahead for another program. With their approval, our team recommended that the next program focus on developing soldiers as instructors for this and future programs. Unfortunately, the incoming group commander decided that the funds were not available for another program. While no explanation was given, the rumble through the grapevine was that he had an army to run and didn't want to hear about martial arts, meditation, and brainwaves.

Visions of Jedi Warrior 2.0

Taking to heart the lessons learned from Jedi Warrior 1.0 and ones gleaned since then, Jedi Warrior 2.0 would most wisely be offered to volunteers who are sincerely interested and self-motivated. These volunteers could be grouped into teams or cohorts for the duration of this learning expedition.

We would certainly raise the bar to have prospective participants demonstrate their interest, readiness, and dedication to engage in such intensive inner training prior to entering the formal program. This would involve some entry requirements, such as previous experience in the study of mind fitness and extraordinary performance, some preliminary reading with reflections or discussions on the relevance to their own lives and missions of what they read, and participation in some introductory sessions or short experiential retreats to check out their levels of maturity, motivation, and engagement.

We would also devote more time to basic mindfulness, advanced relaxation and mind-fitness training, additional biofeedback training earlier in the program, and shift the intensive encampment to later in the program.

For "train the trainer" programs there would be considerably more immersion in study and testing for prospective trainers to gain a deeper understanding of the fundamentals of the applied, embodied psychophysical sciences, and to demonstrate proficiency and fluency in their knowledge of the program domains.

With exciting advances in wearable biofeedback instrumentation, we would weave more peripheral biofeedback and neurofeedback sessions into daily life and into mission simulations in the field. Wearable and networked devices would also allow for the progress of program participants to be remotely monitored and coached from afar.

The synergy of biofeedback training with such biosensitive wearables and virtual reality (VR) simulations could provide a wealth of immersive training scenarios to teach and test soldiers' self-regulation and rapid recovery from stress. Both biofeedback and VR simulations could include multiple individuals. Immersive VR plus biofeedback could also be creatively employed to guide individuals in simulations that teach skillful ways to escape from imprisonment within their own self-simulations into states of deeper empathic resonance with others. This could be especially valuable for increasing the capacity of individuals to establish stronger bonds with those they work with and in preparing for operations where they need to build more empathic and trusting relationships with people from other cultures.

While the embodied somatic learning that aikido brought to the program is extremely important, for most nonmilitary programs, actual on-the-mat aikido training may not be possible or appropriate. There are numerous creative ways to introduce enjoyable and powerful methods of somatic attunement and engagement, working with simulations of how we respond and interact when we feel stressed, out of our comfort zone, vulnerable, or attacked. These can be drawn from a wealth of embodied practices adapted from aikido, such as Leonard Energy Training and similar styles of adapted martial arts practice. We have utilized these methods with thousands of people in a wide variety of settings with inspiring results.

Depending on the purpose, goals, and outcomes that are being targeted and the nature of the population we'd be working with, the format and schedule of future programs will vary. Multiple groups in different locations or online could participate in some modules of the training and then come together for more intensive sessions. Training modules could be segmented and delivered over time or offered in an immersive manner like the first Jedi Warrior program. It will always be wise to get to know the audience and their needs ahead of time. Trust the Force, read the field, and be creative with program design!

Far Horizons and Unlimited Potentials

Sustained training in psychophysical disciplines, sports, or music is bound to result in a wide spectrum of skill levels and realizations among any population engaged in these pursuits. Some will become Olympic gold medalists or virtuosos, while others will realize significantly more modest achievements. In our own case, after fifty-plus years of intensive study and practice in various disciplines, we have certainly realized great benefits and expanded our capacities, yet compared with the realizations and capacities of many of our own teachers, we are humbled.

Given the people and circumstances we were given to work with, Jedi Warrior was a success in many ways and offered a rare and profound glimpse of far greater reaches of human potential and successes that would be possible to realize if the circumstances and participation were optimized.

At the end of the program, our own personal feelings and assessments of the success of the program were mixed. Considering the time and resources we had to work with and the challenges we faced, we were inspired by the progress of these soldiers and grateful for the degree of success we realized though the various domains of training. By the end of the program, our warriors were packing a more powerful arsenal of self-mastery skills and capacities than any adversaries they were likely to encounter and were definitely more capable and better equipped to perform their missions. They were less likely to succumb to poor decisions, mindless inattention, self-sabotaging tendencies, and debilitating maladies that warriors are prone to develop in the course of their traumatic work, and they were more likely to serve the greater good.

Yet, compared with what could have been realized through this training if all the participants were highly motivated, self-selected volunteers with a sincere enthusiasm and dedication to learning as deeply as possible in order to inspire and train others in this vital work, then we certainly fell far short of what could have potentially been realized.

When we are asked, "How far short did you fall from what could have been possible?" we have struggled with how to quantify, or even metaphorically characterize, how far short we fell. The challenge stems from our own good fortune of having worked with many extremely dedicated and disciplined teachers who devoted their lives for many years to deep, intensive training, and realized remarkable levels of success in order to inspire and uplift others. These inspiring mentors from various traditions have raised the bar in our minds regarding what human beings can realize and become. The examples of potentials they offer are truly extraordinary and mind blowing compared with mainstream visions of personal mastery and peak performance that most people are likely to encounter in the media.

Our sights for this program were aimed high at lofty goals inspired by the examples of many remarkable men and women we had studied with and based on a wealth of compelling research on extraordinary human potential from modern and ancient contemplative sciences and wisdom traditions. We designed the training with confidence in the potential for each participant in our program to realize extraordinary levels of embodied wisdom, presence, courage, insight, empathy, compassion, and altruism in service of protecting, defending, and caring for the larger whole, while packing as much strength, fierceness, and firepower as needed given the extreme, high-stakes circumstances that these warriors were preparing for.

We remain confident that each person embodies vast stores of extraordinary human potential. From our experience exploring, mapping, and guiding others in these domains of training, our range of targets for what would have been possible for our soldiers to realize lay far beyond learning to merely master stress, develop greater concentration, widen their windows of tolerance, enhance their self-regulation skills, and develop physical strength and endurance. The potentials we envisioned included these accomplishments along with a much vaster set of targets such as becoming wiser and kinder stewards of planet Earth.

In telling this story, our deepest aspiration is that you will be moved to take to heart the principles, practices, and lessons learned from this program and weave them into the fabric of your own life. Appreciating the magnitude of complex challenges and metacrisis present in our lives and world, may this reading also inspire you, and other visionary readers and leaders, to create and support advanced training programs for those seeking the special kind of courage and extraordinary skills to wisely, kindly, creatively, and fiercely, when necessary, work to benefit others and better prepare themselves to meet and resolve these crises with as much wisdom, compassion, and creativity as possible.

While these programs may be developed for emergency services or military professionals, there is also great relevance for individuals, teams, organizations, and communities in every sector. Since this transformational life-skills training has strong roots in science, technology, and psychosocial education, we would love to see adaptations of the Jedi Warrior curriculum wisely woven into robust educational programs for teenagers and young adults in communities around the globe. Channon offers insight from *Evolutionary Tactics* to close this chapter, saying:

> What are the limits to human potential? The culture imposes a language of the possible. Most humans accept those limits and fail to increase their potential. But where those limits are ignored . . . people bend metal with their minds, walk on fire, calculate faster than a computer, travel to new places in their minds, stop their hearts with no ill effects, and see into the future. There are no limits in the Earth Battalion.[2]

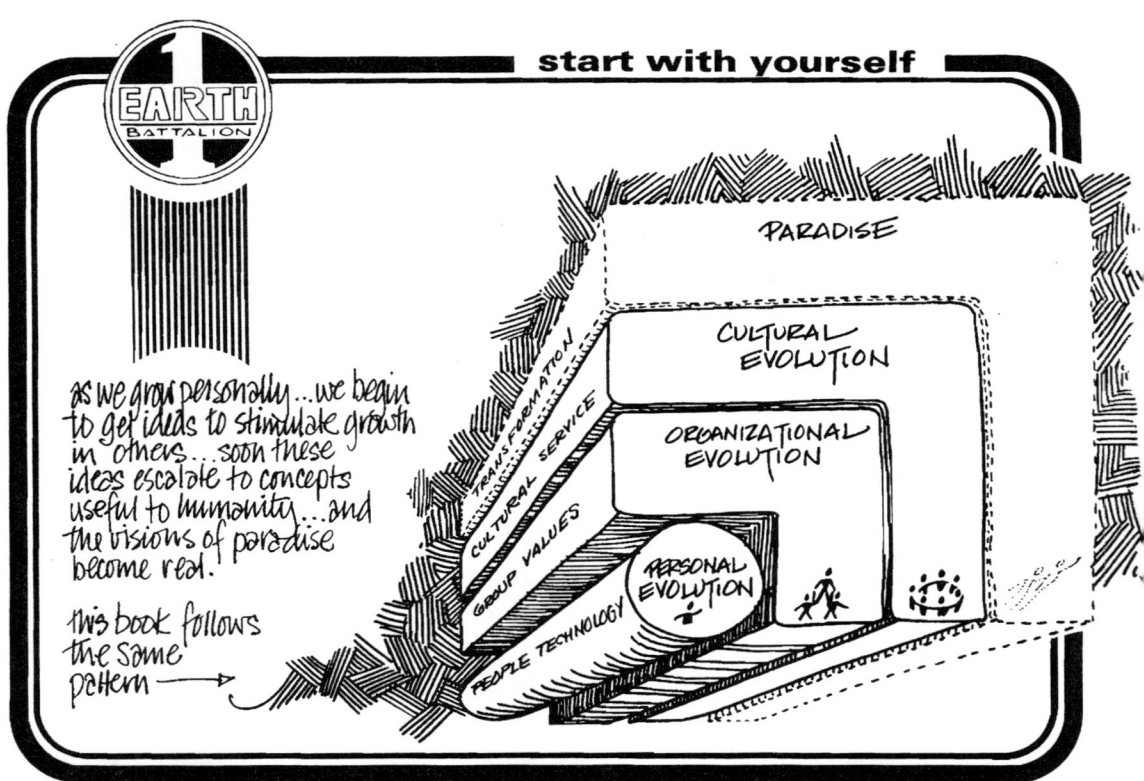

EARTH 1 BATTALION

PARADISE

CULTURAL EVOLUTION

ORGANIZATIONAL EVOLUTION

TRANSFORMATION

CULTURAL SERVICE

GROUP VALUES

PERSONAL EVOLUTION

PEOPLE TECHNOLOGY

as we grow personally...we begin to get ideas to stimulate growth in others...soon these ideas escalate to concepts useful to humanity...and the visions of paradise become real.

this book follows the same pattern →

THE FIRST EARTH BATTALION

EPILOGUE

The Legacy Lives On, New Missions Begin

There are those who are trying to set fire to the world.
We are in danger.
There is time only to work slowly,
There is no time not to love.

DEENA METZGER, "NO TIME NOT TO LOVE"

At this point in the story, you are likely wondering, "What happened next?" Here are some glimpses of what unfolded after the Jedi Warrior program concluded.

In the NATO war games that took place just after our program, one of our teams stood out for its extraordinary performance. They were identified as the most outstanding team in the games for that year. Many of the men we trained moved on into assignments in Delta Force and other Special Operations teams that didn't have forwarding addresses.

Colonel Getty did a stint at the U.S. Army War College at Carlisle Barracks after the program, where he shared his insights from the Jedi Warrior training. He had a talent for conveying his wisdom with a well-targeted question or an inquisitive look, and his field of influence and operations was broad. Following his time at the War College, Colonel Getty was given command of Special Operations in Europe during the later 1980s in the critical period of the rapid and unexpected changes leading up to the fall of the Berlin Wall and the Iron Curtain. He brought along many of the Jedi Warrior graduates to bring their unique talents into the dynamic mix of covert operations taking place in Europe and in Soviet-occupied Eastern Europe during that time.

Three years after the program, Jack, Richard, and Larry delivered a shorter training for a small group of Navy SEALs.

As we connected with some of our Jedi (Trojan Warrior) graduates over the years, they have shared meaningful reflections with us, such as:

"Trojan Warrior was way ahead of its time, and many of us were just too young and bullheaded at the time to appreciate the opportunity and depth of training we received. I've used what I learned to stay warm when I was cold, to focus, and to relax when I've needed to. What I have learned has saved my life on at least one occasion."

"Some of us were too young to really appreciate it until well after the program. At that time we couldn't fully appreciate what the program was giving us, but later, I've found myself relying on many of those skills on many occasions. There have been times when it was just being cold and saying to myself, OK, I can affect this through meditation and breath control."

"The program was fun and exciting, and it was all new to us. In some ways you guys had a real challenge working with us because you know, these guys all just wanted to be in on the fight."

"The idea of meditation for us as soldiers just didn't connect for some of us, even though today so many soldiers rely on these kinds of methods. I think it would have worked better to just call these methods advanced relaxation."

"Later in life, and out on our missions, those skills were incredibly valuable. I have confidence that I can focus my awareness into my body to calm, to focus, to heal, to direct the blood flow."

"You were trying to teach us techniques that we had a hard time identifying with for years. But then years later, those techniques we learned, I've used them in tier one forces and the top special operations where guys were doing meditation and have better performance. . . . It was just that Trojan Warrior was way before its time."

Special Forces in Cold War Berlin

After the program, at least three of our soldiers were recruited into the Physical Security Support Element-Berlin (PSSE-B). Its classified title was the Thirty-Ninth Special Forces "Det A," an elite, undercover Cold War group, operating behind the Iron Curtain and based in West Berlin, which, at that time, was still 110 miles inside the Soviet-controlled German Democratic Republic. Fluent in German, unconventional warfare, clandestine operations, sabotage, counterterrorism, and intelligence tradecraft, the men dressed in civilian clothes and often wore their hair long, blending into the local population in a city awash with spies seeking information at every turn.

If the Soviets invaded Western-held Berlin, the mission of this group of Thirty-Ninth Special Forces soldiers was to deploy "unconventional warfare" to organize and train guerrilla forces to "wreak havoc behind enemy lines" and to "harass and bedevil the communist steamroller," disrupting logistics, rail lines, and key targets and drawing Soviet units away from the front line to combat the threat posed by these freedom fighters, buying time for NATO forces to enter and retake the city.

Their secondary mission was counterterrorism, and members of the detachment participated in the attempted rescue of American hostages in Tehran. These SF soldiers were involved in some of the most sensitive operations of the Cold War. With the collapse of the Berlin Wall in 1989 and the subsequent reunification of Germany, the unit was deactivated, and the program remained highly classified until 2014. This story is well documented in a book by James Stejskal titled *Special Forces in Berlin*.

★ Epilogue ★

Battle of Mogadishu—Black Hawk Down
Delta Sniper Team

On October 3, 1993, a three-man Delta Force sniper team, including the team leader and Jedi alumni Master Sergeant Gary Gordon and Sergeant First Class Brad Halling, along with Sergeant First Class Randall David Shughart, were deployed in Operation Gothic Serpent, a joint-force assault mission to apprehend key advisers to Somali warlord Mohamed Farrah Aidid. The mission failed, and an angry mob raged through the city, surrounding a group of peacekeeping troops on the ground.

During the assault, *Super Six One*, one of the army's Blackhawk helicopters providing insertion and air support to the assault team, was shot down and crashed in the city. A CSAR (Combat Search And Rescue) team was dispatched to the crash site to secure it. Shortly after, a second chopper, *Super Six Four*, was shot down as well. Ranger forces on the ground were not able to assist the downed helicopter crew of the second crash site as they were already engaged in heavy combat with Aidid's militia and were making their way to the first crash site.

As the Delta Force sniper team in a third helicopter hovered over the crash site, Gordon, the sniper team leader, made repeated formal requests to be inserted to provide cover and attempt a rescue for the second downed chopper crew. Mission commanders denied his fervent requests, saying that the situation was too dangerous for the three Delta snipers to effectively protect the Blackhawk crew from the ground. Command's position was that the snipers could be of more assistance by continuing to cover the site from the air.

Driven by concern for his teammates, and an unwritten code never to leave a comrade behind, Gordon concluded that there was no possibility the Blackhawk crew could survive on their own and kept repeating his request until command finally relented and granted permission to attempt a rescue. Before they could be inserted, a crew chief on their

Blackhawk was injured, and Halling took his place on the machine gun, providing air support to protect the men on the ground, leaving only Shughart and Gordon to go in to defend the crew of *Super Six Four*.

Once on the ground, Gordon and Shughart, armed with only their personal weapons and sidearms, had to fight their way to the location of the downed Blackhawk to rescue its crew. By this time, the streets were flooded by enraged Somalis intent on capturing or killing the American servicemen. When they reached the downed *Super Six Four* chopper, Gordon and Shughart extracted the pilot, Chief Warrant Officer Mike Durant, and the other crew members from the aircraft and established defensive positions around the crash site.

Continuing to provide support from above, Halling's helicopter was then hit by a second rocket-propelled grenade, severing his leg above the knee and knocking out the rotor blades of the chopper, which then crashed, leaving Gordon and Shughart without any air support or cover. Speaking with Halling as we were writing this book, he described to us how he found himself in the crashed chopper. Once he realized that they hadn't gone up in flames, he turned his mind to some of the mind-training moves he had learned in our program to calm his heart rate and relax and slow the blood flow so he could focus his mind to find what he needed to create a tourniquet to keep himself from losing any more blood. He ended up making a tourniquet out of his belt and holding it tight all the way to the field hospital. He gratefully affirmed that had it not been for him being able to draw on what he had learned to calm himself to stay present in this way, he may well not have survived.

On the ground, despite heavy casualties inflicted against the Somalis, Gordon and Shughart were finally outnumbered and outgunned. It is believed that Gordon was first to be fatally wounded. Shortly after Shughart returned to take cover in the wreckage, he was killed by Somali gunfire. The mob then overran the crash site and captured the pilot Durant.

Gordon and Shughart were both posthumously awarded the Medal of Honor for their courageous attempts to rescue their endangered colleagues. Halling survived the crash, but his shredded leg was amputated above the knee due to his injuries. He went on to live a productive and meaningful life.

Affirming the wisdom of gratitude for every precious day of our lives, Brad Halling has established an annual birthday Gratitude Run—a ritual of running, which he described in his LinkedIn post:

> Training Run. . . . Preparing for my annual Gratitude run. It is a run I do each year on my Birthday. Gratitude because by God's grace I am alive today and able to run. With the 30th anniversary of the Battle of Mogadishu, this run is very important to me. I will run this year once again for the seventeen men in Task Force Ranger and the two men in the 10th Mountain that did not return. . . . For those who are not here to run. The truth is I do not have a love for running. I run because I can, and it is my expression of gratitude. . . . Nonetheless, on June 10th I will add 1/10th of a mile to last year's run (6 miles). This year I will run 6.1 equaling my age of 61. The idea is that with each year I set a harder goal.

An Affirming Encounter

Years after the program was over, we received a call one day from Sergeant Gerber, one of the men from Bravo Team. "Hey, Joel and Michelle, this is Gerber. Are you surprised to hear from me?" We certainly were surprised! "Amazing. Great to hear from you! What's up?" Gerber replied, "I'm in Port Townsend with my family, and we are heading over to Seattle this afternoon. Can we come by for a visit? I'd love to see you and have you meet my family."

We met up later that day. After all the niceties, Gerber shifted his tone, "I was pretty full of myself during Jedi and had a lot of attitude, and I threw a lot of shit your way. Looking back, I'm sorry for not having showed up with less belligerence and with more engagement. But I have to say, that what I learned from the two of you has saved my life, my marriage, my sanity, and my mission on numerous occasions."

He went on to describe how the techniques he had learned helped him to survive a terrifying situation in Iraq. "When Operation Desert Storm was still in the planning stages, I was dropped into a hide site and dug in doing surveillance of Iraqi troop movements for over a week. The Iraqis were out sweeping the hills to find our scouts, and it was scary to know they were looking for us. At one point we received a coded message from HQ saying that we should plan to dig in as deep as we could because the U.S. would possibly begin its attack with a nuclear blast. That was a super-chilling thought to sit with for all those days. Dug in, listening to my pounding heart, and watching my spinning mind, I relied heavily on many of the practices that I learned from the two of you to keep coming back to ground, to clear and open my mind and maintain my vigilance. It really means a lot to be here, alive, with you, and my wife and kids, and to thank you in person for everything you taught me. I'm a better man and a better soldier because of the work we did together, and . . . ," he paused. "I would imagine that each of the guys being older and wiser now would in their own way likely say the same."

Report from the Field

Ten years after the program ended, we received the following letter from one of the sergeants:

Dear Joel and Michelle,

I just finished a meditation where I focused my thoughts and energy to you. I miss you both and enjoyed the time we spent together a year and a half ago. Although it doesn't seem so long, time has kept marching on.

I have written you for two reasons. First, you asked me a question when I last saw you; what was the one thing that I used most often or most successfully from the things you taught during the Trojan Warrior course? For certain it is the technique of watching your breath. Your thoroughness and clarity of instruction on this technique has stuck with me and serves as a reference point from which I have always started any sort of mental or spiritual work I have done since the course, In the last 10 years I have shared with many people what I learned during the course. It has been the simplest and easiest technique for me to pass on (not necessarily to master!). Imagine the ripples you set in motion!

In the past few months this has been reenforced because I have been meditating daily, often several times a day. Most recently I've been doing a group meditation weekly. We practice visualizations and work on collective problems and healing. It has been very enjoyable and inspiring.

The second reason I write to you is to tell you I am very interested in doing another Trojan Warrior course of sorts. This time as an instructor or a facilitator. It could be to the military again or perhaps a course to motivate burnt out executives. I have been searching for my place and purpose in life for a long time now, and this idea keeps coming back to me as an answer. I have some time left on my contract here and want to start moving in the right direction to make a transition. I respect your opinions and ask you to please meditate on this idea and see what comes to you.

Stay Alive!

Bruce

West Point Briefing

Some years after the program concluded we were invited to offer a special briefing on Jedi Warrior at West Point Military Academy. As we arrived and were greeted by our hosts and those present for the session, it quickly became clear to us that Jedi Warrior seemed to occupy a special, mythical category for these soldiers. There were many wild ideas about what the program entailed and surprisingly few well-informed points of reference. Most of the leaders and cadets had heard of the Jedi Warrior program, yet none seemed aware of its identity as Trojan Warrior. None of the faculty or cadets had a clear sense of how this program came to be, what it involved, how long it was, or how it turned out.

As our presentation progressed, we were met by a sense of amazement. The notion of immersing a small number of the most elite Special Forces troops in the world in a training that involved them pulling no other duty for six months and dedicating an entire month to the encampment, being taught how to control their bodies or to synchronize their brain states with each other, was astounding to the men and women in the audience. As we described the elements of training to them and the results that we realized, they didn't seem to doubt our word but wondered how we had been able to successfully breach so many long-standing boundaries for Special Forces training.

One bright young major on the faculty, with a tall and imposing physical presence, was especially intense and a bit aggressive, buffeting us with a barrage of excellent, challenging questions throughout our briefing. Yet after the session he came up to us, warmly shook our hands, and thanked us, saying, "I'm so inspired to learn more about the real story of this program. The opportunity to do this kind of intensive training has always been a dream of mine, and your account reminds me of my favorite book." Curious, we asked, "So Major, what is your favorite book?" He beamed a big smile, leaned over, and in a slightly hushed voice said, "*The Celestine Prophecy*." We were surprised by his reply as we were quite familiar with this wonderful, fanciful, New Age visionary book about the further reaches of human potential.

After the briefing and a long talk with the faculty and cadets over lunch, Nate Zinnser, the director of High Performance at West Point, invited us to tour his lab and training center. We were impressed by their model of improving performance, which elegantly integrated "cognitive foundations" with goal setting, attention control, stress management, visualization, and imagery to increase the capacity of individuals to perform at higher levels. We were also surprised and delighted to discover that they had quite a bit of high-end biofeedback equipment available for the West Point cadets to train in various modes of self-regulation.

Yet, as we talked with Nate and took time to meet with and listen to the experiences of the cadets who were training in the center, our hearts sank to hear how few of the cadets made use of the resources available in the lab. It seemed that most of the students who came to train at the lab were so exhausted and sleep deprived from the stressful, often overwhelming demands of their military and academic training that when they did make their way to this remarkable lab and sat down to listen to the guided meditations or train with the biofeedback equipment, they usually ended up falling asleep rather than maintaining the wakeful presence of mind necessary to properly train and develop new skills and strengths. While naps are certainly valuable, especially when you are exhausted, they provide little value in terms of promoting the insights necessary for learning new psychophysical skills that increase the power of self-awareness, self-regulation, and self-mastery.

Team Members after Jedi Warrior

Living and Dying Brightly

Following Jedi Warrior, we continued to work with Jack and the team at SportsMind focusing on high-performance leadership and resilient team development with organizations around the globe. Jack Cirie loved the work and brought a fierce dedication to continuing to work deeply on himself to embody the wisdom of a true spirited warrior. His marriage with Anne had come to an end, and he later married Annie Brooke, one of our trainers at

SportsMind, in a pageant of a wedding on Lopez Island where they both rode in on horseback calling each other's names from opposite sides of the valley.

On January 6, 1992, we received a call from Annie saying that Jack had been complaining of a headache that afternoon and his body was showing massive bruises. They had finally rushed him to Harborview Hospital in Seattle when he was beginning to lose consciousness. We dashed off to the hospital to join Annie and Jack's daughters, who were waiting for some diagnosis and plan of treatment. When the doctor came in long-faced with his report, our hearts sunk as we learned that Jack was experiencing massive hemorrhaging due to an insidious type of chronic lymphocytic leukemia, a condition that had killed many veterans of the war in Southeast Asia exposed to Agent Orange, the deadly herbicide that the U.S. Airforce sprayed on millions of acres of lands to defoliate the vegetation and make the Vietcong troops more visible on the ground. The doctor sighed as he explained that many veterans were unaware that they even had this condition until it was too late to treat it, and that Jack's condition was so severe there was nothing he could do to save his life.

With Jack unconscious and on life support, we sat with his family trying to take in the gravity of this dire situation. After some time, we all made the heart stretching decision to remove his life-support and allow Jack's life force to come to completion with his assignment here on Earth, which he had nobly served. At midnight on Epiphany, Jack's final breath was held and witnessed by us all in deep silence with many tears.

We were all in shock, cracked wide open by the utter suddenness of Jack's passing and tenderly said our tearful good-byes. Stepping out from the stark, sterile space and fluorescent lights of the hospital into the fresh, frosty night, the sky was ablaze with stars. Prominent at the crystal-clear midheaven was the brightest star in the sky, Sirius, the Dog Star, which seemed like a fitting heavenly nod to the departing soul of a trickster coyote warrior named Cirie. We remembered Jack's words under another glittering night sky, when he mused, "Believing you can be perfect is the fatal imperfection. Believing you're invulnerable is the ultimate vulnerability. Being a warrior doesn't mean winning or even succeeding. It means risking and failing and risking again, as long as you live."

Richard and Bud

Following the program, Richard Strozzi-Heckler returned to California where he established Rancho Strozzi and the Strozzi Institute, developed a brilliant methodology of training and practice called Strozzi Somatics, and created a thriving international network of coaches and practitioners in this discipline. He went on to help develop and implement the Marine Corps Martial Arts Program and cofounded the Middle East Aikido Project. Richard wrote a book based on his journaling about the Trojan Warrior program titled *In Search of the Warrior Spirit*.

Bud Pōmaika'i Cook, who had initially reached out to us with the invitation to codesign this program for the Special Forces, moved back to Hilo, Hawaii with his wife, Tina, and they started the Maluhia Aikido Dojo and Healing Arts Center. He worked with the University of Hawai'i, Manoa, John A. Burns School of Medicine, on projects related to Hawaiian cultural heritage, trauma, healing, and spirituality and worked as a defense contractor in the Middle East.

Operation Noble Steward

True to spirit after he retired from the army, Jim Channon continued to carry the mantle of commander of the First Earth Battalion. He was frequently invited to return to initiate the army's top brass into the First Earth Battalion. Jim worked toward pivoting the power of the military to protect and preserve the integrity of the vital life-support systems here on planet Earth, affirming Jimmy Carter's vision of the U.S. Armed Forces evolving into a more Earth-stewarding role as it became increasingly clear that war is obsolete. Jim also widely shared his vision of Operation Noble Steward, which would develop military alliances spanning the globe to address the environmental stresses, emerging dangers, and crises on the planet. "We had a Marshall plan after WWII to rebuild Europe and Japan, and today we need something along these lines to recover the Earth's biosphere," he said.

Jim deftly mapped out how the administrative skills that guide and maintain combat missions could be transformed to support complex international projects to protect and regenerate the integrity of biosystems and the natural environment. Transportation units could deploy troops and supplies to areas in need of protection or restoration and help with relocating displaced populations. Intelligence systems could monitor environmental abuse and problem areas and coordinate the distribution of needed resources. Naval vessels could patrol the seas monitoring pollution, resource levels, and depletion. The U.S. Air Force could deliver needed supplies, evacuate, and relocate populations at risk. The U.S. Space Force could keep a watchful eye on weather, atmospheric conditions, and troubled areas on Earth. The Army Corps of Engineers could initiate large scale projects that would be environmentally regenerative rather than destructive. All the while, the military could continue to maintain a high level of combat readiness necessary to deploy as needed. Companies in the military-industrial complex could up their innovation game to develop higher levels of regenerative, life-enhancing technology and services that deliver ever greater value and profits than the old, outmoded, destructive technologies of archaic wars.

As an adept social architect, Jim's greatest achievement was creating vision-inspired communities and organizations. He established Artesia, a creative ecocommunity learning laboratory and ever-evolving three-acre art projects on the island of Hawaii, which he tended for nearly thirty years. We hosted and facilitated many gatherings together in Hawaii and beyond. In the years before his passing, Jim generated a wealth of writings and videos to carry his visions and legacy on. In September of 2017, just before his seventy-eighth birthday, while walking with friends in the gardens of Artesia, he dropped to the earth, shed the chrysalis of his earth suit, and flew off to his next assignment. A documentary on his life, titled *The 1st Earth Battalion,* was completed just months before his death. Go planet!

★ Epilogue ★

Obi-Wan and Princess Leia
Address Parliament

The potency of the Jedi Warrior story has endured and, in many ways, gained mythical strength and potency over time. It seems that the depth, breadth, and scope of our curriculum has never been surpassed, which has assured a certain mythical regard for the stature of the program. Through a cascade of well-timed invitations initiated by our colleagues George Por and Anna Betz in the United Kingdom, we were invited to attend the Mindfulness All-Party Parliamentary Group roundtable at British Parliament and to join their team of advisers for the *Mindful Nation UK Report*. This groundbreaking governmental report recommended that mindfulness be integrated into four domains of British society: health care, workplace, education, and criminal justice.

This in turn led to an invitation to be among an inspiring collection of speakers for a special British parliamentary hearing on the vital role of Mindfulness for Armed Forces, Police, and Emergency Services. The speakers included several British MPs who had served in the military and several leaders of various "blue light" emergency services and police departments. Lieutenant General Walter Piatt, director of the Army Staff, was invited to come, but at the last moment he had to attend to more pressing affairs.

Upon arriving at the parliamentary hearing room, we were informed that the AV support team was missing in action and that none of the presenters would be able to show any slides for their sessions. We exchanged looks of dismay with our colleague Amishi Jha, director of Contemplative Neuroscience and Professor of Psychology at the University of Miami. We had all put a lot of time and attention into compiling our talks into very image-centric presentations that were all locked and loaded, ready to bedazzle and inspire our colleagues at the hearing, and now at the last moment it was clear that wasn't going to happen.

As the hearing began, and the speakers stepped up to the podium one by one, the two of us kept exchanging furtive glances, trying to come up with a plan on the fly without being able to talk with each other as we were seated up front right next to the speakers' podium! It turned out that we were last on the program so the tension had a long time to build. When Clive Lewis, the Labour MP from Norwich South, stood up to introduce us with a review of our bios, his final remarks left the audience in a ker-fuffle of laughter as he concluded his introduction saying, "So without fur-ther ado I'm honored to present you, Obi-Wan and Princess Leia, to tell us about the once-secret Jedi Warrior program for the U.S. Army Special Forces."

Totally winging it, Joel stepped up to open the session by imaginatively inducting everyone into the Jedi Warrior program:

Congratulations! Today is graduation day. You've successfully completed a six-month full-time deployment into Jedi Warrior training. You entered this training six months ago, and since that time, you've been immersed in the most intensive, transformational mindfulness, mind-fitness, and deep resilience program that the military has ever conceived of.

This has involved nearly two months in the field doing mission simula-tions in treacherous environments where you performed at levels that no other Special Forces troops have ever realized. You have taken the prac-tice home to your families, and you've learned to listen to your children and significant others, who, as a data point, have come to us with their letters and their tears thanking us for the impacts that we've had on you. You've been supersaturated in neurofeedback and biofeedback training, learning how to control just about every waveform you can generate in your many dimensional physiologies. You survived a monthlong, silent mindfulness encampment that involved twelve to fifteen hours a day of mindfulness and mind-fitness training, sitting, walking, and ruck-ing meditations. This immersive training prepared you and your teams to deploy on the dreaded Gut Check, a mission simulation, covering ninety to one hundred miles, carrying ninety-pound rucksacks, within seventy-one hours. This included one leg of the thirty-eight miles in twenty-four hours traversing steep mountainous terrain. No Special Forces teams had ever successfully completed this course before—and you and both of your teams aced it!

Off we sailed, summarizing the multidimensional and multidisciplinary terrain we had traversed over the course of the program: three years of planning and six months of delivery, all condensed into a twenty-minute spontaneous review, punctuated by as many anecdotes and data points as we could pack in. Concluding with a brief summary of the meaningful outcomes and impacts of the program, we were met with thunderous applause and many looks and comments of astonishment. In our conversations with colleagues following the session, we amplified and elaborated on the program outcomes.

This parliamentary hearing was quite moving for all involved. Many of the speakers spoke candidly of their personal struggles with service-related trauma, burnout, and PTSD. All had witnessed the heartbreaking toll on their coworkers and families. As speaker after speaker shared their personal stories with great insight, vulnerability, and strength, the vocal quivers of sincerity, concern, and commitment resonated deeply within the hearts, minds, and bodies of everyone present. It was clear from their self-reports and their concern for their colleagues in the military, police, and emergency services, that the stakes for providing this kind of deep transformational skills training work are incredibly high for everyone working or living within these traumatic, high VUCAA professions.

There was agreement that the funds spent providing advanced education to those we send into harm's way is a mere pittance compared to the incalculable costs of neglecting such vital education. The bottom line was a resounding, "How can wise leaders of conscience not invest in providing these kinds of vital skills training for those who are willing to risk and sacrifice so much in their service to our communities and our nations?"

Since this historic hearing, there have been a wide array of international conferences exploring themes related to mindfulness and self-regulation training in the military including: International Mindfulness in Defence Symposium, Mindfulness in the Armed Services: Strengthening Resilience, International Military & Civilian Combat Stress Conference, the International Summit on Military Resilience, and the Defense Centers of Excellence Summit. True to the spirit and vision of the Jedi Warrior Program, these conferences have brought together senior leaders and practitioners from dozens of countries around the globe who are committed to reducing preventable human suffering and finding ways to bring deeper wisdom to supporting professionals working in these fields.[1]

Reflecting on the gathering momentum to expand mindfulness in the military to include its impact on team dynamics and performance, our colleague Jutta Mortlock, founder of the Center for Excellence in Mindfulness Research at City University, London, said:

> Mindfulness and warfare are paradoxical. But mindfulness is a way of being that approaches, not avoids, difficulty and contradictions, in order to understand and overcome suffering. This applies to the mental space within us, but also, and at least as importantly, in the space between you and me, in the space where judgments, prejudice, and ignorance can fester if we're not paying attention. Mindfulness has the potential to transform lives. I am grateful that I'm able to research in the UK Armed Forces how mindfulness may help increase the resilience of individuals and teams operating in extremely challenging contexts.[2]

Jutta has played a pioneering role in speaking to the value of mindfulness for not only enhancing and expanding the capacity for self-care and resiliency skills of individuals, but also for including and highlighting the profound value of training people working on teams to be proactively mindful of one another and their interactions. This explicit focus on collective mindfulness in action was a vital element of Jedi Warrior and is especially important for groups dedicated to caring for the well-being of others, especially in dangerous, high-stress settings such as the military and emergency services.[3]

Jedi Warrior opened the way for a myriad of mindfulness, meditation, mind-fitness, and resilience-based programs to be adopted into military training around the globe.

Exploring Deeper Waters

After Jedi, we returned to our organizational transformation and leadership work at SportsMind for a year. Among other things we completed our first book, *The Fine Arts of Relaxation, Concentration, and Meditation: Ancient Skills for Modern Minds*, and created the world's first digitally recorded self-guided meditation CD, *Self-Guided Relaxation*. We were invited by Michael Murphy to hold a "mini Jedi Warrior training program" workshop at Esalen Institute, introducing some of the advanced methods of mind-fitness and biofeedback training. George Leonard also invited us to bring some of the mind-fitness and personal mastery mind-science training from Jedi into his Leonard Energy Training at Esalen.

During this time, we were also planning for a sabbatical and helping organize a yearlong silent contemplative retreat and research project called the Shamatha Project. The lead scientist on this project was the Venerable Gen Lamrimpa who had been rigorously trained in the most respected monastic universities of Tibet. Genla had devoted nearly seventeen years to deep solitary contemplative retreat and was revered by his peers as an impeccable inner scientist. He was also a close colleague of the Dalai Lama who had requested that he come to America to guide this group of Westerners in a unique yearlong expedition into the depths of inner space.

In some ways, our Shamatha Project was to Western mind science and contemplative science what the first moon shot was for Western material science. Ours would be the first and most rigorous and lengthy of a series of Shamatha Project retreats. Cliff Saron, from UC Davis, who followed us in the role of research director in later, less intensive iterations, wrote that:

> The Shamatha Project is one of the most ambitious and comprehensive longitudinal studies of meditation ever conducted. Investigators are studying how intensive contemplative training benefits mental and physical health . . . and researching the psychological and physiological processes that contribute to possible mental and physical health benefits of meditation. More than 40 scientists from universities throughout the United States and Europe are collaborating in the project and its offshoots, using methods ranging from molecular biology, health psychology, and cognitive neuroscience to anthropology and network science.[4]

For friends who didn't quite understand why we would devote an entire year of our lives to such intensive training in deep silence, we explained it this way:

> If your life were devoted to music and you had the rare and precious opportunity to immerse yourself in refining your skills in playing your instrument in ever more inspiring and profound ways under the guidance of one of the most respected and skilled musicians on the planet, in an environment free from distraction, with the intention that when you emerged from this time and returned to the world, the potency of your music would so deeply touch everyone who heard you play that they would be inspired to learn to play their own instruments in more beautiful and inspiring ways so that they, in turn, would inspire everyone they met to awaken a similar aspiration and engagement . . . wouldn't that be a remarkable opportunity worth pursuing and not to be missed?

As we reentered the world after a year exploring the depths of inner space, we were warmly welcomed back into action with many new portals of possibility opening for us. After a brief time back at SportsMind, we founded Wisdom at Work and were invited by our mentor, Bill Veltrop, to join the core faculty of the International Center for Organization Design. This alliance opened the way for us to deeply connect with thousands of leaders in leading organizations around the globe and to introduce them to the principles of wisdom at work drawn from Jedi Warrior and beyond. When many of these leaders learned about our Jedi Warrior program, they would say, "That's what we need. We need an ultimate warrior training program! Our workplace is like being in a war zone, with bombs being dropped and people getting hurt every day. We need to find wiser alternatives to the widely accepted business-as-usual norms that are killing us and our planet. Do you have a Jedi Warrior program for communities and organizations?"

The credibility offered by our pioneering work with elite Special Forces troops inspired many people and opened many doors for us in the decades that followed. For leaders who might otherwise have lacked the special kind of courage needed to leap into the deeper waters of human potential for their own or their organizations' health and success, the fact that this work had been taken to heart and validated by the Special Forces emboldened them to introduce a deeper kind of advanced personal and team training to their colleagues and organizations.

Trends and Trade-Offs

The multitude of clear and present dangers in our world remind us that there is a myriad of clear and present needs for many more people in diverse walks of life to have the opportunity to learn and develop the courageous skills and strengths we have introduced in this book and in the Jedi Warrior program. The quality of our personal and collective lives, health, well-being, and survivability, may well depend on how deeply and widely this kind of evolutionary education is available and taken to heart.

The legacy of this historic program lives on in countless ways and variations. The pioneering work of Jedi Warrior opened many minds in the military and beyond to new and broader horizons of potentials and possibilities for extraordinary human development in settings and sectors where this would have previously been unlikely. In the years since Jedi Warrior, hundreds of less intensive and less sophisticated programs have been offered, touching the lives of millions of people in branches of the military and other organizations around the globe, each delivering a host of benefits.

With many minds opened by the results and success of Jedi Warrior, a wide variety of programs have followed within the military in the United States and around the world. While most of these focused on aspects of mindfulness, positive psychology, and resilience, as far as we know, none have been as far reaching, vast in scope, and multidisciplinary as Jedi Warrior.

As global awareness of the enduring impacts of trauma on professionals working in the military, emergency services, and health care, has increased, there has also been a growing interest in developing special programs incorporating mindfulness, self-regulation, and resilience training for elite troops, regular military, medical personnel, firefighters, ambulance drivers, EMTs, health care providers, psychologists, and other service providers and first responders at risk. As pandemics, forest fires, floods, and other devastating impacts of climate crisis and social unrest continue to increase, these professionals will be ever more in need of learning and incorporating the more advanced, protective, wise, and empowering personal and team skills that Jedi Warrior relied upon and imparted.

Whereas our training was fully immersive, saturating participants in transformational learnings and developing them as trainers themselves, the trends in later programs offered more of a light misting of these skills and knowledge. Given time, budget, and conceptual constraints, the scope and depth of training has been radically narrowed over the years. Although this has contributed to making training programs more widely accessible, scalable, and affordable, the results are understandably more modest, less enduring, and less transformational for the individuals and organizations involved. An eight-hour mindfulness and resilience program will certainly deliver value and likely save some lives, and making mind-fitness and meditation apps available for all your employees is a great investment for those motivated to get involved, yet such programs will deliver only a tiny glimpse of vastly greater potentials and enduring benefits that could be realized if they were pursued and invested in.

Just consider the value of one brilliant idea emerging from a clear and open mind within a thriving organizational culture that goes on to wide success and brings benefit to the world. Similarly, consider the cost of one glaring but unacknowledged problem, grievous mindless mistake, or miscalculation that ripples out to crash an entire business or destroy the lives of countless people for generations to come. What is the power of one kind, skillful, and disarming empathic response that diffuses the tension in a dangerous situation that might otherwise spiral out of control and escalate into a global conflagration worth? In the long run, the value realized by a training program will reflect the depth of wisdom and investment brought to creating and delivering it, the capacity and realization of the facilitators, and the enthusiasm, curiosity, and engagement that the participants themselves bring to it as well.

Expanding the Scope of Jedi Warrior Training

As we consider widening the impact for Jedi Warrior 2.0 programs, four primary groups stand out who would realize great value in this kind of advanced human development and deep resilience training:

- **Military and emergency services.** Special programs for those who often find themselves in harm's way and need deeper skills in self-awareness, self-regulation, deep resilience, trauma prevention and resolution, empathy and compassion, self-healing, and so on.
- **Activists and humanitarian aid workers.** Given the great peril and urgency of these times, many people are being called to warrior up and

put their lives, safety, and freedom on the line to protect vulnerable people, and local and global ecosystems. These individuals are relying more and more on the wisdom of powerful inner skills to maintain an effective, nonviolent, and compassionate presence while acting courageously and fiercely as needed to reduce harm and destruction.

- **Mainstream organizations and communities.** Skillful adaptations of the ultimate warrior training program could be deployed to inspire a myriad of audiences seeking to be wisely guided and deeply resilient in VUCAA times of deep change and adaptation.

- **Youth programs.** The most highly leveraged application for this training is in helping youth around the globe develop these r/evolutionary skills to prepare them for the increasingly challenging times to come. With design in mind, envision The Jedi Warrior Youth Core, First Earth Battalion for Youth, or other creative possibilities.

The basic curriculum elements that were essential for Jedi Warrior are relevant for any group or organization for whom wisdom, courage, empathy, compassion, mindful presence, somatic intelligence, self-regulation, self-mastery, flow states, and high performance are of value and benefit.

In determining the specific content and ideal schedule for a program, the main design questions to consider are: What are the unique needs or challenges this training program is meeting? What are the purpose and goals for this program? What resources are available to support this initiative? What other considerations need to be addressed to inform a program design for this specific group?

Priority should be given to offering the opportunity to participate in this work to sincerely motivated individuals who step forward out of their own interest to engage in this training. That said, many individuals who may be initially reticent to participate and may not yet comprehend the relevance and privilege of receiving such education up front, are still likely to receive great benefit and would be grateful that they had the opportunity to participate. From our experience, individuals who were initially highly skeptical and hesitant to engage often quickly realize how profoundly practical, meaningful, and relevant this work is for them and their teams. These individuals often become the best advocates, teachers, and coaches for this work within their organizations and communities.

The time involved is an important design factor and will vary from situation to situation. While Jedi Warrior was an immersive, six-month long program, most individuals or program sponsors are unlikely to be able to make that kind of commitment. Great benefit can certainly be realized in shorter, less intensive programs, or in programs that are offered over the span of a year or two and delivered in a progressive series of modules. Online options and elements could be employed for some portions of the training, but actual "boots on the ground" in-person presence will be optimal for much of this work, especially for the immersive retreats and field exercises appropriate to the audience involved.

In lieu of actual "mission simulations," as were used with our soldiers, a wide variety of meaningful field exercises can be creatively woven into program events to test, affirm, and develop greater personal insights and skills, and encourage deepening team connection, alignment, trust, and flow. For programs in mainstream society, creating learning laboratories that offer novel, challenging, and illuminating shared experiences for members of your training cadre can offer new perspectives and meaningful opportunities to test their emerging personal and interpersonal skills. This may involve participating with team members in service projects; field trips to visit and learn with alternative or innovative organizations or diverse communities; treks; rock climbing or ropes course; vision quests; mindfulness-based adventures in nature; engaging in sacred ceremonies that open and expand hearts and minds; or even taking your training cadre to Burning Man, or other immersive festivals, like so many leading Silicon Valley companies have done over the last twenty years! The key is to design these experiences to support the application and integration of the personal and team learnings you are seeking to encourage.

In any setting or organization, it would be ideal to have the facilitators who are delivering the program be deeply experienced within the professions, disciplines, or communities of the participants. In the best-case scenarios, well-qualified and highly motivated graduates of earlier programs will be developed as mentors. This will require their dedication to more intensive study and practice over time.

Postprogram follow-up sessions with training cohorts will help build the sense of a mutually coevolving learning community and encourage the continuity of learning over time. This can be enhanced through the inclusion of participants from other cohorts of the program. Our learning communities include many friends and colleagues that have continued to deepen in these learnings together for decades, along with a continual flow of new participants.

Next-Gen Jedi

Given the state of the world and likely trends, the wisest investment in sharing lessons learned from Jedi Warrior would certainly be programs for youth. Faced with growing up in an increasingly disrupted and VUCAA world, developing the courage, insights, skills, perspectives, and confidence offered by such transformational, embodied, contemplatively informed, awareness-based mind-fitness and resilience training will be inexpressibly valuable in preparing and inspiring youth to be well prepared and of service as they grow into their lives.

We have glimpsed the power of this kind of transformational inner education with youth in many settings around the globe, and we envision the main audience for this special kind of higher education to be teenagers and young adults. It has been so rewarding to mentor students in high school "mindfulness clubs" and to work with entire student bodies and faculty groups from a variety of schools and school districts and departments at universities. The ages of students who have found value in this inner learning has ranged from kindergarten to postgraduate.

The ideal scenario for curriculum development is to integrate mind-body training into classes related to health, fitness, science and technology, and social and emotional learning modules. These are wise and natural blends. While there are a growing number of school programs that offer some mindfulness, social, emotional, and ethical learning, and positive psychology, it seems that integrating biofeedback and embodied somatic intelligence aspects into their programs remains a future frontier.

While such an empowering curriculum could run for a single term, it is optimal to offer this education as an enlightening curriculum for life spanning our entire education, an ongoing progressive series of modules. We have seen some remarkable schools where every class with every teacher and subject integrated some potent elements of this kind of inner, empowering, transformational education. Many of the students we mentored in various schools and universities have gone on to inspire thousands of other students and colleagues over decades. This work, as it ripples its benefits into the world, is a powerful force.

The Long Gaze beyond the Horizon

In the final stage of writing this book, the Union of Concerned Scientists advanced the Doomsday Clock to just eighty-nine seconds before midnight. The wisdom of *Evolutionary Tactics*, the First Earth Battalion, aikido and martial science, contemplative science, and the Jedi Warrior ideals have never been more relevant and precious to our lives than they are now in these times of colliding existential threats. In the light of the Great Unraveling, it is crystal clear that a special kind of courage, care, and commitment is needed and that we are all called to warrior up to live as a force for good for the benefit of all.

Sitting here on our lanai on the northern tip of the island of Hawaii, immersed in natural beauty looking down the rolling green mountain slopes and out across the sparkling sea toward the summit of Haleakala, the House of the Sun, on Maui, we look back at this journey of a lifetime we have shared and marvel at the gifts, blessings, challenges, and opportunities that have shaped our lives and world to bring this Jedi Warrior story to life and this book to your hands. About a mile down the mountain, the cupola of Jim Channon's house peeks out above the trees like the spire of a Thai chedi, reminding us of the bright beacon of Jim's creative spirit rooting us on from beyond the veil to continue to dedicate our lives to being noble stewards applying evolutionary tactics and furthering the r/evolution in consciousness, always doing our best to mirror heaven here on Earth for the benefit of all.

Imagine sitting here with us, looking out across the shimmering waves, while looking inwardly together, reflecting on this journey we have shared through our words entering and entraining your mind, unfurling this story before your inner eyes. Savor and appreciate the lessons learned and taken to heart in reading this book—the images and stories that linger in your mind, the deep questions and aspirations that have awakened within you. Envision how many lives have been blessed by the widening ripples of Jedi Warrior's enduring legacy emanating out into our world across time, and how different our world would be if many more of the soldiers, leaders, first responders, humanitarian aid workers, caregivers, teachers, and students of our world had the opportunity to study, learn, take to heart, and embody what these fortunate twenty-five Jedi Warriors learned, and then went on to inspire others who would inspire others—for generations to come.

On with the R/evolution!

Go Planet!

Vi Cit Tecum

EARTH 1 BATTALION

mother Earth... my life support system..
as a soldier.. I must drink your blue
water.. live inside your red clay and
eat your green skin___.
I pray..... my boots will always kiss
your face and my footsteps match
your heartbeat...

carry my body thru space and time...
you are my connection to the
universe ..and all that comes after.
I am yours and you are mine
I salute you___

EARTH PRAYER

THE FIRST EARTH BATTALION

AFTERWORD

The Spirit of Dedication

As you sense the insights and aspirations that are aglow and aflow within you after having read this book, we invite you in the spirit of dedication to gather all that is good, true, noble, and helpful into the depths of your being like waves of energy and light and to shine this light into the continuum of your awakening spirit in a manner that will continue to guide your way and inspire your journey forever more. Gathering all this inspiration into your heart, radiate this goodness into the hearts of all beings to activate and awaken within them the special kind of courage they need to live whole-heartedly for the benefit of all.

> *Let's take a moment to remember why we are here. Let's remember our love for this beautiful planet. Let's remember our love for all humanity in all corners of the world. As we act today, may we find the courage to bring a sense of love and peace and appreciation to everyone we encounter and every word we speak. We are here for all of us.*
>
> EXTINCTION REBELLION,
> "DECLARATION OF SOLEMN INTENT"

Acknowledgments

This book has come into being like a lake fed by many streams that flow from many lakes that, in turn, have been fed by many streams.

Our deepest thanks go first and foremost to Bud Pōmaika'i Cook who opened the door for us to enter into this profound project, for his trust in us, friendship, inspiration, vision, and dedication to living true to the heart-warrior spirit of *Dō*. May his leadership and vision for igniting this bundle of potentials be honored.

We offer our heartfelt salute to Colonel Kenneth W. Getty for his friendship and inspiration as the guiding military presence stewarding this program. This book came about primarily in response to his sincere request to us to write it and share a broader, deeper perspective of this story than has previously been available.

We deeply honor the twenty-five soldiers from the Tenth Special Forces Group who participated in this historic program for their willingness to go where no teams of Special Forces troops had ever gone before. May their pioneering spirit shine forth as a beacon to guide countless generations to come of awakening warriors to dedicate their lives to Earth and service for the good of all.

Heartfelt appreciation to Sergeant Major Brad Halling, for his courage, insight, inspiration, moving stories, and illuminations regarding the battle of Mogadishu and the PSSE of the 410th Special Forces Detachment. Thanks also to Colonel Fred Krawchuk for his wise counsel in framing this story.

Special thanks go to Lieutenant Colonel James B. Channon, commander of the First Earth Battalion, for his enduring visionary friendship, inspiration, support, and wizardly creative collaboration. We are grateful to Jim for his permission, blessings, and generous encouragement to incorporate his artwork and excerpts from his illuminating "cult classic," *Evolutionary Tactics: A Manual for the First Earth Battalion*, into this book, and to his family for their permission and blessing as well.

Deepest gratitude to Richard Grossinger from Inner Traditions, for his vision and inspiration to call this book into being, and for his wisdom, kindness, patience, expertise, and persistence in getting us to commit to writing it. Special thanks also to Ehud Sperling, and to our brilliant editorial team, including Jeanie Levitan, Courtney B. Jenkins, Chris Cappelluti, Beth Wojiski, Katherine Mueller, Manzanita Carpenter, Ashley Kolesnik and the whole production team at Inner Traditions. Heartfelt appreciation to Karin de Weille for her inspiration, friendship, care, and insightful editorial suggestions.

Deep bows to our colleagues and core team members, Lieutenant Col. Jack Cirie and Sensei Richard Strozzi-Heckler, for their wholehearted dedication to ennobling the warrior spirit, and for their essential roles in helping to deliver this epic program, and to our SportsMind team: Chris Majer, Larry Burback, Horst Abraham, and Mike Blondell for their dedication to the success of Jedi Warrior. May the ripples of benefit and inspiration from our collaboration continue to open hearts and minds for generations to come.

Heartfelt thanks to George Leonard and Michael Murphy, as friends, mentors, and pioneers who opened the vast frontiers of the human potential movement, and for their encouragement, inspiration, and guidance in visioning and delivering this program.

Hats off to Dr. James V. Hardt, Founder of Biocybernaut Institute, Inc., for his friendship, neuro-wizardly wisdom and engineering, and skills in processing mountains of data.

Deep gratitude to our many advisers, mentors, friends, and guest presenters who have been guiding lights on this epic journey, including Brother David Steindl-Rast, Gary Zukav; Randy Cherner; Bira Almeda; and colleagues from the Council Grove Conference; Institute of Noetic Science; The Mindfulness Initiative; and The Mind and Life Institute.

We especially want to acknowledge the inspiration of the Dalai Lama, Kyabje Zong Rinpoche; Professor Ngawang Thondup Narkyid (Kuno); Kalu Rinpoche; Geshe Lhundrub Sopa, Chaiwat Thirapantu; Ven. Rina Sircar, Ven. Taungpulu Sayadaw, and Ram Dass, whose wisdom and kindness also inspired this program and this book.

Our profound gratitude to the teachings and shining examples of: Joanna Macy, Roshi Joan Halifax, Angeles Arrien, Margaret Wheatley, Greta Thunberg, Roger Hallam, Amy Goodman, Dan Siegel, Thomas Hubl, Gabor Maté, Stephen Porges, Jutta Tobias Mortlock, Amishi Jha, Elizabeth Stanley, Chris Ruane, M.P., and Chadd ʻOnohi Paishon and the Polynesian Voyaging Society for their courage in showing the way to vaster horizons.

In closing, we'd like to honor George Lucas for giving the ennobling Jedi Warrior meme to the world, and offer a deep bow to the subtle, inspiring presence of Manjushri, the Awakened Wisdom Warrior archetype depicted as wielding a flaming double edged sword of wisdom that adeptly cuts through all delusions that give rise to fear and suffering, while gently holding at his heart the stem of a lotus that blossoms at his left ear, revealing his deep listening to the profound wisdom of the natural world with the noble intent to liberate all suffering beings.

And to you dear reader, we offer our deepest appreciations for hearing the call and following your guidance to delve into this book. May the many treasures encoded here unfurl in your mind in ways that open your vision and will to live with deeper courage, wisdom, and compassion in service of the good of all.

Dwight Eisenhower said:

"Someday people are going to want peace so badly that the governments of the world will have to stand back and let them have it"

Someday the soldiers of the world may come to their highest ideals and realize that only they can agree to disarm the world time bomb.

THE FIRST EARTH BATTALION

Notes

Introduction: A Special Kind of Courage

1. James Channon, *Evolutionary Tactics: A Manual for the First Earth Battalion* (Privately published, 1982).
2. Elizabeth A. Stanley, "Cultivating the Mind of a Warrior," *Inquiring Mind* 30, no. 2 (Spring 2014).
3. Stanley, "Cultivating the Mind of a Warrior."
4. Sheila Ostrander and Lyn Schroeder, *Psychic Discoveries behind the Iron Curtain* (New York: Bantam Books, 1971).
5. Alan Senauke and Barbara Gates, "Mental Armor: Interview with Neuroscientist Amishi Jha," *Inquiring Mind* 30, no. 2 (Spring 2014).
6. Lt. Walter Piatt, Colonel Deydre Teyen, and Amy Adler, "Leading with Attention: Mindfulness Takes Hold as Army Embraces the Now," AUSA website, March 19, 2021.
7. Channon, *Evolutionary Tactics.*
8. Channon, *Evolutionary Tactics.*
9. D. Mike Malone, forward to "The First Earth Battalion: Ideas and Ideals for Soldiers Everywhere," by James Channon (declassified U.S. Army internal concept paper, 1979).
10. Channon, *Evolutionary Tactics.*
11. Asher Miller and Richard Heinberg, *Welcome to the Great Unraveling: Navigating the Polycrisis of Environmental and Social Breakdown* (Post Carbon Institute, 2023).
12. Joanna Macy and Chris Johnson, *Active Hope; How to Face the Mess We're in with Unexpected Resilience and Creative Power* (Novato, CA: New World Library, 2022).

13. Thanks to Sebastian "Basti" Nienaber who during our European Learning Expedition in 2019 suggested adding an additional A to VUCA for absurdity.

14. Glenn Albrecht, *Earth Emotions: New Words for a New World* (Ithaca, NY: Cornell University Press, 2019).

15. *Hinduism Today*, "Meditating Green Berets," March 1, 1988.

16. Channon, "First Earth Battalion."

Chapter 1: The Genesis of Jedi Warrior

1. James Channon, *Evolutionary Tactics: A Manual for the First Earth Battalion* (Privately published, 1982).

Chapter 2: The First Earth Battalion, Birthplace of Jedi Warrior

1. Nick Kotz, Nancy B. Nathan, and Cathryn Donohoe, "Where Have All the Warriors Gone?" *Washingtonian*, May 21, 2015.

2. Kotz, Nathan, and Donohoe, "Where Have All the Warriors Gone?"

3. James Channon, *Evolutionary Tactics: A Manual for the First Earth Battalion* (Privately published, 1982).

4. Channon, *Evolutionary Tactics*.

5. D. Mike Malone, introduction to "The First Earth Battalion: Ideas and Ideals for Soldiers Everywhere," by James Channon (declassified U.S. Army internal concept paper, 1979).

6. Channon, "First Earth Battalion."

Chapter 3: Tenuous Times

1. Bulletin of the Atomic Scientists, Doomsday Clock.

2. Wikipedia, "Vasily Arkhipov."

3. John F. Kennedy: Presidential Library and Museum, "Excerpt, Commencement Address at the American University, 10 June, 1963," Archives.

4. Judith Ehrlich and Rick Goldsmith, *The Most Dangerous Man in America: Dan Ellsberg and the Pentagon Papers*, documentary, 92 mins. (First Run Features, 2009).

5. Judith Ehrlich and Rick Goldsmith, *The Most Dangerous Man in America: Dan Ellsberg and the Pentagon Papers*.

6. George Leonard, introduction to *In Search of the Warrior Spirit*, by Richard Strozzi Heckler (Berkeley, CA: North Atlantic Books, 2011).

7. The Fourteenth Dalai Lama, speaking at Harvard University, 1984.

Chapter 4: Emergent Human Technologies for the Special Forces

1. Charlene Spretnak, "Naming the Cultural Forces That Push Us toward War," *Journal of Humanistic Psychology* 23, no. 3 (Summer 1983): 104–14.

2. Joel and Michelle Levey, Trojan Warrior briefing notes.

3. Lt. Gen. Walter Piatt, Colonel Deydre Teyen, and Amy Adler, "Leading with Attention: Mindfulness Takes Hold as Army Embraces the Now," AUSA website, March 19, 2021.

4. Gabor Maté, *The Myth of Normal* (New York: Avery, 2022).

Chapter 5: The Embodied Wisdom of Awakening Warrior

1. Daniel Siegel, *Pocket Guide to Interpersonal Neurobiology: An Integrative Handbook of the Mind* (Norton Series on Interpersonal Neurobiology) (W. W. Norton & Company. Kindle Edition), 199.

2. Thomas Hübl and Julie Jordan Avritt, *Healing Collective Trauma* (Boulder, CO: Sounds True, 2020), 178.

3. American College of Cardiology, "Getting Good Sleep Could Add Years to Your Life: Having Five Low-Risk Sleep Habits May Have Long-Term Benefits," American College of Cardiology website, February 23, 2023.

4. Gavin Dahl, "More Troops Hospitalized for Mental Health than Any Other Reason," Rawstory website, May 15, 2010.

5. Alan Senauke and Barbara Gates, "Interview with Neuroscientist Amishi Jha: Mental Armor," *Inquiring Mind* 30, no. 2 (Spring 2014).

6. Elizabeth Stanley, "Cultivating the Mind of a Warrior," *Inquiring Mind* 30, no. 2 (Spring 2014).

7. S. Shipko, W. A. Alvarez, and N. Noviello, "Towards a Teleological Model of Alexithymia: Alexithymia and Post-Traumatic Stress Disorder," *Psychotherapy and Psychosomatics* 39, no. 2 (1983): 122–126.

8. R. Yehuda, A. Steiner, B. Kahana, L. Binder-Brynes, S. M. Southwick, S. Zemelman, E. L. Giller, "Alexithymia in Holocaust Survivors with and without PTSD," *Journal of Traumatic Stress* 10, no. 1 (January 1997): 83–100.

9. Otto Scharmer and Katrin Kaefer, *Leading from the Emerging Future: From Ego-System to Eco-System Economies* (Oakland, CA: Berret-Koeller Publishers, 2013).

10. Jon Ramer, "Mighty Compassion: Breaking Our Collective Spell," Evolutionary Leaders website.

11. Paul Levy, *Wetiko: Healing the Mind Virus That Plagues the World* (Rochester, VT: Inner Traditions, 202.

Chapter 6: Wise Counsel

1. Bill D. Schul, "Exploration of Inner Space," *Southwest Review* 57, no. 1 (Winter 1972): 30–39.

2. Wikipedia, "Esalen Institute."

3. International Campaign for Tibet, "Least-Free Country: Tibet at Bottom of Global Rankings," March 9, 2023.

4. WINN (What Is Needed Now), "To Honor Kuno: Professor Ngawangdhondup Narkyid, 1931–2017," March 3, 2017.

5. The 13th Dalai Lama, "The Backyard Bodhisattva," by Lama Surya Das, on Surya website, accessed April 4, 2024.

Chapter 7: High Stakes, High Risks

1. Ronald H. Spector, "French Rule Ended, Vietnam Divided," *Encyclopedia Britannica*, last updated September 6, 2024.

Chapter 9: The Subtle Transformational Power of Aikido

1. Morihei Ueshiba, as quoted in Kisshomaru Ueshiba, *Aikido* (Tokyo: Hozansha, 1985).

2. Mark Nepo, *The Endless Practice: Becoming Who You Were Born to Be* (New York: Simon and Schuster, 2015), 302–3.

3. Winfried Wagner, *Aikido: The Trinity of Conflict Transformation* (New York: Springer, 2014).

4. Morihei Ueshiba, "The Memoir of the Master," AikiWeb.

✶ Notes ✶

Chapter 10: Caution! Entering Mind Field

1. Elmer E. Green, "Beyond Psychophysics," *Subtle Energies & Energy Medicine* 10, no. 1 (1999): 368.
2. Joanna Macy, "Faith and Ecology," *Resurgence & Ecology* 123 (July–August 1987): 20.
3. Robert G. Jahn and Brenda Dunne, "The PEAR Proposition," *Explore (NY)* 3, no. 3 (May–June 2007): 205–26.
4. Barbara B. Brown, *Stress and the Art of Biofeedback* (New York: Harper and Row, 1981).
5. Mindfulness All-Party Parliamentary Group (MAPPG), *Mindful Nation UK* (Report), The Mindfulness Initiative, October 2015.
6. Viktor E. Frankl, *Man's Search for Meaning* (Boston: Beacon Press, 1946).

Chapter 11: The Encampment

1. Diado-ji Yusan, *Primer of Bushido: The Way of the Warrior* (Valencia, CA: Ohara, 1984).
2. Richard Strozzi-Heckler, *In Search of the Warrior Spirit* (Berkeley, CA: North Atlantic Books, 2011), 104.
3. Strozzi-Heckler, *In Search of the Warrior Spirit*, 104.
4. Strozzi-Heckler, *In Search of the Warrior Spirit*, 106.
5. Strozzi-Heckler, *In Search of the Warrior Spirit*, 110.

Chapter 12: Mastery and Mystery

1. Aldous Huxley, *The Doors of Perception* (London: Chatto and Windus, 1954).
2. Richard Strozzi-Heckler, *In Search of the Warrior Spirit* (Berkeley, CA: North Atlantic Books, 2011), 144–45.
3. Francisco J. Varela, *Ethical Know-How: Action, Wisdom, and Cognition* (Stanford, Ca: Stanford University Press, 1999).
4. Joanna Macy, "Joanna Macy: A Wild Love for the World," On Being with Krista Tippett (interview), April 25, 2019.
5. Martin Luther King Jr., "Letter from Birmingham Jail."
6. Thomas Merton, "Statement from his final address, during a conference on East-West monastic dialogue, delivered just two hours before his death (10 December 1968)," quoted in *Religious Education* 73 (1978): 292.

7. Robert O. Becker. The Body Electric: Electromagnetism And The Foundation Of Life, (New York: William Murrow Paperback, 1998).

8. R. Buckminster Fuller, "Guinea Pig B: The 56 Year Experiment," in *Inventions: The Patented Works of R. Buckminster Fuller* (New York: St. Martin's Press, 1983); and Amy Edmondson, *A Fuller Explanation: The Synergetic Geometry of R. Buckminster Fuller* (Pueblo, CO: EmergentWorld Press, 1987), 3.

9. Koichi Tohei, *Aikido: The Arts of Self Defense* (Tokyo: Rikugei, 1961).

Chapter 13: Taking the Practice to Heart

1. Joanna Macy, "Joanna Macy at Bioneers 2009," Vimeo, 16:47, December 1, 2009.

2. Compassion Institute, "Our Team: Guiding the Mission of Compassion Institute."

3. Thomas Merton, *Conjectures of a Guilty Bystander* (New York: Image, 1966), 153–55.

4. Merton, *Conjectures*, 155.

5. See Joel and Michelle Levey, Wisdom at Work, "Great Compassion."

6. See Joel and Michelle Levey, Wisdom at Work, "Great Compassion."

7. Daniel Goleman, "Superhumans: The remarkable Brain Waves of High-Level Meditators," The Well, Big Think, John Templeton Foundation, video, 4 min., September 13, 1018.

8. Goleman, "Superhumans."

9. Thanks to Rick Hanson for illuminating these neuropsych nuances during his online seminar at The Dalai Lama Global Vision Summit 2021: The Power of Compassion.

10. Matthieu Ricard. Notes from Ricard's teachings at the Power and Care conference in Brussells, sponsored by Mind and Life Europe, 2016.

11. Tilopa, "The Ganges Mahāmudrā Instructions," Lotsawa House, translated by Ina Bieler, 2017.

12. Excerpted from notes and interview from the Trojan Warrior program, 1986.

Chapter 15: Awakening Warriors

1. Richard Strozzi-Heckler, *In Search of the Warrior Spirit: Teaching Awareness Disciplines to the Military* (Berkeley, CA: Blue Snake Books, 2007), 204.

2. Strozzi-Heckler, *In Search of the Warrior Spirit*, 238.

3. William James, "The Moral Equivalent of War," Lecture 11 in *Memories and Studies* (New York: Longman Green and Co., 1911): 367–296.

4. Strozzi-Heckler, *In Search of the Warrior Spirit*, 247

5. Bira Almeida, *Capoeira, A Brazilian Art Form: History, Philosophy, and Practice* (New York: Penguin Random House, 1981).

6. Almeida, *Capoeira: A Brazilian Art Form.*

7. Strozzi-Heckler, *In Search of the Warrior Spirit*, 261.

Chapter 17: A Wealth of Lessons Learned

1. Data sources and quotes cited in this chapter are from notes and interviews gathered in preparation for preparing the *Trojan Warrior After-Action Report* for the U.S. Army, 1986.

2. James Channon, *Evolutionary Tactics: A Manual for the First Earth Battalion* (Privately published, 1982).

Epilogue: The Legacy Lives On, New Missions Begin

1. The Mindfulness Initiative, "Mindfulness in the Armed Forces," October 23, 2022.

2. Jutta Tobias Morlock quoted in Shamin Quadir, "Mindfulness in the Armed Services: Strengthening Resilience," City University of London, October 31, 2022.

3. The Mindfulness Initiative, "Mindfulness in the Armed Forces."

4. Clifford Saron, "The Shamatha Project," The Saron Lab website; and Wisdom at Work, "Shamatha Project."

Index

★ Index ★

About the Authors

Joel Levey and Michelle Levey developed and delivered advanced biopsy-bernautic training for the historic U.S. Army Special Forces' once secret Trojan Warrior program (aka Jedi Warrior). The Leveys have devoted their lives to exploring the interfusion of modern neurobiological and ancient contemplative transformational sciences by skillfully blending mindful presence, integrative medicine, neurofeedback, cyberphysiology, interpersonal neurobiology, systems thinking, and deep ecology. They have worked with hundreds of leading organizations and communities around the globe to inspire people to expand their capacity to bring a deeper wisdom, compassion, resilience, and collective, creative intelligence to life, work, and relationships.

Their clients include NASA; NOAA; U.S. Surgeon General's Office; U.S. Army Special Forces; U.S. Navy; Google; British Parliament; National Institutes of Health; National Health Service; Intel; MD Anderson Cancer Center; World Bank; West Point Military Academy; Forest Ethics;

Compassionate Action Network; Compassion Games International; Stanford Research Institute International; Washington Athletic Club; St. Francis Hospice; MIT; Clinton Global Initiative; World Government Summit; and World Business Academy. They served as core faculty for the International Center for Organization Design (ICOD) and as cochairpersons for the Center for Corporate Culture and Organizational Health at the Institute for Health and Productivity Management (IHPM). The Leveys were honored to participate in the Mindfulness All-Party Parliamentary Group at British Parliament, served as advisers for the historic *Mindful Nation UK* report, and presented at the parliamentary hearing on the vital role of mindfulness in the military and emergency blue-light services. They serve as Stewards of Collective Wisdom and Contemplative Science for the First Earth Battalion. The Dalai Lama, an advisor on several of their projects, encouraged the Leveys in their work, saying: "You are presently engaged in work that has great prospects for bringing the inner sciences of transformation to a very wide section of people who may not under ordinary circumstances come into contact with these teachings."

The Leveys have studied closely with many of the world's most respected teachers in both modern and ancient mind science and contemplative science traditions. Honored by the Institute of Noetic Sciences as leading "teachers of transformation," they have served as clinical faculty at the University of Minnesota Medical School and Bastyr University where they taught programs on contemplative science and mind-body medicine, and also taught special graduate programs for Mahidol University in Thailand; Indian Institute of Management; and Antioch University. Michelle and Joel also directed clinical programs related to mindfulness, deep resilience, stress mastery, and biofeedback for Group Health and Children's Medical Centers in Seattle, and serve as contemplative mentors to the Art Monastery Project.

The Leveys' published works include *Living in Balance: A Mindful Guide for Thriving in a Complex World*, which won the Nautilus Award;

Mindfulness, Meditation, and Mind-Fitness; *Wisdom at Work*; *The Fine Arts of Relaxation, Concentration, and Meditation: Ancient Skills for Modern Minds*; and *VUCA Savvy Leadership: Thriving in Complex Times*.

Founders of Wisdom at Work, based in both Seattle and Hawaii, and Bodhi Tree EcoDharma Sanctuary, Joel and Michelle Levey live in Seattle and on the island of Hawaii and work with communities and organizations around the globe. To learn more or to invite them to lecture or teach, please visit their website at WisdomAtWork. You can also find them on YouTube (wisdomatwork), Facebook (LeveysWisdomAtWork), X (#WisdomAtWork), Bluesky (@WisdomAtWork.bsky.social) and Instagram (joellevey).

Books of Related Interest

The Hidden Power of Aikido
Transcending Conflict and Cultivating Inner Peace
by Susan Perry, Ph.D.

Aikido practitioner and 6th-degree blackbelt Susan Perry, Ph.D., shows how Aikido can help peacefully resolve difficulties that arise with intimidating and unpredictable people, those who are stubborn or don't listen, insincere people who want something from you, and chaotic situations. Includes Aikido's step-by-step protocol for deescalation.

The Art of Mastery
Principles of Effective Interaction
by Peter Ralston

Peter Ralston explores the foundational skills and operating principles that empower mastery, including accurate perceptive-awareness and effective interaction. Sharing methods to overcome the major obstacles to mastery, he presents a step-by-step breakdown of the principle of effective interaction and explains how to adapt when situations are not aligned with your objectives.

Aikido: The Art of Transformation
The Life and Teachings of Robert Nadeau
*by Teja Bell, Laurin Herr, Richard Moon,
Bob Noha, Susan Spence, and Elaine Yoder*

An influential figure in the development of Aikido in America, Robert Nadeau is one of the few American direct disciples of Aikido's founder Morihei Ueshiba Osensei. This book, written by his students, explains Nadeau's unique teaching, his core concepts, and basic practices centered on energy refinement, direct experience, and inner transformation.

Scan the QR code and save 25% at InnerTraditions.com.
Browse over 2,000 titles on spirituality, the occult, ancient mysteries, new science, holistic health, and natural medicine.

INNER TRADITIONS
Books for the Spiritual & Healing Journey
— SINCE 1975 • ROCHESTER, VERMONT —
InnerTraditions.com • (800) 246-8648